The Making of United States Foreign Policy

The Making of
United States Foreign Policy

BURTON M. SAPIN

THE BROOKINGS INSTITUTION

Washington, D.C.

THE BROOKINGS INSTITUTION is an independent organization devoted to nonpartisan research, education, and publication
in economics, government, foreign policy, and the social sciences
generally. Its principal purposes are to aid in the development of sound
public policies and to promote public understanding of issues of national
importance.

The Institution was founded December 8, 1927, to merge the activities of
the Institute for Government Research, founded in 1916, the Institute of
Economics, founded in 1922, and the Robert Brookings Graduate School of
Economics and Government, founded in 1924.

The general administration of the Institution is the responsibility of a self-
perpetuating Board of Trustees. The trustees are likewise charged with maintaining the independence of the staff and fostering the most favorable conditions for creative research and education. The immediate direction of the
policies, program, and staff of the Institution is vested in the President, assisted by the division directors and an advisory council, chosen from the
professional staff of the Institution.

In publishing a study, the Institution presents it as a competent treatment
of a subject worthy of public consideration. The interpretations and conclusions in such publications are those of the author or authors and do not
purport to represent the views of the other staff members, officers, or trustees
of the Brookings Institution.

08652

Foreword

The organization of the United States government to deal with foreign policy has undergone continuing review and reform since 1945. The first Hoover Commission provided a major assessment in 1948. Congressional committees have periodically examined the structure. In recent years, the most extensive congressional attention has been reflected in the work of several subcommittees of the Senate Government Operations Committee, chaired by Senator Henry M. Jackson. Personnel problems have received special attention from time to time, notably by the advisory committees chaired by Dr. Henry M. Wriston and former Secretary of State Christian Herter.

The Brookings Institution has long been interested in this field. Its first major postwar study was a report on *Administration of United States Aid for a European Recovery Program,* submitted to the Senate Foreign Relations Committee in January 1948. In 1951, at the request of the Bureau of the Budget, the Institution prepared a major study on *The Administration of Foreign Affairs and Overseas Operations.* A report on *Administrative Aspects of United States Foreign Assistance Programs* was prepared in 1956 for the Senate's Special Committee to Study the Foreign Aid Program. In 1959, at the request of the Senate Foreign Relations Committee, the Institution prepared a report on *The Formulation and Administration of United States Foreign Policy.*

The author of the present study was a member of the research group for the 1959 report, which was prepared under the supervision of H. Field Haviland, Jr., now Director of the Institution's Foreign Policy Studies Division. At the conclusion of that study, it was decided that there was need for a more detailed treatment of the subject which is presented in this volume. Although the 1959 report was the point of departure, Mr. Sapin's study is substantially a new book.

Mr. Sapin has taught at Princeton University, Vanderbilt University, and the Massachusetts Institute of Technology. In the fall of

1961, he joined the Department of State where he became a member of the Politico-Military Affairs Staff attached to the Office of the Deputy Under Secretary of State for Political Affairs. He returned to academic life on the faculty of the University of Minnesota in July 1965. His publications include: (with Richard C. Snyder) *The Role of the Military in American Foreign Policy* (1954) and (with Richard C. Snyder and H. W. Bruck) *Decision-Making as an Approach to the Study of International Politics* (1954).

The Institution and the author benefited from the counsel of an advisory committee composed of the following: Colonel DeWitt C. Armstrong III, Roger W. Jones, Charles O. Lerche, Jr., Herman Pollack, James N. Rosenau, and Francis O. Wilcox. Two members of the Senior Staff of the Institution, Robert E. Asher and Karl Mathiasen III, also reviewed the manuscript. The index was prepared by Helen Eisenhart.

At an earlier stage of his work, Mr. Sapin received extensive critical comments from Professors Rosenau and James A. Robinson, Mr. Timothy W. Stanley, and Colonel Armstrong.

From 1959 to 1965, Mr. Sapin discussed aspects of the study with several hundred government officials. Some of these discussions were formal interviews; many others were informal conversations. In this and other ways, many who must remain anonymous have contributed generously to the present study. To the extent that Mr. Sapin's book captures a sense of the structure and functioning of the United States foreign policy machinery, much of the credit belongs to these participants in the foreign policy-making process.

The Institution is grateful to the United States Senate Committee on Foreign Relations, which supported the original study out of which this volume grew, and to the Ford Foundation, whose grant for general support provided the funds for the present work.

The views expressed are those of the author and do not purport to represent the views of the staff members, officers, or trustees of the Brookings Institution, the Ford Foundation, or of any governmental organization. The Department of State is not involved in or responsible for this work.

Robert D. Calkins
President

January 1966
Washington, D. C.

Contents

Appendixes

1

Introduction

DURING THE PAST twenty-five years, a solid national consensus has developed in support of the belief that the United States must actively pursue its national interests in the world beyond its boundaries if Americans are to enjoy the fruits of freedom and prosperity at home. At the same time, it has become clear that the world of the mid-twentieth century is so greatly troubled and so rapidly changing that even the most ambitious and generous mustering of American resources can at best reduce, rather than eliminate, problems abroad. The leverage the United States can exert on situations overseas is always limited and sometimes almost nonexistent, and many difficulties in foreign relations are not a result of either bad intentions or poor performance.

But while the characteristics of the contemporary international scene are of fundamental importance in shaping the contours of American foreign policy, they are not completely determining. They do not compel or assure particular responses to particular problems. United States foreign policy actions reflect the priorities attached to interests and objectives, the interpretations given to international situations and problems, the limitations that may be imposed by the broad range of domestic factors usually labeled political, and the organizational apparatus within which these foreign policy activities are carried on. In brief, an important part of the explanation for American foreign policy actions lies in the nature of American society and the functioning of its political system and its national governmental machinery.

Given that assumption, the study of United States foreign policy

1

organization and processes takes on an added significance—and fascination. The United States is confronted by international problems and responsibilities that are as challenging as any ever faced by any nation; it must meet these challenges with a governmental structure and system that most observers find far from ideal, indeed quite inadequate.

Focus of the Study

This study is focused on the formulation and administration of United States foreign policy. It will not attempt an exhaustive canvass of all the foreign affairs activities carried on by all the agencies of the federal government. Attention will be directed to major foreign policy decision making, particularly within the executive branch, and important overseas programs.

Foreign policy and domestic policy no longer represent easily separable and essentially independent clusters of executive and legislative units, problem areas, and governmental programs. This creates added difficulties for foreign policy, and for domestic policy as well. It is relatively easy, however, to distinguish between those executive agencies that are concerned mainly with foreign affairs and those that deal primarily with domestic affairs.

There is also ambiguity in such terms as foreign policy, military or national defense policy, and national security policy. National security policy can be regarded as the most comprehensive since the security of the nation involves not only its foreign relations and its military posture but also—among other things—the state of the economy, the availability of certain natural resources, the skills and education of the population, and even major social patterns and characteristics.

Foreign policy and military policy are then subcategories of national security policy, with many complex interrelations. Foreign policy decisions and commitments affect military responsibilities and even capabilities. Similarly, the posture and policies of the military establishment affect the international position of the United States in many important ways. What were once thought of as purely military matters, such as force levels, choices among weapons systems, or the level of the military budget, have significant foreign policy implications.

The national security machinery at the presidential level will be carefully examined in this study. The organization and decision processes of the military establishment represent a massive and highly challenging subject of study in themselves. For present purposes, however, it will be necessary only to sketch them in broad outline, focusing on the more direct links to the foreign policy process.

The various executive units concerned specifically and directly with aspects of official United States foreign relations will be referred to as the *foreign policy organization;* to convey a sense of activity or process the terms *foreign policy system* or *foreign policy process* will be used. For broader references that include the military establishment, the term *national security organization* will be used.[1]

One purpose of this study is to provide a reasonably up-to-date description of present organizational arrangements, and primary attention will be devoted to them and their recent antecedents. The emphasis is on structure and function, though processes are not ignored. At the same time, it is clear that preoccupation with contemporaneity is no substitute for the probing of continuing organizational problems that run through a variety of organizational forms and reforms.

At this point, the start of a long journey through the corridors of United States foreign policy making, a few preliminary comments seem to be called for. First, the executive agencies involved in

[1] The wide range of agencies and complicated and perplexing problems involved in American national security policy making is reflected in the work of the Subcommittee on National Policy Machinery of the Senate Government Operations Committee. From 1959 through 1961 this subcommittee, chaired by Senator Henry M. Jackson (D-Wash.) and aided by an able staff, engaged in a thoroughgoing study and evaluation of major problems in this field, providing the interested observer with a rich source of relevant materials. These materials are now conveniently assembled in three volumes. When the subcommittee's hearings and staff studies are referred to in the present study, they will be cited as Subcommittee on National Policy Machinery, *Organizing for National Security.*

A second stage of this subcommittee's work was undertaken by the same group of senators. The second Jackson subcommittee, which began its work in May 1962, was called the Subcommittee on National Security Staffing and Operations, and its subject was the administration of national security. It is cited in this study as Subcommittee on National Security Staffing and Operations, *Administration of National Security.*

In early 1965, the subcommittee began the third phase of its inquiries in the national security field. Its new name was Subcommittee on National Security and International Operations and its new subject, the conduct of national security policy.

foreign policy are, from a sociological perspective, complex orga- nizations or bureaucracies, and they have many of the character- istics associated with nongovernmental bureaucracies. These include a well-defined structure of authority, a rather elaborate division of labor, an extensive communications network to tie the various parts and levels of the organization together, and personnel who are re- cruited and dealt with primarily on the basis of merit or achievement and whose working relationships are essentially formalized and routin- ized. For present purposes, it suffices to say that the modern bureau- cracy should, ideally, provide an instrument through which large numbers of men can join forces to carry out major tasks more effec- tively than they otherwise could. Indeed, in many instances, such an organization provides the only way a particular function can be per- formed.

Unfortunately, most large bureaucracies, including agencies of the federal government, fall short of this ideal, and the term "bureaucra- cy" becomes a label of abuse, aimed at those organizations that are led and operated so poorly that their size does become a major handicap. They are consequently sluggish and unwieldy, lacking the capacity for vigorous action and quick response.

For the purposes of foreign policy making, two basic points should be underscored. These large organizations are necessary to do some of the jobs, and they have their equivalents outside the government. Fur- thermore, there is no reason why they cannot be so led and organized that they perform their functions with reasonable efficiency and dis- patch.

Governmental bureaucracies, including the foreign policy agencies, do operate under some limiting conditions that most nongovernmen- tal bureaucracies do not have to face. For one thing, agency and, sometimes, subagency powers and responsibilities are specified by stat- ute and thus can only be modified by Congress. The same is often true of agency organizational and personnel arrangements. For better or for worse, the hiring and the firing of career employees in government are hedged around with many more safeguards and requirements than in private business. In addition, the foreign policy agencies, and the rest of the executive branch, must operate under the continuing, critical and sometimes harsh scrutiny of the legislature, the mass media, and interested citizen groups. The comparison could be extended further, but the conclusion is clear: beyond the usual difficulties of large organizations, governmental agencies have some added problems and limitations of their own.[2]

The Role of Organization

While recognizing that the international environment does not completely determine American foreign policy responses, many observers inside as well as outside the government are inclined to be skeptical about the role of organizational arrangements. They doubt whether variations in the division of organizational labor, the particular functions specified and provided for, the relationships established among various organizational units, and the communications facilities and networks that link them make much difference in substantive policies and actions.

Skeptics point to the confused quality that appears to characterize much decision making in times of major crisis. Orderly procedures and precisely defined organizational roles seem to be replaced by the efforts of a handful of key officials whose behavior gives little indication that they are relying on or are even in close touch with the organizations they formally head.

The role of organization is even more briefly dismissed by those who simply take the view that "it is people rather than organization that count." This is not the place to attempt a definitive rebuttal of such a view. However, it may be useful at this point to suggest some of the fundamental ways in which organizational structure and functions affect the foreign policy processes and actions of the United States.

First of all, the allocation of powers and responsibilities to certain agencies and the specifying of particular relationships among them by statute or executive order represent significant facts of life within the governmental structure. By no means do these provide the complete picture of who is actually doing what—and certainly not how well—but

[2] The organizational aspects of foreign policy making are analyzed much more extensively and systematically in Richard C. Snyder, H. W. Bruck, and Burton Sapin, *Decision-Making as an Approach to the Study of International Politics*, Foreign Policy Analysis Series No. 3 (Princeton University, 1954). This study has been republished in *Foreign Policy Decision-Making* (Free Press of Glencoe, 1962), by the same authors.

they do establish a basic framework. For some agencies or organizational units, this framework may provide the necessary leverage to try to get a job done; for others, it may represent the barriers that must be circumvented if they are to accomplish what they regard as their own organizational purposes. While a formal assignment of certain responsibilities to the Secretary of State does strengthen his ability and that of his department to provide foreign policy leadership to the rest of the government, it obviously cannot guarantee the effectiveness of that leadership.

Furthermore, the establishment of some new or expanded organizational unit to carry out a specified function is one way of indicating recognition of a need for increased effort. The presence of the organization, again, does not guarantee the desired results, but it does provide increased resources to accomplish them as well as concrete evidence of a greater concern. This might be said about the Arms Control and Disarmament Agency established by President John F. Kennedy in 1961. It was a way of focusing greater governmental attention on this problem area. The director of the new agency was further armed, organizationally speaking, by the establishment of a direct relationship between him and the President.

The fact that the men at the working levels of the foreign policy organization often seem to be ignored in crisis situations does not necessarily mean that they are not playing a role. For one thing, there is no reason why they or their efforts should be visible to the outside observer, for example, the newspaperman. Few newspapermen would be able in any event to recognize most officials below the Assistant Secretary level. Furthermore, if the organization has been doing its work well prior to a crisis, its heads may well be able to operate in semi-isolation once the crisis is upon them. They will have read or be able to draw upon relevant intelligence estimates, policy analyses, and planning documents. They can tap the necessary staff expertise as required. While all of these things must be available, they are not necessarily visible to the outside observer.

The making of tough, basic policy choices by top-level decision makers is, in any event, just the beginning of a complex flow of activities. There are usually a great many follow-up actions required which are ordinarily passed down to subordinate levels, if for no other reason than that the men at the top cannot physically do it all themselves.

Some of the toughest choices are often made in these processes of implementation.

Statutory prescriptions, executive orders, and organization charts and manuals provide at least one authoritative set of statements about what agencies and organizations are supposed to be doing, and how. They are not a complete guide to the nature of the work being done, and certainly not to its quality. They do represent a necessary point of departure, if only to check the extent of deviation in actual practice. They may even provide a model, an organizational ideal toward which to aim.

Organizational characteristics take on fuller meaning in terms of the qualities of the political and career personnel who staff the foreign policy organization and the domestic political requirements that impinge upon it. Organizations must be manned, relationships between them interpreted and carried out, and leadership provided. These things do not, however, occur in a structural or functional vacuum. A framework of organizational units already exists, with assigned responsibilities and relationships prescribed in great detail. These organizational arrangements, the purposes they are designed to accomplish, and the problems they generate affect foreign policy decisions.

Evaluating Organizational Performance

Over the past twenty-five years, considerable attention has been directed to the foreign policy organization by individual scholars, private research organizations, and a variety of officially sponsored or supported study groups. A number of very useful studies have appeared, and in recent years some major contributions have been added.

From the scholarly point of view, however, this body of literature has suffered from important shortcomings. Even in terms of the modest accomplishments of the social sciences in general, the research in this field has not been sufficiently scientific, that is, little attention has been given to organizing research around explicit hypotheses and theoretical formulations or to improving research methods. Furthermore, relatively little effort has been made to link the study of governmental bureaucracies to the substantial research and theory-building efforts of

sociologists and others in the field of nongovernmental bureaucracies—
to try to identify similar patterns and problems and explain significant
differences.

Beyond this, the major studies of U.S. governmental machinery—
for example, those by the Brownlow Committee and the two Hoover
Commissions—do not seem to have built systematically on one another's work.[3] Nor have they been followed up to determine whether
the implementation of recommended changes produced over time the
results predicted or hoped for. Indeed, in some of these reports, the
relationship between "recommended reform A" and "desired conse-
sequence B" seems to be hopefully assumed rather than persuasively
demonstrated.[4]

Finally, most studies of the foreign policy and national security organizations have been quite inadequate in moving from the level of
description and analysis to evaluation and prescription. There has
been no shortage of judgments and recommendations, but the intellectual bases for them have often been either unclear or, when clear,
not persuasive. Evaluation is a legitimate—some would say necessary—
part of the scholarly enterprise. The present study has its share of
judgments; hopefully, the bases for them will be made quite clear to
the reader.

It must be conceded at the start that the inadequacies in reliable,
widely accepted knowledge about large organizations, whether governmental or nongovernmental, make it difficult to establish models of
organizational excellence in terms of which to evaluate the American
foreign policy organization. Some of the distinctive limitations imposed by the American political system—quite detailed legislative
enactments and budgetary control, the high turnover rate of politically-appointed executives, and the pressures of the domestic political setting—add to the difficulty and raise serious questions about the practical
utility of trying to blueprint the ideal organizational arrangements for
U.S. foreign policy machinery. It would certainly be naive to assume

---

[3] The President's Committee on Administrative Management (1937) and the two
U. S. Commissions on Organization of the Executive Branch of the Government,
1947-49 and 1953-55.

[4] See the comments in Richard C. Snyder and James A. Robinson, *National and
International Decision-Making,* A Report to the Committee on Research for Peace
(Institute for International Order, 1961), pp. 82-83.

that there is one set of organizational roles and relationships clearly and demonstrably preferable to all others.

This study will instead attempt to identify functions that the foreign policy organization should be able to perform and organizational roles and relationships that seem appropriate in terms of the international and domestic political settings within which it must operate. These will provide the bases of judgment for the study. Each chapter will include a discussion of criteria relevant to the particular agency or functional area.

The question of how well particular organizational arrangements stand up against the criteria specified will tend to be answered in rather impressionistic terms. Ideally, this should not be the case. It should be possible to posit empirical hypotheses and indices, gather data accordingly, and then draw appropriate conclusions. For the most part, this kind of material does not exist in the literature on the subject, and it has not been possible to develop it in detail for this study. Thus, the judgments reached will reflect the views of thoughtful observers inside and outside the foreign policy organization and some of my own experiences and observations as a working bureaucrat in the Department of State.

Requirements that Reflect the International Environment

The nature of the international environment not only significantly limits the choices and the leverage of the United States in its foreign relations but also calls for some distinctive responses on the part of the U.S. foreign policy organization. To begin with, over the last twenty years foreign affairs have become much more operational and programmatic. The United States is no longer primarily an observer overseas; it seeks very actively to influence a wide range of people and situations. This entails not only the varied military, economic, information, cultural, and scientific programs that have become so familiar in the last two decades but also a much more active, influencing role in the traditional government-to-government relations carried on by U.S. diplomats.

It has also become increasingly clear that the foreign policy business cannot be carried on as a 9-to-5 enterprise. It is a round-the-clock operation. Important problems may arise at any time of day or night, in any part of the world. Foreign policy agencies must be operated and staffed accordingly. Furthermore, the revolutionary telescoping of time and space during the last decade requires not only a posture of continuing alert and readiness to respond but the ability to do so quickly and effectively. While these comments obviously apply to the military, they are almost equally applicable to the full range of foreign policy activities.

The very diversity and extent of foreign policy activities carried on today produce their own set of organizational requirements. These are rather familiar, calling for unified policy direction both at home and overseas, and careful, continuing attention to program details so that these activities reinforce rather than degrade overall effectiveness. The requirements are more easily stated than satisfied.

There are many more sovereign nations to deal with today than twenty-five or even ten years ago. Included among them are several dozen new nations woefully inexperienced in international politics and woefully ill-equipped, politically or organizationally, to deal with its problems. The sheer increase adds substantially to the foreign policy workload just in terms of the number of overseas embassies and missions and country desks in Washington to be established and manned. And, because few countries in the world are capable of applying to the problems of international politics the intellectual and organizational resources of the United States, this country finds itself, in effect, doing much of the foreign policy thinking (though not the decision making!) for nations around the world. This is not chauvinistic pride but a fact of contemporary international life that most American and foreign diplomats, if they are willing to be candid, will concede.

Not only are there many more nations, but there are new and important multilateral forums. In addition to the complex of organizations, councils, committees, programs, and meetings subsumed under the United Nations label, there are a number of important regional organizations concerned with military security, economic development, and peacekeeping. The most important dealings with other nations sometimes take place within one or more of these international organizations.

Each international agency has its own particular history, procedures, and problems that now have to be understood and weighed in the process of formulating foreign policy. This is a requirement almost wholly separate from the continuing need for country-to-country relations, that is, it is an added rather than a substituted requirement. These organizations are no longer mere debating societies. With the willing or reluctant agreement of member-states, even the United Nations organs have undertaken important programs and activities—economic and technical assistance to the underdeveloped countries, international peacekeeping missions, and, in the Congo from 1961 to 1964, a major contribution to the functioning and very survival of what might be called a territorial entity trying to become a nation.

This is at best a partial listing of some of the international needs and characteristics to which the foreign policy organization must be responsive. Some of the more detailed organizational and personnel implications will be developed in later chapters. Nothing has been said about those requirements generated by domestic needs and pressures; they will be discussed to some extent in the chapters on Congress and the President.

An Approach to Organizational Reform

Often, the evaluation of a situation or activity is but a prelude to recommendations for improving it. This is perfectly reasonable, and the option to prescribe as well as judge will be exercised from time to time in this study. I am, however, quite skeptical about the efficacy of grand designs or sweeping proposals for change in the foreign policy organization.

As was suggested above, it is difficult to accept the notion that there is one set of organizational arrangements and relationships ideally suited to meet the needs of the foreign policy organization. For one thing, its effectiveness is significantly limited by deeply ingrained characteristics of American government and politics. For another, the periodic changes in the presidency and the even more frequent turnover in political leadership of the executive departments bring into positions of power new men, with different personalities, attitudes, and leadership styles. With these new men come changes in how the organization is viewed and what is expected of it, and in the ability of its leaders to mobilize its resources. It is also true that even after a major organizational reshuffling, most of the same career people are usually still on the job.

Given the lack of relevant doctrine or theory firmly grounded in empirical investigation, organizational changes are often made without due attention to broader consequences. "It is easier to devise machinery for particular purposes than to consider its total impact as an addition to the already existing structure; the motivations for additions have in fact been particularistic. . . . To keep the structure adequate and up to date requires continuing attention to the mainline of operating command, as well as to staff offices and aids."[5] Furthermore, efforts to fix some of these changes by statute often introduce unnecessary rigidity into what should be a flexible situation, forcing responsible executive officials into organizational molds not of their own choosing and often not to their own taste.

It would be absurd to argue that organizational reforms and adjustments are never useful. Sometimes the need for them is painfully clear. Even then, there is usually a price to be paid. The boxes on the organization chart represent human beings who must learn to carry on their business in the new organizational setup. Each important organizational change involves disruption, readjustment, and some loss of momentum.

As with all else, some organizational changes make more sense than others. For example, proposed organizational arrangements or procedures may represent advances in administrative techniques or relevant technology. An illustration of the former is the concept of an executive secretariat, designed to monitor and control the flow of papers to and from ranking officials in an agency. This is one way of attempting to establish more orderly and systematic decision-making procedures, winnowing the flow of papers to senior officials and assuring their review by the relevant units within the agency. An executive secretariat was one of the organizational contributions that General George C. Marshall made to the State Department in the course of his tenure as Secretary of State from 1947 to 1949.

[5] H. Field Haviland, Jr. and Associates, *The Formulation and Administration of United States Foreign Policy*, A Report for the Committee on Foreign Relations of the United States Senate (Brookings Institution, 1960), p. 43. As was indicated in the Foreword, this study provided the inspiration and point of departure for the present study.

There are many examples of relevant technological advances. In an age marked by striking improvements in the possibilities of direct and rapid telephone and radio communications, the Department of State and the other foreign affairs agencies should not have to rely on commercial cable and telephone lines, as they have to a considerable extent, for the exchange of urgent messages with missions overseas. Part of the problem has been the limited funds available for improvements in communications facilities. The inadequacies in these facilities were brought home sharply at the time of the Cuban crisis in October 1962, and steps were taken shortly thereafter by President Kennedy to strengthen governmental communications, particularly the international system.[6]

Similarly, advances in such fields as computers and microfilming open up fascinating possibilities for meeting a long-standing problem of large organizations—how to draw upon the information stored in files accurately and rapidly as needed. Devices already available make possible almost instantaneous information retrieval. It is not surprising, but somewhat reassuring, to learn that one of the most ambitious and complete information retrieval systems has been installed in the headquarters of the Central Intelligence Agency.

One further category of acceptable organizational innovations should be mentioned. Sometimes, as noted above, organizational change is involved in the effort to introduce a new function, program, or perspective into the structure or to strengthen one that is already present. The latter may be accomplished by elevation in the bureaucratic hierarchy (and thereby, it is hoped, greater power and prestige), increased capabilities in the form of more men and a larger budget, or a more independent position in the organization (so that competing units will less easily be able to block or hinder its activities).

Evaluation of this kind of change will depend upon one's view, first, of the function or perspective being strengthened and, second, of the likelihood that the change will accomplish the desired result. Examples in this category would include the establishment of a Politico-

[6] These steps were reported to the Senate Subcommittee on National Security Staffing and Operations on December 23, 1963, by the Bureau of the Budget. See *Administration of National Security*, Hearings, 88 Cong. 1 sess. (1963), Pt. 6, pp. 421-27. The Department of State also submitted a report on its communications capabilities and problems to the subcommittee on April 20, 1964. See *ibid.*, Pt. 8, pp. 505-09.

Military Affairs staff in the State Department in the spring of 1961, the appointment of a science adviser to the President in 1957, and the much larger and more independent Arms Control and Disarmament Agency that appeared at the end of 1961. These and other examples will be discussed and evaluated later in the book.

The study of United States foreign policy making is a rather unsatisfactory business for those who crave simple, once-and-for-all solutions to problems. Neither the substantive dilemmas nor the organizational problems are susceptible to that kind of treatment. The limits on what is known and what men can do suggest a rather modest, empirical approach to organizational adjustment, with new additions retained and strengthened as they demonstrate their value and less healthy developments pruned from time to time. In organization as in policy, an overall strategy or approach may be useful in setting general directions, but the specific steps must almost inevitably be more limited and tentative.

Finally, the best of organizational and political circumstances can never guarantee "right" decisions. There may be no "right" decision possible, in the sense of one that would somehow advance the interests of the United States. Foreign policy makers are always dealing on the basis of incomplete knowledge with an uncertain world, a world where chance events may prove significant and important factors are completely beyond their control. Thus, there is almost always a discretionary area where judgments must be made. Some mistakes or errors, however defined, are inevitable. Others are not—and this, briefly, is the justification for serious attention to the structure, functions, processes, and personnel of the foreign policy organization.

2

Some Fundamental Characteristics
of the System

SOME GENERAL CHARACTERISTICS of the foreign policy organization
cut across the whole range of executive departments and agencies,
presidential staff units, and overseas programs and operations involved
in American foreign policy. These help point up some of the underlying problems and therefore seem worthy of separate consideration
as a prelude to the discussion of specific organizational units.

The Organizational Revolution

The emergence of the United States as unquestioned world leader
over the past twenty years has revolutionized American foreign policy
organization as well as American international responsibilities and
commitments. As suggested in Chapter 1, the extent of the changes
reflects the character of the world with which the United States must
cope as well as the mere fact of its leadership.

Organizationally, the new tools of statecraft appear as major new
programs and agencies: a vast intelligence apparatus built almost from
scratch, massive economic and military assistance programs metamor-
phosed organizationally more in sixteen years than staid domestic
agencies in sixty, the projection abroad of American information and
the American image, and so on. Cultural and educational exchange
has become increasingly important, as has the role of science for

15

peaceful and military purposes. And just when it seemed as if the possibilities for new programs and agencies had been exhausted, the Peace Corps appeared upon the scene.

The traditional agencies and agents of American foreign policy—the Department of State and the military establishment—have expanded significantly, the military enormously. The expansion has not been only quantitative, in terms of more people, more organizational subdivisions, and much larger budgets. Even more significant have been the fundamental changes in the nature of the work to be done. In addition, many other executive agencies now have major international dimensions to their programs—the Treasury, Commerce, Agriculture, and Labor Departments, the Atomic Energy Commission, and the National Aeronautics and Space Administration, to name some of the more important.

This notable expansion in the number and size of executive agencies in the foreign policy business requires that all their activities be viewed in a broader perspective and given some unified direction. At the highest level this must be a presidential concern; it has been expressed in the establishment and development of the National Security Council as well as other presidential committees, staff positions, and advisory groups. At lower governmental levels all sorts of interdepartmental committees and other coordinating devices have been designed to link related activities in independent executive bodies.

The pace of organizational change has been quite rapid. It has been marked by the setting up of new agencies and new policy-making and coordinating machinery, and by the almost daily modification and reorganization of ongoing organizations, all confronted by quite novel problems of great enormity and complexity. This experimental approach has by no means been limited to the White House. Periodically, the military establishment, the Department of State, and the foreign aid program have been reappraised and reorganized.

Although the National Security Council was established less than two decades ago, its organization and mode of operation have undergone a series of modifications and renovations. In the course of the Eisenhower Administration, the Council machinery expanded considerably. This bureaucratic growth was in turn sharply trimmed by the Kennedy Administration during its first months in office. Some of it has already blossomed again during the last few years in somewhat different forms and forums and with different labels.

In spite of shortcomings and handicaps of one kind and another, there have in fact been some impressive achievements since 1947 in the development of machinery for the formulation and implementation of foreign policy and national security policy. The National Security Council represents an important concept and achievement. The gathering and interpretation of intelligence have advanced a considerable distance from the crudities and confusions of the immediate postwar period. Professionally competent agencies have been developed in the overseas information and economic aid fields. Both the State and Defense Departments are far better equipped to cope with their mid-twentieth century responsibilities than they were ten years ago. Indeed, the whole foreign policy organization is characterized by an increasingly assured and professional approach to the peculiarly difficult international problems of the day.

All of this is not to be interpreted as the counsel of smugness and self-satisfaction. However, in a society where the emphasis seems to be on loud and strident criticism, it seems appropriate to be reminded of the distance already traveled as well as how much still lies ahead.

The Interdepartmental Nature of Important Problems

It has been said that there are no longer any strictly departmental problems, that all important policy problems in the federal government are inter- or cross-departmental. This is certainly the case in the foreign policy field. The responsibilities and programs of many agencies, and their special knowledge and skills, bring them squarely into the foreign policy process. Their involvement is unavoidable and essentially desirable; it reflects the complex nature of contemporary international politics.

At the same time, questions arise—of defining boundary lines between agency responsibilities and allocating roles in the decision-making process. No answers to these questions can satisfy everyone. Each agency, preoccupied with its own problems and responsibilities, is bound to think that others are encroaching on its special precincts, and that its own broader prerogatives are being ignored. There may be general agreement that an agency's role in policy making be roughly proportionate to the extent of its involvement and interests. The State and Defense Departments, however, are wary lest an admission card to the foreign policy process imply an equal voice and equal rights for all; the lesser agencies fear that they will be ignored or kept at arm's length.

There are other characteristic reactions. A typical State Department view is that many agencies with programs and activities relevant to foreign policy are not sufficiently sensitive to foreign policy considerations. Commerce, Agriculture, the Atomic Energy Commission, the Space Administration, and the Defense Department, among others, criticize the State Department for an automatically negative attitude toward activities that have even the slightest possibility of adverse effects abroad. However, no one seriously questions the legitimacy of this broad involvement of executive agencies in foreign affairs.

Although such terms as "communication," "coordination," and "integration" have tended to become shopworn clichés, they do point to fundamental organizational and intellectual requirements of contemporary foreign policy. Differences of opinion exist about how these requirements for policy agreement and program coordination can be most effectively met both in Washington and abroad, and during the last dozen or so years the government has been involved in an extensive learning process. There are implications for personnel as well. If most of the business of foreign policy is cross-departmental, the participating agencies need at least some staff people equipped by training and experience to think and operate across departmental and professional boundaries.

This stress on *inter*departmental relations should not obscure the fact that these requirements for policy and program coordination, and the communication and negotiation they usually demand, apply equally to *intra*departmental policy and program development. Differing geographic and functional perspectives and responsibilities are bound to produce somewhat different answers to policy questions. Even the bonds of departmental loyalty and broad personal acquaintance cannot eliminate them.

There is a somewhat related point that should be noted. Perhaps as another function of the breadth and complexity of contemporary foreign policy, particular "areas of policy" have their own, largely separate groups of policy officials.[1] These groups can be distinguished for purposes of analysis, but their membership cuts across agency lines and can be conceived of as including legislators and even politically active people outside the government.

A few key officials—the President, the Secretaries of State and Defense, perhaps the President's Special Assistant for National Security Affairs—are necessarily involved in almost all important foreign policy and national security problems. It is not surprising, however, that an executive official, or even a congressman, whose responsibilities and interests lie in disarmament policy, NATO, economic development in Latin America, or the destinies of the newly independent states of sub-Saharan Africa would have neither the time nor the inclination to get involved in another major policy area—unless he suddenly found it impinging on his own. These semi-autonomous policy areas underscore the cross-departmental character of contemporary foreign policy making and the imperatives of overall policy direction and meaningful linkages among implementing programs and activities.

The Role of Top Leadership

The burdens of the top leadership of the foreign policy organization are onerous, probably much more so than the demands placed on either their counterparts in other governments, or American executives outside the government. These top leaders must be highly sensitive and responsive to the needs, concerns, and interests of their boss—the President. The centrality of foreign policy problems and the President's responsibility for coping with them make this an overriding requirement that usually takes precedence over all else. It is bound to be highly demanding of time and energy, irrespective of the President's personality and working style. A presidential request or inquiry is not something to be dealt with in good time. And as these top leaders attempt to respond to the President's needs and wishes, the priorities

[1] The term "areas of policy" is borrowed from Roger Hilsman. See his discussion in "The Foreign Policy Consensus: An Interim Research Report," *Journal of Conflict Resolution*, Vol. III (December 1959), pp. 374-79.

they set inevitably reverberate through their organizations, establishing one important part of the workload.

The foreign policy leaders feel the pressures of the domestic political environment indirectly through the President. They also feel them directly—in their various and demanding relationships with Congress, in their contacts with various interest groups, and in their speeches, press conferences, and other statements designed to gain public support for United States foreign policy. Both the indirect and direct play of domestic political forces and pressures is reflected well down the line of the foreign policy organization.

If the foreign policy leaders have important relationships up to the President and out to the wider domestic political setting, they have almost equally critical relationships with one another and with the large bureaucratic organizations they preside over. When one of the major foreign policy actors—the President, the Secretary or Under Secretary of State, the Secretary of Defense, or the Administrator of the Agency for International Development—is at the center of the public stage, one can easily forget the substantial organizational machinery that supports his statements and actions. On the other hand, a stroll through the seemingly endless corridors of the Pentagon or the greatly expanded New State Department Building may lead one to wonder how the top leadership can keep from being swallowed up by the bureaucracy, and how any action at all can emerge from such organizational colossi.

There is, obviously, a strong reciprocal dependence between the politically responsible leadership at the top and the largely career-staffed organizations beneath. There are also important differences—in position, responsibilities, and perspective, and in background, training, and skills. The leadership's actions and decisions rest to a considerable extent on the preparatory labors and recommendations of the organization. On the other hand, the prerogative is always theirs to ignore staff studies and staff advice. Although top leaders are often in the position of essentially ratifying the work of their subordinates, the final choices are still theirs. Sometimes, they will modify staff recommendations, or even reject them. They may even ignore the organization completely. The basic truth is that their interests and concerns are not always those of the bureaucracy. Indeed, as a colleague once put it, there are times when the top of the policy-making iceberg disappears into the clouds, and staffs are completely cut off from any knowledge of what is being discussed and from any opportunity to influence directly the nature of the decisions reached.

The energy, effectiveness, and morale of the organization depend to a considerable extent on how it is led and directed, on the top leaders' sense of purpose, their will and resolve in facing difficult problems and making tough decisions, their energy in pursuit of agreed objectives, their sense of the organizational resources available to them, and their ability to use these effectively.

These qualities, which are in large measure beyond the immediate control of the working levels of the organization, establish its general "tone" and determine how effectively its capabilities will be put to use. The mere existence of the capabilities is not enough. At the same time, from the perspective of the top leaders, it may seem that they are substantially hampered by the inadequacies of the organization. This very combination of mutual dependence and differing interests between top leadership and staff assures that each will have a a somewhat different view of how it is serving and being served by the other.

The roles of ranking foreign policy officials and the relations among them are a more intriguing subject, if only because of the identifiable public personalities involved. As is the case with the top leadership-career organization relationship, the subject is of interest and concern far beyond the foreign policy organization or even government organization in general.

Relevant research has been concerned with the interaction between office and person, between the formal description of a job and the way some individual actually performs in it. It seems reasonable to hypothesize that at the upper echelons of any organization, particularly in the line-of-command positions, the role that an officeholder actually plays will depend less on the formal definition of his responsibilities and more on his personality, skills, and attitudes, the interests and abilities of his immediate colleagues, and their attitudes toward him. At lower levels, job responsibilities are usually defined more narrowly and specifically, with less room for individual interpretation and maneuver.

At the level of the President's relationships with his agency heads, the evidence is pretty clear. The allocation of responsibilities between a particular President and Secretary of State provides some dramatic illustrations. For example, one can contrast the broad mandate of responsibility that President Eisenhower gave John Foster Dulles with the much more limited scope that President Franklin Roosevelt allowed Secretary of State Cordell Hull.

The point applies equally within departments. The division of foreign policy labors in the State Department among the Secretary, the two Under Secretaries, and the Deputy Under Secretary for Political Affairs depends on individual abilities, attitudes, and personal relationships rather than on anything that can be specified in an organization manual. For example, during both the Eisenhower and Kennedy Administrations, a capable Under Secretary of State for Economic Affairs was promoted to the position of ranking Under Secretary; in both instances, he brought his economic functions to the new position.[2]

This is not to suggest that the essence of foreign policy making lies in personalities and personal relationships. It does seem appropriate in an organizational study, however, to note the limits of organizational arrangements. The fact is that at times difficulties in the policy-making process may well be explained by examining personal relationships and attitudes.

A relationship of mutual confidence and respect between the Secretaries of State and Defense may do more to improve and facilitate State-Defense relations than a dozen executive orders. This is true also of the Secretary of State's relationship with a number of other agencies and their heads—the Agency for International Development, the Arms Control and Disarmament Agency, the Peace Corps, and the United States Information Agency. Although the Secretary of State is the ranking foreign policy official beneath the President, and has varying degrees of authority over these agencies, he is not in a position to exercise detailed control and supervision of them.

At the same time, there is the need for closely coordinated policies and actions. This cannot be accomplished by appropriate admonitions in organization manuals and directives; mutual respect, good working relations, and basic policy agreement among the major agency heads and ranking subordinates are needed. These factors should certainly be a prime consideration in the making of major appointments al-

[2] Douglas Dillon and George W. Ball.

though, of course, these are not things that can always be accurately predicted. The principle is equally applicable to the key positions in the United States missions abroad. The notions of "team" and "teamwork" may have become political slogans in recent years, but they do point to some basic—although sometimes subtle—organizational realities.

Preoccupation with the Current and Immediate

The effects of continuing organizational change and the heavy burdens of top leadership are accentuated by a persistent problem of American government—the rapid turnover of personnel in top positions. This occurs when a new President enters office, of course, but it also occurs with great frequency between presidential changes of power. Perhaps these factors contribute to another basic characteristic of American foreign policy making—a continuing preoccupation with the current and the immediate.

The foreign policy process is marked by an ever-present sense of rush and urgency, of sharp and immediate threats to policies and programs posed by opposition both domestic and foreign. The system is primarily preoccupied with day-to-day problems, with putting out the fire immediately at hand, whether this be a new crisis in Southeast Asia or Central Africa, a controversial speech by a European leader that requires a response, or a sharp cut in foreign aid funds voted by a House Appropriations subcommittee. One gets little sense of a leisured pace, of very many moments available for contemplation and reflection. Furthermore, the higher one moves up the organizational structure, the more pronounced these "crisis" characteristics become.

It is difficult to imagine the British—or even the French or the Soviets—operating with quite this style and tempo. Why is this characteristic so strikingly American? For one thing, the external problems of the United States are fantastically difficult and complex; in truth, there is no equivalent in earlier periods. Not only are there extremely powerful, hostile nations challenging the United States in a wide range of areas and situations, but the problems of negotiation, conciliation, and coordinated action with allied, associated, and neutralist nations provide dilemmas and difficulties aplenty.

Further, the nature of the American constitutional and political system adds substantial burdens. Relations with Congress are crucial and time-consuming. High-level officials must spend a considerable portion of their working year testifying before congressional committees. Policies and programs requiring appropriations must undergo yearly scrutiny, and there is always uncertainty about the results. Partisan, domestically-oriented politics inevitably becomes interwoven with foreign and military policy. Depending on one's point of view at any particular time, the partisan political element may be considered statesmanlike and responsible or narrow and irresponsible—but introduced it often is.

Some observers would at this point add comments about the American character or the American style and suggest that many American executives are used to—and even enjoy—this sense of ever-present crisis and urgency, this need for immediate action and lots of it, and their seventy-hour weeks. Possibly, many officials would not want contemplative moments and would not know what to do if these were built into their schedules.[3]

If there is any validity in the foregoing, what difference does it make? In this study it is assumed that major foreign policy problems will be more adequately dealt with if there is time to reflect, if decisions are approached with an understanding in depth of what is involved, and furthermore, if problems are viewed in a broader policy context and from a longer-term perspective. The foreign policy organization should have the capacity to anticipate policy problems and prepare accordingly; its leaders need some time to profit from these preparations. It is clear that the characteristics of the American system and the American style noted above are not completely compatible with these intellectual requirements.

It should be emphasized that this general statement, which is elaborated in Chapter 10, is not meant to present a black-and-white picture. For one thing, operating and thinking are not mutually exclusive. Furthermore, profound thought and keen analysis are by no

[3] W. W. Rostow has written some fascinating essays on the American national style and its expression in the United States role in world affairs. See, for example, "The National Style," in Elting E. Morison (ed.), *The American Style* (Harper, 1958), pp. 246-313; and *The United States in the World Arena* (Harper, 1960), *passim*.

means strangers to the foreign policy organization. There are, however, substantial handicaps to overcome.[4]

In some areas, these handicaps do not seem to be subject to much alteration in the immediate future. The role of Congress and the burdens of executive-legislative relations fall in this category, as does party politics. To the extent that the handicaps are matters of working style, there would seem to be some room for modification and improvement. Even here, the grounds for optimism are limited. Thoughtful outside observers deplore the hectic pace and the many overseas journeys of the Secretary of State. However much Secretaries of State may acknowledge the point in principle, they seem unable to do very much about it in practice.

Decision Processes and Patterns

The study of foreign policy decision-making in the United States tends to leave one with a contradictory set of impressions. In part this may be explained by the diverse agencies and activities involved in foreign policy making and the variety of patterns that characterize decision making.[5]

Differences in how and where—and by whom—decisions are made reflect the nature of the problem being dealt with and the importance attached to it, particularly by senior officials. This assessment involves subjective judgments as well as objective criteria. Importance may be measured in quite fundamental terms, that is, whether basic national security interests and objectives are considered to be at stake. Once this judgment is made as far as the United States is concerned, poli-

[4] Former Secretary of State Dean Acheson has argued that if the Secretary of State, or any other high official for that matter, feels strongly enough about his need to think deeply about the problems that confront him, there is no reason why he cannot do so. See "Thoughts About Thought in High Places," *New York Times Magazine*, Oct. 11, 1959, pp. 20 ff. This essay has been reprinted in *Organizing for National Security*, Vol. 2, Studies and Background Materials submitted to the Senate Government Operations Committee by its Subcommittee on National Policy Machinery (1961), pp. 290-96.

[5] The apparent confusion is also explained in part by the absence of substantial, relevant quantitative data on most of these matters as well as of carefully defined case studies. One must settle, therefore, for qualitative impressions and judgments rather than conclusions expressed in more precise, even quantitative terms.

cy makers must then consider how other nations view the importance of a situation. The size of relevant programs and the funds involved are also bases for assessing importance. So is the interest shown by the President. These factors influence the level of the organization at which decision making will take place and the number of officials and agencies that will get involved.

It was suggested in Chapter 1 that in times of crisis, the foreign policy organization may appear particularly disordered and confused.[6] This may be a surface observation that does not take into account the quiet support that professional staffs are providing to the few key officials in the spotlight. Furthermore, if normal organizational channels and routines are being ignored, this, too, is not necessarily as disorderly as it may appear. Habits of cooperation and good working relations built up by the responsible officials and their staffs in quieter periods may make it possible to short-circuit normal procedures in a crisis period.

In the governmental bureaucracy, a low priority problem may drag along for weeks at a time because people, particularly senior people, are busy with more urgent matters. The pressure to get the matter resolved is simply not there. But once that pressure is generated by some change in circumstances, the whole decision-making process can be greatly accelerated, and with little damage to the substance of what is being decided. In such cases, the essential organizational relationships have been developed and most of the thinking about the problem has already been done. It can, therefore, quickly be brought to resolution.

It must be conceded that not all crisis decision making can be explained in these terms. At times, situations get a bit hectic, and *ad hoc* efforts take the place of more disciplined and orderly processes. It would, nevertheless, be a gross distortion to describe the decision-mak-

---

[6] This is the impression that many journalistic observers get, and reflect to their readers. Given the perspective of the newspaperman, who focuses his attention primarily on the comings and goings (and comments) of a few key officials at the top, this is an understandable reaction. It is likely to be further reinforced by some of the ways in which the newspaperman plies his trade and is in turn manipulated by his news sources—for example, intentional and unintentional leaks to the press and off-the-record "backgrounders" by senior officials. For a thoughtful and sophisticated variation on this theme, see Max Frankel, "Origins of Foreign Policy: Secrets, Errors and Vision," *New York Times*, June 29, 1964.

ing activities of the total foreign policy organization in terms of the behavior of a few top officials in some crisis situations.

This view ignores the elaborate machinery that has been developed and frequently used since World War II for the making of high-level foreign policy decisions. It also ignores the substantial staff support activity, mentioned above, that is usually available for the making of critical decisions. In an orderly, even routine, fashion, intelligence estimates and deeper intelligence studies, planning papers, and policy analyses are systematically prepared by formally designated staffs. Reporting and analysis from the field missions of the foreign affairs agencies and from the military commands flow into Washington on a regular basis. Requests for supplementary information and analysis are made all the time by Washington agencies. If crisis decision making sometimes gives the impression of a foreign policy organization without structure and order, the more routine, continuing activities connected with foreign policy making leave the strong impression of system and rationality. Both pictures are incomplete; each without the other is misleading.

High-level decision making is not always crisis decision making. Top officials must approve a great variety of documents that establish policy guidelines and implementing strategies in various fields. They must approve budgets and are often called upon to decide very specific and difficult budgetary questions. The toughest decisions are often the implementing choices rather than those that demand opting for one fundamental course of action rather than another.

Apart from the situations of high crisis, where decisions are made by a hard core of key officials—such as the Cuban missile crisis of October 1962 and the decision to intervene in Korea in 1950—decision-making processes tend to be handled through rather well-established organizational channels and in terms of normal bureaucratic routines. Typically, foreign policy documents—which may range from outgoing telegrams to proposed country foreign assistance programs to contingency planning papers—must go through a process of intra- and interagency clearance before they reach the organizational level at which final approval can be given. "Clearance" is a system for assuring that all those with relevant responsibilities have seen and approved the document in question. It is a system that can be abused, but it does attempt to provide for an orderly process of consultation under circumstances where a minimum of several organizational units, and sometimes many more, are interested in most problems.

It should not be assumed that the more routine decision-making processes are necessarily slower than the crisis versions. Telegrams coming into the Department of State from overseas missions often must be answered on the same day—and are.

It was suggested earlier in the chapter that semi-autonomous "areas of policy" can be distinguished which have their own organizational subsystems and sets of interested officials. Decision-making patterns often vary from one of these policy areas to another. In part, this reflects the personalized nature of the responsibilities assigned to senior officials. For example, the Assistant Secretary of State responsible for one geographic area may be very highly regarded by the Secretary of State and the President. He may therefore be given more autonomy in his day-to-day work and also be admitted into the inmost decision-making circles more frequently than colleagues of equal rank in the State Department. Special presidential interest in a problem usually produces more active involvement of the White House national security staff.

Decision-making patterns within particular policy fields do, then, reflect the extent of interest at high policy levels as well as the abilities and reputations of responsible political and career officials at the next few organizational levels below. They may also be influenced by the nature of the formal decision-making machinery available in the particular policy field. Both points are illustrated by the establishment of a high-ranking Special Group (Counter-Insurgency) at the beginning of 1962. The existence of the Group, Attorney General Robert Kennedy's membership in it, and President Kennedy's strong interest combined to give the counter-insurgency problem a focus and sense of urgency that it probably would not have otherwise had.

Interagency committees, task forces, and coordinating groups are not always so fortunate in their high-level membership and the high-level attention devoted to them. Even such support cannot guarantee their continuing usefulness. As will be seen in the discussion of specific committees in later chapters, there is a tendency for committees to become overly routinized in their work while losing the strong sense of purpose that may have motivated them originally. Sometimes, the problem may be that they have performed their assigned task so well that they should be abolished, but aren't. As in the carrying on of any other complex organizational activity, committees are an essential element—and a continuing problem—in foreign policy making.[7]

No discussion of foreign policy decision making, even as an executive branch process, would be complete without some comments on its political dimensions. The fact that domestic political forces and pressures reach into the foreign policy organization in a variety of ways has already been noted. What is referred to here are the political elements that characterize decision making within executive agencies.

While the insight is not new, scholars like Samuel P. Huntington, Richard E. Neustadt,[8] and Roger Hilsman have been most helpful in providing substantial illustration and systematic analysis to underscore its significance in the processes of foreign and military policy making.

Hilsman emphasizes that the "rational" model of the policy-making process is a highly simplified version of what usually takes place. He argues that in the case of "major national issues" the "making of policy in government . . . *is essentially a political process,* even when it takes place entirely inside the government, screened from the voter's view, or even when it takes place entirely within one agency of the government."[9] In his view, a processs that is "essentially political" has three characteristics. These include: (1) "the reconciliation both of a

[7] Arthur W. Macmahon comments: "A committee is the fitting device when a number of agencies have a substantial concern in a series of related problems of policy upon which all should have a chance to comment and which, as a continuing matter, will require recurrent consultation over a considerable period of time." *Administration in Foreign Affairs* (University of Alabama Press, 1953), pp. 205-06.

The role of committees in complex organizations is a subject that has been extensively treated by students of bureaucracy and public administration. From the point of view of American foreign policy making, useful references would be: Macmahon, *op. cit.,* Chap. 4; The Brookings Institution, *The Administration of Foreign Affairs and Overseas Operations* (Government Printing Office, 1951), Chap. IX; and a letter, dated Dec. 2, 1963, written by Donald Wilson, then Deputy Director of the U. S. Information Agency, to Senator Henry M. Jackson, in *Administration of National Security,* Hearings before the Subcommittee on National Security Staffing and Operations of the Senate Government Operations Committee, 88 Cong. 1 sess. (1963), Pt. 6, pp. 429-32.

[8] Neustadt has written perceptively, and with rich illustrative detail, about significant political dimensions in the work of the President. See *Presidential Power* (John Wiley, 1960).

[9] Hilsman, in *Journal of Conflict Resolution,* p. 365. Emphasis added.

diversity of values and goals and of alternative means and policies";
(2) "competing groups who are identified with these alternative goals
and policies"; and (3) the dependence of the final decision as much on
"the relative power of these participating groups . . . as the cogency and
wisdom of the arguments used in support of the policy adopted."[10]

The basic point in the analyses of both Hilsman and Huntington
is that where important disagreements on policies or programs exist
within the executive branch, or even within particular departments,
the resolution of these differences involves controversy, bargaining, ap-
peals to higher authority, and perhaps efforts to obtain support outside the executive branch. Furthermore, the end result will be as much
a function of the power of those involved as of the intellectual merits
of their respective positions. Such disagreements, it is believed, cannot
usually be resolved by study and analysis. Two key factors intertwine:
the organizational and personal stakes are likely to be too great and,
furthermore, the merits of the issues are not usually that clear-cut.

The most obvious examples of "political" conflict, in this sense,
within the executive branch are probably found in the making of military policy. Decision making on major military programs generates a
series of political struggles within the military establishment and,
more broadly, within the national security organization.[11]

There are also examples and case studies to be found in the foreign
policy field, although Hilsman has overstated his case. The decisions
on Cuba in the spring of 1961 certainly reflected a great deal of political struggle within the executive branch. Perhaps this explains why it
was not possible for the United States government to decide on either
a full commitment of its prestige and resources or no involvement at

[10] *Ibid.* Huntington approaches the question of major military policy making (or,
as he calls it, "strategic planning") in a similar way. What Hilsman labels "political,"
Huntington calls "legislative": "Strategic programs are thus decided upon in the
Executive rather than in Congress. The process of decision within the Executive,
however, bears many striking resemblances to the process of decision in Congress.
It retains a peculiarly legislative flavor." See "Strategic Planning and the Political
Process," *Foreign Affairs,* Vol. 38 (January 1960), pp. 288-89. Huntington has de-
veloped this analysis more fully in *The Common Defense* (Columbia University
Press, 1961), particularly Chap. III.

[11] Huntington dissects and documents this process thoroughly and brilliantly in
The Common Defense, op. cit. One has the sense that this particular characteristic
of military policy making has been less evident during the tenure of Defense Secretary Robert McNamara, perhaps because he has used his own position of authority
so effectively.

all. On the other hand, the decision to intervene in Korea in 1950 seems to have had wide and substantial backing among the agencies involved. All that can be said is that where such differences do exist, they are likely to trigger conflicts of a political nature within the executive branch, and the policy consequences will reflect these elements as well as rational analyses of the problem.

Intellectual Creativity in a Bureaucracy

In a sense, all the characteristics discussed above point toward one of the fundamental problems of the foreign policy organization. Put in general terms, how are intellectual integrity, keen analytical abilities, creativity of thought, and a longer-term perspective on problems to be maintained in a complex bureaucratic and political structure?

It has already been pointed out that the foreign policy organization is characterized by the presence of a large number of agencies with relevant responsibilities and skills and perspectives, which in turn necessitates rather elaborate machinery and procedures to facilitate coordination and integration of policy development, decision making, and program implementation.

In terms of their general purpose and function, these activities cannot be questioned. However, in their detailed operation, they are not completely compatible with the intellectual needs of the system. The necessity to coordinate and to integrate perspectives and programs often produces the watering down of differences—in intelligence estimates, analyses of problems, and policy and program recommendations. Dulling the sharp edges of intellectual disagreement is often the price of interdepartmental agreement and cooperation. Sometimes it is a price well worth paying, in terms of the solution arrived at as well as the facilitation of the government's business. Sometimes it is not.

Another consequence of the intradepartmental and interdepartmental clearances and concurrences which are the working procedures of coordination is a certain inertia in the system. This should not be exaggerated because, as was suggested above, it is possible to produce decisions very quickly if the need is seen as sufficiently great. Nevertheless, the bureaucratic processes are often both slow and cumbersome unless prodded by a sharp sense of urgency.

There is also a point at which the production, distribution, exchange, and revision of papers—all, again, necessary in this kind of intellectual activity—become absolutely overwhelming. The drafting and redrafting, the subtle nuances of meaning and interpretation, the considerable number of people who have a hand in the drafting of a particular paper, the clearances and concurrences that must be obtained—clearly, this massive paperwork becomes at a certain point stifling and unproductive. The value of additional contributions by new hands rapidly diminishes and in the end must be far outweighed by the costs of delay and under-employment of highly skilled people.

This in turn suggests another problem. Does a system with these characteristics tend to discourage its brighter, more creative, and imaginative career officials so that a substantial proportion of them eventually leave government service? Do many of those who stay tend to lose their élan, or simply their motivation to put out their best effort? When one refers to the "military mind" or the "bureaucrat" in the stereotyped sense, the implication is that long years of service in a large organization have resulted in a smoothing-down of the rough edges of individuality and originality, a certain narrowness and rigidity of view, a lack of receptivity to new or unconventional ideas, and perhaps excessive caution and loss of initiative. No doubt some would say that there is, in this sense, a "Foreign Service mind." Is it inevitable that the frustrations and inhibitions imposed by the large organization discourage many from remaining and stifle the intellectual originality and brilliance of those that do?

There is a question about how much intellectual originality the foreign policy organization needs. Much of its work calls for applied, operational intelligence rather than highly imaginative or innovative effort. Such application of intellect to practical, working problems is certainly in the pragmatic American tradition.[12]

These are broad questions and generalizations. Certainly for those deeply interested in contemporary problems of foreign policy and national security, there is a kind of excitement to be found in working on these problems that is simply not available elsewhere. This stimulation may more than compensate for the burdens of life in the bu-

[12] See W. W. Rostow's comments in his essays on the American style cited above. Rostow acknowledges the American capacity for adaptive response but suggests that America's present world position demands a capacity for broad innovation not notably evidenced in American historical development.

reaucracy. Undoubtedly, it does for many. It is also clear that these characteristics of the modern complex organization have a far wider range of applicability than the foreign policy organization of the United States; they are problems to be faced in many fields of employment.

Perhaps, as Mr. Rostow has suggested, some things can be done to help re-establish the importance of the individual in the bureaucratic structure, even in Washington.[13] In any event, the nature of the American system is such that if the men at the top are not satisfied with the quality of the intellectual efforts within the organization, they have considerable freedom to look beyond it, for both ideas and "idea men." This in turn creates further problems—for the morale and sense of commitment of men in the career services. The fundamental problem remains, and there seems to be no easy solution.

These have been tentative and impressionistic characterizations of the foreign policy organization. Perhaps some of their implications will be seen more clearly as specific agencies and functional problems are examined in the chapters that follow.

[13] See Rostow's interesting discussion in *The United States in the World Arena*, pp. 493-502, "Bureaucracy, Innovation, and the Individual."

The general problem of intellectual creativity in a bureaucratic structure is approached somewhat differently but discussed provocatively and insightfully in an essay by Henry A. Kissinger, "The Policymaker and the Intellectual," *The Reporter*, Vol. 20, No. 5 (March 5, 1959), pp. 30-35. Kissinger's essay has been reprinted in *Organizing for National Security*, Vol. 2, pp. 254-66. It also appears in an excellent collection of readings edited by Professors Andrew M. Scott and Raymond H. Dawson, *Readings in the Making of American Foreign Policy* (Macmillan, 1965), pp. 320-33.

3

The Congressional Setting

EXECUTIVE DOMINANCE in foreign policy is both traditional and constitutional. Conditions of life in the mid-twentieth century have in many ways increased and underscored that dominance. On the other hand, the centrality of foreign policy and national security problems in the governmental process, and in the federal budget, has produced an interesting and ironical result: the legislature's role in foreign policy making is secondary, and yet quite powerful. Congress represents the most important part of the political setting within which the foreign policy machinery of the executive branch must operate. While it is not normally in a position to take the initiative in the formulation of policy,[1] Congress can and often does modify policy significantly in detail and, upon occasion, exercises a kind of veto on certain lines of policy choice.

The focus of this study does not permit treatment of those political forces and processes lying outside the formal governmental structure. The latter may be thought of as the broader political setting within which the national government must operate, imposing its own limits on the choices open to executive and legislature alike but, particularly

[1] For a case study of congressional initiative in the foreign policy field, see James A. Robinson, *The Monroney Resolution: Congressional Initiative in Foreign Policy-Making* (Henry Holt, 1959). Professor Robinson has pursued this interest in a larger study, *Congress and Foreign Policy-Making* (Dorsey Press, 1962). See particularly Chaps. Three, Four, and Seven of that study. Robinson inclines to the view that greater congressional initiative in foreign policy is not only desirable but feasible. In my view, he underestimates the fundamental nature of the obstacles and places too great a weight on the role definitions and behavior of some key senators, for example, Lyndon Johnson's performance as Senate majority leader.

in the foreign policy field, not exercising important initiative. A wide variety of people, organizations, activities, and attitudes are encompassed. There are many relationships and connections within this broader political setting, as well as between it and units and officials within the legislative and executive branches. The concept of "setting" is not meant to imply a series of watertight rings surrounding and limiting the rings within. In a highly pluralistic society like the United States, there are many channels and outlets for the expression of views on foreign policy problems and for efforts to influence official decisions.

The vigorous scholarly research on American political processes during the past thirty or forty years has raised serious doubts about the traditional image of the democratic citizen in action. The evidence suggests that the moods and views of the "mass public" set only the very broadest limits on policy direction. At the same time, the views of certain opinion leaders—businessmen, trade union officials, newspaper editors and publishers, and leading figures of church, education, medicine, and the bar—may, on some occasions and for some issues, have a very specific impact on policy decisions. These views and preferences may be brought to bear directly on the foreign policy organization or be expressed through certain influential members of Congress.[2]

These comments are not meant to imply a "power elite" hypothesis about United States foreign policy making. While neither the processes nor the results are ideal, there is open political activity and debate aplenty on foreign policy and national security issues. The average citizen may not be paying much attention, but a great volume of words is directed at him at least implicitly on the assumption that his views are important and are therefore worth trying to influence.

In sum, the interactions and interrelations among the executive, the legislature, and the politically relevant units and activities beyond them are very complex and characterized by many different techniques of political persuasion; they have greatly varying consequences for foreign policy decisions. Thus, an analysis of the role of Congress

[2] A systematic effort to set forth the variety of channels and processes that link public views and foreign policy is found in James N. Rosenau, *Public Opinion and Foreign Policy* (Random House, 1961). Professor Rosenau has also provided us with a probing general analysis of the nature and functioning of these leadership groups along with a case study in what he calls "the mobilization of public support." See *National Leadership and Foreign Policy* (Princeton University Press, 1963).

in foreign policy must be concerned not merely with executive-legislative relations but equally with the relations of both with the political world beyond.

Bases for Evaluation

Some of the obstacles to a meaningful evaluation of the organization and processes of foreign policy making in general are illustrated with particular sharpness in an analysis of the role of Congress.

The very structure of Congress presents difficulties. Compared to the executive branch, Congress has relatively little hierarchical organization. There are party leaders, presiding officers, and committee chairmen, but they are not in a position of clear authority, like the President or his department heads. There is no one official or group of officials to whom certain tests of leadership can be logically and rigidly applied. Congress is also marked by a diffusion of responsibility for the functions it performs, however significant or influential the actions of certain committees may in fact be. In contrast, there are some precise allocations of power and responsibility among the agencies of the executive branch and, therefore, a more clearly defined basis for assessing their operations.

It should be possible to set forth the basic functions that Congress does or should perform. However, lists of these functions tend to be unexceptionable and not very helpful. It is not so much a question of *what* Congress should do, but *how* it does it, or how it *should* do it. Presumably, the kind of congressional performance prescribed will be based on assumptions about both the conditions and requisites of contemporary international politics and the role of the democratic legislature as it has developed in the American political system.

The complex problems and needs of a modern industrial society and great world power have substantially strengthened a characteristic built into the American system by the checks and balances of the Constitution, namely, the considerable overlap in the functions of the legislative and executive branches. It is true that the President alone is vested with the "executive power" to see that "the laws be faithfully executed," and that Congress is endowed with "all legislative powers." Nevertheless, the major portion of their functions is shared.

Both are significantly concerned with broad domestic and foreign policies and programs, the major policy choices of war, peace, and cold war, and the detailed execution of these policies and programs. From the point of view of the executive, the basis for congressional potency lies in its exclusive prerogatives of legislative authorization and appropriation. From the congressional viewpoint, this ultimate power is considerably diluted in fact—particularly in the foreign policy-national security area—by the complexities of the problems, the continuing need for speed and secrecy, and the obvious advantages of the executive with regard to both.

In terms that are .rather general, the basic functions of Congress can be set forth as follows:

    1. It has a responsibility to identify and inquire into problems that may call for legislative action.

    2. It shares with the Executive the function of framing broad national objectives.

    3. It can help to estimate the relative merits of alternative approaches to dealing with various problems.

    4. It may give attention, on a selective basis, to questions of detail related to broader issues.

    5. It has the exclusive responsibility for enacting authorization and appropriation legislation.

    6. It can help, as part of its investigatory function, to evaluate the performance of the Executive, again on a selective basis.[3]

Putting the matter in somewhat different terms, in the field of foreign policy Congress has a responsibility for the careful scrutiny and critical discussion of policies and programs that will normally be initiated and developed by the executive as well as for the continuing surveillance of executive implementation of these programs. If Congress performs these functions effectively, it should contribute to the clarification of basic policy issues and problems and should also help keep the executive agencies more alert, more efficiently run, and sharper in their own intellectual processes. Finally, legislative debate of the major issues before Congress should serve as a highly important

---

[3] This list is quoted verbatim from H. Field Haviland, Jr. and Associates, *The Formulation and Administration of United States Foreign Policy,* A Report for the Committee on Foreign Relations of the United States Senate (Brookings Institution, 1960), p. 24. The present chapter draws to some extent from Chap. II of that study, particularly pp. 22-24, 27-28, 29-31, and 37-39.

contribution to public understanding and discussion. Thus, aside from the difficult business of trying to develop policies and programs of its own, Congress should be critically analyzing and evaluating those of the executive, keeping a watchful eye on executive performance, and contributing significantly to public discussion of the issues.

All of this is still rather general. Is it possible to be more specific and even quantitative? One simple and crude basis for evaluating congressional performance in the foreign policy and national defense fields would be to compare it with the legislative programs and budgetary requests of the executive and to find it inadequate to the extent that legislative response deviated from the executive request. This idea is rather absurd, although some executive officials might view it with a kind of wistful interest. It does provide a reminder that the labors of the Congress have some very specific and even quantitative end products in the form of statutes enacted, monies appropriated, and taxes levied. These can be evaluated in terms of the intellectual qualities of the statutes enacted, the nature of congressional modifications of the original proposals of the executive branch, the relationship between programs authorized and money actually appropriated for them, and, of course, the relationship between expenditures voted and taxes levied. The diffusion of power and responsibility within Congress makes it difficult to evaluate individual and even committee performance, but some crude, overall judgments should be possible.

There are also basic organizational criteria applicable to an evaluation of congressional performance. There is a division of labor within each house, based primarily on the committee system. Highly relevant to this discussion are the questions of how clearly responsibilities for functional areas and policy problems are allocated among the committees, and of what procedures for consultation and coordination are employed when committee responsibilities overlap, as they inevitably do. So is the question of the speed with which the legislative proposals of the executive are worked through the total legislative process. Clearly, speed is not an end in itself, but in an era of swift changes and unexpected developments, government's ability to respond with dispatch can be extremely important and, for many matters, this ability is highly dependent on Congress.

One acid test applied to the formulation of public policy, whether foreign or domestic, is the nature of the relationship between policies recommended or pursued and the amounts of money recommended or allocated in these policy areas. Putting the problem in organizational terms, it is the relationship between substantive policy making and policy makers and the budgetary processes and personnel through which the abstractions of policy are translated into specific programs and activities. This is a fundamental question in the analysis of executive policy making; it is also an important and legitimate question in the study of Congress.

Basic Characteristics

Perhaps the best way to introduce this brief analysis of the world's most powerful and important legislative body is with some broad brushstroke characterizations. It has already been remarked that power and responsibility for legislative action are widely diffused within Congress. Certain individual legislators, furthermore, have considerable ability to influence legislative end results while some, perhaps most, of their colleagues are as individuals relatively uninfluential. These positions of influence are not necessarily related to broad-based support among fellow legislators, to good relations with the President or some executive agency, or to a strong popular standing with large countrywide constituencies.

It should also be noted that the division of labor, organizational structure, and institutionalized patterns and procedures of the House and Senate provide ample opportunity for the defeat (either by vote or by committee pigeonholing), modification or, some would say, emasculation of proposed legislation. In this sense, as an institution better suited to opposition and naysaying than to positive action, the Congress of the United States can be fairly labeled a conservative body.

It is a bicameral legislature, where both houses must approve identical bills before the legislature can act or, rather, enact. The Constitution provides for some differentiation of roles, and at one time the Senate's treaty-approval and appointment-confirmation powers gave it and its Foreign Relations Committee a certain pre-eminence in the foreign affairs field. It is generally agreed that this pre-eminence has sharply waned if not completely disappeared with the advent of multibillion dollar national security budgets and the increasing intermixture of foreign and domestic policies.

The Committee Structure

The major legislative work of both houses takes place in a series of formally organized and constituted committees, broken down primarily by subject matter. In some committees, notably the House Appropriations Committee, the work of well-established subcommittees is quite important. The committees are the key to congressional behavior; their decisions, more often than not, become the decisions of each house.

The role of the committee chairmen in the functioning of these committees is central. Normally, they have the key voice in the hiring and firing of staff personnel (for the majority members); often, these staff people tend to become in effect an extension of the chairman's personal staff. The chairmen usually take responsibility for scheduling committee meetings, and are most influential in the choice of subjects for investigation and in the decisions made about legislation under consideration. But beyond the powers gained through their formal role as chairmen, these men are usually powerful because of lengthy service and experience, close ties with the party leadership, the considerable deference with which they are treated by executive officials, and, often, mastery of the substantive policy problems with which their committees deal, based on long experience. Seniority in committees is based on length of service on the committee, and the chairmanship, with quite rare exceptions, goes to that legislator of the majority party who has served longest on the committee.

The Senate Foreign Relations Committee is still the premier congressional committee in the foreign policy field, extremely influential both with its Senate colleagues and with the foreign policy officials of the executive branch. The House Foreign Affairs Committee has in recent years risen in prestige and in the quality of representatives interested in serving on it, but it still does not carry the influence in the House that its counterpart does in the Senate.

Each committee has established consultative subcommittees designed to provide for continuing communication with the executive branch about more specific policy matters. Some are organized along geographic lines—for example, Far East, Latin America, Africa—parallel to the regional bureaus of the State Department. Others have a functional or problem focus, such as the Senate Subcommittee on Disarmament. The latter is an example of a subcommittee that has been very active in its field of policy interest. Another example of the use of this device was the intimate collaboration between the Senate subcommittee concerned with Far Eastern affairs and the then Ambassador John Foster Dulles and his State Department staff in shaping the Japanese peace settlement in 1951 and 1952.[4]

The widening impact of international affairs is reflected in Congress in the fact that more than half of the thirty-six standing committees of the two houses now deal regularly with issues of international significance. Those committees concerned with military policy and the military establishment have a particularly important jurisdiction. And while the role of the Armed Services Committees therein is considerable, it is by no means all-inclusive. Professor Huntington notes that a majority of the congressional committees "become involved in one way or another with military affairs," but he labels six of them the "principal instrumentalities."[5]

The presence of both military appropriations subcommittees on Huntington's list is but one illustration of the substantial power of the Appropriations Committees. In theory, one might assume that these committees would not be concerned with the substance of policy but only the cost of what has already been authorized. Policy and the amount of money spent to carry it out are, however, not so easily separable. In fact, the Appropriations Committees regularly and openly make substantive policy judgments, and their right to do so is not generally questioned. Presumably, these judgments are translated into their budgetary decisions.

Where the authorizing legislation establishes rather general guidelines—such as the personnel ceilings set for the military services—the Appropriations Committees are not substantially limited and indeed become the principal instruments of legislative control. But even when programs are authorized annually with precise expenditure figures at-

[4] See Bernard C. Cohen, *The Political Process and Foreign Policy: The Making of the Japanese Peace Settlement* (Princeton University Press, 1957), Chap. 8.

[5] Samuel P. Huntington, *The Soldier and the State* (Belknap Press of Harvard University Press, 1957), p. 403. In addition to the two Armed Services Committees, he includes the House and Senate military appropriations subcommittees, the House Government Operations Committee, and the Senate Foreign Relations Committee.

tached, such as foreign aid, the two committees feel free to make their independent budgetary judgments.

In other words, the fact that programs must first be authorized by legislation originating in such substantive committees as Foreign Relations and then implemented through separate appropriations acts that are the responsibility of the Appropriations Committees means that policies and programs are subjected to a kind of legislative double jeopardy. In the process, they are almost certain to be modified and, occasionally, sharply altered. Furthermore, since the expenditures authorized in effect represent ceilings, the amounts actually appropriated are bound to be lower. This is generally understood and expected. The critical question is always, how much lower?

Each Appropriations Committee is a holding company for powerful subcommittees that dominate the financial decisions about their respective fields. Considerable influence is wielded by the chairmen of these subcommittees. The subcommittee decisions about their portions of the budget are usually ratified without extensive deliberation by the full committees. Congressional judgment about the budget as a whole is in turn the sum of its actions on the series of separate appropriations measures, compiled at the end of a legislative session. The appropriations process, then, illustrates par excellence the influence that a relative handful of men can have in determining the essential shape of legislation in Congress.

In the foreign policy field specifically, this state of affairs is underscored by the considerable influence of two Democratic Congressmen who have had a goodly share of public attention: John Rooney, from a district in Brooklyn, and Otto Passman, representing a rural constituency in Louisiana. Congressman Rooney chairs the House Appropriations subcommittee concerned with Department of State appropriations while Mr. Passman is chairman of the subcommittee on the foreign aid program. Thus, Mr. Rooney's skepticism about the size of State Department representation allowances abroad[6] and Mr. Passman's general skepticism about foreign economic aid[7] become

---

[6] See the analysis by William L. Rivers, "The Foreign Policy of John J. Rooney," *The Reporter*, Vol. 24, No. 13 (June 22, 1961), pp. 36-38.

[7] Mr. Passman was, not surprisingly, one of the leading congressional opponents of the late President Kennedy's effort, in legislation proposed in 1961, to put foreign economic development aid on a long-term authorization and financing basis. Indeed, the Congressman at one point claimed that the Kennedy Administration had offered

significant factors in determining the funds that will be voted by the full committee and by the House itself in these fields.

The House Appropriations subcommittees work much of the time in executive session, in virtual isolation from one another and from the related substantive committees. The Senate group also employs subcommittees for conducting most of its business, but, in contrast to the House unit, the full committee considers foreign aid appropriations and a larger proportion of its business is conducted in public. The rules of the Senate, which provide for representation of the substantive committees on the related Appropriations subcommittees, and the fact that all committee members serve on another important committee (which is not usually the case in the House), provide at least the basis for some blending of fiscal and substantive judgments by the Senate group.

Among the other committees with important foreign policy interests, the Senate Government Operations Committee should be mentioned. As indicated in Chapter 1, successive subcommittees of this committee, under Senator Henry Jackson's leadership, have been engaged since 1959 in a thoroughgoing study of the major problems of the national security organization. The House Government Operations Committee, particularly its Military Operations Subcommittee, has played a useful role in the critical scrutiny of the military establishment.

The relatively new House Committee on Science and Astronautics and the Senate Committee on Aeronautical and Space Sciences have been given jurisdiction over the rapidly expanding and increasingly expensive field of space exploration, one with obviously significant military and foreign policy implications. The expanding peaceful as well as military uses of atomic energy involve the very important and

---

to drop the controversial long-term financing aspect of its proposed legislation if Mr. Passman would resign as chairman of the subcommittee handling foreign aid appropriations. See *New York Times*, Aug. 5, 1961.

Mr. Passman's confrontations with the White House on foreign aid have by no means been limited to the Kennedy Administration. In the 1964 session of Congress, he met his first major legislative defeat on the foreign aid program at the hands of the Johnson Administration. His subcommittee, the full Appropriations Committee and the House of Representatives in turn rejected his pleas for a major cut in the Administration's aid request. For one account of what took place, see Elizabeth Brenner Drew, "Mr. Passman Meets His Match," *The Reporter*, Vol. 31, No. 9 (Nov. 19, 1964), pp. 40-43.

influential Joint Committee on Atomic Energy in military and foreign affairs problems.

The economic and financial aspects of foreign policy involve a number of congressional committees whose primary focus and concerns are domestic. Since the agricultural attachés who serve abroad are by legislative enactment separate from the Foreign Service, they come under the jurisdiction of the Agriculture Committees. Much more important, these committees are concerned with the use of domestic agricultural surpluses as part of the United States program of foreign economic aid, the so-called Public Law 480 assistance. Promotion of the foreign trade of the United States is a continuing interest of the Commerce Committees while the Export-Import Bank comes under the jurisdiction of the Banking and Currency Committees.

The revenue-raising responsibilities of the House Ways and Means Committee and the Senate Finance Committee bring tariffs within their jurisdiction, and this puts them in a key position with regard to United States foreign economic policy. Periodic reminders of their power are provided by the legislative battles that take place each time the President's tariff-cutting and tariff-negotiating powers under the reciprocal trade treaty program come up for renewal. In 1962, in the context of the developing European Common Market, the Kennedy Administration laid heavy emphasis on the renewal and widening of the President's powers. Because several important domestic proposals also fell within the jurisdiction of the Ways and Means Committee, its chairman, Wilbur Mills (Democrat, Arkansas), previously little known to the public, was assiduously courted by the Administration and widely profiled by the Washington press corps.

The obvious question with regard to these committees—deeply rooted in the domestic scene and primarily oriented to domestic problems —is their ability, and their willingness, to weigh the foreign policy implications of their decisions. The number and variety of congressional committees whose responsibilities impinge on the foreign policy field raise an equally fundamental question, namely, the extent to which these overlapping and interrelated responsibilities are matched by appropriate coordination and communication among the committees.

Something of an answer to this question has already been provided regarding the relationship of substantive committees and the corresponding Appropriations subcommittees. Occasionally, committees do work together, or special committees are established to work in overlapping policy areas. An example of the latter is the Senate Special Committee to Study the Foreign Aid Program, which was active in 1956 and 1957, and which drew its membership from the Committees on Foreign Relations, Appropriations, and Armed Services. But most of the committees and their staffs work quite independently of one another; each carefully guards its jurisdiction. Where functions are closely related, there is even likely to be a sense of rivalry. In some instances, even subcommittees have become largely independent entities, pursuing inquiries and engaging in other activities over which the parent committees exercise only nominal control. The barriers to communication are somewhat offset by the directing influence of legislative and executive leadership, personal ties among members and staffs, and the fact that a senator usually serves on at least two major committees. Much more is needed to improve communication and cooperation among the committees.

Several references have been made to committee staffs. These are quite small and vary considerably in their professional competence and the degree to which they are considered nonpartisan employees of the committee. Under the terms of the Legislative Reorganization Act of 1946, the Senate Foreign Relations Committee and the House Foreign Affairs Committee are each authorized to employ four professional staff members and six clerks.

Over the last ten or fifteen years, the Senate Foreign Relations Committee staff has built up a reputation for professional and essentially nonpartisan competence. It is also said to have very good working relations with the State Department and the other executive foreign policy agencies. To some in Congress who are highly critical of American foreign policy, such close relations with the executive are viewed with concern, even suspicion.

Senators and representatives are also allocated funds for personal staffs. These vary in terms of the size of the constituency. Most congressmen have legislative or administrative assistants as well as secretarial help. In addition, Congress has its own research staff in the Legislative Reference Service of the Library of Congress. Included on this staff are approximately fifteen people who might be classed as foreign policy experts. Congressmen and congressional committees are free to draw on them for such research and analysis as they may require.

Congressional committees also make considerable demands on executive agencies for special studies and back-up information relevant to proposed legislation and appropriations. They are also free to contract for outside research studies; this has been done increasingly in recent years by the Senate Foreign Relations Committee among others.

These are rather modest staff resources, particularly in view of the massive and complex problems to be dealt with in the foreign policy-national security field. Clearly, Congress cannot hope to match the executive. However, the congressional approach to recruiting and retaining staff, and mustering those intellectual resources that are available, does seem unnecessarily helter-skelter and haphazard.

The Party Machinery

The committee structure and parliamentary processes of both houses are given energy and direction by the legislative machinery of the two parties, nowhere acknowledged in statute but crucial nevertheless. Each party has its elected leadership in each house, which is likely to have greater influence on party policies and tactics than caucuses of all the members. The parties—guided by their leaders, whips, and key committee chairmen—decide on the proportioning of committee seats between the two parties and the assigning of party members to committee vacancies. The party leaders control to a large extent the calendars of their respective houses. They attempt to develop something of a legislative program and strategy for their party. Its nature will depend, of course, on which party controls the presidency and, thus, the executive branch, and whether that same party has majority control of the two houses.

Lyndon Johnson's wide reputation as one of the great Senate majority leaders of modern times dramatizes the nature of party functions and party discipline in Congress. Johnson's skill as a legislative tactician was said to have rested on his superb ability to charm, cajole, persuade, bargain with, and, where necessary and feasible, pressure his colleagues into following particular courses of action or accepting compromise solutions. He was also credited with being better able than most to find areas of agreement among those who differed. Without accepting the applicability of the Lyndon Johnson model in detail or for all situations, at least some of the ingredients of this approach seem inevitable, given an American Congress not characterized by the strong party discipline (enforceable by potent political sanctions) and therefore the reliable party-line voting normally found in the British House of Commons.

Top party leaders rarely exert their influence at the level of committee activity. They are careful to respect the prerogatives of chairmen and ranking committee members. On the floor, they usually support the bipartisan coalition in charge of a measure. When either house threatens to engage in what they consider to be a major aberration, or when the achievement of agreement is difficult, they employ their leadership resources more vigorously. Seldom do party meetings discuss foreign policy issues and relate these to party policy or to broader legislative strategy. Perhaps this reflects a general assumption that voting records on specific foreign policy questions normally have little to do with political survival in the constituencies.[8]

Party leaders are drawn into some of the executive-legislative consultations on foreign affairs, particularly those in which the President is involved, and in ways, usually unpublicized, work to promote responsible agreement on foreign policy issues both within Congress and between the two branches. On more important issues, there is usually some bipartisan consultation. Observers have commented on the considerable attention given to Democratic leaders Lyndon Johnson and Sam Rayburn on foreign and military policy issues by President Eisenhower, particularly after the retirement of Senator Walter George, Democratic chairman of the Senate Foreign Relations Committee. It is true that Eisenhower had an opposition Congress to contend with. But, in the first year of the Kennedy Administration, it was noted that Mr. Kennedy was consulting very closely with the two Republican minority leaders, Representative Charles Halleck and Senator Everett Dirksen, particularly the latter. Given his background, it was not surprising to see Lyndon Johnson continuing this pattern as President.

Scholars analyzing the motivations, decision processes, and voting behavior of representatives and senators have catalogued a number of influential factors: the nature of the constituency and how its views

[8] Voting on specific measures should be distinguished from a general posture on foreign affairs. For example, a legislator with a consistently neo-isolationist voting record would find it difficult to survive in a strongly internationalist district although, even here, there would be exceptions.

are perceived and interpreted; personal judgments and preferences; pressure groups outside of the legislature; reference groups within the legislature; kind of mail received; and, finally, party affiliation—which may at times involve a choice among several party factions, or between legislative party leaders and the President. Typically, a fundamental concern of the congressman is to make certain that the interests he believes he represents are adequately protected and promoted. When those interests are not involved or are more or less evenly balanced, the member is freer to act in accordance with his personal views. This is often the case with foreign policy issues.

There are votes within Congress which rather strongly reflect party lines. In other areas of public policy, laws are rather consistently enacted, or not enacted, on the basis of informal if nevertheless powerful interparty coalitions. Most widely referred to, of course, is the coalition of Southern Democrats and most Republicans in opposition to certain "liberal" social and economic legislation.[9] For a long time, "internationalist" foreign policy measures received their strongest support from Democrats plus East and West Coast Republicans. The "isolationist" or "unilateralist" trend among Southern Democrats in recent years[10] has tended to be offset by the waning of Midwest Republican isolationism.

On certain matters, votes will reflect most strongly conditions and preferences in the members' districts. This will certainly be the case where some social or economic problem has widespread consequences, generating strong feeling within a constituency. Such economic issues as legislation for depressed areas and agricultural price supports would fall in this category. Economic consequences may also be a factor in

[9] An interesting phenomenon observed in the first session of the Eighty-Seventh Congress, in the spring of 1961, was an informal coalition in the House of liberal Democrats and roughly two or three dozen Republicans representing large urban areas in the Northeast supporting most of President Kennedy's domestic reform program. The small Republican group sometimes provided the President's margin of victory.

[10] A fascinating and solidly documented study of this development is Charles O. Lerche, Jr., *The Uncertain South* (Quadrangle Books, 1964). The term "unilateralist" is Professor Lerche's. His point is that few people at present favor American withdrawal from world affairs. The key distinction is between those who prefer maximum American freedom of action, the "unilateralists," and those who emphasize the interdependence of nations for purposes of security and prosperity, the "multilateralists."

the fate of certain weapons systems, and the substantial contracts to produce them that benefit certain areas. The voting of Southern Democrats on civil rights legislation also illustrates the point, although there have been some notable exceptions. This kind of political pressure and urgency does not usually affect specific foreign policy issues.

The views and programs espoused and pushed by party leaders, executive as well as legislative, are but one among a number of factors motivating the individual member. The party leaders are not helpless: there are still some patronage and favors to be dispensed; choice and less-than-choice committee assignments to be distributed; possible future support by the leadership for a legislator's pet project or a measure to aid his district. However, the leadership is not usually in a position to threaten the ultimate political sanction: defeat at the next election. On the other hand, there are times when the legislator must face the threat of such defeat if he goes along with the leadership.

Congress, then, is characterized by the great influence of certain key individuals. The House and Senate can be labelled conservative bodies in that their structure, procedures, and, to some extent, their traditions facilitate the obstruction and the destruction of proposed legislation, without the presence of the unifying and expediting force of highly disciplined legislative party units.

Legislative-Executive Relations

An elementary yet fundamental point of departure for understanding the American system of government is that it is based on a separation of the three major governmental powers, substantially modified by a system of constitutional checks and balances binding the branches inextricably to one another. Indeed, if any one of the three branches were ever grimly determined to bring the processes of the national government to a serious if not complete halt, it could undoubtedly do so. If conflict and mutual distrust between legislature and executive are built into the American system, as they undoubtedly are, so is the necessity for cooperation and joint action.

It has already been pointed out that the division of governmental labor between executive and legislature is by no means as clear-cut as the labels would suggest. Consistently since the days of the New Deal, the President has been expected to present a legislative program to each session of Congress. Congress often has a considerable impact on the detailed manner in which the laws of the land are administered by executive agencies through its investigations, hearings on appropriations and other measures, detailed provisos and stipulations written into legislative enactments, and the close working relations between certain congressional committees and certain executive agencies and subagency units.

The very high cost of foreign and military policy programs, the fading of the line between domestic and foreign policy, and the growing impact of international developments on the domestic scene (as well as vice versa) have made Congress an active participant in the foreign policy process. It is concerned not only with major policy choices and major international agreements but with such vital programmatic elements as economic development, military assistance, agricultural surplus disposal, and cultural and educational exchange.

At the same time, there are major obstacles that tend to frustrate and limit the legislative role—the growing volume and complexity of international transactions, the speed and flexibility with which many foreign policy matters must be handled, the limiting effect of having to work in harness with other countries, and the secrecy that conceals many of these activities.

The adjustment of Congress and the executive to this new state of affairs has been pragmatic. Executive-legislative relations have come to involve hundreds of public and private contacts between the two branches at many levels. There are the formal occasions of presidential addresses to Congress, and the regular, informal contacts between the President and his own party leaders—as well as important opposition leaders—in Congress. There is the heavy traffic to Capitol Hill of executive officials come to testify before congressional committees. These officials range from the secretaries of major departments to middle-level career officials, military as well as civilian. Top leaders and their staffs expend tremendous amounts of time and energy in preparing and delivering testimony. One former Secretary of State has estimated that during his tenure of office he never devoted less than one-sixth of his time to dealing with Congress, and, for months at a time, this function consumed most of his efforts.[11] Other high-ranking civilian and military officials would tell a similar story.

[11] Dean Acheson, *A Citizen Looks at Congress* (Harper, 1957), pp. 64-70.

While relying heavily on top leadership for important testimony, agencies usually have full-time professional staffs to manage contacts and relations with "the Hill." The Department of Defense and each of the military services maintain legislative liaison units, including some liaison officers available at the Capitol itself. The Department of State elevated its top legislative liaison officer to Assistant Secretary rank in 1949, and he now has a small professional staff (approximately ten people) to assist him. Because of the interdepartmental character of the Mutual Security Program (including both economic and military assistance), a staff was developed in the office of the Under Secretary of State for Economic Affairs during the last few years of the Eisenhower Administration with overall responsibility for coordinating the program's legislative presentation. This function and related legislative liaison activities are now the responsibility of the new Agency for International Development. The President usually has at least one major aide whose primary responsibility is congressional relations and who acts on the President's behalf to gather support for his legislative program.

Among the other techniques that have been developed to facilitate legislative-executive cooperation are the consultative subcommittees of the foreign affairs committees already referred to, special briefing sessions by executive officials for legislators, appointment of some representatives and senators as members of United States delegations to international meetings, and joint legislative-executive commissions like the two Hoover Commissions to deal with certain major problem areas.

There are a host of less formal contacts. Common problems may be discussed over breakfast or lunch by the President or the Secretary of State with a group of congressional leaders or with some key figures from the foreign affairs or armed services committees. Informal consultations also take place frequently between professional staff members of these and other committees and substantive policy officials or legislative liaison specialists from executive departments. They may involve plans for future hearings or the tactical maneuvers designed to support legislation under active consideration. A Senator or Representative from a key committee is likely to have little difficulty in seeing or talking to some high-level State or Defense Department official if he has some problem on his mind that he would like to discuss with him.

The executive obviously needs congressional understanding and support and in recent years has made a considerable effort to obtain it through some of the devices and techniques discussed in this section. At the same time, Congress—or, certainly, individual congressmen—has constitutional and political incentives to find chinks in the executive armor. It is not reasonable, and probably not even desirable, to expect congressional-executive relations to achieve some idyllic and unpolitical state of total amity and understanding.

Congress, the Executive, and the Public

Both members of Congress and politically responsible leaders of the executive branch are concerned about and eager to influence the various dimensions of public attitudes and activities relevant to foreign policy. Both attempt to keep well informed about public views, and both have various formal and informal liaison activities that keep them in touch with key groups and persons active in the foreign policy field. Executive and legislative motivations do differ somewhat. At least a part of the legislative interest in public views is a matter of political calculation and survival. The President will undoubtedly share this interest, although his constituency is much wider, but he and his executive colleagues are at the same time concerned about the broad base of popular support for policies and programs they are pursuing.

Executive agencies, occasional congressional committees, and individual congressmen engage in activities explicitly designed to educate the public, or the more politically attentive groups within it, about national security and foreign policy problems. These efforts include studies, hearings, liaison with interested organizations, public speaking engagements, and publication programs. Some of them have been very impressive and have borne fruit in obvious public response. Nevertheless, it seems fair to say that the activities of public officials, particularly the legislators, that have most significant consequences in terms of public attitudes and understanding are not those self-consciously designed for this purpose. Congressional debate and discussion of major policy issues, whether in committee hearings, on the floor of either house, or in public and in the forums of the mass media, seem more important factors in molding public views than most hearings and studies specially tailored for that purpose.

In a sense, the same thing can be said about the executive. The tone and quality of presidential addresses are likely to be far more significant in their impact on public views than the public affairs and public relations activities of the various departments, however worthy and commendable these may be.

Senators and representatives are in a position to play one very useful role not open to the executive, namely, that of responsible critic of policy. They can clarify basic issues for the public and, beyond that, identify alternative courses of action to the ones actually being pursued. Unfortunately, few legislators choose to exercise this prerogative in the foreign policy field. One notable exception was the effort by Senator J. William Fulbright, Democratic Chairman of the Foreign Relations Committee, to draw attention in late March of 1964 to what he regarded as some "old myths and new realities" of American foreign policy. The speech created quite a stir. This may well be explained by the rarity of such initiatives since the Senator's views, while not reflecting current official policy on some problems, could hardly be called extreme.[12]

In sum, the level of political discourse in the country, as established by the public utterances of important legislative and executive officials, between as well as during election campaigns, would seem to be a far more fundamental determinant of public views than specific programs of public information and education. Equally basic in this picture, however, is the set of culturally-influenced attitudes and values that the bulk of the citizenry bring to their political actions and reactions. Clearly, these are not likely to be radically changed, at least in the short run, by either the level of political discourse or the strenuous efforts of public affairs specialists.

Major Problems

The United States Congress is a particularly difficult political institution to characterize accurately, to evaluate in some overall fashion— and to reform. The words and actions of the committees and individ-

---

[12] The speech and several others made during the same period have been published in somewhat amplified form in J. W. Fulbright, *Old Myths and New Realities and Other Commentaries* (Random House, 1964).

uals who make it up range from the most impressive, mature, and statesmanlike to the most tawdry, irresponsible, and self-seeking. At its best, it is a match for the finest intellectual, administrative, and political performances of the executive; at its worst, it is very bad indeed. It is limited by the fact that its members represent hundreds of local constituencies around the country whose interests and horizons are inevitably narrower than something that might be labelled the broader national interest. On the other hand, service in Congress does tend to broaden the horizons of its individual members.

Much of what Congress does and can do, as well as the way that it is perceived by outside observers, depends on the attitudes and performance of the President and the executive branch. It is interesting to note that many of the political liberals who had few kind words to say for Congress and saw it as almost exclusively a negative and obstructive force in the days of vigorous presidential leadership during the New Deal and Fair Deal administrations of Franklin Roosevelt and Harry Truman began to turn towards it during the two Eisenhower terms to rectify what they viewed as the latter's sins of omission and commission.

As a matter of fact, Mr. Eisenhower's relations with Congress, particularly during his second term, provided a somewhat novel lesson for the student of executive-legislative relations: namely, that a President of Mr. Eisenhower's predispositions and reluctances, buttressed by the immense political and administrative powers of the office in mid-twentieth century, can only be pushed and cajoled to a certain point by an impatient legislature, even when the opposition party controls both houses. Particularly in the foreign policy and national defense fields, there are important limits to what Congress can do or force the executive to do. This is especially true when it comes to *increasing* rather than *limiting* executive efforts.

In foreign affairs, Congress probably serves best as discussant, critic, sharp-eyed investigator, and watchdog rather than as policy initiator and formulator. If seemingly major inadequacies of executive analysis or effort are encountered, Congress is not likely to be in a position to do very much about them, with one exception—reducing appropriations. For a number of reasons, the same situation does not hold quite so true for domestic policy problems.

Frustrations, of course, do find a way of expressing themselves.

This is probably a good part of the explanation for the heavy cuts in the funds voted for foreign aid during the 1962 and 1963 sessions of Congress. Growing numbers of senators and representatives have become increasingly concerned and doubtful about the purposes, the administration, and the effectiveness abroad of United States economic and military aid programs. Since they are simply not in a position to examine these programs in great detail and pinpoint areas of difficulty and possible waste, their reaction is to cut the aid appropriations sharply and let the executive identify marginal programs and wasteful procedures in the process of making do with less.[13]

This is not an attempt to justify the size of the cuts, or the amendments passed in 1963 and 1964 that were designed to limit in some very specific ways the executive's discretion in carrying out the program. However, it is useful to look at these actions from the congressional perspective and recognize that these crude budgetary slashes represent one of the few potent ways for legislators to express their concerns in the foreign policy field.

Finally, while such overall judgments are difficult to make and to demonstrate persuasively, it seems a fair conclusion that Congress has not been a major handicap in the pursuit of United States national security and foreign policies since the beginning of World War II. Everyone can think of horrendous examples of irresponsible individuals seemingly hell-bent on destroying what they claimed to be protecting, of the widely-publicized cuts in foreign aid appropriations just mentioned, of executive officials unnecessarily badgered, investigated and calumnied, of narrow domestic economic interests threatening larger national economic policies abroad, and of vital issues beclouded rather than clarified in congressional debate. Nevertheless, a careful look at how United States foreign policies and programs have fared in Congress in the postwar years leads to the conclusion that they have on the whole been consistently and rather responsibly supported.

All major policies, programs, and treaty arrangements calling for congressional approval have received it. In the military field, Congress has on the average voted at least as much money as that requested by the executive. Indeed, in recent years Congress has developed a

[13] For an interesting case study of an earlier foreign aid bill, see H. Field Haviland, Jr., "Foreign Aid and the Policy Process: 1957," *American Political Science Review*, Vol. 52 (September 1958), pp. 689-724.

pattern of voting additional funds not requested by the executive and
then trying unsuccessfully to force the executive to spend them. The
foreign aid program has not fared so well, being in a number of ways
an ideal political target. Even here, the appropriations cuts made by
Congress have until the past few years constituted energetic par-
ing rather than radical surgery. The unsuccessful effort to put the economic development program on a long-term financing basis was led
by, among others, Senator Fulbright of the Foreign Relations Committee. Furthermore, standing or special congressional committees have
sometimes led the way in educating the public, and their own colleagues, about the need for some new program or major changes in
old ones.

National Security and the Requisites of Partisanship and Tradition

It is only realistic, in asking how the functioning of Congress in relation to foreign policy can be improved, to recognize that certain patterns represent for the present and into a rather distant future "giv-
ens", unlikely to be substantially modified. The seniority rule provides
one such example; the considerable latitude and discretion granted to
committees and their chairmen is another. The lack of disciplined legislative parties on the British model will also continue to be criticized
more than changed. Within the limits imposed by these patterns, however, there is still considerable room for useful modification and adjustment.

The student of contemporary United States foreign policy making
may well ponder on ways to improve the speed and statesmanlike
manner with which Congress dispatches foreign policy business. In a
basic sense, Congress is searching for patterns and procedures that will
at one and the same time expedite urgent national security business
and yet not upset too seriously its traditional ways of working. The
requisites of national security must struggle against the constant pull
of political requirements towards domestic concerns, the stress on partisan tactics, the resistance to centralized party direction, and the inclination to distrust the executive.

For example, bipartisanship in foreign policy, as seen from the
congressional perspective, involves arrangements that will produce the
necessary interparty agreement on fundamental policy directions and

implementing programs without foreclosing either party's prerogative to criticize the views and actions of the other and, where possible, to reap political advantage. The party that controls the presidency and thus must take primary responsibility for foreign policy decisions usually wants, and sometimes needs, the support of the other party for major measures and decisions. It would, on the other hand, like to take credit for major achievements. The party not in control of the executive is under considerable pressure, patriotic as well as political, to go along with the President and his foreign policy. However, its leaders are unwilling to put themselves into his hands completely, and can justify this posture not merely in terms of the partisan advantage it may bring them but also as part of the fundamental watchdog role of a loyal but critical opposition.

Academic students of this problem have attempted to clarify the various usages of the term "bipartisan" and to relate these definitions to actual states of affairs. In some cases, they have even suggested new terms that more aptly describe prevailing conditions. A possible next step is to prescribe conditions that would better meet the demands of national security and of healthy party competition in a democratic society and, perhaps, to suggest a more self-conscious approach to bipartisanship on the part of the legislators that would bring this more satisfactory state of affairs into being.[14]

Members of Congress do not completely share these concerns. Their interests are more pragmatic. There seems to be a fairly widespread acceptance of the need for national and governmental unity on basic policies and programs. The boundary line between this sacrosanct area and the area that is fair game for partisan criticism and debate is not and cannot be a clear one, however, even by academic definition. The critical opposition is bound to define the area of bipartisan agreement more narrowly than the party responsible for foreign policy. It is almost inevitable that cries will be heard periodically from one side or the other that the bipartisan spirit or principle is being violated. Yet, there would seem to be no possible way of defining these areas in terms clear, precise, and acceptable to all. Am-

---

[14] Two important studies of bipartisanship are Cecil V. Crabb, Jr., *Bipartisan Foreign Policy, Myth or Reality?* (Row, Peterson, 1957) and H. Bradford Westerfield, *Foreign Policy and Party Politics: Pearl Harbor to Korea* (Yale University Press, 1955).

biguity is inevitable, and so are occasional partisan disputes about the honesty and responsibility with which the other party is playing its bipartisan role.

In good part, the problem of bipartisanship is one of executive-legislative relations, not merely of arrangements within Congress. The executive wants to develop as broad a base of support as possible for its national security policies and programs. If the President's party is in a minority in one or both houses of Congress, the need for this kind of support is painfully clear. However, given the nature of American political parties, the need is almost as great when the President's party has a majority in both houses. In any event, the fact that the bipartisan problem involves the legislature's relations with the executive adds to the uncertainties, the lingering suspicion and distrust, and the occasional outbursts of vigorous partisanship, charges, countercharges, and all the rest. The partisan elements are bound to be sharpened when presidential as well as congressional politics are involved.

Bipartisan arrangements have also tended to be limited by the presence of individuals in both parties who refuse to "go along." Given the room for maneuver that American legislators, and particularly senators, possess, mavericks can on occasion cause considerable difficulties. Nevertheless, when all the handicaps are added up, it must be concluded that the major directions of postwar United States foreign policy and most of the implementing programs and decisions have had substantial bipartisan support in Congress and that partisan strife has not represented a major problem in foreign policy.

Indeed, it can be argued that bipartisanship has been too successful, that there is too little criticism of either the basic premises or the detailed implementation of United States policy, and that at times the price of bipartisan support has been the foreclosing of lines of policy choice and the imposing of too great a rigidity, too great a conservatism, on United States policy.[15]

It is, in any event, naive to hope for a clear-cut once-and-for-all solution of the bipartisan problem. Legislative politicians will rightfully refuse to be bound by any set formula and will continue to insist on their own right to define proper rules and boundaries of partisanship

---

[15] Without necessarily espousing the point of view just stated, Paul Seabury suggests some of the dangers of bipartisanship in his *Power, Freedom and Diplomacy* (Random House, 1963) pp. 229–31.

and bipartisanship, and to operate in the congressional arena accordingly. Continuing ambiguity and disputations on the subject are inevitable and unlikely to be dissipated by even the most logical and brilliant of academic analyses.

Security Requirements and the Legislative Role

Traditionally, Congress has been interested in opening up for discussion subjects that executive departments would just as soon forget, and bringing to light possibly embarrassing states of affairs that executive officials are trying to keep quiet or which they may not even be aware of. A well-established convention in the American system is that the President does not appear to testify before congressional committees. However, a continuing point of tension and disagreement is the right of his subordinates in the executive branch to claim "executive privilege," on the basis of which they can refuse to make certain documents and information available to congressional committees, including their conversations with the President.

In more recent times, security requirements have provided an additional basis on which the executive can refuse to make available to congressmen and committees certain highly sensitive information. It should be added that, from Congress' point of view, information is rarely withheld on security grounds. Security-classified material is provided as a matter of course to the appropriate congressional committees and subcommittees meeting in executive session.

Some commentators outside of Congress as well as within[16] have complained that many documents are overclassified, that often the basis for their being classified at all is not as a protection against potential enemies abroad but rather critics at home. Even those who are most critical of security and classification practices in the executive branch do concede the need for some such system and complain about executive sloppiness or lack of discretion in handling certain classified data. For example, a standard criticism directed at the military services is that as part of the competition for support of one service's weapon system against a similar system developed by another, the ser-

[16] One legislative critic, Representative John Moss (Democrat, California), has been chairman for a number of years of the very active Government Information Subcommittee of the House Government Operations Committee.

vices release information on these systems, not otherwise available, that is extremely useful to other nations.

Perhaps the foreign policy-national security activities which congressmen are most reluctant to scrutinize closely—and indeed loath even to learn too much about—are the operations of the Central Intelligence Agency (CIA). Congressional attitudes about the intelligence agency epitomize one of the dilemmas of the democratic legislature in the modern world. Probably more than any other legislative body, Congress oversees the work of the executive with close and critical attention. There is, at the same time, a keen awareness of the need for some legislative surveillance of CIA's activities. However, because many of these activities are so sensitive and susceptible to great damage through public exposure, inadvertent or not, there is a great reluctance to get substantially involved, as for example by establishing a joint congressional committee on the model of the Joint Committee on Atomic Energy.

Those in the executive and elsewhere who oppose the establishment of such a committee argue that the analogy with the Atomic Energy Commission is not an accurate one. They seem to feel that the several members of the Armed Services Committees who are informally responsible for scrutinizing the activities of the intelligence agency are enough of a legislative watchdog and that this is one area where the executive branch must essentially be its own watchdog. The various pros and cons of this particular aspect of the congressional role in national security policy making have been carefully considered elsewhere.[17] What is relevant for present purposes is the view of Congress caught between its traditional style of open debate and freewheeling investigation and the legitimate secrecy and security requirements of contemporary international politics.

Useful Changes Short of Constitutional Reform

Some of the obstacles to strengthening the role of Congress in for-

[17] See Harry Howe Ransom, *Central Intelligence and National Security* (Harvard University Press, 1958), Chap. VII. In a more recent study of defense and intelligence policy making, Professor Ransom has pursued the broader problem of the compatibility of defense and democracy. See his *Can American Democracy Survive Cold War?* (Doubleday Anchor Books, 1964).

eign policy making have been made clear, as have some of the dilemmas that confront Congress in any attempt to modify traditional patterns and practices in the light of contemporary needs. Are there any areas for improvement left once the presence of these formidable obstacles is accepted? Not only can an affirmative answer be given, but it can also be argued that no fundamental changes in congressional structure or procedures are required to bring about some useful improvements, and no constitutional amendments need be passed.

As trite and obvious as it may sound, basic to the whole picture are the attitudes of the congressmen themselves. In the field of foreign policy, attitudes have changed substantially, and sometimes dramatically, during the past twenty years. They continue to change. The views of senators and representatives on foreign policy issues continue to be modified by service in Congress, by extended service on particular committees, and by travel. It does not seem unreasonable to assume that they will continue to change in the direction of greater sophistication, understanding, and patience, and perhaps in a willingness to devote increasingly larger proportions of their time to those issues and problems that are central to the survival of the nation.

Each Representative and Senator faces the question of how he should distribute his time and energy. These individual allocations have a direct bearing on the effectiveness of Congress as a whole. The burdens of public service are enormous, and members of Congress are in general overworked. As every member knows, however, detached analysis would reveal that a large proportion of his energies is allocated to relatively peripheral activities that have accumulated from the practices and habits of a simpler past. It would be both politically risky, and probably generally undesirable, for congressmen to renounce these "service" activities completely. However, it would seem reasonable for them to try to limit these as far as possible, rather than almost to thrive on them as a kind of busywork way of avoiding the tougher problems that confront Congress daily.

It is also important that congressional leaders and committee chairmen accept and implement certain premises basic to effective United States foreign policy making—that the coordination of related responsibilities and programs is a fundamental requirement, that substantive and budgetary policy issues are closely related and must be dealt with accordingly, and that organizational arrangements cannot assure a grasp of the intellectual complexities and subtleties of policy. The particular devices and techniques through which these premises are translated into legislative arrangements must meet the test of practical usefulness, as distinguished from theoretical appeal. There is no reason to expect magical results from the establishment of a joint congressional committee on national security designed to coordinate the related activities of the dozen or fifteen congressional committees significantly concerned with foreign policy and national security problems. Similarly, strengthening the staff resources of the two foreign relations committees, and of the Foreign Affairs Division of the Legislative Reference Service of the Library of Congress, is probably a sensible idea, but the needs for expertise on the legislative side can probably be met in other ways, as they have already been in some instances.[18]

Some of the proponents of long-term financing of the foreign aid program (through authorization to borrow up to a specified amount from the Treasury during a two-, three-, or five-year period) probably expect more impressive improvements than will in fact be forthcoming. On the other hand, congressional opponents of this change certainly exaggerate the dangers involved. Congress can always amend statutes it has enacted, and the executive branch, it seems safe to say, will be all too eager to keep in the good graces of Congress and will quickly if not always happily supply the reports and information the latter requests.

The unnecessary duplication of efforts and the substantial overlapping of responsibilities are among the administrative sins of the executive branch to which the legislature is most alert and which it most heartily deplores. And yet the present congressional system of authorizing and appropriating committees is a rather striking example of a similar flaw, if flaw it be. The two distinct legislative processes represent not only a double legislative scrutiny of many governmental programs and a double burden for busy executive officials who must testify before both sets of committees in both houses, but also an increased workload for the legislators, who must consider both kinds of bills.

---

[18] These two proposals, and others, are discussed at somewhat greater length in *The Formulation and Administration of United States Foreign Policy*, pp. 32-34 and 37-38.

Arguments can be offered in defense of the present system. For example, an informal division of labor does tend to develop between the substantive committees and the related Appropriations subcommittees. Nevertheless, if these units are not to be simply combined, arrangements must be made to link their efforts more closely. Such a pattern has already been developed in the Senate, with several members of the substantive committees sitting as members of the related Appropriations subcommittees. This is a modest and sensible way of meeting the problem. There are others. The important point is that the underlying premise is a sound one.

That Congress does not view its committee arrangements as sacrosanct was demonstrated in 1946 when the Legislative Reorganization Act was passed. Under its terms, the number of committees in each house was reduced, and the military and naval affairs committees, among others, combined. Perhaps it is time for another congressional scrutiny of its committee structure. In a period when the pressure on top foreign policy and national defense leaders is so great and the demands on their time so many, it seems rather absurd and wasteful that they should be required to give similar testimony before parallel committees in each house. The increasing number of congressional committees with national security responsibilities adds further to this burden. Would it be excessively damaging to congressional *amour-propre* if certain hearings were held on a joint basis by the two committees concerned with foreign affairs or armed services? The same question can be raised about testimony before the two Appropriations Committees.

The point of these comments is that if Congress wishes to improve its contributions to the national security policy process, it can make modest adjustments in its working procedures that will not only increase efficiency but do so at little or no cost to its power and prerogatives, or the vigorous performance of its traditional functions. All that may be threatened is the power of some of the lesser hierarchs—subcommittee chairmen and the like—and they would probably oppose such proposals. Unfortunately, such opposition would represent a major roadblock to the successful introduction of these changes.

Looking at Congress from a longer-term perspective, some of the fundamental changes now taking place in the American political landscape should have consequences for foreign as well as domestic policy. Increasing urbanization and industrialization, for example, and the requirement recently imposed by Supreme Court decision that congressional districts be roughly equal in population[19] should eventually produce fewer rural rotten boroughs and give the urban and suburban areas of the country a more powerful voice in Congress. In balance, this should contribute to greater congressional interest and competence in foreign affairs. Like the rest of the government and the nation, Congress should increasingly reflect the seasoning and maturity brought about by an exposure to international complexities measured in decades rather than years. Finally, the improving quality of those who now seek and gain public office should over time manifest itself in the work of Congress.

[19] *Wesberry v. Sanders*, 376 U. S. 1 (1964).

4

The President and the National Security Organization

GIVEN THE GREATLY EXPANDED ROLE of the federal government in American life, primary leadership and initiative in developing policies as well as carrying out programs must come from the President and the executive branch. Such shadings of doubt as may exist about this fact of political life with regard to domestic matters inevitably disappear when foreign and military policies are considered. In these areas, the Constitution—by both direct statement and interpretation—and the requisites of international politics in mid-twentieth century place primary responsibility for policy leadership and program direction squarely in the hands of the President.

What Model for Presidential Performance?

Each President will define his role and responsibilities somewhat differently and fulfill them in a manner that reflects or is at least compatible with his own needs, temperament, and operating style. This includes the way in which he organizes and uses the White House and Executive Office staffs; he will muster them and adapt their capabilities to meet his own needs and problems, rather than those of his predecessor or anyone else. In this sense, it is pointless to try to develop some ideal organization of the presidency. This obvious truth would hardly be worth repeating were it not for the fact that it is forgotten by overeager exponents of particular organizational panaceas.

There is a balance to be struck. Over the last twenty or twenty-five years, the President's swiftly expanding responsibilities have been accompanied by efforts to make his tasks more manageable, not to say feasible, by providing him with staff assistance of various kinds. These range from an expanded group of personal assistants to special staffs and offices designed to facilitate the general direction of individual departments and the necessary presidential coordination and control of important interdepartmental problems.

Some of these have proved their worth over time. Many critics carp at specific actions of the Bureau of the Budget, but few would recommend that its functions and the assistance it provides the President should be eliminated. Similarly, General Eisenhower's addition of a Special Assistant for National Security Affairs to the presidential staff has survived his Administration and seems likely to become a permanent fixture. In short, the increasing institutionalization of the presidency represents to a considerable extent an effort to protect the President (in the best sense of the word)—to free him, to enable him to master the major dimensions of the problems that confront him.

Nevertheless, considerable skepticism is in order with regard to grandiose plans to alter the nature of the presidency. Unless the President is prepared in effect to abdicate a significant portion of his responsibilities to others, the presidency is a tough, trying job, and there is no set of organizational devices that can change that state of affairs. Most presidents have felt the need for advice and assistance from sources outside of the formal organizational channels. Woodrow Wilson had his Colonel House and Franklin Roosevelt his Harry Hopkins. President Kennedy had a devoted brother, much of whose assistance had nothing to do with the latter's formal position as Attorney General.

It is to be expected, furthermore, that the President will try to help himself in other ways if the organizational machinery or the personnel of the Executive Office or of one of his major departments is not giving him what he thinks he needs. And he will do so whether or not his move disturbs the abstract logic of an organization chart or an orderly scheme for the flow of national security policy papers.

An example of a President's reaching out for assistance was the appointment of General Maxwell Taylor as President Kennedy's military adviser in the spring of 1961, following the abortive landing in Cuba. Apparently, Mr. Kennedy felt the need for an able and experienced military officer to advise him directly on some of the military aspects of the critical problems he was confronting daily. Concern was expressed by some that the presence on the President's immediate staff of a former Army Chief of Staff, one with widely-known, controversial views on military policy questions, would downgrade the Joint Chiefs of Staff in their role as principal military advisers to the President. It was indicated in the weeks following General Taylor's appointment that this was not the President's intent, although this was somewhat belied by Taylor's appointment as chairman of the Joint Chiefs of Staff in July 1962.

Thus, if the President was not satisfied with the military analysis and advice that he was getting through the formal organizational channels available to him, he did not seem to regard it as inappropriate to look elsewhere and, in this case, to bring into his own immediate staff the kind of skill and competence he believed he needed. Given the awesome responsibilities of the President, the desirability of such a prerogative seems undeniable. At the same time, a President should recognize the price he may have to pay for this assistance—in the form of duplication or confusion of functions, demoralization of line agencies, or increased tension and rivalry between them and the presidential staff.

There is no ingenuity of organizational arrangement or brilliance of organizational doctrine that can prevent situations of this kind from arising periodically. In the end, the President must be able to arrange his immediate staff and make use of the units of the Executive Office in a way that he finds most congenial to *his* working style and *his* needs.

Operating within such an organizational framework, the President must face the more fundamental problem of how he goes about accomplishing his purposes with the greatest possible effectiveness. It is easy to talk about the need for presidential leadership and initiative, to say that the President must provide the executive branch, Congress, and the nation with a clear sense of direction, that the President must coordinate and integrate the various departmental programs and activities so that they add up to a consistent and self-reinforcing set of national purposes, policies, and programs. These prescriptions are so general, however, that they provide only the vaguest outlines of a model for presidential behavior.

So many factors enter into the success of presidential policies, and so few of them are within the President's power to command or control, that it would be naive to attempt to set forth a series of copybook maxims for the guidance of American chief executives. However, because the presidential role is so central, it may be useful to try to spell out some elements of style and behavior that would seem to be desirable attributes for *any* incumbent of the presidency—now and in the foreseeable future.

Professor Richard E. Neustadt's brilliant essay on the political dimensions of the presidency has clarified some of the sources of the President's power to persuade and influence, and some of the ways in which this power may be diluted. Neustadt shares the view of most students of American government that the power of the President is an essential motive force in accomplishing the purposes of that government. He is, therefore, deeply concerned that presidential power be marshalled and wielded as effectively as possible.

The President, he suggests, must be conscious of the power stakes involved in his various actions and decisions and determined to protect his own power position. He cannot count on anyone else to do it for him. Since this type of political sophistication, or intuitive sense, is not easily come by, Professor Neustadt concludes that the White House is no place for an amateur, that its resident must be a professional politician.[1]

This is still not a very precise prescription and, indeed, the President is not always going to find his power stakes in a particular situation as easy to determine as in the examples Neustadt has chosen for his book. Even in these instances, such as Mr. Truman's decision to let United Nations military forces cross the Thirty-Eighth Parallel during the Korean War, it is no doubt easier to see the power risks *post facto* than it was at the time. Even if the power stakes do seem crystal clear, there may be other elements in the situation that push strongly in a

[1] Neustadt's analysis and supporting case studies are found in *Presidential Power* (John Wiley, 1960). It is interesting to observe that Dwight Eisenhower, the amateur in politics, was succeeded in the presidency by two highly effective politicians, John F. Kennedy and Lyndon B. Johnson. By Neustadt's use of the term, or just about anyone's, they would certainly be called professionals.

contrary direction. In effect, Neustadt is providing more an illuminating general analysis than he is a specific prescription for the power-sensitive President.

Given the great complexity of most contemporary foreign and military policy issues, it seems even more important that the contemporary President have a capacity to grasp the essential nature of these problems and, with the help of the knowledge and analysis available to him, make assured and measured decisions about them.

It is no easier to prescribe for the development of this policy-analyzing and policy-deciding capacity than it was for the nurturing of the political-power sense. However, if a President is to have some "feel" for the problems with which he is dealing and the policy issues about which he must decide, it seems highly desirable that he involve himself to some extent in the discussions about them. In this way, he will get some of the flavor of relevant and perhaps conflicting interpretations of events and situations, varying values and objectives to be served, and alternative courses of action.

His role should not be merely one of making the final decisions, important as that is, or of making the tough choices where there are strong tugs in a number of policy directions. In organizational terms, this means that he must be in direct, continuing contact not only with the heads of the great departments of the government but also with some of their key subordinate officials. He cannot allow his contact with these officials, or with the major policy issues, to be mediated exclusively through his Executive Office staff personnel.

If these requirements are met and if the President sees his role as that of active participant in the policy process, he should be able to energize the system from his position at the top of the executive hierarchy. He will not simply wait for ideas and materials to flow up through the governmental structure to him. Rather, there should be a continuing two-way interaction between the President and the executive agencies, with the President sending down requests and, on occasion, ideas and suggestions of his own—"needling" his associates and subordinates with the pinpricks of his own curiosity and concerns.

When the President is operating in this way, the concepts of policy leadership, energy, and sense of direction take on more concrete meaning. The whole governmental system should thereby be stimulated and the levels of performance and creativity throughout the structure raised.

This is a basic function of presidential leadership; most of the work must be done elsewhere.

The limits of what can be accomplished by this active presidential participation must also be underscored. The President plays a number of major roles in American political life. Many of the demands consequently imposed upon his time and attention are compelling, difficult to avoid; the total effect is overwhelming. Thus, even in the crucial military and foreign policy areas, the number of matters to which he can give serious attention is quite limited.

The combination of events abroad and the nature of the personalities, skills, and interpersonal relationships of the President and his key advisers and department heads will help determine where presidential attention is focused. For example, it is probably true that under Mr. Kennedy's leadership, Secretary of Defense Robert McNamara and his major subordinates in the Defense Department had a greater range of policy discretion than did Secretary of State Rusk; the opposite was apparently true in General Eisenhower's relations with his several Secretaries of Defense compared with his relationship with Mr. Dulles.

It must furthermore be emphasized that neither a particular working style nor a particular set of institutional arrangements can protect the President from having to face up to some very difficult choices, confronted sometimes by ambiguous situations interpreted in a variety of ways and sometimes by conflicting advice from a number of trusted advisers. Here, the President must fall back on the subtle factors of intellect, values, imagination, and moral sense that go by the names of judgment, intuition, creativity, or wisdom. When such crossroads choices must be made, a bit of luck will do him no harm either.

Mr. Kennedy's decisions in connection with the abortive landing of anti-Castro Cubans in the spring of 1961 highlight this point dramatically. Until this fiasco, the proponents of a vigorous political and intellectual President had looked on in wide-eyed admiration as the new President proceeded to function in a manner that many had longed for during the Eisenhower incumbency. After the Bay of Pigs, they were reminded sharply that the President earns his keep by a few key decisions wisely made as well as by a more generally vigorous performance of his functions. The much more challenging and dangerous Cuban missile crisis in October 1962 reinforced the point, this time to Mr. Kennedy's credit. Nothing can protect the President of the United

States from those difficult and lonely moments when he alone must make fundamental decisions, using those resources of intellect and character that lie within him.

However one explains and interprets the detailed playing out of the two Cuban dramas, and however one parcels out blame and praise therefor, both series of events underscore another fundamental point—that no matter how keen, how shrewd or how politically sensitive he may be, the contemporary President cannot wholly protect himself from the actions and inaction—and from the bad as well as good advice—of his subordinates in the executive branch. In that sense, he is bound to be, in part, a captive of those around him. He can maximize his freedom of choice and maneuver by insisting that the policy disagreements of his subordinates be brought to him clearly, in undiluted form, and, furthermore, as Professor Neustadt has suggested, he can attempt to develop his own alternative sources of intelligence and advice, both inside and outside the government.

The Cuban crisis in the fall of 1962 dramatized another dimension of the burdens of the contemporary President. As Professor Neustadt characterized it in testimony before the second Jackson subcommittee, presidential decision making now involves "the risk of irreversibility become irremediable" or, stated more baldly, the possibility that some presidential act could in fact plunge us into the thermonuclear abyss. Neustadt suggests that while others may recognize this burden intellectually, the President "actually experiences it emotionally." In this way, the President is set apart from everyone else, even his closest advisers.[2]

This new element in presidential responsibility is linked to the acquisition of a substantial nuclear weapons and delivery capability by the Soviet Union. Thus, it was presumably experienced to some extent by President Eisenhower in the last years of his incumbency, and more fully by President Kennedy and, now, President Johnson. Professor Neustadt may be overdramatizing the point since much will depend on the temperament and perceptions that individual presidents bring to this responsibility.

It is clear that the experiences of presidents before Franklin Roose-

[2] For Professor Neustadt's comments on this point, see *Administration of National Security*, Hearings before the Subcommittee on National Security Staffing and Operations of the Senate Government Operations Subcommittee, 88 Cong. 1 sess. (1963), Pt. 1, pp. 76-78.

velt have sharply declining relevance for the contemporary incumbent. Even the jump from Roosevelt to the Truman period after World War II seems large. Now still another chapter has been added to a continuing development.

Eisenhower and Kennedy: New Perspectives on the Presidency

This is the endless fascination in the study of the American presidency. Just when it seems that the last possible variation has been observed and the last word on the subject said, a new study, or a new President, or a new set of problems, comes along to add some novel facets or perspectives. Since the President of the United States is by almost any standard the most powerful executive leader in the democratic world, bearing the most overwhelming set of responsibilities, and since he carries out his functions in a complicated, diffuse, and highly pluralistic political and constitutional system, it is not surprising that the interactions of office, man, and circumstance continue to produce interesting new combinations and variations on more familiar themes.

Any brief comments on the incumbency of General Eisenhower and the tragically foreshortened tenure of President Kennedy are bound to be impressionistic and to lack the depth and profundity that historical perspective can, hopefully, provide. Nevertheless, they do present the opportunity to discuss and dramatize some of the basic characteristics and problems of the contemporary presidency.

It is interesting to observe the impact of the man on the office and, equally, the impact of the political and organizational requirements of the office on the man. It seemed as if President Eisenhower would have liked to hark back to a traditional—some would say Republican—approach to his office, emphasizing the separation of powers and the congressional prerogative to legislate and appropriate. Long before his first term of office was over, however, Eisenhower was berating Congress and challenging it to pass his legislative program, in very much the style of some of his Democratic predecessors. Indeed, in dealing with the Democratic Eighty-Sixth Congress in 1959 and 1960, he made vigorous and skillful use of the presidential veto power.

At the same time, Mr. Eisenhower inevitably brought some of his previous experiences and orientation as a lifelong professional soldier to the presidency. The Cabinet, the National Security Council machinery, and the White House staff were more formally and elaborately organized than they ever had been. It is generally held that Mr. Eisenhower, in the military staff tradition, expected policy papers to be brought before him that had been fully "staffed out" with the interested agencies, and that incorporated policy recommendations supported by all.

There is some disagreement about the extent to which major policy papers were brought before Mr. Eisenhower with important policy differences for him to settle. Leaving aside this question, it does seem clear that he was not inclined to delve too deeply into the intellectual subtleties and ramifications of particular problems, or to read widely in the governmental and nongovernmental materials that provided the underpinning for the policy papers before him, or to probe the relationships among the various major lines of policy that he was interested in pursuing. Furthermore, he gave certain of his Cabinet members very wide latitude in developing and carrying out policy in their particular areas of responsibility. This was clearly the case in foreign policy as long as John Foster Dulles was Secretary of State. Although Harry Truman leaned very heavily on his Secretary of State, Dean Acheson, Mr. Dulles undoubtedly had much greater freedom to maneuver than did Mr. Acheson.

A proposal that was given considerable attention in the last few years of the Eisenhower Administration, and apparently had the support of Secretary Dulles and Mr. Eisenhower himself, was the establishment of a new position, First Secretary of the Government. It was assumed that the First Secretary would act on the President's behalf as a kind of Deputy President or Prime Minister for Foreign Affairs, giving policy leadership and direction to the many agencies and programs involved in foreign affairs, but operating from the White House and not in direct charge of any of these agencies.

The First Secretary proposal reflected the relationship between President Eisenhower and Secretary of State Dulles, and Mr. Dulles' belief that he could have performed as foreign policy maker more effectively if he had not been tied to his specific duties as Secretary of State but had instead been located at the White House level. In terms of his sense of the kind of policy-making role he would have liked to play, and the kind of President Mr. Eisenhower was, Mr. Dulles may have been right. To infer from this particular set of circumstances a major long-term reform in the organization of the presidency seems quite mistaken.[3]

In Mr. Eisenhower's conception of the presidency, there seemed to be something of the flavor of the French Presidency pre-Charles de Gaulle, that is, an official symbolizing the government and the nation but in a sense separate from political and governmental processes. Mr. Eisenhower's attitude toward the vast executive branch he headed seemed more of a "me-they" than a "we" attitude. While occasionally stirred or persuaded into political action, and at times quite effective when once engaged in political combat, he was obviously not very happy about this particular aspect of the presidential role. He tended to have the traditional American attitude that politics was essentially a dirty business and consequently played his political role most reluctantly, often ineffectively, and at times with the sort of lack of candor and sense of propriety that he himself deplored in others.[4]

Proponents of a vigorous twentieth-century American President—and Senator John F. Kennedy was certainly among them—found the Eisenhower performance woefully inadequate. Mr. Kennedy was without doubt the most self-conscious and intellectually-oriented President

[3] The criticism directed at this proposal from a number of sources is highly persuasive. Fundamentally, it is questioned whether an official short of the President, sitting above the Cabinet and above the line departments, could—no matter how influential his policy advice—exercise effective control over the Secretaries of State and Defense and the substantial bureaucracies available to them. It can be argued that the Secretary of State's command of a major line department and his direct link to some of the operations he is supposed to control are advantages rather than handicaps in performing the policy leadership role. Furthermore, could a First Secretary perform his assigned role effectively without threatening or, indeed, assuming the prerogatives of the President himself? For further discussion of the First Secretary idea, see H. Field Haviland, Jr. and Associates, *The Formulation and Administration of United States Foreign Policy*, A Report for the Committee on Foreign Relations of the United States Senate (Brookings Institution, 1960), pp. 48-56. Also highly relevant is Governor Nelson Rockefeller's testimony before the Subcommittee on National Policy Machinery of the Senate Government Operations Committee. See *Organizing for National Security*, Vol. 1, Hearings, 86 Cong. 2 sess. (1960), pp. 942-1001, and *ibid.*, Vol. 3, Staff Reports and Recommendations (1961), "Super-Cabinet Officers and Superstaffs," pp. 11-24.

[4] See the comments by a perceptive if not too friendly observer in Neustadt, *Presidential Power*, pp. 163-71 and, indeed, throughout the whole volume.

since Woodrow Wilson. Not only had he read and been impressed by Professor Neustadt's study of presidential power, but he also asked Neustadt to work on some of the problems of transition from the Eisenhower Administration to his own and later retained him as a part-time consultant on organizational problems facing the new administration.

Mr. Kennedy came to the presidency well-versed in the relevant theories and doctrine about its nature and keenly aware of some of its recent organizational problems. By personal working style and temperament as well as by intellectual orientation, he was not only determined but bound to be a very different kind of President from Dwight Eisenhower. As a man of considerable intellectual curiosity and attainments, Mr. Kennedy would not be satisfied with ratifying the choices of others or being left with yes-or-no decisions. He would want to understand the complexities and subtleties of the issues he was called upon to decide. Indeed, in the early months of his Administration, it was reported that no Assistant Secretary of State was immune from a direct call from the President inquiring about some specific problem. It was said that on such issues as Laos, Cuba, and the Congo, the President was at least as well-informed as any of his Cabinet officers.

Mr. Kennedy and his advisers were unhappy about the proliferation of committee machinery and staff procedures that had grown up in the national security-foreign policy field under the Eisenhower Administration. Mr. Kennedy proceeded to abolish most of it. It was made clear that the new President was skeptical about the usefulness of large, formal, and regularized committee meetings. He preferred to meet with what were in effect *ad hoc* task forces composed of the officials responsible for dealing with the particular problem that might be at hand. In the lexicon of the new Administration, "committee" became a negative word, and the business of government began to be conducted by a series of "task forces." If Mr. Eisenhower's presidential style reflected his military background, some critical observers felt that the White House under Kennedy had something of the free-wheeling, loose-knit atmosphere of a Senator's office.

At the same time, it became clear rather quickly that it was impossible for anyone, no matter how brilliant or curious, or how swift and voracious a reader, to master the details of the many crucial problems and issues that thrust themselves continually at the American President. The new President was forced to learn the inevitable lesson of selectivity, of focussing his attention on certain key problems and leaving others primarily in the hands of trusted subordinates.

Similarly, it soon became obvious that while the Eisenhower Administration might have overelaborated the machinery and overloaded it with the flow of formal papers, the National Security Council and its Planning Board as well as the Operations Coordinating Board had performed some useful functions in the development and implementation of national security policy. Since most of this structure had been abolished, some other means had to be found for accomplishing these tasks.

In the less than three years of the Kennedy presidency, a number of new high-level policy committees, working groups, and task forces appeared upon the scene, accompanied by the almost inevitable requirements for plans, policy guidelines, action programs, and periodic reports. Perhaps they merely made prophetic the comment of a high official of the Kennedy Administration who, in defending the dismantling of the Eisenhower national security machinery, commented that "If we are going to have weeds, we'd rather have our own weeds and not theirs." At the same time, it must be noted that these new committees tended on the whole to be more narrowly task-oriented than their predecessors. Mr. Kennedy's approach to policy making continued to be less formalized and more *ad hoc,* and pressure was directed at the line departments, particularly the State Department, to exercise leadership in developing interdepartmental policy views and recommended programs.

The Executive Office of the President

The Executive Office of the President, established in 1939, was designed to assist the President in maintaining policy leadership and broad control over the increasing number of executive agencies and their greatly expanding programs and activities. The Executive Office was to be (as it still is) the President's staff agency, giving him sources of information, analysis, and advice independent of the executive departments, following up decisions or situations of interest to him, attempting to coordinate individual departmental programs—and budgets—in terms of overall presidential policies.[5]

As presidential and executive branch responsibilities have expanded substantially since 1939, the Executive Office has followed suit. Today the Executive Office, while still of minuscule proportions compared to the large executive departments, has itself become a rather substantial collection of staff units. Its title is a misnomer if from it is derived the picture of a single, cohesive organization. Total personnel at present numbers over fifteen hundred.[6] They fully occupy the large building adjoining the White House to the west that housed in simpler times the State, War, and Navy Departments.

The six major units of the Executive Office are well-known: the White House Office; the Bureau of the Budget; the Council of Economic Advisers; the Office of Emergency Planning; the Office of Science and Technology; and the National Security Council. The National Aeronautics and Space Council is also included within the Executive Office. For foreign policy purposes, the White House Office, the Budget Bureau, and the National Security Council are most important and are discussed in detail in the present chapter. The Space Council and the Office of Science and Technology are treated in Chapter 8.

The Office of Emergency Planning represents the latest stage of development of a presidential staff unit that has gone through a series of metamorphoses, never gaining major stature as an organization but never quite dying either. The Office of Defense Mobilization, established during the Korean War, eventually absorbed its predecessor agency, the National Security Resources Board. It was combined with the civil defense agency during the last years of the Eisenhower Administration to become the Office of Civil and Defense Mobilization, retaining its status as a presidential staff unit with its Director entitled by statutory prescription to a seat on the National Security Council.

When President Kennedy, in July 1961, turned responsibilities for

[5] Some of the descriptive material in this section is adapted from *The Formulation and Administration of U.S. Foreign Policy*, Chap. III.

[6] The actual figure for the fiscal year ending June 1964 was 1542. Estimates for the 1965 and 1966 fiscal years were 1580 and 1660 respectively. All of these include Executive Mansion and Grounds personnel (less than a hundred). More detailed figures are available in *The Budget of the United States Government for the Fiscal Year Ending June 30, 1966* (1965), Appendix, pp. 49-62.

civil defense over to the Defense Department, such remaining functions as stockpiling and planning for disaster relief and for national mobilization in times of major crisis were left in the hands of a reconstituted staff agency called the Office of Emergency Planning. This Office is also concerned with the problem of assuring the continuity of civilian elements of the government in times of extreme crisis—for example, a nuclear attack on the United States.

The work of the Council of Economic Advisers is focussed on the American economy. Obviously, the state of that economy both affects and is affected by economic developments abroad. In this fundamental sense, the studies and advice of the Council have foreign policy implications. On such issues as U.S. foreign trade policy or the present balance-of-payments difficulties, its advice could loom large.

White House Office

"White House Office" is the label given to that group of presidential staff assistants who work directly for the President, rather than for one of the other six Executive Office units already mentioned. However, even the White House Office can no longer be conceived of as a small, intimate operation. At present, its total staff numbers more than 250.[7]

One aspect of Mr. Eisenhower's effort to put the operations of the presidency on a more systematically organized basis was the designation of one of his aides as the Assistant to the President. Particularly during the tenure of ex-New Hampshire Governor Sherman Adams, this official worked as a virtual chief of staff of the White House Office. Mr. Kennedy did not give any of his aides such a designation, and apparently no one Kennedy assistant functioned in such a role. Early experience with President Johnson's modus operandi suggests that he, too, will put no one aide in such a position.

Another Eisenhower innovation not retained by Mr. Kennedy was the Staff Secretary. This official, an Army brigadier general who had worked for General Eisenhower in NATO headquarters, was responsible for a variety of secretariat functions, including supervision of the preparation and flow of White House paperwork, checking on the im-

---

[7] The average for fiscal year 1964 was 263. The estimates for fiscal 1965 and 1966 were, respectively, 262 and 260. *Ibid.*

plementation of presidential decisions, marshaling the daily intelligence reports for the President and preparing "staff notes" to alert Mr. Eisenhower to emerging problems and events.

The establishment of a small Cabinet secretariat in 1954, responsible for the preparatory and follow-up work surrounding Cabinet deliberations, was an Eisenhower change that seemed to make sense, if only for the sake of an accurate record of decisions taken. Given Mr. Kennedy's lack of interest in regular Cabinet or National Security Council meetings as forums for policy decisions, the practical usefulness of the device seemed much diluted. While one presidential assistant continued to be given the title of Secretary to the Cabinet, the secretariat as such was not retained.

Special presidential aides, like special presidential coordinating devices, come and go. Mr. Eisenhower had Special Assistants for Security Operations Coordination and Foreign Economic Policy during the last few years of his Administration. They departed the scene at the start of the Kennedy Administration along with the high-level committees, the Operations Coordinating Board, and the Council for Foreign Economic Policy, which they represented. Mr. Kennedy did not replace General Taylor with another special military aide. His staff did include special assistants for metropolitan Washington problems and cultural affairs.

The Bureau of the Budget

The Bureau of the Budget is the oldest of the presidential staff units and in fact predates the Executive Office itself. It was originally established in the Treasury Department in 1921 and was moved over to the Executive Office when the latter came into being in 1939. While it is not easy to compare the usefulness of organizational units, it is probably true that the Bureau's functions could be least easily dispensed with or handled some place short of the Executive Office. The Bureau's assigned functions make its importance clear: overall coordination and preparation of the executive branch budget, review and clearance of all departmental legislative proposals before they are sent to Congress, and general responsibility for improving organization and management within the executive branch.

These assignments are not merely *pro forma*. The Bureau's Legislative Reference Division—not to be confused with the Legislative Reference Service of the Library of Congress—can and does return proposed legislation to departments for revision or clarification; it may even reject some proposals as not consistent with the President's program or as otherwise ill-conceived. The President has even vetoed a congressional enactment that was favored by one of his own departments on the basis—at least in part—of contrary advice from the Budget Bureau. The Bureau's responsibility for organizational improvement involves it in important organizational changes proposed for or by the various executive agencies.

The heart of the Bureau's responsibilities lies in the budgetary field. After the budget units within each of the executive agencies have gone over the requests of their various subdivisions and pruned and chopped in terms of the preliminary budget guidelines with which they have been provided by the Bureau, the agency budgets are submitted to the Budget Bureau. Its examiners scrutinize them in terms of the policies and specific figures determined by the President and his top advisers. The Bureau, working closely with the President, pulls together these complicated materials and prepares the massive document submitted to Congress.[8]

This, obviously, is a highly simplified explanation of a most complicated process, one of the key processes in the American governmental system. Many important national security policy issues, particularly in the fields of national defense and foreign aid, tend to become translated into budgetary terms and to be settled in the course of the budgetary cycle. This is in one sense quite reasonable, even inevitable. Broad policies are translated into specific programs which are in turn translated into expenditures to be proposed to Congress for its approval or disapproval. Given the limited funds and many worthy programs and projects competing for support, difficult choices must be made in establishing priorities and allocating resources.

In this process, executive budget units as well as Appropriations

[8] A standard reference on this subject is Arthur Smithies, *The Budgetary Process in the United States* (McGraw-Hill, 1955). For a more recent analysis concerned with the budgetary process as political behavior, see Aaron Wildavsky, *The Politics of the Budgetary Process* (Little, Brown, 1964). The first Jackson subcommittee also gave considerable attention to this topic. See *Organizing for National Security*, Hearings, 87 Cong. 1 sess. (1961), Vol. 1, pp. 1003-1134, and a staff study, *The Bureau of the Budget and the Budgetary Process*, Vol. 3, pp. 89-100.

subcommittees are in a position to make independent policy judgments and then to translate these into budgetary decisions. Sometimes they do. It is the exercising of this prerogative by budget units that most disturbs operating agencies and divisions, who are reluctant to accept this as a necessary part of the budgetary function. It should be added that on the more important policy questions, budget staffs must presumably be able to sell their views to authoritative policy makers like the President or heads of agencies.

In the national security field, the International and Military Divisions of the Budget Bureau play the most important roles. In money terms, the major concern of the International Division is the foreign aid program. The Military Division works closely with the Comptroller of the Defense Department on the largest and most difficult part of the whole federal budget—the military.

No doubt the size and importance of the military budget explain the exceptional relationship that exists between the Budget Bureau and the Defense Comptroller. The Defense Department is the only executive agency where there is direct participation of representatives of the Bureau of the Budget in the budget preparation process. Each fall, members of the Military Division staff move over to the Pentagon and work with the Comptroller's staff on the military budget documents. It is probably fair to say, however, that the Defense Comptroller is more influential, and the Budget Bureau less so, than during the Eisenhower Administration.

The precise amounts of money allocated to the State Department for the upkeep of United States diplomatic and consular missions are unlikely to have a direct effect on the state of relations with particular countries. On the other hand, the meaning and effectiveness of foreign aid and informational and cultural programs are more closely linked to the funds voted. In those cases, the budgetary translation is significant and can become the basis for considerable modification of accepted policies and programs. In this sense, budgetary decisions— whether by the executive on funds to be requested of Congress or by Congress on the funds it actually provides—are political as that term was defined in Chapter 2. They involve conflicting values and goals, competing agencies and interests and, often, the need for resolution by the President himself.

The impressive array of staff functions performed by the Bureau

on the President's behalf has led to harsh cries of outrage and indigna-
tion, particularly on matters of money. The Bureau is by no means
the most popular agency in Washington. Given the "political" nature
of budgetary decisions and the fact that the President cannot oversee
the work of the Bureau in great detail, some have suggested that the
Bureau actually has substantial decision-making power, resting on and
shielded by the power of the President but in fact independently
wielded.

During the Eisenhower Administration, with its strong orientation
to the value of a balanced budget, such charges—particularly with regard to the military budget—were commonplace. Some Pentagon circles were deeply concerned that the Budget Bureau was substituting its
own judgments about military matters for those of the military chiefs
of staff and other professionals.[9]

This is difficult to assess in definitive terms. Undoubtedly the Budget Bureau can be a potent factor in presidential program and budgetary decision making. However, the President does have other staff aides
who can alert him to any major Bureau decisions that go against his
own policy and program preferences. Furthermore, his agency heads
have opportunities to question their budgetary allocations at a number of points in the budgetary process, and most of them exercise this
prerogative at one point or another. An agency head who believes that
an important program is likely to be damaged significantly by cuts
in its budget can always appeal directly to the President; this, too, is
frequently done.[10] The Budget Bureau has lost its share of bureaucratic battles.

The role that the Bureau plays at any particular time is a function
of the operating style and policy views of the President and his relationship with the Bureau and its Director as well as of the skills and

[9] In this connection, much depends on how one defines the special purview and
competence of the professional military man and the range of possible civilian expertise in military matters. For a discussion of the role of the Budget Bureau at
that time, see *Major Defense Matters and the Role of Budget Bureau in Formulation and Execution of Defense Budget*, Hearings before the Preparedness Investigating Subcommittee of the Senate Committee on Armed Services, 86 Cong. 1 sess.
(1959), Pt. 2, May 20 and June 17, 1959.

[10] In the case of the military establishment, the Joint Chiefs of Staff can also
voice their concerns directly to the President (and the Congress), while recognizing
that in so doing they may incur the displeasure of their civilian chiefs in the
Pentagon.

attitudes of the Bureau's own staff. The largely negative role attributed to the Bureau during the Eisenhower Administration reflected the policy views and conservative fiscal orientation of the President and his key advisers. The same is true for the especially broad and potent policy role attributed to the Treasury Department under Eisenhower. Under other circumstances, the Bureau can play a more positive role, encouraging needed organizational changes or the rethinking of basic policy and program premises by the departments.[11]

Ideally, the Bureau is a major staff arm of the President, trying to enforce his policy views and translate them into specific programs and amounts of money. This involves needling the departments and engaging in vigorous dispute with them. It can also mean close, informal, and mutually advantageous cooperation and consultation on difficult problems.

The National Security Council

Within his first month or two in office, Mr. Kennedy abolished most of the high-level interdepartmental committees that had been set up in the Executive Office to coordinate or formulate policy in various foreign affairs fields. Among the casualties were the two major subsidiary units of the National Security Council, the Operations Coordinating Board and the Planning Board, and the various subordinate units and activities they in turn had spawned. The Council itself was retained, along with the office of Special Assistant to the President for National Security Affairs. The professional secretariats that had been attached to the National Security Council-Planning Board complex and to the Operations Coordinating Board were largely disbanded. Mr. Kennedy held less frequent and regular meetings of both the Security Council and the Cabinet,[12] preferring smaller, *ad hoc* sessions with groups of advisers and departmental officials responsible for particular problem areas.

[11] For a report on the role of the Bureau of the Budget in the Johnson Administration and an assessment of its influence therein, see Alan L. Otten, "Powerful Pygmy," *Wall Street Journal*, Dec. 10, 1964.

[12] See the article by Carroll Kilpatrick, "Is Kennedy Correct In Use of Cabinet?" *Washington Post*, March 25, 1962. Kilpatrick reported that at the time of writing, Kennedy had held 15 Cabinet meetings and 23 meetings of the National Security Council.

Before attempting to analyze and evaluate the role of the National Security Council in foreign policy decision making, it may be useful to sketch its development briefly. It was originally established under the terms of the National Security Act of 1947. Its statutory members are the President, the Vice President, the Secretary of State, the Secretary of Defense, and the Director of the Office of Emergency Planning. Sitting as statutory advisers to the Council are the Director of the Central Intelligence Agency and the Chairman of the Joint Chiefs of Staff.

As can be seen from its statutory membership, the Council is in fact an inner Cabinet or a Cabinet committee for national security policy rather than a staff agency in the usual sense. In formal terms, it is the highest committee in the government for the resolution of national security questions; its views can only be advisory to the President, who alone makes the final decisions. In actual operation, the Council has been concerned with major policy decisions of longer-term import rather than with current, day-to-day problems and activities. In spite of the fact that it was originally fathered in the military establishment, its primary focus has been foreign rather than military policy, although the latter is by no means completely excluded.

From 1950 until early 1961, a second-level group connected with the Council did much of the work involved in preparing the policy papers to be acted on by the Council and the President. This group was known as the Senior Staff under President Truman and became the Planning Board under President Eisenhower. Each member of the National Security Council was represented on the Planning Board by one of his departmental officials, usually of Assistant Secretary rank. In the last few years of the Eisenhower Administration, these officials in turn relied on a group of their subordinates, known as the Planning Board Assistants, to do much of the detailed drafting of the papers.

In late 1953 the Operations Coordinating Board (OCB) was established by an executive order and made a part of the national security organization at the presidential level; it did not formally become a part of the National Security Council structure until July 1957. The OCB was an outgrowth of the Psychological Strategy Board, established in 1951, and in part reflected a concern to maximize the psychological impact of United States policy. Its prescribed function was to spell out the policies established by the National Security Council in terms of more detailed agency programs and to attempt to assure that these programs were mutually reinforcing and implemented to produce maximum advantage. The Operations Plans produced by the Board, however, apparently enumerated ongoing agency programs for the most part.[13]

The core membership of departmental representatives on the Coordinating Board included an Under Secretary of State, the Deputy Secretary of Defense, and the Directors of the Central Intelligence Agency, the then International Cooperation Administration, and the United States Information Agency. The OCB members also had their group of Board Assistants to do preliminary labors for them. Detailed scrutiny of policy execution in various geographical and functional areas was actually carried out by approximately fifty OCB working groups. These were interdepartmental committees of working-level officials with one professional staff person from the Coordinating Board's secretariat sitting with each working group.

Another Eisenhower innovation in the National Security Council system was to establish in 1953, as part of his own immediate staff, the position of Special Assistant to the President for National Security Affairs. Under Mr. Eisenhower, this official played a key role in the work and meetings of the Council, acted as chairman of the Planning Board meetings (previously the function of the executive secretary of the Council staff) and, after serving as a member, was made chairman of the Operations Coordinating Board in January 1960 (a position previously assigned to the Under Secretary of State).

Because of the Special Assistant's close working relation with Mr. Eisenhower and because of the highly experienced and able men who held the position—Robert Cutler, Dillon Anderson, and Gordon Gray —the Special Assistant was, during the Eisenhower Administration, an important figure in the deliberations of the National Security Council and the Planning Board and in national security policy making at the presidential level.[14]

In 1957, the position of Special Assistant to the President for Security Operations Coordination was established. This official served as

[13] The Kennedy decision to abolish the Operations Coordinating Board, and the broader problems of policy execution and implementation that the Board attempted to cope with, are discussed in Chapter 9.

[14] Some of the description and analysis of the National Security Council in the present chapter is drawn from an appendix prepared by the author for *The Formulation and Administration of U. S. Foreign Policy*. See App. B, "The Organization and Procedures of the National Security Council Mechanism," pp. 162-71. The hearings held by Senator Jackson's Subcommittee on National Policy Machinery provide a rich

Vice-Chairman of the Operations Coordinating Board and in addition attended meetings of the Security Council and the Planning Board. His position was clearly subordinate to the Special Assistant for National Security Affairs. It was abolished by Mr. Kennedy.

From its inception, the National Security Council had a small professional staff attached to it, headed by an executive secretary, performing primarily secretariat functions—arranging the agenda for meetings, providing and distributing supporting papers (including records of actions taken at Council meetings), and facilitating negotiations among participants. It also did a certain amount of independent analysis of the policy papers going through the Council machinery, a function expanded somewhat during the Eisenhower Administration.

Mr. Gordon Gray, the last Eisenhower Special Assistant for National Security Affairs, reported that the secretariat provided him with an "objective analysis of every policy paper" that went through the Planning Board to the Council. While it did "not itself make policy recommendations," it did "scrutinize departmental proposals and suggest policy alternatives or additions that merit consideration."[15]

The Operations Coordinating Board had its own professional staff, which was formally a part of the overall National Security Council staff but had its own Executive Officer and seemed to operate pretty much as a separate unit. The Executive Officer attended meetings of the Coordinating Board, chaired meetings of the Board Assistants, and was responsible for general supervision of the activities of the Board working groups. As noted above, members of his staff participated in the work of all of these groups.

Mr. Kennedy discarded most of this machinery. He did continue the position of Special Assistant for National Security Affairs and appointed to it McGeorge Bundy, then Dean of Harvard College. While the Special Assistant under Eisenhower came to preside over a rather

---

source of data on the Council structure and processes. In addition, see the collection of *Selected Materials* and *Organizational History of the National Security Council*, prepared for the subcommittee by two members of the Council secretariat, the then Executive Secretary, Mr. James S. Lay, Jr., and Mr. Robert H. Johnson, in *Organizing for National Security*, Vol. 2 (1961), pp. 115-298 and 413-68.

[15] Gordon Gray, "Role of the National Security Council in the Formulation of National Policy," unpublished paper prepared for delivery at the 1959 meeting of the American Political Science Association in Washington, D. C. This paper was reprinted in the collection of *Selected Materials* prepared for the Subcommittee on National Policy Machinery. See *Organizing for National Security*, Vol. 2, p. 188.

elaborate cluster of committees, staffs, and secretariats and served the President primarily through his formal role at the center of this machinery, Mr. Bundy acted more as a personal aide to Mr. Kennedy on national security and foreign policy matters. This relationship continued under President Johnson until Mr. Bundy resigned in early 1966 to become head of the Ford Foundation.

While Mr. Bundy as Special Assistant did attend the National Security Council and other high-level meetings and did systematically follow up on their decisions, his concerns were much broader. He followed important national security problems and situations on the President's behalf, reflecting the President's views where appropriate, seeing that departments were implementing decisions and considering important problems, and making sure that necessary information and reports were reaching the President in timely fashion. Clearly, such a role permits considerable influence on certain policy decisions.

Rather than devoting its primary efforts to servicing the formal National Security Council machinery, the relatively small staff remaining from the earlier NSC and OCB secretariats performs coordinating, following-up, and information-gathering tasks for the President and the Special Assistant. Some of the staff have been assigned geographic and functional areas of responsibility and keep in close touch with those in the State Department and elsewhere in the foreign policy organization with parallel responsibilities. They should be able to reflect White House views and at the same time keep the Special Assistant fully abreast of what is and is not being done in the line foreign policy agencies. In effect, the present national security staff has become an extension of the President's personal staff rather than a part of the institutional apparatus connected with the National Security Council.

The contrasting operating styles of Kennedy and Eisenhower are also revealed by the actual working procedures of the Council under the two men.[16] As has already been noted, the Council machinery expanded considerably under Mr. Eisenhower. Furthermore, an elabo-

[16] In contrasting the Eisenhower and Kennedy approaches to use of the National Security Council, it should be remembered that Harry Truman was the first President who had this mechanism available to him. Particularly in the period before the Korean War, Mr. Truman apparently regarded it as a forum where some of his top officials could discuss major national security problems, and do so more effectively, without the inhibiting effect of his presence. See *Organizational History of the National Security Council, ibid.* p. 421.

rate procedure was developed for the preparation of policy papers, and such documents were systematically produced and recorded. The Council met regularly once a week, as did the Coordinating Board. The Planning Board met at least two afternoons a week.

In its weekly two-hour meetings, the Council typically disposed of four or five policy papers. This led critics to infer, probably with some justice, that there was little time for probing policy discussions, that about all the President and the Council could do was to make basic decisions and perhaps resolve occasional sharp conflicts between the departments. (Of course, on the right problems, that would be quite a bit.) Most of the work, including the tentative reaching of decisions, had to be done at lower levels. Most of it was actually performed in the departments. Under Mr. Kennedy, the routine preparation and consideration of such policy papers was dropped.

By the close of the Eisenhower Administration, the National Security Council structure and processes were under substantial criticism. It was said that they had become too routine, too mechanical. Many policy papers were being produced, but they did not seem to provide much concrete guidance. The number of people attending the meetings had gradually expanded. Not only had the seven statutory members and advisers been joined on a regular basis by the Secretary of the Treasury, the Director of the Bureau of the Budget, and the Chairman of the Atomic Energy Commission, but a considerable number of other officials, including some presidential staff aides, were normally present. It was estimated that at least twenty people were regularly in attendance at Council meetings, hardly the setting for frank discussion of national security policy issues.

During the last year or two of the Eisenhower Administration, there were efforts to meet these criticisms. The requirements for reports and plans by the Operations Coordinating Board were simplified and the paperwork substantially reduced. There was also an effort to bring more open discussion into the Council forum earlier by the use of such devices as "discussion papers" that were meant to stimulate discussion on policy matters rather than decide them.

Thus, the Kennedy changes, while certainly sharp, did not represent a completely new or unexpected turn of events. They had in fact been forecast by the critiques of the Eisenhower operations, although Mr. Kennedy and his advisers must be given credit for being willing to make a clean sweep of much of the apparatus rather than trying to modify it.

In a letter written to Senator Henry Jackson in September 1961, McGeorge Bundy indicated rather clearly the view of the Kennedy Administration toward national security policy making at the presidential level and the path that it would indeed follow in the succeeding two years. He noted that many matters that used to flow routinely to the National Security Council were now being settled in other ways and in other forums. Furthermore—and this is a pattern that continued to be important—some were being settled at levels below the President.

While admitting that Mr. Kennedy convened the Council much less frequently and had in fact downgraded its policy-making role, Bundy emphasized that even in its more influential days, it had never been "the only instrument of counsel and decision available to the President in dealing with the problems of . . . national security." Many of the crucial decisions of the Eisenhower and Truman Administrations had been made outside its framework. "The National Security Council is one instrument among many; it must never be made an end in itself."[17]

Between 1961 and 1963, a number of new instruments of policy making and operational coordination appeared upon the scene. Most of them did in fact function at the sub-Cabinet level or lower. They ranged from the Special Group (Counter-Insurgency)—to focus governmental attention and expedite programs in that field—to Berlin and Vietnam Task Forces and an interagency Youth Committee. They also included policy committees on Latin America and Africa, chaired by the Assistant Secretaries of State for those regions. At the time of the Cuban crisis of October 1962, an Executive Committee (EX-COMM) of the National Security Council was established to provide a hard-core decision-making group for that problem. The EXCOMM device was also used in dealing with certain other key problems over the next year or two.

[17] *Organizing for National Security*, Vol. 1, Hearings, p. 1336. The text of this letter appears on pp. 1335-38. Other Kennedy Administration officials elaborated this point of view on national security policy making in testimony before the subcommittee in the summer of 1961. For the testimony of Secretaries Rusk and McNamara and Budget Bureau Director David Bell, see Hearings, pp. 1133-1333.

In all of these cases as well as in the operation of the National Security Council itself, the bulk of the work in preparing papers and implementing decisions fell on the participating departments. This had also been true for the Council under Eisenhower, with the important difference that the work of the departments was mediated by the Planning and Coordinating Boards and their Board Assistants. The pattern under Mr. Kennedy was to place responsibility for the necessary policy formulation and program implementation directly on the departments involved and to ask one of them to provide leadership and coordination for each specific problem or situation. Particular emphasis was placed on the leadership role of the Department of State.

If the Eisenhower system had seemed overly routinized, the Kennedy approach struck some observers as too free-wheeling, too disorderly, too diffuse. It certainly placed added burdens and pressures on the departments, particularly the Department of State. It was also clear that the disappearance of most of the Eisenhower National Security Council machinery had not meant an end to interagency policy-making and policy-implementing mechanisms and forums. What some might have considered a void had been quickly filled, but in a manner more congenial to the needs and style of the new President.

Major Problems

The President's values, his qualities of character and intellect, his capacity for leadership, his political skills, his definition of his own role, and the way he performs it—these are fundamental determinants of the working of the American government and of American politics. They are at the same time matters over which the student of organization has little control, however much he may philosophize or theorize about them.

As far as the organization of the presidency is concerned, the author's general point of view has already been stated. Simply put, there can be no ideal organization of the presidency. Each President's personality, style of work, and definition of his job will lead him in different directions. It does not seem likely that a particular set of organizational arrangements will draw an incumbent into a role performance that runs against the whole grain of his personality and past experiences. What he doesn't find helpful or actively dislikes, he will either modify or ignore. Thus, there is no point in trying to set forth a detailed blueprint of what the ideal Executive Office might look like.

Organizational Assistance for the President: Some General Considerations

There are, nevertheless, some functions that any set of organizational arrangements must perform, some requirements that must be met, and it may be useful to try to suggest them. Before doing so, a few words should be said about the underlying approach.[18] There are two general kinds of choices to be made. First, and less important, is the question of how much of the Executive Office structure should be embodied in statutory enactment rather than executive orders and the like. The position in this study has been made perfectly clear—as part of a modest and tentative approach to the Executive Office, caution should be exercised in fixing Executive Office changes in statute.

The other kind of choice is more controversial. Where does one strike the balance between building up the staff organization immediately available to the President and, on the other hand, relying on the efforts of the major line departments and agencies? The bias in this study is toward relying on the departments rather than building up a substantial staff structure at the presidential level. This was in general the position taken by President Kennedy and his Administration and perhaps reflects the influence of that point of view.

On the other hand, the thrust of the Coffey and Rock study, among others, is in the opposite direction—that the many needs of the contemporary President should be met by building up the responsibilities and capabilities of the various Executive Office units and, indeed, by adding to them. If the present study reflects a Kennedy influence, it seems fair to say that the Coffey and Rock study, published in the last days of the Eisenhower Administration, bears the mark of that Administration and some of its needs, practices, and organizational arrangements.

[18] A broader and more thoroughgoing discussion of the organization of the presidency is found in J. I. Coffey and Vincent P. Rock, "The Presidential Staff" (National Planning Association, Dec. 15, 1960, mimeo.). This study presents some very interesting proposals and analyses, but its general approach differs from the one taken here, as will be seen in the discussion that follows.

Some of the specific recommendations made by Coffey and Rock seem eminently sensible, and it is not possible to take exception to most of the presidential needs they set forth. The more basic question is whether it is desirable, or even feasible, to try to satisfy them by building up the presidential staff. One of the flaws in such proposals is their assumption that because people are recruited to do a particular job in a particular way, they are actually going to be able to do it. Being a member of a presidential staff does not turn someone into a superman. If the jobs to be performed are difficult and sophisticated, and if the departments seem unwilling or perhaps unable to perform them, why should it be assumed that they will be any more easily performed at the presidential staff level?

It is conceivable that, over time, it would be possible to build up a highly prestigious career service at the presidential staff level, but it certainly does not exist today. This suggests that rather than being able to recruit supermen, the presidential staff units may not even be able to recruit as able people as the departments can. Even the Bureau of the Budget, venerable and well established, finds it difficult to hold on to its abler career officials. For many, the challenges and responsibilities of the operating line agencies are more appealing than staff work, no matter how lofty the level at which it is being performed. After a while, there is a desire to get into "the action" rather than stand above or beside it.

Furthermore, the fact that a unit is set up to do a particular job is no guarantee that it is going to do it well. One can have planning staffs that plan poorly or not at all, science staffs that do not have the respect of their professional colleagues, and so on down the line. It is not just a question of identifying a functional need and then establishing a staff structure to deal with it. There is no reason to assume that it will do the job that has to be done.

In his study of presidential power, Professor Neustadt pointed out that to some extent the executive departments, and their heads, are by the very nature of their functions "natural enemies" of the President.[19] This can become another strong argument for building up the presi-

[19] Neustadt, *op. cit.*, pp. 39-40. The term appears in Charles G. Dawes' comment, quoted by Neustadt, that "the members of the Cabinet are a President's natural enemies."

dential staff—to protect the President from his Cabinet members and their departments and, furthermore, to enable the President to jog the departments, to get them to do what they are supposed to be doing but either cannot or do not want to do.

To be frank, this seems like a rather caricatured view of the great departments of the government. They have their own narrower problems and inhibiting pressures, but they are also subject to a wide range of pressures from the President and their political chiefs who are, after all, his appointees. Furthermore, in the foreign policy-national security field, the leading agencies—the Department of State, Central Intelligence, the Information Agency, the Agency for International Development and, to a lesser extent, the Defense Department—do not have any substantial domestic clienteles. They are presumably less subject to the pressures that tend to counter the will of the President in some of the domestically-oriented agencies. The State Department and the Secretary of State, in particular, have always been closely linked to the President; it is a little difficult to conceive of them as the President's enemies. If the President is prepared to exercise his leadership and use the State Department effectively, it can be viewed in some ways as a large-scale extension of his own staff.

Some of the functions proposed for the presidential staff by Coffey and Rock—for example, linking policies, programs, and budgets more closely and systematically; improving the use by the government of the social sciences and, more generally, of scientific knowledge and research; coordinating more effectively all domestic and foreign information programs—represent needs of the government as a whole rather than simply those of the President. If this is so, the answer would seem to lie in improved handling of these functions by the operating agencies rather than in adding presidential staff units. It is difficult to see why a challenging problem that is not being satisfactorily met by a responsible line department, which is presumably organized and equipped to deal with it, will be handled more satisfactorily by a presidential unit.

The President's perspective on national problems is almost by definition broader than anyone else's, either in Congress or in the agencies of the executive branch. But it is difficult to see how one can derive from this premise the assurance that anyone working on a presidential staff will have the same perspective or the same balanced view, or the ability to formulate a version of the "national interest" superior to that emanating from the departments. Because a presidential staff man works directly for the President, one may assume that he will be somewhat more responsive to the latter's wishes than a civil servant or a military officer in the Pentagon or Foggy Bottom. However, as the presidential staff begins to take on considerable dimensions of its own, why should it be assumed that key staff people will not develop their own particular interests and points of view, which may at times diverge from those of the President? Is it generally agreed that Sherman Adams was the completely self-effacing and self-restrained instrument of Mr. Eisenhower's wishes?

The President's position and perspective do not guarantee that he will always be broader-gauged or wiser in his judgments than the departments. Sometimes they may be right and the President wrong. If this is the case for the President himself, there is certainly no reason to assume by definition the superior wisdom or perspective of the presidential staff. From this critical point of view, the apparatus proposed or implied by the Coffey and Rock analysis sounds as if it might stifle or overwhelm the President, rather than free and strengthen him.

In sum, all other things being equal, as much as possible should be delegated to the departments and done by them. They have the relevant operating responsibilities, and they are, presumably, equipped organizationally and intellectually to do the big jobs. If they are not doing them, the President should find out why and try to do something about it. He does need immediately available staff assistance for this kind of job. Only as a last resort should he move the function or problem into the Executive Office and try to handle it from there. Particularly in the national security and foreign policy fields, the President should work directly and intimately with the Secretaries of State and Defense and their higher echelon officials.

To take an example from one field, in the absence of a strong civilian scientific capability in the Defense Department, the office of the President's Science Adviser at one time had a particularly important role to play in military policy making. Is this preferable to the present situation where the Secretary of Defense has a strong scientific and engineering staff of his own? Similarly, the scientific knowledge of the

Science Adviser and the President's Science Advisory Committee can be no substitute for a scientific and research capability in the Arms Control and Disarmament Agency itself.[20]

Requirements for National Security Organization at the Presidential Level

During the last few years of the Eisenhower Administration, the National Security Council became the subject of considerable discussion, heated controversy, scholarly research and analysis, and finally Senate investigation, by the Subcommittee on National Policy Machinery already mentioned. In the course of this debate, the shortcomings of the Council as an organizational device were charged with much of the responsibility for failures and inadequacies of United States foreign policy, just as in an earlier period the Council had been viewed as the reassuring summit of the policy organization, a kind of American "Politburo."

All of this was patently absurd, and the absurdity was quickly underscored in the early months of the Kennedy Administration. With many of the supposedly hobbling committees and procedures of the Council eliminated, the new Administration found that the major policy problems it faced—Cuba, Berlin, Laos, Vietnam, and the Congo —were as intractable as before. About all that could be said was that the previous inadequacies in the policy-making machinery may have helped them get that bad—and that would be difficult to demonstrate.

It would be grossly unfair to accuse Mr. Kennedy and his advisers of having assumed that the heart of United States policy troubles lay in the national security machinery elaborated under the Eisenhower

---

[20] The Presidential Special Assistant for Science and Technology (or Science Adviser, as he is often called) and his staff represent a kind of Executive Office success story. When originally established in 1957, the innovation was greeted with considerable skepticism, but the Science Adviser, his very small staff and the governmental and outside advisory committees serviced by it proved extremely useful in bringing scientific knowledge to bear on policy problems. In May 1962, the unit was expanded into an Office of Science and Technology, with somewhat larger staff and broader functions but still located within the Executive Office. This example would seem to support the argument for gradual accretion rather than grand designs in the organization of the Executive Office. The new science office and its predecessor are discussed in more detail in Chap. 8.

Administration. Their major criticisms of the previous administration had been directed at substantive policies, not organizational arrangements. However, the policy problems and experiences of the new Administration during its first year in office made crystal clear what some observers had insisted on all along—that if there had been major failures or weaknesses in United States foreign and defense policies, the essential explanation lay elsewhere than in the structure and operation of the National Security Council and its subsidiary units.

Rather than discuss past problems and future possibilities of the Council *per se,* it might be more useful to indicate some of the requirements that *any* set of national security arrangements at the presidential level should satisfy. The past experience of the Council and its related units is certainly relevant, and will be referred to, but for present purposes, the analysis will primarily set forth fundamental requirements to be met—and each President to his own organizational devices.

Crucial to the policy process are systematic policy analysis, the creative development of policy alternatives, the anticipation of situations likely to become problems if not dealt with forehandedly, and long-range programming and planning. These are appropriately the primary concern of the departments, working separately and together.[21]

It is of fundamental importance that particular policies and programs be seen in relation to one another, not as a series of separate entities or episodes. This is an obvious requirement, but it can easily be forgotten in the press of successive crises and the difficult choices that must be made daily. One way of trying to meet it is by a series of interdepartmental committees and other coordinating arrangements, with some ranking body like the National Security Council to oversee the total national security terrain. Indeed, one of the criticisms of the Eisenhower organization at the end was that pieces of the same problem were being dealt with in a variety of forums. There were too many committees, with overlapping functions but separate staffs, that were not being properly coordinated.[22]

The same criticism was directed at Mr. Kennedy, given the prolif-

---

[21] See the more detailed discussion in Chap. 10.

[22] See Coffey and Rock, *op. cit.,* Chaps. VIII, X, and XI. They recommend that committees be combined where appropriate and that a single secretariat be set up to service all the high-level interdepartmental committees.

eration of high-level committees and task forces noted above as well as his preference for *ad hoc* decision-making bodies. In Kennedy's case, furthermore, there was no designated forum for the broad overview of policy problems. Obviously, the responsibilities of some officials, like the Secretary of State or the Secretary of Defense, cut across almost all national security problems. It was argued by Kennedy Administration spokesmen that the Secretary of State can and should perform this integrating function on the President's behalf in the foreign policy field.[23]

The need for an integrated approach to policy formulation and decision making is matched by an equivalent need for coordination in the execution of policies. Where the Eisenhower Administration looked at least in part to the Operations Coordinating Board structure, the Kennedy Administration was inclined to place responsibility on the departments, particularly on the State Department in the foreign policy field. In both cases, it is important to be clear about who is to do what.

It is therefore desirable that decisions made and responsibilities allocated be set forth in writing. While there seems little doubt that the Eisenhower Administration went too far in developing and formalizing the requirements for written papers and documents, it is not surprising to note that the President's national security decisions are still embodied in writing, usually by the Special Assistant for National Security Affairs, and follow-up memoranda are still sent to the responsible agencies. Clearly, the time is long since past when even the most free-wheeling President can count on informal understandings and what he and others can remember—or choose to remember—to carry on the work.

[23] Those who favor substantially expanded staff resources at the presidential level insist that this integrating function can only be effectively performed at that level. Undoubtedly, at a minimum, a vigilant presidential staff is necessary. It should also be noted that emphasis on the leadership role of the Secretary and the Department of State does not imply a posture of passive reliance on the part of the President and his White House and Executive Office staffs. By their actions, the latter may try to prompt and encourage this leadership and even help to support the State Department in its dealings with the other major foreign policy agencies. On the other hand, they may eventually lose patience and despair of effective State Department leadership. In other words, emphasis on State Department leadership by no means implies the abdication of leadership at the presidential and Executive Office level.

One of the original reasons for establishing the National Security Council was the belief that the United States lacked an explicit, clearly-defined set of statements embodying not merely general policy, but also what this policy implied for specific areas and problems. This was, and probably still is, a need strongly felt in many parts of the government. One of the roles of the National Security Council up to the Kennedy Administration was to develop and keep up-to-date papers setting forth policy in important geographical and functional areas, including basic military-strategic policy. Since these papers had the approval of the President, they presumably represented official United States policy. Although papers with similar purposes continued to be produced under the Kennedy Administration, the approach and format differed substantially; they were usually developed and agreed to at the departmental level rather than approved formally by the National Security Council and the President.

The setting of major policy guidelines and directions is an important policy-making function. The pre-Kennedy National Security Council not only produced fairly general statements indicating the course the United States should pursue in some particular country or region but also made rather specific choices, such as the decision to develop a thermonuclear bomb on a "crash" basis or, one might speculate, fairly fundamental policy determinations about West Berlin or the development of certain weapons systems by the military establishment.

The more general types of policy statements tend to sound either quite vague or perhaps so obvious as hardly to need stating. These, no doubt, called forth some of the critical comments about the vagueness, generality, and even ambiguity of many of the National Security Council's policy papers. Successor documents under Mr. Kennedy elicited similar reactions. It is clear that when a specific situation arises which is supposedly covered by one of these policy papers, the complexities and peculiarities of the situation often mean that the previously prepared, rather general policy statement provides little specific guidance.

Such papers should not be expected to provide all the answers, or even most of them, when a specific contingency arises. There may still be considerable advantage, however, in having thought about, researched, analyzed, and discussed the general area in advance and made some general determinations about it.[24]

There are several other more subtle functions often credited to the National Security Council structure as it operated under President Eisenhower, even by those who were skeptical about its major policy role. For one thing, it provided an institutional mechanism which assured that the responsible heads of the major national security agencies and the key presidential advisers in this field would, along with the President himself, examine many of the crucial national security problems facing the United States from a number of significant personal and departmental perspectives. Perhaps the requirements for such attention are so clear and the necessary habits so well developed that this kind of institutional "insurance" once provided by the National Security Council is no longer necessary.

Another subsidiary function often conceded to the Council was the "educating" of some of the key officials of the executive branch, giving them a fuller sense of the nature of significant national security problems and, at the same time, building broad understanding and agreement among these leaders about major policy lines. In a complicated governmental structure facing extremely difficult problems, with top officials rushed and busy, with a rather high rate of both political and career personnel turnover, this may be more important than a first glance might suggest. Mr. Kennedy was reported to have used occasional Cabinet and National Security Council meetings for precisely this purpose—to inform his Cabinet officers and other high officials about the line of policy he was taking on some very important matter —perhaps one that cut across the responsibilities of several departments—and to spell out the rationale that underlay it. Press reports in early 1965 suggested that President Johnson is using Cabinet meetings for similar purposes, though on a far broader range of subject matter than national security problems, and to stimulate Cabinet implementation as well as understanding of his policies.

This is at best a partial listing of the requirements of the national security organization at the presidential level, even in the foreign policy field. It suggests that the National Security Council performed some useful, even necessary, functions in the past. However, it is the

[24] This question is discussed in more detail in Chap. 10.

functions rather than the particular organizational mechanism that performs them which are of the essence. If they are not performed by the Council or the Cabinet, they must be taken care of somewhere, somehow. Whether tidier, more systematically developed arrangements result in more effective performance is an open question.

Finally, there can be no doubt that the President needs some independent staff capability of his own to follow up on problems and decisions, to obtain necessary information and studies from the agencies, to alert him quickly to what needs doing, and to prod the departments on his behalf. But this presidential staff can be no substitute for the will, vigor, and intellect of the President himself, nor for the quality of the officials he appoints to lead the great national security departments of the government.

5

The Department of State

BY STATUTORY AND ADMINISTRATIVE prescription as well as by current governmental operating doctrine, the Department of State is the premier foreign policy agency of the United States. Under the President's direction and control, it is responsible for the overall state of relations between the United States government and all the other national governments in the world.[1] Accordingly, it is responsible for developing United States foreign policies and for assuring that the activities of other governmental agencies directed abroad fully reflect those policies and are best designed to maximize their effectiveness.

Historically, the Secretary of State has been the ranking officer of the Cabinet and a senior policy adviser to the President. In the past fifteen years, with international affairs the central problem in national policy, his role has grown increasingly broader and more important. To many thoughtful observers, the Secretary of State has seemed the logical man, short of the President, to develop national strategy in foreign affairs and to integrate the many strands that enter into national security policy. In this sense, he and his Department have been viewed as the ranking national security agency, taking precedence over the Secretary and Department of Defense. Although it is a difficult thing to measure, this view has been reflected to a considerable extent in the Department of State's role under Presidents Truman, Eisenhower, Kennedy and, now, Johnson.[2]

[1] For the sake of brevity and simplicity, let us assume that this includes relations with dependent territories and those that take place within the hundreds of international organizations and other international bodies.

[2] The first two Jackson subcommittees were, at the same time, strong advocates

101

The President's relations with his Secretary of State are central. His opinions about the quality and effectiveness of the Department of State as an organization are also important. If he sees his Secretary of State as his senior adviser and operating deputy for foreign policy and national security, many other things will fall into place. If he has doubts or reservations, the Secretary and the Department will have to struggle much harder to establish their policy primacy, and may not succeed. Since recent presidents have been inclined to look toward their Secretaries of State, the essential challenge has been to their effective performance of the leadership role.

The Department of State's functions of foreign policy direction and coordination are given formal expression through a variety of statutes and regulations. The other foreign affairs agencies of the government—the Agency for International Development, the Information Agency, the Arms Control and Disarmament Agency, and the Peace Corps—are placed by statute and executive order under varying degrees of policy direction and guidance by the Secretary of State.

Under what is known as the Circular 175 procedure, the Secretary of State or a State Department official delegated by him must approve the initiation of all negotiations with foreign governments designed to reach formal, written agreements with them. The agreements themselves, no matter how technical the subject matter or which governmental agency has primary interest, must also be approved by the State Department.[3]

---

of the prime role of the Secretary of State in national security policy and critical observers of the performance of the Department of State. For example, see Subcommittee on National Policy Machinery of the Senate Government Operations Committee, *Organizing for National Security,* Vol. 3, Staff Reports and Recommendations (1961), "The Secretary of State and the National Security Policy Process," pp. 41-56; and the Staff Reports of the Subcommittee on National Security Staffing and Operations of the Senate Government Operations Committee, *Basic Issues,* 88 Cong. 1 sess. (1963), and *The Secretary of State,* 88 Cong. 2 sess. (1964).

Don K. Price has commented thoughtfully on these questions in the volume he edited for the American Assembly. See *The Secretary of State* (Prentice-Hall, 1960), Chap. 7, "The Secretary and Our Unwritten Constitution." The other essays in the volume are also quite relevant to the present chapter, particularly those by Dean Acheson, Henry M. Wriston, and John S. Dickey.

[3] For a more detailed explanation of the Circular 175 procedure, see Richard B. Bilder, "The Office of the Legal Adviser: The State Department Lawyer and Foreign Affairs," *American Journal of International Law,* Vol. 56 (July 1962), pp. 651-52.

Quite often, the Department of State's representative is designated chairman of interdepartmental committees in the foreign affairs field. These are set up to consider highly specialized as well as broad policy matters, including such varied problems, for example, as the exchange of classified military information with foreign nations, international aviation policy, and international athletics. In some cases, the State Department provides secretariat support for the work of these committees.

The State Department also gives direction to foreign policy through the requirement—established by presidential order—that all speeches, statements, articles, and the like by officials of the federal government relating to foreign policy and foreign relations must be cleared with the Department of State before delivery or publication. This applies to political as well as career officials in all other agencies, including the Department of Defense.

Presidential directives have strongly reaffirmed the leadership role of U.S. ambassadors over the full range of U.S. governmental activities carried on in the countries to which they are accredited (with the major exception of military field forces). Although U.S. ambassadors are the President's personal representatives, they direct their communications to the Secretary of State and do most of their day-to-day business with the Department. Furthermore, almost all the career officials appointed as ambassadors are Foreign Service Officers.

The Department of State does share the foreign affairs field, both at home and abroad, with a veritable host of other offices and agencies, ranging from high-level White House staffs and the Department of Defense to the Agriculture, Labor, and Commerce Departments, not to mention the Department of Health, Education, and Welfare and the Federal Aviation Agency. The job of providing foreign policy leadership and guidance to all of them is highly demanding and, it should be emphasized, must be worked at on a daily, continuing basis. It is not something that can be done once or on periodic occasions and then promptly forgotten. It must be carried on in connection with many specific, even quite minor, problems and questions, by all levels of the organization from the Secretary of State to the country desk officer.

The other agencies generally understand the rationale for this State Department role and are prepared in principle to accept it. A standard complaint is about the way the role is played rather than the appropriateness of the role itself. Perhaps they are just playing with words. In any event, some of the problems of defining areas of responsibility precisely are discussed later in the book. Beyond this particular point of friction, an opinion widely held in these other agencies and by many outside observers as well is that the Department of State simply does not have the organizational efficiency or the personnel with the necessary skills and experience to do the job. It is a commonplace for students of the U.S. foreign policy organization to deplore the Department's shortcomings and at the same time concede that it is the logical and appropriate choice for foreign policy leadership.

The Foreign Service—the Department's primary body of professional officers in Washington as well as overseas and the traditional agent of the nation's foreign policy—has had its share of critical attention. Its skills and training have been found inadequate to many present needs. Some critics have felt that while the Foreign Service might have enough officers with the poise and intelligence needed for the traditional diplomatic functions of representation, reporting, and negotiation, it did not have, in adequate supply, men with the intellectual toughness and capacity for profound analysis, the range of specialized skills and knowledge, and the managerial and program-direction abilities required to meet the foreign policy problems of the day.

The phenomenon of an executive department being simultaneously criticized, even scorned, and yet looked to for leadership is an intriguing one. Since the present study also assumes the desirability of State Department leadership in foreign policy and national security policy, the nature and adequacy of the Department's performance will be examined in this and several succeeding chapters.

A Brief Historical Sketch

Some of the present problems of the Department can perhaps be better understood if a number of facts of recent history are kept in mind. First, during the middle and late 1930's and through the Second World War, major foreign policy decisions were being made by President Franklin Roosevelt, and both the Department and its chief, Secretary Cordell Hull, were often in the position of responding to the ideas and initiatives of others elsewhere in the government, whether White House aides, military leaders, or the Secretary of the Treasury.

During the war, the Foreign Service was unable to do any long-term recruiting of career personnel. At the close of the war, the Department inherited some of the functions and personnel of such war-time agencies as the Office of Strategic Services and the Office of War Information. In addition, approximately 165 people were brought into the middle levels of the Foreign Service under the provisions of a special Manpower Act of 1946, and the State Department thus began its own postwar increase in size. While substantial in proportionate terms, it still left the Department as one of the smaller major agencies in Washington.[4]

By the Department's own choice, the postwar occupations of Germany and Japan were set up under the direct control of the military establishment, although presumably acting under the policy guidance of State. While a civilian High Commissioner who reported to the State Department took charge in Germany in 1949, the military were in control of the Japanese occupation until ratification of the Japanese peace treaty in 1952. At the same time, when the foreign economic aid program was first established in 1948, Congress placed it in the hands of a new and independent agency.

From the start of the postwar period in 1946, the Department was troubled by the basic problem of what to do about its personnel arrangements: how to resolve in some more satisfactory way the division between the Foreign Service, conceived of and recruited as an elite officer corps of diplomatic "generalists," and its Civil Service professionals working in Washington and providing the Department with

---

[4] Among the ten Cabinet-level departments, only the Justice Department, at present, has a smaller budget than the Department of State. (In fiscal year 1964, $347 million was expended for the State Department and $328 million for the Justice Department.) Only the Labor Department, with slightly more than 9,000 employees, has fewer on its rolls than the State Department. The State Department's staff of less than 25,000 includes overseas as well as domestic employees, among them approximately 10,000 foreign nationals locally employed overseas. It should be noted that neither the budget nor the employment figures for the State Department include the Agency for International Development, the Peace Corps, or the independent United States Information Agency. (These data are drawn from *The Budget of the United States Government for the Fiscal Year Ending June 30, 1966* [1965].)

many of its more specialized skills and talents. The continuing, less than satisfactory efforts to deal with the problem from 1946 to 1954 contributed to a sense of uncertainty and insecurity on the part of many of these officials. The decisive resolution of this problem taken by Secretary Dulles upon the heels of the Wriston Report in 1954 was more upsetting than reassuring.[5]

This sense of uncertainty and anxiety was greatly sharpened for many officers by the attacks from various quarters on the loyalty and competence of Department and Foreign Service career officers in the early 1950's. It is generally agreed that these attacks on career personnel, and the particularly bitter attacks on Secretary Dean Acheson during this period, were highly damaging to the Department's morale as well as to its prestige among important elements of the public.

In recent years, the quality and prestige of the Department have been moving steadily upward. This development, however, must be viewed against the events of the not too distant past just noted. The Department of State has for the greater part of the past thirty years suffered the indignities of a secondary role; it has often been ignored in what it regarded as its own proper province of foreign affairs. In addition, its staff has suffered severe strains and sharp changes—in number, internal organization, recruitment and training, and morale and sense of purpose.[6]

---

[5] Secretary of State's Public Committee on Personnel, *Toward A Stronger Foreign Service* (June 1954). Dr. Henry M. Wriston, then President of Brown University, was chairman of the committee.

[6] Until the appearance of Robert E. Elder's book, *The Policy Machine* (Syracuse University Press, 1960), it might have been said with reasonable accuracy that no good book had been written on the organization of the State Department since World War II, or perhaps even World War I. A number of books, like the McCamy, Macmahon, and Brookings Institution studies cited below, had incorporated useful materials on the Department into larger studies of the administration of foreign affairs. Given the central position of the Department in U.S. foreign policy making, this strikes one as an amazing state of affairs.

Professor Elder's book, as he himself candidly admits, provides only a partial remedy. It has a great deal of useful descriptive material on the Department's structure and processes. In those areas he describes—for example, the country desks, intelligence, policy planning, and legislative liaison—Elder does communicate a concrete sense of how the work is done. On the other hand, certain major bureaus of the Department are not treated at all, and decision making at the highest levels gets relatively little treatment.

What Organization for Foreign Policy Leadership?

The Department of State and the Foreign Service continue to carry the main burden of representing the United States abroad. The Foreign Service represents the largest pool of foreign affairs talent available to the government, whatever its inadequacies of the moment. In other words, the tendency to look to the Department for foreign policy leadership is not just a matter of habit or tradition but does reflect some practical facts about its functions and its capabilities.

There is some tendency for observers to forget this workaday role of the Department overseas. Perhaps this helps account for the somewhat oversimplified question of administrative doctrine that was much discussed and debated in the ten or fifteen years after the war, though less so in recent years. The basic problem posed was whether the Department of State should be primarily a policy-formulating agency, leaving policy implementation (in the form of the new economic, informational, cultural, and military programs) to others, or whether it should undertake active responsibility for at least some of these programs. This basic question of role and responsibility was sometimes phrased, again oversimply, as the choice between being primarily a foreign policy *staff* agency for the President and the Secretary of State or a major *line* operating agency. Even at this stage, the desirability of the Department of State's foreign policy leadership tended to be assumed. The disagreement was over how best to accomplish it.

Discussion revolved to some extent around the question of the compatibility of the policy-control and policy-implementation functions: in effect, can an organization like State effectively carry out the former if it is burdened with the latter? For those persuaded about the compatibility and even the desirability of both being carried on by a single foreign affairs agency, the more fundamental question seemed to be whether the Department had available or could recruit the personnel with the requisite abilities and perspectives to handle the detailed direction of major overseas programs.[7]

[7] Much more elaborate discussion of this question, and some varying perspectives on the State Department, are to be found in three earlier major studies of the U.S.

In practice, various programs have moved into and out of the Department with apparently little attention to the consistency of administrative doctrine. At the start of the Eisenhower Administration in 1953, the overseas information program was removed from its position as a relatively autonomous unit within the Department and established as an independent agency. The various economic aid programs were brought together under an independent Foreign Operations Administration, including the technical assistance program which had also operated previously as a relatively autonomous unit within State.

At present, the economic aid program, in its most recent organizational transformation called the Agency for International Development (AID), is an autonomous unit within the State Department. Its predecessor agency, the International Cooperation Administration (ICA), completing a cycle of organizational travels, had been brought under the State Department in 1958. For most practical purposes, AID, like ICA, acts like an independent agency.

The United States Information Agency (USIA) continues to operate as a fully independent agency, although it receives its policy guidance from State and the two agencies work very closely together. In fact, relations between the public affairs and geographic policy units in State and their opposite numbers in USIA are generally considered to be far more satisfactory at present than they were when USIA was a unit within the Department.

These brief bits of organizational history suggest that the effective operational answer to the question of an appropriate role for the Department of State is not necessarily to be found in the persuasiveness of abstract arguments on either side of the question. Furthermore, since specific organizational arrangements have not always produced

---

foreign policy organization: James L. McCamy, *The Administration of American Foreign Affairs* (Alfred A. Knopf, 1950); The Brookings Institution, *The Administration of Foreign Affairs and Overseas Operations,* A Report Prepared for the U.S. Bureau of the Budget (U.S. Government Printing Office, June 1951); and Arthur W. Macmahon, *Administration in Foreign Affairs* (University of Alabama Press, 1953). Macmahon's book, in particular, is still well worth reading.

Basic documents on this question, and on the organization of the State Department, are the reports of the Hoover Commission and its Task Force on Foreign Affairs. See Commission on Organization of the Executive Branch of the Government, *Foreign Affairs,* A Report to the Congress, February 1949 (1949); and Task Force Report on *Foreign Affairs* [Appendix H], prepared for the Commission on Organization of the Executive Branch of the Government, January 1949 (1949).

the predicted results, it seems reasonable to focus instead on the organizational consequences viewed as desirable, keeping an open mind about the specific administrative arrangements that might accomplish them.

On the broad objectives, there is general agreement. Clear policy directions must be formulated and supported by strong policy leadership. Implementing programs and activities that fully reflect and express these policies must be developed and carried out in close relation to one another and with full awareness of the larger policy framework. And yet the necessary discretion and room to maneuver must be available to the operating units in the field. This is a generalized statement of the ideal. As these general requirements are spelled out in specific situations, it is clear that they will not always be completely compatible. At times, a program or situation may demand a great deal of freedom for the operating units in the field. At other times, the essential need may be for tight, closely integrated policy control from Washington.

On the more specific question of the Department of State's role in the foreign policy process, a number of basic points should be stressed. First, the Department is, and always has been, an operating agency. Its major "program," if you will, is the broad range of diplomatic reporting and analysis and consular functions that it carries on at close to three hundred separate posts around the world.

Furthermore, putting some agency or unit in formal charge of the activities carried on in other major organizational units does not guarantee effective control. The history of military establishment organization since the so-called "unification" of 1947 should make this perfectly clear. What is really involved here is a range of possible authority relationships, from formal independence (which may be combined with active policy guidance, as in the case of an independent USIA) to the autonomy of one of State's own regional bureaus. In none of these cases can formal authority assure actual responsiveness, although it would be naive to deny that it can help. Moreover, as Arthur Macmahon put it a number of years ago: "Operations require autonomy of some kind. Therefore, no matter whether they are conducted inside the department or outside, it is necessary to learn the art of policy guidance without undue interference."[8]

[8] Macmahon, *op. cit.*, pp. 69-70.

If the State Department is to play the role of policy leadership and overall program guidance and coordination effectively, it needs more than formal grants of authority and presidential backing—although these are fundamental. The leadership role must be firmly grasped, and the arduous labors necessary to make it effective must be accepted and carried out. It is neither possible nor desirable to stay at arm's length from operations; on the other hand, it is not practical to "ki-bitz" all the details. Striking the proper balance requires the development of organizational habits and the accumulation of relevant skills and experience, not only by the State Department but also by the other major agencies in the foreign policy organization. These are matters for more detailed discussion in the pages and chapters that follow.

Organizational Structure and Processes

In 1947, the Department moved into a severely modern building in the so-called Foggy Bottom section of Washington, originally meant to house the War Department. In 1959 and 1960 the Department brought most of its units under one roof as it moved into a new addition that formed a massive "L" around the original building and more than quintupled its floor space. In one sense, the new building symbolizes the contemporary Department of State. Its mammoth size and antiseptic modern architecture[9] underscore far better than a dozen pages of text the fact that the Department has many of the familiar characteristics of the very large, modern, complex organization. There are well-established procedures and routines for assigning decisional responsibility and for making decisions, for communicating a variety of messages within the Department and outside of it, across the oceans and across the Potomac, and for gathering, interpreting and disseminating intelligence.

[9] One witty observer, a former State Department official, has described the new State Department Building as having the appearance of the world's "best-appointed penitentiary." As he notes, it stands in marked contrast to some of the striking and imaginative examples of modern architectural design to be found in some of the newly-built American embassies abroad, for example, in India. See Charlton Ogburn, Jr.'s perceptive essay, "The Department of State," *Holiday*, Vol. 30 (December 1961), p. 183.

Assistance for the Secretary

At the level of the Secretary, there is, first of all, an Executive Secretariat whose primary job is: (1) to control the flow of papers coming to the Secretary and the Under Secretaries of State from within the Department, other agencies, and American diplomatic posts abroad; and (2) to follow up on decisions and papers going from these top officials to the rest of the Department to see that they are properly carried out.

This brief description of the work of the Secretariat (S/S in the Department's system of symbol-abbreviations) does little justice to the variety and complexity of its burdens. The Secretariat is also responsible for the preparation of a number of reports and summaries of current policy decisions and important incoming and outgoing messages that are distributed within the Department. It is the major formal communications channel between the State Department and the White House. But its primary function is to protect the Secretary from the vast flow of written material which is in a sense the lifeblood of the structure for making foreign policy, to enable the Secretary to "stay on top of" all of this material, neither being overwhelmed by it nor ignoring crucial items.

The Secretariat is also responsible at present for the functioning of the Operations Center, which was originally set up as a separate unit at the Secretary level of the Department in April 1961, shortly after the Bay of Pigs. Establishment of this Center apparently reflected the Kennedy Administration's dissatisfaction with the Department's communications, administrative, and other facilities for dealing with new or continuing crises of major proportions. While it no longer has the major role in organizing governmental response to foreign policy crises ascribed to it in the first months of its existence,[10] the Operations Center continues to serve a number of quite useful purposes. It provides the Department with special communications facilities, including links to the military establishment's communications network; the organizational basis for establishing and servicing special task

[10] See, for example, Max Frankel, "Center for Crises—And Flaps," *New York Times Magazine*, Oct. 1, 1961, pp. 69-71.

forces that may be set up to cope with crises; and watch officers who are on duty twenty-four hours a day.[11]

The Secretary is by no means completely dependent on the Secretariat. Usually, he has personal assistants who have no formal connection with the Secretariat. In addition, the Secretary is likely to have several high-ranking officials working directly for him; they may act as troubleshooters or speechwriters, or deal with special problems in which he is particularly interested.

In addition to the Under Secretary, who ranks immediately below the Secretary, there is a second Under Secretary who is sometimes designated as Under Secretary of State for Political Affairs and sometimes as Under Secretary for Economic Affairs.[12] There are also two Deputy Under Secretaries, one for political affairs and the other for administration. Heading the major regional and functional bureaus of the Department are approximately fourteen additional officials of Assistant Secretary rank or the equivalent.

Attached directly to the Office of the Secretary is the Policy Planning Council, headed by an official of Assistant Secretary rank. The present Chairman of the Planning Council is also the Counselor of the Department, a position to be distinguished from the Legal Adviser.[13]

[11] For an authoritative account of the present functions and facilities of the Operations Center, see William B. Connett, Jr., "Operations Center—Locus of 'Crisis Management,'" *Department of State News Letter*, No. 40 (August 1964), pp. 16-18. Mr. Connett, a Foreign Service Officer, is a former Director of the Operations Center. It might be noted that the *Department of State News Letter*, which serves in effect as the "house organ" of the Department, is an extremely useful source of information on organizational and personnel developments.

[12] The designation and functions of the second Under Secretary depend on the interests and organizational role of the ranking Under Secretary, as well as the interests and abilities of particular incumbents. Thomas C. Mann was sworn in as Under Secretary for Economic Affairs in March 1965. His two immediate predecessors, W. Averell Harriman and George C. McGhee, were both designated Under Secretary for Political Affairs.

[13] The position of Counselor had previously been a separate one, and it is said that the two were combined in 1961 to make another Assistant Secretary position available, since the Department is allotted a fixed number by statute. In the past, the Counselor has been a kind of Assistant Secretary of State without portfolio. The position had been held in the postwar years by a series of very able Foreign Service Officers—including Charles E. Bohlen, George F. Kennan, Douglas MacArthur II, and G. Frederick Reinhardt, who worked closely with the Secretary in a troubleshooting capacity. In addition, the Counselor sometimes acted on the Secretary's behalf as governmentwide coordinator for a major foreign policy operation. The

Prior to 1961, the Policy Planning Council was known as the Policy Planning Staff, and it was headed by a Director rather than a Chairman. These changes in nomenclature were apparently not accompanied by significant changes in the functions performed by the group.

The Policy Planning Staff itself was originally established in 1947, with long-range planning viewed as one of its primary functions.[14] It has always been a part of the Secretary's Office, and it is said that when Dean Acheson was Secretary of State, he would occasionally come over and join in the informal discussions of the Staff. The Staff or Council has quite consciously been kept small in size. In the past, it usually numbered ten or twelve. The feeling was that to increase the size of the group much beyond this number would destroy the intellectual intimacy and stimulation, and group rapport, which have been regarded as among the Staff's major assets and hallmarks. In the past few years, the Council has grown a bit larger; its present authorized strength is eighteen, including two military exchange officers.

The Policy Planning Council has two broad and related functions: (1) to act as a source of policy advice for the Secretary; and (2) to engage in the long-range consideration and analysis of policy problems. During the Eisenhower Administration, when the National Security Council was more active, it was also the focal point for State Department participation in the work of the National Security Council and its supporting Planning Board.

This list of functions is not very revealing. The more precise role and influence of the Council depend to a considerable extent on the needs of the Secretary and his view of the Council, and on the abilities and attitudes of its chief.

Council members do not spend all their time preparing long-range "think-pieces." Each is usually assigned some regional area or functional problem that he follows regularly; he keeps in close touch with

---

highly personal nature of the position is further suggested by the fact that in 1960 the Counselor was assisted in performing his duties by only one Foreign Service Officer.

[14] This discussion of the Policy Planning Council is adapted, with some modifications, from H. Field Haviland, Jr. and Associates, *The Formulation and Administration of United States Foreign Policy*, A Report for the Committee on Foreign Relations of the United States Senate (Brookings Institution, 1960), p. 98. The broader problem of foreign policy planning is dealt with in Chap. 10.

the relevant operating unit, and often participates in its staff meetings. Council members are expected to introduce a broader and longer-range policy perspective into current policy deliberations, thus linking their planning function directly to current problems and decision making.

The usefulness of this contribution now seems to be quite widely accepted in the Department. The operating units are often too busy coping with immediate situations to develop this kind of perspective. On the other hand, from the point of view of the Planning Council members, a balance has to be struck between their responsibilities for longer-range analyses and the detailed involvement in current problems. No doubt this presents a continuing dilemma for them. The lure of the immediate crisis is hard to resist.

Historically, the performance and influence of the Staff have varied considerably, and certain difficulties have plagued it through most of its existence. As a small group of able officers, its members have frequently been drafted for operational duties, such as writing speeches and current policy statements. Such activities can, again, be useful in keeping the Staff in touch with current affairs, but they do reduce the time available for consideration of longer-range problems. The same can be said for the burdens involved in servicing the Department of State's participation in the National Security Council during its more active Eisenhower phase.

It should be added that foreign policy planning is entering a more active and ambitious phase, both within the State Department and elsewhere in the foreign policy organization. This development is discussed in detail in Chapter 10 along with more extended consideration of the planning process itself.

The Secretary of State is not limited by physical proximity in his contacts with the senior officials of his Department. A Secretary may develop particularly close working relations with certain of his Under and Assistant Secretaries and see relatively little of others. Much will depend on the nature and urgency of the substantive problems before the Department. For example, during a period of great turmoil and crisis in the Near East, there is bound to be close and continuing consultation with the Assistant Secretary for Near Eastern and South Asian Affairs. The same could be said about any geographic area where major trouble has erupted.

At his staff meetings, held up to recently three times a week at 9:15 a.m., the Secretary meets with all his high-ranking officials (usually of Assistant Secretary rank and higher), giving them an opportunity to bring matters before their colleagues and the Secretary.[15] What can be accomplished, however, is severely limited by the size of the group and the relatively short time available (usually less than forty-five minutes) for the global review of problems that takes place. For this reason, other regular meetings of senior officials are held, often chaired by an Under Secretary.

The use of regular staff meetings as a device for intra-organizational and intra-unit communication is well established in the Department. The Assistant Secretaries hold regular meetings, weekly and sometimes more frequently, with their office directors and other top Bureau officials. The office directors in turn hold similar meetings with their key subordinates. These meetings help assure a regular flow of communication up and down the various levels of the system and also help keep the various members of each organizational unit informed about their colleagues' concerns at any particular point in time.

Decision Processes

It has already been made clear that the Department of State operates with many of the procedures of any large organization. Its decision-making activities and communications problems are, if anything, even more complex than those of most large organizations, governmental or private. There is, for example, the whole system of communications with U.S. missions abroad—ranging from the coding and decoding of telegrams, the comings and goings of diplomatic couriers with their pouches of airgrams and other messages and reports, and the rules for the distribution of messages with widely varying substantive content both within the Department and to other agencies like the Defense Department and the Central Intelligence Agency.

There are endless drafts of outgoing cables and policy papers, intelligence reports, and memoranda of conversation as well as more in-

[15] Under Secretary Dean Rusk, there has been some experimentation in frequency and functions of these sessions and the particular officials invited to attend them.

formal devices like luncheon meetings and clearances given over the telephone. There are many intra- and inter-departmental committees ranging from the well-known units at the presidential and Cabinet levels to the working-level groups dealing with modest, limited, and frequently rather technical subjects. The periodic campaigns to eliminate superfluous committees can only hold down the number. At any one time the Department of State is likely to be involved in upwards of one hundred formally-constituted interdepartmental committees.

Operating under well-established rules, the communications people send the *action copy* of an incoming telegram or despatch (to use the Department's spelling) to the appropriate bureau and information copies to other departmental units and outside agencies that have an interest in the matter. Under the present departmental concept of *action responsibility,* one bureau or office is usually given responsibility for dealing with a particular problem or request; when a matter of major policy is involved, it may be taken over by the Secretary or one of the Under Secretaries, or by the Assistant Secretary of the bureau primarily involved.

The effort is to make clear where responsibility lies. It is then incumbent upon the responsible bureau and officials to see that the matter is checked out and appropriate documents "cleared" with other interested offices and officials. This means getting either positive approval or at least an initialled willingness to let the item go through to the next highest level or to the level at which formal action can be taken. (As in many other bureaucracies, the man who finally signs the document and sends it out over his signature is usually not the one who has drafted it.)

Such a system would seem to leave considerable room for "end-running" officials and units with differing views, for pushing papers through without "clearing" with all the interested parties. As a matter of fact, this is not a major problem. For one thing, the Executive Secretariat checks papers very carefully before submitting them to the Secretary. Furthermore, an official or a unit that has been bypassed once on some matter in which it has an interest will raise such an uproar and make life so difficult for those who have tried to "end-run" them that it is not likely to happen a second time. It should be noted that departmental officers usually have no difficulty in identifying other offices that have a legitimate interest in a particular problem.[16]

Who gets involved in the handling of a problem will depend upon a number of factors and how they interrelate at a particular time: the characteristics of the "triggering" event itself; how it is perceived by various people; its timing; and the attitudes, information, and styles of organizational work of certain key officials—as well as their preoccupation with other matters. A geographic desk officer may find himself right in the middle of a major foreign policy crisis and play an important role in its resolution. On the other hand, he may have most of the relevant data at hand and yet find that the Secretary of State has taken hold of the problem personally and perhaps is dealing with it as if the desk officer and his knowledge in depth did not even exist. However, for the most part, it can be assumed that there are organizational "circles" of decision making, that the desk officer may fade into the background (remaining available to perform supporting labors of detail) if an Assistant Secretary takes charge of a problem, and that there may even be problems dealt with by the various agency heads and the President to which Assistant Secretaries are not privy.[17]

The Bureaus

A classic question in public administration, in foreign policy making as elsewhere, has been whether agencies should be organized along primarily geographic or functional lines. Both kinds of perspectives must be included, but the question is which should be given primary emphasis and policy responsibility. While the State Department has some important functional activities and units, its dominant mode of organization is geographic. (See Chart 1.) Even some of its functional

[16] See Elder, op. cit., pp. 34-41, for a more detailed account of clearance and coordination processes, particularly as seen from the perspective of the country desk officer. Elder's whole chapter on the desk officer, pp. 19-44, is extremely useful for its graphic description, among other things. Probably the best description in print of how the Department's policy-making business is actually carried on is Charlton Ogburn, Jr.'s essay in The Formulation and Administration of U.S. Foreign Policy, App. C, "The Flow of Policymaking in the Department of State," pp. 172-77. This essay has been reprinted in App. A of the present study.

[17] See the somewhat more detailed discussion of decision-making problems and relationships in Chap. 2, particularly the sections titled "The Role of Top Leadership" and "Decision Processes and Patterns."

CHART 1. Department of State, April 1965

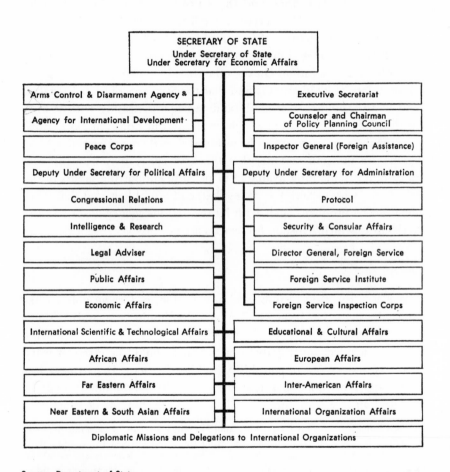

SECRETARY OF STATE
Under Secretary of State
Under Secretary for Economic Affairs

Arms Control & Disarmament Agency ᵃ	Executive Secretariat
Agency for International Development	Counselor and Chairman of Policy Planning Council
Peace Corps	Inspector General (Foreign Assistance)
Deputy Under Secretary for Political Affairs	Deputy Under Secretary for Administration
Congressional Relations	Protocol
Intelligence & Research	Security & Consular Affairs
Legal Adviser	Director General, Foreign Service
Public Affairs	Foreign Service Institute
Economic Affairs	Foreign Service Inspection Corps
International Scientific & Technological Affairs	Educational & Cultural Affairs
African Affairs	European Affairs
Far Eastern Affairs	Inter-American Affairs
Near Eastern & South Asian Affairs	International Organization Affairs
Diplomatic Missions and Delegations to International Organizations	

Source: Department of State.
ᵃ A separate agency whose Director reports directly to the Secretary of State and serves as principal adviser to the Secretary of State and the President on arms control and disarmament.

118

units, like the Bureau of Educational and Cultural Affairs, are subdivided on a geographic basis. This organizational characterization of the State Department also applies, in essence, to the United States Information Agency and the Agency for International Development.

The major business of the State Department is conducted by a series of geographic and functional bureaus. Each of the five geographic bureaus—for Europe, Latin America, Africa, the Far East, and the Near East and South Asia—has a somewhat distinctive tradition, character, and point of view. Each also has cadres of Foreign Service Officers who have spent a major part of their careers working either in the bureau in Washington or in field posts within the bureau's geographic bailiwick.

The geographic bureaus usually have the dominating influence on most policy questions that concern the countries within their areas of responsibility. There are important exceptions in certain functional fields with worldwide implications, such as international trade policy or the peaceful uses of atomic energy. Furthermore, on questions of any importance or sensitivity, the bureaus must consult with and accept the policy guidance of the Secretary or one of the Under Secretaries. The policy influence of the geographic bureau in those circumstances will rest to a considerable extent on the relationship of the Assistant Secretary heading the bureau with the ranking officials of the Department. It can also be hypothesized that the bureaus are not major sources of policy innovation, but rather are most influential on questions arising within the established policy framework.

The geographic bureaus also have their rivalries and differences of policy view. Sometimes these differences mirror differences between the areas for which they are responsible. One example would be the somewhat varying perspectives on the remaining problems of colonialism in southern Africa of the Bureau of European Affairs, some of whose "clients" are still heavily involved in that area, and the Bureau of African Affairs. It should be noted that the two bureaus do not (and should not if there is appropriate organizational discipline) disagree on basic policy objectives. However, tactical disagreements can be just as significant and just as difficult to settle.

The Assistant Secretaries of State heading the geographic and functional bureaus usually have two or three Deputy Assistant Secretaries to help them direct the work of their bureaus. One of these officials serves, in effect, as senior deputy. Supervisory duties may be divided among them on either a functional (for example, political or economic) or a geographic (that is, subregional) basis.

The geographic bureaus are broken down into a series of geographic subunits, each called an Office and headed by an Office Director and a deputy. These are in turn subdivided into groups of either one or a few countries, each headed by an officer-in-charge. At the bottom of the structure is the desk officer dealing on a day-to-day basis with the problems arising out of United States relations with one particular country. The functional bureaus are similarly organized, with subunits broken down by problem areas instead of countries.

One of the more interesting developments of the last fifteen years in the organization of the Department has been the integration or closer connection of a number of functional specialties—economics, legal advice, public affairs, military affairs—with the geographic bureaus. Each bureau has on its staff a public affairs adviser whose function is to evaluate problems and policy decisions in terms of public reactions to them both abroad and in the United States, and to recommend what can and should be said about them publicly. These officials are "housed" with the bureaus in which they work, and are usually either State Department Foreign Service Officers or officers on detail from the United States Information Agency. At the same time, they are in continuing touch with their colleagues in the Bureau of Public Affairs and, through them, with the Information Agency. Presumably, this should enable them to get the broader public affairs picture within which the actions of their particular unit must fit.

Assistant Legal Advisers are specifically designated for each of the major geographic and functional areas represented by the bureaus and work closely with these bureaus, even though they are physically "housed" with and are part of the Legal Adviser's staff.[18] Officials with economics training and interests are to be found at just about all levels of the geographic bureaus, whether or not they are specifically des-

---

[18] The organizational role and functioning of the Legal Adviser and his staff are thoroughly and thoughtfully discussed in the article by Richard B. Bilder cited above. See "The Office of the Legal Adviser: The State Department Lawyer and Foreign Affairs," *American Journal of International Law,* Vol. 56 (July 1962), pp. 633-84. In the course of explaining the work of the Legal Adviser's Office, Mr. Bilder makes some more generally relevant observations about State Department decision making.

ignated as economic affairs officers. Bureaus have either an office or an officer responsible for politico-military affairs. Although the nature of this function varies from one bureau to another, it tends to be concerned with such matters as military assistance programs and regional military pacts.

This last comment suggests another characteristic of the geographic bureaus that should be underscored. At present, all five have offices specifically set up to handle regional affairs. In fact, at the present time, European Affairs (EUR) and Inter-American Affairs (ARA) have two, one for political and security affairs and the other for economic affairs. The European Bureau's Office of Atlantic Political-Military Affairs (RPM) has an even more specific major function—supporting U.S. political participation in the North Atlantic Treaty Organization.

It is clear that in a period when most problems and policies cut across single-country lines and when this fact is reflected in a variety of regional arrangements—political, military and economic—an office of regional affairs is going to be dealing with many of the important problems confronting a bureau and may sometimes be in the best position to integrate the bureau's policies regarding them.

The responsibilities of the functional bureaus of the Department vary widely. The *Bureau of Congressional Relations* and the *Bureau of Public Affairs* are designed to deal with the two major aspects of the Department's domestic political setting—the legislature and the public.[19] Through its responsibilities for developing public affairs guidance and its close working relationship with the Information Agency, the Bureau of Public Affairs is also concerned with the projection of the U.S. image abroad. The work of the *Bureau of Educational and Cultural Affairs* falls in the same general category. Both are discussed in Chapter 7.

The *Bureau of International Organization Affairs* deals with problems that enter the forums of the United Nations. Since the precise role to be given the United Nations in United States foreign policy is itself a continuing policy question and since it is often difficult to

[19] Some of the functions of the Bureau of Public Affairs are discussed by Elder, *op. cit.*, Chaps. 6 and 7. In Chap. 5, Elder describes the work of the congressional relations staff, which is also treated at length in James A. Robinson, *Congress and Foreign Policy-Making* (Dorsey Press, 1962), Chaps. 5 and 6.

draw a clear line between the political and procedural intricacies of the United Nations and the substantive problems dealt with therein, this Bureau's policy interests and influence are broader than its formal functions might lead one to expect.[20]

The *Bureau of Economic Affairs* is responsible for certain economic problems that cut across country and regional lines—international trade agreements, the balance of payments, international transportation and communications questions, and the marketing of certain basic and widely-produced commodities. Its responsibilities call for considerable bureaucratic negotiating, intradepartmentally with the geographic bureaus and interdepartmentally with such agencies as the Treasury, Commerce, and Agriculture Departments.

The *Bureau of Intelligence and Research* prepares reports and studies for distribution within the Department and is also a major participant in the activities of the governmentwide "intelligence community." There are major problems with regard to the role of the Bureau within the Department and the activities of the "intelligence community" more generally. These are discussed in Chapter 10.

Relations with the Military Establishment

The Department of State's relations with the Department of Defense are central to United States foreign policy and, more broadly, to overall national security policy. State's relations with the military establishment can be characterized as substantial and varied. They take place at just about every organizational level, from Secretary to desk officer, from the forum of the National Security Council to the *ad hoc* working-level committee, overseas as well as in Washington. The subject matter ranges from major national security policy decisions to the "nuts and bolts" of specific country military aid programs.

Given the fundamental importance of this relationship, the State Department's politico-military capabilities had long been regarded by many as inadequate. It was believed that there was need of a unit specifically responsible for keeping an eye on overall relations with the military establishment and reviewing the total defense effort from a foreign policy viewpoint, and, equally important, providing advice and

[20] Its functions are discussed in somewhat greater detail in Chap. 9.

staff support to senior officials on important politico-military problems and developing policy on politico-military questions that cut across or perhaps fell between bureau responsibilities. In May 1961 such a Politico-Military Affairs staff was established. It is headed by a Deputy Assistant Secretary for Politico-Military Affairs, who is attached to the office of the Deputy Under Secretary for Political Affairs.[21]

The link to the Deputy Under Secretary for Political Affairs was not accidental. For a number of years, he has been the senior official in the Department charged with overall responsibilities in the politico-military field. In the past, responsibilities have not been well defined and have been discharged with varying degrees of vigor and interest by different incumbents. Since 1950 or 1951, however, the Deputy Under Secretary or some other ranking State Department official has met on a regular basis with the Joint Chiefs of Staff. These meetings provide an occasion for informal exchanges of views on problems of common concern that do not usually require immediate action. The Deputy Under Secretary was formerly accompanied by the Director of the Policy Planning Staff and one or two other senior officials. The Deputy Assistant Secretary of State for Politico-Military Affairs is now among the State Department officials present at these meetings. The Assistant Secretary of Defense for International Security Affairs also participates in them.

While some organizational support was previously provided to the Deputy Under Secretary in his politico-military role by special assistants and others, the new staff gives him much more substantial backing. It also provides the military establishment with a central point of contact within State where it can raise policy questions or ask for information without having to deal separately with a number of State Department units or waste time trying to find the right one. In this

---

[21] For a detailed account of the organization and functions of this staff, see Burton M. Sapin, "The Politico-Military Affairs Staff: Its Organization and Its Duties," *Department of State News Letter*, No. 30 (October 1963), pp. 24-26. I served as a member of this staff from June 1962 to June 1965.

A broader look at the State Department's increasing efforts in the politico-military field is to be found in a paper prepared for the second Jackson subcommittee by the Office of the Deputy Under Secretary for Political Affairs. See *Administration of National Security*, Hearings, Pt. 6, "Memorandum on the Department of State's Politico-Military Organization and Staffing," pp. 413-19. This memorandum appears as App. B in the present study.

sense, the Politico-Military Affairs staff performs the same kind of function for Defense in the State Department that Defense's Office of International Security Affairs does for State in the Pentagon.

While the Politico-Military Affairs staff has extensive dealings with the military establishment, it by no means represents the sole authorized State Department channel. The Policy Planning Council has had a continuing and substantial interest in politico-military problems and has its own direct contacts. The country desks and politico-military affairs units of the five geographic bureaus conduct considerable business with the Office of International Security Affairs, much of it in connection with the military assistance program which the latter directs. There are also questions of troop deployments, military base rights, status of forces agreements, and military overflight rights. Politico-military problems like Berlin, Vietnam, and the strategy for the defense of Western Europe bring the responsible State Department geographic units into direct contact not only with the Office of International Security Affairs but also with the Joint Staff of the Joint Chiefs of Staff.

The bulk of Department of Defense contacts with the Department of State is handled by the Office of International Security Affairs. The Assistant Secretary of Defense heading this office has executive authority in this area through functions delegated to him by the Secretary of Defense. This means that there is relatively little direct contact between State and the three service staffs. When it is necessary, however, and when personal acquaintance or good working relations developed over time make it possible, State Department desk officers and military service action officers may try to expedite matters by dealing directly with one another. Obviously, this is more likely to occur when policy implementation details come up than when major policy questions are being considered.[22]

An emphasis on current operational questions characterizes the whole spectrum of State-military establishment relations. At lower organizational levels, a great deal of the interaction between Foreign Service desk officers and Pentagon officials has to do with specific aspects of the military assistance programs being carried on in various

---

[22] The role of Defense in the foreign policy organization is discussed in Chap. 6.

countries. In the past, little attention has been devoted to joint State-Defense efforts to develop long-range policy analysis and planning, either in terms of upcoming problems as seen from the perspective of the foreign affairs official or as viewed from the equally relevant perspective of impending developments in weapons systems, force levels, and troop dispositions. This is now beginning to change.

One notable indication of the change is increasing recognition that the State Department has a legitimate and important role to play in the making of military policy. A major development in this connection is Department of State review of the proposed military budget each year before it is submitted by the Secretary of Defense to the President.[23]

Whatever the shortcomings may be, the need for close State-Defense relations is no longer seriously questioned within either agency, although there is the inevitable uneasiness about boundary lines between questions that are clearly "political" and those that are clearly "military"—and the increasingly large group in between. Inevitably, most people are inclined to feel that the other fellow gets outside of his proper bailiwick more than he should, but this is not one of the really serious problems facing these agencies.

What would seem to be more fundamental are: first, whether the departments are jointly addressing themselves to the right problems; second, whether their relations are satisfactorily organized; and, third, whether both agencies have sufficient personnel equipped with the skills, attitudes, and perspectives to deal effectively with the difficult politico-military problems that they must jointly face.

Major Problems

Broadly speaking, the Department of State is confronted by two fundamental and closely related organizational challenges. The first involves the recruitment, training, assignment, and retention of appropriately skilled and motivated personnel—political appointee as

[23] The State Department's role in military policy making is discussed further in Chap. 6.

well as career official. Personnel problems of the foreign policy organization are discussed in Chapter 11, but there are some distinctive aspects of the Department's personnel situation that should be noted here. The second challenge involves the Department's ability to carry out its role of foreign policy leadership vigorously and effectively.

The interrelation of the two is obvious. The Department cannot perform effectively as policy leader in the foreign policy and national security fields without a wide range of skills and talents available to it, particularly within its career service. On the other hand, even the most skilled and experienced of personnel will feel frustrated and in the end are bound to be severely handicapped if certain basic organizational and political requirements are not fulfilled. These include a reasonably clear definition and allocation of responsibilities, the unequivocal support of the President, strong leadership by the Secretary and his ranking aides within the Department as well as elsewhere in the executive branch, and finally, organizational arrangements that facilitate both thoughtful policy analysis and the necessary decisive action.

Personnel

In the personnel field, the Department has been greatly concerned since the end of the Second World War with the relationship between these two separate services that had developed in the Department over an approximately twenty-year period. The Foreign Service manned the overseas posts and some of the positions in Washington while Civil Service employees occupied most of the Washington positions, including many of the specialized jobs in the intelligence, economic, and administrative bureaus. The problem was complicated by the blurring of the distinction between Foreign Service Officers and Foreign Service Staff personnel. Some of the latter, supposedly narrow technicians, were doing the work of Foreign Service Officers.

A series of studies and reports, by both outside groups and groups within the Department, all pointed in the same general direction—eventual amalgamation or integration, partial or complete, of the Foreign and Departmental (Civil) Services. Progress in this direction had been quite gradual, some would have said almost imperceptible, until the issuance of the Wriston Report in June 1954 and its vigorous implementation soon thereafter by Secretary Dulles. "Wristonization," as the program of greatly accelerated amalgamation of Civil Service personnel into the Foreign Service[24] came to be called, is now an accomplished fact, but its consequences and repercussions are still keenly felt within the Department and are still a matter of considerable debate and dissatisfaction in some quarters.

It is generally agreed that, in the short run at least, the Department weakened itself by Wristonization of some of its Civil Service professionals. For example, experienced economists and intelligence analysts working in rather highly specialized fields were sent out to overseas assignments that often did not make full use of their particular skills. At the same time, it has not been easy to replace them in Washington either with appropriately skilled Foreign Service Officers or by outside recruitment.

While adjustments have been and will be made to deal with unfortunate inclusions and exclusions, a major reversal of the program is out of the question. Indeed, the Department is likely to try to complete the logic of the Wriston reforms by unifying the Foreign Service and what remains of the Civil Service employees under a single personnel system.[25]

What can be said with certainty about the developments of the last dozen years is that if Foreign Service Officers were ever characterized by homogeneous qualities—whether social or educational background or attitude—this has unquestionably been altered. The total Officer Corps numbered approximately 3,600 in June 1965. The Wriston program alone brought approximately 1,500 Civil Service, Foreign Service Reserve, and Foreign Service Staff officers into the Foreign Service in the

[24] In actual fact, more Foreign Service Staff personnel than Civil Service officers came into the Foreign Service Officer Corps under the Wriston program. Between 1954 and 1957, the numbers were 802 from the staff corps, 631 from Departmental Civil Service and 69 Foreign Service Reserve officers. See William Barnes and John Heath Morgan, *The Foreign Service of the United States* (Government Printing Office, 1961), p. 281. This volume suffers some of the shortcomings of an officially prepared document; it is cautious or noncommittal on matters of any controversy. On the other hand, it is a useful historical survey and has some interesting charts and statistical summaries among its appendices.

[25] Congressman Wayne L. Hays (Democrat, Ohio) introduced a bill in early 1965 that would have exactly this effect for all employees in the State Department. It is described in more detail in Chap. 11.

mid-1950's. Several hundred additional lateral entrants have been accepted since then. The Department of State has also appointed more than 700 junior officers to the Foreign Service in just the past four years (and is likely to add at least 100 or 150 new officers each year).

Closer examination of the Department's present personnel situation suggests that, as is often the case, the issue that has been most controversial is not the most fundamental. Long after the feelings roused by the Wristonization program have died down, the Department will still be attempting to cope satisfactorily with what is often termed, in rather gross and unfortunate oversimplification, the problem of the generalist versus the specialist.

In brief, the Department must find some satisfactory way of recruiting and retaining officers with a wide range of functional, linguistic, and area skills while at the same time continuing to train and maintain officers capable of handling the more traditional Foreign Service tasks of diplomatic representation and negotiation, and political and economic reporting and analysis. The Foreign Service has thought of the latter as generalists: it may be more useful to think of them as constituting at least several types of specialists. It should also be noted that these two general categories are by no means mutually exclusive. Functional specialists may make superb diplomats and ambassadors: the "new diplomat" needs at least some exposure to several of the recent additions to the foreign affairs business.

Linguistic skill has for a long time been considered an important asset for the Foreign Service Officer. In the early years of the twentieth century, Congress authorized the recruitment of student interpreters to be trained in Chinese and Japanese. In the 1920's and 1930's, selected Foreign Service Officers received training in Chinese, Japanese, Russian, Turkish and Arabic.[26]

At present, the Department is engaged in a vigorous program of language training, closely geared to overseas assignments. There is a parallel emphasis on foreign area training. The Foreign Service Institute offers courses in more than fifty languages, including such exotic tongues as Swahili, Cambodian, and Hindi, not to mention Arabic, Polish, Korean, and Hebrew. Outside language scholars and teachers have been quite favorably impressed by some of the teaching de-

[26] See Barnes and Morgan, op. cit., pp. 156-57 and 211-12.

vices and materials developed by the Institute in this field. As a matter of policy, Foreign Service Officers are encouraged to develop a professionally useful proficiency in two foreign languages before they reach senior levels. Interested and able younger officers are offered incentives to study languages of the Middle East, Asia, Africa, or Eastern Europe, in which proficiency is in short supply in the Foreign Service.

In addition, junior officers entering the Foreign Service are provided in-grade salary increases if they can at the time of entrance demonstrate minimum professional proficiency in one or more foreign languages. These language policies also apply to the Foreign Service Officers of the United States Information Agency.[27]

With the increasing importance of scientific developments in international affairs, it can be assumed that the Department will need a certain number of officers sophisticated in some of the data, theories, and technological products emerging from the work in the natural sciences. Similarly, the area where military affairs and foreign affairs converge is a substantial one. It has in the past represented an area of weakness for State, but in recent years a number of steps have been taken that should increase substantially the number of Foreign Service Officers adept at dealing with politico-military questions. These steps are discussed in Chapter 11.

There has been less reluctance to acknowledge the need for a large group of officers skilled in one or another of the major branches of economics, but the Department has been far from successful in recruiting adequate numbers of such specialists and, as was noted above, suffered important losses in this field as a consequence of the Wriston program.[28]

In some cases, there is no doubt that a Foreign Service Officer can follow a career pattern in which he combines a functional or area specialty with the more traditional diplomatic activities and responsibilities. However, some of the specialists needed will not fit easily into

[27] For a more detailed discussion of recent improvements in the language training and skills of Foreign Service officers, see the article by Howard E. Sollenberger, Dean of the School of Language and Area Studies, Foreign Service Institute, "Languages and the Foreign Service," Department of State News Letter, No. 50 (June 1965), pp. 4 ff.

[28] The various fields of required personnel specialization and expertise are discussed at greater length in Chap. 11.

traditional patterns of assignment and promotion. If the Department accepts the need for such specialists, it must devise methods for recruiting and promoting which will not handicap them against those who follow more traditional career patterns. Stated more positively, the Department must assure a channel up to the very highest positions in the Service for those with the requisite ability.

The availability of traditional and specialized skills and knowledge does not exhaust the intellectual requirements that are imposed upon the Department. A key question, discussed in broader terms in Chapter 2, is whether the necessary intellectual discipline, integrity, and creativity in the analysis of foreign policy problems can be encouraged and developed among sufficient officers to provide, as it were, a pool or leaven of first-rate policy analysts within the Department.

It is clear that the professional personnel of the Department of State, and particularly the Foreign Service, must take on a number of quite new and difficult kinds of assignments if the Department is in fact to lead in the foreign policy-national security field. It is still an open question whether they have or can develop the necessary skills, experience, and motivation to do so successfully.

The Department's Leadership Role

The doctrine of State Department foreign policy leadership has broad acceptance within the government. It had the backing of Mr. Kennedy and his two immediate predecessors in the presidency. President Johnson has made clear his support. All four have accepted the general doctrine and worked well with their Secretaries of State, but have had some reservations about the Department of State as an organization.

By law and executive order, the Secretary of State holds some measure of control or authority over a number of the other major units in the foreign policy organization—the Agency for International Development, the Information Agency, the Arms Control and Disarmament Agency, and the Peace Corps. The nature of the Secretary's control is by no means unambiguous, but if he has the full support of the President, it is enough to give him and his Department a solid basis for leadership and guidance of these agencies. The Secretary is on more of an equal footing with the Secretaries of Defense and Treasury and the Director of the Central Intelligence Agency. Even here, if the foreign policy aspect of a problem is primary, the Secretary should be in a position to exercise leadership and win most, if not all, of the major policy arguments.

As has already been made clear, there is no particular administrative structure or set of organizational arrangements that can guarantee this result. For example, it is widely agreed that State has a much closer working relationship with the independent United States Information Agency than it does with the Agency for International Development, which is by law a part of its own organizational structure. Given presidential backing and the formal support already supplied by statute and regulation, what is required is a certain set of attitudes on the part of the Secretary and his top aides (essentially shared by the career personnel), and the necessary range of skills and talents to play the leadership role effectively and vigorously on a daily, working basis.

The role of the Secretary is crucial, just as is the President's at the highest level. If the Secretary of State's view of his role, and that of his Department, is relatively narrow and circumscribed, this will limit what the Department can do. In the face of Secretary Dulles' reported lack of interest in military policy questions, those of his colleagues in the Department who were deeply concerned with the foreign policy implications of major military policy decisions were less able to exert influence than they would otherwise have been.

That particular men vary in their special interests and concerns may from time to time handicap effective State Department leadership in foreign policy. However, the role of the Secretary of State as the operating head of a major executive department has a more basic complication, one that is shared to some extent by his senior subordinates in the State Department. In no other executive department of the government do the Secretary, the Under Secretaries, and the Assistant Secretaries have so much direct dealing with the President and feel so directly and continuously the pressure of the latter's views and concerns. Since these are bound to take precedence over all else, the ability of the Secretary of State and his senior colleagues to give effective leadership to their Department, and on its behalf, is further limited.

What about those agencies that should be led or guided by the

State Department's foreign policy views? Are they prepared to accede to State's leadership role? At one level, it can be said that if the conditions specified above prevail, they really do not have much choice. The role of the other agencies depends to a considerable extent on the way State plays its role. Clearly, in these matters it is not possible to arrive at a perfect state of harmony. Even at best the State Department cannot win all the policy battles and, for the sake of the national interest, it probably should not.

The State Department possesses no special magic or highly esoteric knowledge in foreign affairs, but it should have the broadest perspective on U.S. relations with other nations: it does have the longest and most extensive experience in dealing with them. It should be in the best position, short of the President, to provide the policy framework within which to judge the activities of other United States agencies that involve the views, responsibilities, or interests of one or more foreign governments.

The State Department is in any event responsible for doing so. When another agency's activities have a significant foreign relations aspect, the State Department's job is to assess likely foreign reactions and consequences and put these in the broader context of United States interests and policies abroad. If it concludes that, on balance, a proposed action would not be to the net advantage of the United States abroad, this view should be governing on those matters where the foreign relations aspect is important. For its part, the State Department must beware the automatic negative, the "don't-rock-the-boat" approach. It must manifest understanding and sympathy for the overseas activities and programs of other agencies and a capacity to weigh their net advantages or disadvantages judiciously against the anticipated foreign policy consequences.

If, after such scrutiny, the government's final decision still moves in a direction opposed by State, there is at least the assurance that it has met this kind of critical examination. If too many crucial national security decisions begin to be made by the President against the advice of the Secretary and Department of State, the President will probably start looking for a new Secretary of State and will no doubt start wondering whether State can, after all, do the job required for foreign policy leadership.

In the past, the Department has seemed less than fully effective in carrying out this role. Undoubtedly much of the explanation lies in factors beyond its control. Since World War II, it has had to adjust to substantial changes and the emergence of powerful rival agencies in a very short period. During and after the war, there was the rapidly expanding role of the military establishment. Soon after came the appearance and rapid growth of the Central Intelligence Agency. Then there was the economic aid program in its various organizational guises. Recently, "scientific" agencies like the Atomic Energy Commission and the National Aeronautics and Space Administration have moved upon the scene with policies and programs that have important international aspects. These agencies were not always impressed with State's prior claims and experience in the foreign affairs field; at the same time, they have not always demonstrated a sophisticated grasp of the relationship of their activities to overall American foreign policy.

For its part, the Department tended to respond to these new agencies, new programs, new skills, and new personnel in the foreign policy field by remaining essentially assured of its own primacy and unexcelled foreign policy competence—resenting the intrusion and activities of these new units but at the same time making relatively little effort to master the new programs and some of the new skills.

In addition, the State Department sometimes resisted innovations in the policy-making structure by claiming either that the function in question did not need to be performed or that the Department was already taking care of it in a satisfactory fashion. Others disagreed, and thus the State Department found itself in the position of first resisting and then accepting with little enthusiasm the National Security Council structure, the Operations Coordinating Board, and, one might add, the long-range planning responsibility.

There were weaknesses of conception and structure in all of these organizational innovations. Nevertheless, others saw significant needs inadequately provided for by the system, and both the National Security Council and the Operations Coordinating Board were efforts to fill such needs. The view of many involved in foreign and national security policy making was that these units needed and would have responded to State's vigorous leadership, but in good part did not get it. President Kennedy made it clear in abolishing the Operations Coordinating Board structure that he viewed the functions it was supposed to perform as essential. He indicated that he would look primarily to the State Department to carry them out in the future.

Overseas, the need for strong policy leadership and direction, and for the administration of political, cultural, economic, information, and military programs so that they are mutually reinforcing in the achievement of policy objectives, is symbolized in the concepts of the "country team" and the "executive ambassador." Here again, assuming that the ambassador is the logical choice to do the job and that he does have a special relationship to the State Department (as well as to the President of the United States), the importance of the training and career experiences given to officers in the Foreign Service, and in the AID and USIA services as well, becomes clear.

As with the rest of the foreign policy-making field, the problems of policy direction and program coordination overseas grow more complicated rather than less so. In addition to the economic aid agencies, cultural and informational activities, military assistance (and the American forces stationed in some countries), the work of intelligence units, and the attachés that represent the Agriculture and Treasury Departments, representatives of other agencies—for example, the Atomic Energy Commission—are now being sent abroad.

In evaluating the State Department's capacity to deal with these problems over the next decade, its substantial achievements during the past fifteen years in strengthening its organizational machinery and broadening its personnel base and programs should be kept in mind. The present ferment going on within the Department suggests that it may yet surprise and delight those of its critics who simultaneously deplore its inadequacies and yet concede the logic of its role as foreign policy leader.[29]

[29] In early March 1966, the White House announced that increased powers would be given to the Secretary and Department of State to "direct" the overseas activities of all government agencies, excluding military operations. One mechanism established to assist the Secretary of State was a Senior Interdepartmental Group, chaired by the Under Secretary of State. As always, it must be cautioned that substantive effectiveness in foreign policy leadership requires more than organizational directives or statements of good intentions. For an account of the new developments, see *New York Times*, March 5, 1966.

6

The Role of the Military Establishment

MILITARY FORCE remains a highly potent factor on the world scene. In some situations, a military test of strength continues to be the final arbiter of disagreement among nations. Where the violent resolution of differences is not an actuality, it is usually a possibility; military strength-in-being must therefore be available to deter other nations from opting for either the threat or the use of force. The widening spectrum of warfare introduces further complications. At the one extreme, thermonuclear weapons pose the threat of worldwide mass destruction; at the other, insurgency and guerrilla warfare in the underdeveloped countries represent unconventional problems requiring immediate, innovative response.

The central role of the United States in such an environment establishes the fundamental interdependence of its foreign and military policies. The international commitments of the United States provide the broad framework within which the responsibilities of the military establishment must be developed. On the other hand, a significant altering in the balance of national military capabilities—perhaps brought about by the appearance of a new weapons system—may limit the foreign policy objectives that can be pursued or the commitments that can be made. Irrespective of technological breakthroughs, inadequacies in national military strength may make it difficult or impossible to opt for certain courses of foreign policy action.

This interdependence is manifested in other ways. The use of military instruments of policy—the stationing of U.S. forces abroad, the training and equipping of the military forces of allied nations, the involvement in combined international military activities—is a fundamental necessity, but such actions in turn have their own costs and difficulties. Requisite treaties and agreements must be negotiated, military objectives balanced with other objectives, and host country sensibilities soothed—to name just a few.

Foreign policy purposes may demand military programs and activities that do not seem warranted by "purely" military factors. This is a standard military complaint about some U.S. military assistance programs. On the other hand, the enhancement of military capabilities—for example, by establishing a base in another country—may clash with broader foreign policy objectives.

The interrelations of foreign and military policy can also be suggested somewhat more concretely by cataloguing some of the major problem areas of U.S. foreign policy: the future of NATO—both as a military alliance and a political configuration; the Berlin situation; internal defense and anti-guerrilla warfare in some of the underdeveloped areas; the particularly difficult problem of Vietnam; arms control and disarmament; the sharing of nuclear weapons and information with allied nations; the relationship between stationing large contingents of armed forces abroad and recent balance of payments difficulties; and the recurring dilemma of military assistance to strategically placed but ideologically unattractive countries.

Foreign policy establishes the broad outlines within which the defense establishment must do its work, and more specific guidelines for the use of military instruments of policy. A wide variety of military programs, forces, and activities helps implement foreign policy decisions. In addition to the positioning of forces abroad and aiding and collaborating with the armed forces of other nations, these may range from "showing the flag" in some sensitive corner of the world to a "show of force" in a crisis situation to the actual commitment to combat. Beyond these specific implementing activities, the overall military posture of the United States has significant implications for foreign policy. The size and vulnerability of strategic deterrent forces, the defense capability against nuclear missile attack, and the capacity to meet "limited war" and "sublimited war" situations are all of fundamental importance in determining the strength and flexibility of United States policy.

Organizationally, this interdependence is reflected in the intimate, day-to-day collaboration of the foreign policy agencies and the military establishment in dealing, at every organizational level, with a host of major problems and minor difficulties—in Washington, in the diplomatic missions abroad, and in the headquarters of overseas military commands. There is no doubt about the need for regular, continuing military participation in foreign policy making and execution. This substantial intermixture of problems and responsibilities makes it clear that military policy making—the fundamental choices about weapons systems and military forces, as well as the planning for various military contingencies that may confront the United States—is a matter of fundamental concern for foreign policy makers and one in which they have a legitimate and useful role to play.

Thus, while the primary concern of this chapter is with the participation of the military establishment in the foreign policy process, some attention will also be given to the basic aspects of military organization and decision making because they are so central to the foreign policy position of the United States.[1]

Bases for Evaluation

The organizational structure and performance of the military establishment have been evaluated by many critics and observers.

[1] Four studies provide an informative introduction to the organizational structure, processes, and problems of the American military establishment. William R. Kintner and his associates have identified and analyzed major functions and major problems in the contemporary Department of Defense in their *Forging A New Sword* (Harper, 1958). Paul Y. Hammond gives these problems sixty years of historical perspective in *Organizing for Defense: The American Military Establishment in the Twentieth Century* (Princeton University Press, 1961). As previously noted in Chap. 2, Samuel P. Huntington has analyzed the politics of military policy making since World War II, both within the military establishment and outside of it, in *The Common Defense*. In *The Soldier and The State* (Belknap Press of Harvard University Press, 1957), Huntington discusses American civil-military relations in the context of American ideology and the requisites of military professionalism. A useful earlier book that also gives some attention to national security organization at the presidential level is Timothy W. Stanley, *American Defense and National Security* (Public Affairs Press, 1956).

Among them, Colonel (now Professor) Kintner and his colleagues are noteworthy for having tried to specify and define the criteria that might provide a "measure of performance" for the military establishment.[2]

Because the military establishment is by far the largest and most costly unit in the federal government, "economy" and "efficiency" are inevitably criteria given heavy emphasis, particularly by those who must appropriate funds and periodically seek the approval of the electorate. The difficulty comes in translating these general concepts into specific organizational arrangements, budgetary procedures, and substantive program choices.

If "economy" implies the most effective use of available resources, the simple fact that budgets have been cut or savings made provides no proof that economy has been introduced. A reduction in military force levels which makes it more difficult to respond to a particular contingency or necessitates an expensive "crash" program when a crisis develops can only be labelled "economy" in a very narrow sense of the term. As long as general usage of that term is so fuzzy, it is well-nigh impossible to translate it into specific policies and programs equally persuasive and satisfactory to all.[3]

For present purposes it will suffice to comment briefly on the concept of civilian control and on the question of an appropriate role for the military in foreign policy making.

[2] See Kintner, *et al., op. cit.,* Chap. Two, entitled "The Measure of Performance." Among the "eight basic requirements for the operational performance of the Department of Defense" set forth are: "civilian control"; "maximum readiness"; "sound strategic doctrine"; "orderly innovation"; and "maximum cost efficiency." Unfortunately, as such question-begging adjectives as "sound," "orderly," "flexible," and "maximum" suggest, Kintner and his associates have not moved very far in refinement of their criteria.

[3] A much more sophisticated approach to the problem of allocating limited resources among competing programs is possible and is employed in developing the defense budget. See the extended treatment given this problem by two economists in Charles J. Hitch and Roland N. McKean, *The Economics of Defense in the Nuclear Age* (Harvard University Press, 1960). Stated oversimply, the authors contend that at any given level of military expenditures, with any given set of policy goals and assumptions, their system of analysis will produce a more rational allocation of resources than the approaches previously employed by the military. In 1961, Mr. Hitch was given the opportunity to apply his theories when he was appointed Comptroller of the Defense Department.

Civilian Control

The specific criterion most frequently applied in discussions of the military establishment is the traditional American concept of civilian supremacy or, put the other way, of military subordination to the civil power. Unfortunately, as with other venerable concepts, the term has often been used with more emotion than clarity, and a number of shibboleths and clichés have grown up around it. Its essential meaning, and guiding purpose, is that major policy decisions regarding the military establishment should be made by the politically responsible civilian leadership, both executive and legislative.

A number of points about this definition should be emphasized. First of all, there is no one set of institutional or organizational arrangements that can ensure effective civilian control. Formal grants of authority to civilian officials and formal subordination of military officers are not enough. Civilian political officials must provide knowledgeable and vigorous leadership; civilians and military officers alike must have a clear understanding of the meaning, implications, and limitations of military professionalism.[4]

The rationale for civilian supremacy should be made clear. Some of the points apply equally well to the relationship of the politically responsible civilian leadership and the career *civilian* services. In a democratic system, major policy decisions should be made by politically responsible leaders, whether these leaders are dealing with military officers, Foreign Service Officers, or civil servants in the Agriculture or Commerce Departments. It is as appropriate for the career civil servant as for the military officer to avoid involvement in partisan politics and, at the same time, to be protected from involvement or ex-

---

[4] While most of the material in this chapter is new, some sections, particularly those dealing with military participation in foreign policy making, are adapted from H. Field Haviland, Jr. and Associates, *The Formulation and Administration of United States Foreign Policy*, A Report for the Committee on Foreign Relations of the United States Senate (Brookings Institution, 1960), Chap. V, pp. 80-91. The concept of civilian control is discussed and analyzed at length in Burton M. Sapin and Richard C. Snyder, *The Role of the Military in American Foreign Policy* (Doubleday, 1954), Chaps. 4-6, and in Huntington, *The Soldier and the State*, particularly Chaps. 1-4, 7, and 12-17.

ploitation in the political arena. From this point of view, it may be regarded as unfortunate that both career military and career civilians are required to testify before congressional committees along with their politically appointed superiors.

Perhaps it is worth adding that effective control by politically responsible civilians does not guarantee the wisdom of substantive decisions. Indeed, one of the burdens that career officials must be prepared to bear is to see their political superiors embarking on courses of action that they regard as painfully ill-advised. They may even believe—as military officers often have—that their civilian superiors are moving beyond the policy realm into matters of detail calling for professional judgment rather than political decision. Once again, this is a distinction difficult to fix and maintain on a once-and-for-all basis. Furthermore, it is up to the responsible civilian to decide in the end where this line is appropriately drawn. In such circumstances, career civilian and military officers must take such comfort as they can from the possibility that their politically responsible bosses may even prove to be right, as has happened on occasion in the past.

There are two points of special concern about the career military officer, and it is these that have made civilian supremacy over the military a far more important theme in American political life than control over their civilian counterparts. First, the military establishment controls society's most powerful weapons of physical coercion. Second, there is considerable contemporary as well as historical evidence that this coercive power may be used by the military to overturn a political system. While this aspect of the problem did concern the Founding Fathers, it is not seen as a threat in contemporary America.

However, some credence is still given to the concept of the "military mind," the notion that a lengthy period of professional service in one of the armed forces tends to produce a frame of mind narrow and rigid in thought patterns, one that oversimplifies problems and their solutions, is somewhat authoritarian in procedures and values, insensitive to the nonmilitary factors in situations, inclined to the use of force—in sum, not completely compatible with basic democratic values. It is this assumption about military thinking that gives the civilian control concept its continuing potency in the thinking of many Americans in and out of public life.

There is at present considerable skepticism, which is shared by the author, that the "military mind," as defined, represents the dominant mode of thought within the U.S. military establishment. At the least, career military officers may be assumed to share the fundamental values of American society as a whole, as well as special attitudes and values stemming from long service in a particular bureaucratic structure. Twenty-five years of substantial and impressive military participation in the major policies and programs of the nation seem to have reduced traditional fears and anxieties. These have been replaced to a considerable extent by a growing acceptance of the necessity of the military role and a positive appreciation of the contribution made by the professional soldier and the military establishment to the nation's security.

Given the nature of American government and society as well as the demands of military professionalism, civilian control continues to be a fundamental requirement. However, it no longer dominates thinking about the military establishment. The substantive performance of the military organization and its professional officers is now generally viewed as far more important. The maintenance of civilian control is assumed to be secure.

Appropriate Role in Foreign Policy Making

The usual concern about military participation in foreign policy making has been that the military perspective not dominate what might be thought of as a broader, politico-diplomatic point of view. This view could be justified in a number of ways. First of all, since military force represents merely one among a number of policy instruments, the military should have as limited a role in determining the overall policy framework or "grand strategy" as any other policy instrument. Second, if the "military mind" assumption were viewed as having any validity at all, it would be important to subordinate military attitudes and values to broader and more sophisticated political perspectives.

While it is true that military force is only one among a number of foreign policy instruments, it has at least two claims to special distinction: first, it is by far the most costly; and, second, under present conditions, major mistakes in the military area could be fatal. In addition, while typical military officer views on foreign policy problems are probably less sophisticated and broad-gauged than those of civilian foreign affairs agencies and officials, the military establishment does have an impressive number of officers broadly experienced and trained in politico-diplomatic matters.

As suggested above, this study assumes Department of State leadership, under the President's direction, in foreign policy formulation and decision making and, at the same time, substantial military participation in foreign policy making. It is not possible to set clear, fixed boundary lines between those questions that are the legitimate concern of the military and those that are not. This will always have to be a matter of interdepartmental negotiation and, no doubt, irritation.

A question about which there has been less agreement is the appropriate role for foreign policy makers in major military decision making. Under present conditions, many major military decisions have foreign policy implications. These would seem to be as much the concern of officials responsible for the nation's foreign policy as major foreign policy decisions are rightfully the concern of military policy makers. In both these cases, it is much easier to agree on the general principle than to assure its effective implementation. The two agencies must be sensitive to each other's legitimate concerns and develop the necessary organizational arrangements and cooperative working relations.[5] A great deal will depend on the skills and attitudes of the personnel involved in these State-Defense relations, both at high policy and desk officer levels.

Major Organizational Characteristics

Before attempting to characterize the organization of the military establishment, it may be useful to comment briefly on the nature of

[5] See the comments on the question of the role of the foreign policy maker in military policy by the then Secretary of State Christian Herter and Secretary of Defense Thomas Gates in their testimony in June 1960 before the first Jackson subcommittee in *Organizing for National Security*, Hearings before the Subcommittee on National Policy Machinery of the Senate Committee on Government Operations (1961), Vol. 1, pp. 696-720 and 728-58.

the substantive problems which are the military's responsibility. The military establishment has always had two basic missions: to deter war and, if war did come, to fight and win it. Traditionally, the American military have been primarily concerned with the latter. Their primary job was to make plans and prepare forces so that the United States could win any war in which it was involved. The emphasis has now shifted. The primary responsibility of the military establishment is to *deter* war—whether nuclear or non-nuclear, limited or unlimited.

The quality of the military's research and development, and the weapons systems that emerge therefrom, are of fundamental importance in this connection. It is probably not too much of an exaggeration to say that the success of the military establishment under contemporary conditions depends as much on its supply of military scientists and weapons engineers, and military staff officers sophisticated in international politics, as on a large supply of able combat officers.

The fantastically swift rate of contemporary scientific and technological development and its competitive character among nations pose one set of problems in the development of military weapons. There are other difficult calculations and choices involved: uncertainties about what the "state of the art" will permit, how long it will take to bring a weapons system from the idea stage into full operational readiness, how much capability to meet the contingencies of the present and immediate future should be sacrificed for the sake of larger investments in the development of more advanced weapons, and so on. These calculations are further complicated by the fact that there are not always widely accepted answers to all of the technological questions. For example, it is often not possible to state precisely in advance all the important performance characteristics of a weapon.

As another major dimension of its work, the military establishment must anticipate a very broad range of possible contingencies which may call for action on its part. It cannot be prepared to deal adequately with all or even most of them. Inevitably, there are only limited resources available to deal with seemingly unlimited possibilities. Again, difficult choices, assessing likelihood and establishing priorities, are called for.

As Professor Janowitz has pointed out, major changes in the nature of contemporary military responsibilities and military technology have tended to blur considerably the distinction between military and civilian skills and problems; consequently, military institutions have been "civilianized."[6] There are many traditionally "military" problems to which civilian scientists, scholars, and even political leaders have contributed quite creatively and, similarly, traditionally "civilian" or "political" problem areas where some of the most impressive thought and analysis has been contributed by military officers.

It is not surprising that creative thinking about military problems should emerge from those groups intimately concerned with some of the forces producing change: the physical scientists, engineers, and mathematicians, particularly those who have become deeply involved in weapons systems technology and engineering; the game theorists, who have developed a theoretical-mathematical approach to conflict situations; and the economists, who have traditionally been concerned with the rational allocation of limited resources.

Separate Services and Integrated Functions

From the organizational point of view, the most significant development in the nature of military functions is that the differentiation in terms of the natural elements of land, sea, and air—reflected in the existence of a separate Army, Navy, and Air Force—no longer corresponds to military realities, if it ever did. On the other hand, although considerable modifications and limitations have been imposed upon the three services, they continue to exist as separate entities. The development of the military establishment since 1946 could be characterized as a continuing effort to devise organizational arrangements that would reflect both the interdependence and separateness of the services.

The trend has been strongly in the direction of integrating related functions, unifying command structures and, perhaps most important, centralizing decision-making power and responsibility in the hands of a civilian Secretary of Defense and the substantial Office of the Secretary

[6] For a very useful analysis of some of the contemporary problems and dilemmas that confront the professional officer in the United States, see Morris Janowitz, *The Professional Soldier* (Free Press of Glencoe, 1960), particularly Chaps. 1-4. Janowitz has also commented on contemporary patterns and problems in the military establishment in his research inventory for the American Sociological Society, *Sociology and the Military Establishment* (Russell Sage Foundation, 1959).

of Defense (OSD) that has grown up under him in the past dozen years.

There are at least three important ways in which the traditional military division of labor is inadequate to meet present needs. Many items of supply, including even some weapons systems, are or should be common to all three services and most economically procured on a common basis. Even more broadly, problems of logistics and supply cannot be prudently dealt with on an individual service basis. These premises have been increasingly recognized in moves ranging from the establishment of a joint Defense Supply Agency, to the concept of one service acting as executive procurement agent for all three on a particular product, to joint Navy-Air Force procurement of the same fighter plane.

What is true of service and technical functions is even more relevant to military operations. During World War II, each military theater was under the overall command of one officer. The same pattern has been continued in the postwar period, for obvious reasons. For example, U.S. air, sea, and land forces in Europe are all designed to serve the same purpose, namely, to defend Western Europe from attack from the East. There is good military-geographic logic, then, in placing them under the command of a single Commander-in-Chief, United States Forces in Europe (CINCEUR in the abbreviated nomenclature of the military establishment). This logic has been carried one step further in Europe with the designation of one officer, the Supreme Allied Commander, Europe (or SACEUR), to command all NATO forces in Europe. So far he has always been the American CINCEUR.

While all these factors have contributed to the general unifying trend within the military establishment, another has served specifically to enhance the power of the Secretary of Defense. Probably the most fundamental way in which the contemporary revolution in weapons technology has affected the three services is in the allocation of basic combat functions. There are a number of fields in which there is a substantial overlap of service interest and involvement. For example, all three services contribute to air defense, and the Air Force, as well as the Navy, plays a role in antisubmarine warfare. In almost any conceivable limited war situation, all three services will be heavily involved.

These military functions have had their share of interservice disputes, including the questions of command-and-control and budgetary allocations, but the greatest difficulties have come in some of the newer areas of military activity that did not seem to fall obviously within one service's traditional jurisdiction. At the same time, these were often the very areas most generously dealt with in the overall military budget. Control over nuclear weapons and, even more basically, at least a share in the strategic-deterrent function, have at one time or another thrown each of the services into competition and controversy with the others. The strategic deterrence mission aroused particularly keen rivalry: the fact that each of the services had the capability to develop and operate intermediate-range and intercontinental ballistic missiles could only serve to sharpen the intensity of the competition.

This is not the appropriate place to weigh the merits of these disputes. The point is that the inability of the three services to reach clear-cut agreement on the allocation of roles and missions, the control of particular weapons systems, the division of military budgets, and the shape of a national military strategy not only accelerated the centralizing trend in the making of major military decisions, but also put that decision-making power increasingly into the hands of the Secretary of Defense.[7]

It might be said that the power of the Secretary to make major military policy decisions is established by the civilian supremacy concept, and furthermore, that in a period when these military decisions are so complex and so fraught with implications for the very existence of the nation, it is even more important that they be made by the politically responsible civilian official, the Secretary of Defense. However, these concepts will not suffice to explain the range and depth of his present control, which undoubtedly represents the most noteworthy development in the organization of the military establishment since 1947. It has been matched to some extent by the expanding role of the

[7] From the point of view of civil-military relations, this interservice conflict might be regarded as a phenomenon with some desirable consequences. As Samuel Huntington puts it: "Potential conflict between civil and military institutions was sublimated and deflected into conflict among military groups. Interservice controversy substituted for civil-military controversy, and interservice controversy became a key aspect in the maintenance of civilian control." (*The Common Defense*, p. 378.)

Joint Chiefs of Staff and, more particularly, of the chairman of the Joint Chiefs and the Joint Staff that serves them. These changes are discussed later in this chapter.

The Expanding Role of the Secretary of Defense

As originally established in the National Security Act of 1947, the role of the Secretary of Defense was quite limited. His powers of direction and control were stated in general terms, and all powers and duties not specifically granted to him were reserved to the individual service Secretaries, whose departments were to be administered as individual executive departments. He was authorized to appoint not more than three civilian special assistants to advise and assist him.[8]

In the 1949 amendments to the act, the role of the Secretary as principal assistant to the President in all matters relating to the Defense Department was stressed, and he was provided by statute with a Deputy Secretary and three Assistant Secretaries. Furthermore, as Professor Smithies notes, the Secretary's budgetary responsibilities for the military establishment were emphasized "with the creation of the Comptroller of the Department of Defense as his principal budgetary adviser"[9] and, more generally, by the addition to the original act of a Title IV concerned with promoting economy and efficiency through budgetary and fiscal procedures.

In President Eisenhower's Reorganization Plan No. 6 of 1953, further efforts were made to strengthen the Secretary by providing him with six additional Assistant Secretaries and, also, by replacing several interdepartmental boards, like the Munitions and the Research and Development Boards, with Assistant Secretaries. In his message, the

[8] See Sec. 202, National Security Act of 1947 (Public Law 253, 61 Stat. 500). This limited role and staff support for the Secretary of Defense were originally favored by the then Secretary of the Navy, James Forrestal, who became the first Secretary of Defense. The problems and frustrations that led Forrestal to modify his views in the direction of a stronger Secretary of Defense are documented in *The Forrestal Diaries* (Viking, 1951), edited by Walter Millis with the collaboration of E. S. Duffield.

[9] Arthur Smithies, *The Budgetary Process in the United States* (McGraw-Hill, 1955), p. 255. For the full text of the act, see National Security Act Amendments of 1949 (Public Law 216, 63 Stat. 578).

President stressed the key role of the Secretary in directing the military establishment.[10]

Even before the Defense Reorganization Act of 1958, the Secretary was exercising progressively greater control over military policy in a number of ways. First, he was formally the President's principal assistant on military matters. Furthermore, after the 1949 act, he was the only civilian representative of the military establishment sitting on the National Security Council. His Assistant Secretaries of Defense and their staffs were presumably in a position to provide him with the information and advice that would make his control of policy meaningful in such functional areas as manpower, supply and logistics, research and development, and international security affairs. But perhaps the most significant instrument of power was his increasingly firm control over the military budget and the allocations to the services made therein.[11]

The 1958 act added considerably to the Secretary's role. It clarified his authority vis-à-vis the three service departments by stating that they were to be "separately organized" (the previous term was "separately administered") but to "function under the direction, authority, and control" of the Secretary. The Secretary had already been placed in the chain of command from the President to the unified and specified commands in the field by the Reorganization Plan of 1953; this was continued in the 1958 act even though these commands were made directly responsible to the Joint Chiefs of Staff.[12]

Much more significant were the substantial powers given to the Secretary to transfer, reassign, abolish, and consolidate functions

[10] For the texts of the plan and the President's message, see *New York Times*, May 1, 1953.

[11] See Professor Smithies' discussion of the defense budget, *op. cit.*, Chap. XI, particularly pp. 240-65. Reflections of the Secretary's budgetary power, often not too happily viewed, are to be found in the memoirs of such retired Army generals as Matthew Ridgway, James Gavin, and Maxwell Taylor (brought back from retirement to serve successively as Military Assistant to the President, Chairman of the Joint Chiefs of Staff, and U. S. Ambassador to Vietnam).

[12] A unified command is one in which the units of all the services in a particular area are under the command of one officer, usually representing the service of predominant interest in that area. Examples would be: the unified commands in the Pacific and the Atlantic headed by Navy admirals (their formal titles are Commander-in-Chief, Pacific, and Commander-in-Chief, Atlantic, or, in military shorthand, CINCPAC and CINCLANT, respectively); the European Command, now

among the services. While a somewhat cumbersome procedure was established for the transfer of functions established by statute (primarily combatant functions), the Secretary was given complete discretion in assigning the development and operational use of new weapons or weapons systems to one or more of the services and in providing for "the carrying out of any supply or service activity common to more than one military department by a single agency or such other organizational entities as he deems appropriate." The Secretary and the Director of Defense Research and Engineering were given broad powers of direction and control over all research and development activities in the Department of Defense.[13]

The trend has also been to appropriate increasingly larger sums directly to the Secretary or to units under his control. For example, the Advanced Research Projects Agency (ARPA) is under direct control of the Secretary and has funds appropriated to it for research that for one reason or another is not being done or cannot be done by one of the services. It has included such fields as space, special metals, chemical technology, and defense against missiles. ARPA, in turn, can actually contract with one of the services[14] for a specific research project.

Armed with a rather broad legislative mandate and supported by a substantial, civilian-led and largely civilian-staffed organization of his own—the Office of the Secretary of Defense (OSD)—the Secretary is the dominating figure in the Pentagon. How he defines his role and uses his power will be a matter of his own personality and working style

---

under an Army general (CINCEUR); and the Southern Command (CINCSO is the term for its commanding general) in the Panama Canal Zone, with Caribbean and Latin American responsibilities.

Specified commands are units of one of the services or special task forces which are deemed important enough to be under the operational control of the Joint Chiefs of Staff. Perhaps the most significant present example is the Strategic Air Command (SAC).

[13] Department of Defense Reorganization Act of 1958 (Public Law 85-599, 72 Stat. 514). Major organizational responsibilities and relationships within the military establishment, as provided for in the presently governing statutes, are set forth in two Department of Defense directives: 5100.1, dated December 31, 1958, "Functions of the Department of Defense and its Major Components"; and 5158.1, dated December 31, 1958, "Organization of the Joint Chiefs of Staff and Relationships with the Office of the Secretary of Defense."

[14] See for example, the report by Louis Kraar in the *Wall Street Journal*, April 27, 1962.

and his relationships with the key people at his level and above him—
the President, the Secretary of State, perhaps the chairman of the
Joint Chiefs of Staff. He can, as some secretaries have done, define his
role in relatively narrow terms—to make major policy decisions and
supervise the overall management of the services. This would leave his
military and civilian subordinates with considerable discretion in implementing policy decisions. He can, on the other hand, if he has the
full support of the President, play to the hilt his role as Deputy Commander-in-Chief, concerning himself with the details of organization
and operations and the comparative merits of weapons systems as well
as broader policy and budget choices.

The present Secretary of Defense, Robert McNamara, has chosen
the latter option. It also seems fair to say that Mr. McNamara has
demonstrated the intellectual capacity and the leadership and management skills to carry out this role with great vigor and effectiveness. On
the other hand, if Secretary McNamara seems ideally equipped for his
job, the thirteen or fourteen years of legislative and organizational development since 1947 were probably necessary to provide him with the
powers and the organizational tools that he wields so effectively. He
will undoubtedly leave his distinctive mark on the job and on the military establishment. But the firm, sure grasp he has taken on the making of major military policy decisions and on the detailed management of the defense establishment should be recognized as but further
steps in the line of development just sketched. Perhaps this is one of
those rare instances where the right man was chosen at the right time
for the right job.

In addition to making vigorous use of the powers he already had,
Mr. McNamara has also continued the trend of centralizing functions
and responsibilities under either the Secretary or the Joint Chiefs of
Staff. A joint Defense Supply Agency responsible directly to the Secretary was established to procure and distribute many items common to
the three services. A joint Defense Intelligence Agency was established
and made responsible directly to the Joint Chiefs of Staff. In an effort to
strengthen the ability of the United States to respond to military contingencies short of an all-out nuclear war, a Strike Command (STRI-
COM) was set up as a unified command reporting directly to the Joint
Chiefs. Ordinarily, STRICOM is not in direct command of military

field forces; its mission is to plan and, if necessary, direct the rapid, efficient movement of combat-ready Army, Navy, and Tactical Air Command units to meet any situation around the world that may require their presence.

McNamara also established an Office of Organizational and Management Planning and attached it directly to his own staff. This unit was charged with the continuing scrutiny of the military establishment organization. In July 1964 a number of administrative and management functions performed on behalf of the Secretary of Defense were consolidated into one organization under the direction of an Assistant Secretary of Defense for Administration. The Organizational and Management Planning staff was made a part of this new office, and its director appointed to the new position of Assistant Secretary of Defense (Administration).[15]

It is clear that Secretary McNamara views the tightening up of the massive military structure as a fundamental problem that must be dealt with on a continuing basis. Reorganizations of the military establishment since 1947 have tended to concentrate on the top of the superstructure, the Office of the Secretary of Defense and the Joint Chiefs of Staff, with little attention directed to the structure of the individual services. These are now beginning to get their share of attention. For example, in a move regarded by many as long overdue, the seven traditional technical services of the Army have been abolished and replaced by a centralized Army Materiel Command.[16]

It is worth noting that all of these changes have been carried out without a single major legislative change; Mr. McNamara has operated within the framework of the powers granted him by the 1958 act. In response to congressional queries, he has indicated that, while keeping an open mind on the subject, he has not felt the need as yet for any legislative changes in the act. Congress and, more specifically, the Armed Services Committees have expressed concern about the increasing centralization of power and responsibility for military matters in Mr. McNamara's hands, and about what they regard as a strong trend toward the merging of the three services into a single service. While

---

[15] See Department of Defense Directive No. 5110.1, July 11, 1964, "Assistant Secretary of Defense (Administration)."

[16] See John G. Norris' account in the *Washington Post*, July 3, 1962.

CHART 2. Department of Defense, April 15, 1965

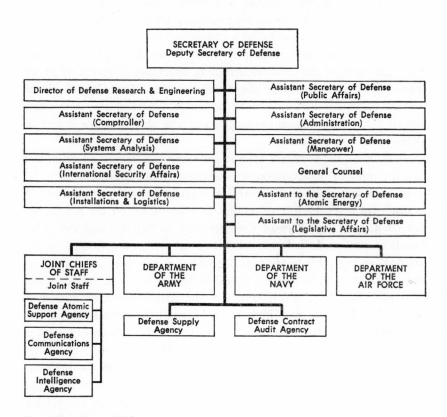

Source: Department of Defense.

many would regard these as essentially desirable developments, they have traditionally been viewed with suspicion and hostility in Congress. As of this writing, key congressmen have been willing to accept Mr. McNamara's reassurances, but it would not be surprising to see the pendulum swing in the other direction and some legislative binders placed on the Secretary of Defense.[17]

The Joint Chiefs of Staff

The Office of the Secretary of Defense, with its eight Assistant Secretaries and four or five other ranking officials and its 2,000-odd military and civilian employees, represents one major source of assistance and advice to the Secretary. The other is what might be termed the Joint Chiefs of Staff-Joint Staff complex, under which can be included several of the joint service agencies—the Defense Atomic Support Agency, the Defense Communications Agency, and the Defense Intelligence Agency (see Chart 2).

As stated in the relevant sections of the National Security Act, the Joint Chiefs of Staff (JCS) "constitute the immediate military staff of the Secretary of Defense." They are also the "principal military advisers to the President, the National Security Council, and the Secretary of Defense." This duality in role should be noted. While the Joint

[17] Whatever Congress may do, it should be noted that not all observers are reassured by the developments in the role of the Secretary of Defense and the organization and functions of the Office of the Secretary (OSD) just catalogued; nor are they fully satisfied with Mr. McNamara's performance as Secretary of Defense. See, for example, Hanson W. Baldwin, "Slow-down in the Pentagon," *Foreign Affairs*, Vol. 43 (January 1965), pp. 262-80, and John C. Ries, *The Management of Defense* (Johns Hopkins Press, 1964).

Mr. Baldwin and Professor Ries both deplore what they regard as the over-centralization of operating responsibilities in the Secretary of Defense and the greatly expanded Office of the Secretary that has developed to support him. Ries believes that the fundamental intellectual error involved is the assumption that effective central policy control (which he regards as a desirable goal) is best accomplished by increased centralization of operating responsibilities and functions. His own view is that the more detailed operations are controlled from the top, the less it is possible to maintain effective central control.

It is not possible to pursue these complex questions of organizational theory and practice. I believe, however, that Professor Ries and Mr. Baldwin have oversimplified considerably the effects of organizational arrangements on policy making in the Pentagon and not done justice to the improvements in the quality of analysis that underlies the making of important decisions.

Chiefs are a major staff arm of the Secretary of Defense, they are at the same time principal military advisers to the President; they have independent access to the President.

In essence, the Joint Chiefs of Staff are responsible for translating the nation's national security and foreign policies into military force goals and into overall strategic planning for and direction of these forces. This role is given greater substance by the direct command relationship that now exists between the Joint Chiefs, acting on behalf of the Secretary of Defense and the President, and the unified and specified military commands in the field.

If OSD and JCS units both serve the Secretary of Defense, it may well be asked how their functions are differentiated. In general, the OSD units are assumed to be concerned primarily with policy while the Joint Chiefs of Staff, the Joint Staff, and the three service staffs are primarily responsible for translating policy into military activities and operations. The Pentagon military staffs are not themselves in command of military line units; in that sense, they too are policy outfits. But they are at least several steps closer to military operations than the OSD staffs usually are.

In any event, the distinction is a difficult one to maintain. Those involved in policy making at any level inevitably get involved in the "details" of the levels below them because this is where the meaning of their policies is spelled out. Thus, the work of related OSD and Joint Chiefs of Staff units does overlap to a considerable extent, and representatives of each are likely to be working together on any important problem, with the individual service staffs also represented or at least consulted where they have an interest. The import of these relationships for the international security affairs field will be discussed at greater length below.

It may be useful to sketch briefly the development of the Joint Chiefs since the end of World War II. Although the Joint Chiefs of Staff came into being during the war, their existence as a corporate body was first given statutory recognition in the National Security Act of 1947. Since that time, a number of significant changes have taken place. In the 1949 act, the position of chairman was first established. Since then, there has been a gradual trend in the direction of strengthening the role and position of the chairman vis-à-vis his JCS colleagues. In part this has come about as a consequence of statutory changes in his functions, but it has also resulted from close working relations between the chairman and the Secretary of Defense, reinforced by the failure of the Joint Chiefs to agree on certain key policy questions. Under such conditions, a chairman trusted and respected by the Secretary is likely to be asked for his own views and advice. This was certainly the situation with Admiral Arthur Radford and then General Nathan Twining during the Eisenhower Administration.[18]

The chairman is formally charged with: (1) furnishing the Secretary with periodic progress reports on important items being considered by the Chiefs; (2) keeping the Secretary informed on issues about which agreement among the Chiefs has not been reached; (3) managing the Joint Staff and its Director on behalf of the Joint Chiefs; and (4) selecting and fixing the tenure of the Director in consultation with the Chiefs and with the approval of the Secretary.[19] Thus, the increasing centralization of decisional power in the hands of the Secretary has been accompanied by the expanding role and influence of the chairman of the JCS, even though any thought of a single chief of staff for the armed services is strenuously resisted from many quarters.

Among other important developments in the role of the Joint Chiefs has been the change in their relationship to the unified and specified commands noted above. Whereas in the past the chief of staff of one of the three services was assigned command responsibility as executive agent for the Chiefs, there is now a direct chain of command running from the President through the Secretary of Defense and the Joint Chiefs to these various commands in the field. (All major combat units are assigned to one of these commands.) Formally speaking, the Chiefs serve as advisers and military staff to the President and the Secretary in relation to the unified and specified commands, but, in effect, day-to-day control and responsibility is in their hands.

To enable the JCS to handle this expanded set of responsibilities, the authorized strength of the Joint Staff that serves them was doubled in size in the 1958 act, from 200 to 400 officers. At the same time, the

[18] See, for example, General Maxwell D. Taylor's comments in *The Uncertain Trumpet* (Harper, 1960), particularly Chaps. VI-VII. General Taylor's own appointment as chairman in the fall of 1962 presented the interesting case of an officer who had established a close working relationship with the President before assuming the position of chairman.

[19] Department of Defense Directive 5158.1, section II-F.

structure of the Joint Staff was changed from the earlier grouping of joint committees on various subjects to a more standard military staff organization with J-1 through J-6 directorates dealing with personnel, intelligence, operations, logistics, and plans and policy. However, roughly equal numbers of officers are still assigned to these units from each of the services.

One interesting innovation in the functioning of the Joint Chiefs that was introduced by Secretary of Defense Thomas Gates in the last year or two of the Eisenhower Administration has been retained by Mr. McNamara. As Secretary Gates described it to Senator Jackson's subcommittee: "A procedure was instituted whereby the Secretary of Defense and the Deputy Secretary of Defense sit with the Joint Chiefs weekly, usually on Monday afternoon, and more frequently if desirable, to discuss major issues."[20] It was the first time that such a regular exchange of views had been provided for.

Since a standard criticism of the Joint Chiefs in the postwar period has been their inability to deal effectively and expeditiously with certain basic policy issues, these regular meetings are presumably designed to bring the most difficult problems before the Secretary and Deputy Secretary at an early stage in their consideration.[21]

International Security Affairs

A Secretary of Defense with the powers described above is inevitably a major figure in the foreign policy-making process. The exact nature of his role will depend on what his primary interests are, how he

[20] *Organizing for National Security,* Vol. 1, Hearings, p. 730. For related testimony by Mr. Gates, see also pp. 729-30, 739, and 749-50.

[21] Whether these meetings are a genuinely useful device for improving communication between the Joint Chiefs and the Secretary or essentially another way of strengthening the decision-making role of the Secretary is hard for the outside observer to judge. This involvement of the two senior civilian officials in the previously sacrosanct discussions of the Joint Chiefs seems essentially healthy for both parties concerned. It may be argued, on the other hand, that the Chiefs should be left to arrive at independent military judgments, which can then be evaluated and acted upon by the civilian chiefs in terms of broader, nonmilitary considerations. This was not, however, the way the system was in fact working, so a regularly established exchange of views should prove productive.

interprets his role, and what kind of reciprocal relationships and attitudes exist among the President, the Secretary of State, senior White House national security aides, the chairman of the Joint Chiefs of Staff, and the Defense Secretary himself. Certainly on those foreign policy questions that have a major military dimension (or those military matters with significant foreign policy implications), a vigorous and interested Secretary of Defense (like Mr. NcNamara) can play a most important role, even a more important one than the Secretary of State himself.

Two recent situations may help illustrate the point. Without implying that Secretary McNamara was the most influential policy official during the sequence of events that followed the discovery of Soviet ballistic missile installations in Cuba in the fall of 1962, the central role of the varied military instruments applied to that situation or poised for use in it made the military establishment and the Secretary of Defense key figures in one of the major foreign policy crises of the postwar period.

The uproar created in Great Britain in December 1962 by the decision of the United States to cancel further development work and future production on the Skybolt air-to-surface intermediate-range ballistic missile illustrates perfectly the foreign policy consequences of a major U. S. military policy decision. Since the United States had agreed to supply Skybolts for Britain's jet bomber fleet and since the British government viewed this weapon as necessary to Britain's policy of maintaining an independent strategic-nuclear capability, the U. S. government found itself in a first-class foreign policy dilemma with its closest ally. The fact that the crisis was resolved by U. S. agreement to supply another missile, the Polaris, to the British further underscores the interdependence of the foreign and military policy realms.

As another example of this basic point, the Secretary of Defense participates at least once a year, along with the Secretary of State, in the semi-annual ministerial meetings of the North Atlantic Treaty Organization. Secretary McNamara has taken a leading role in explaining U. S. policy to the other NATO nations and, furthermore, in exhorting them to increase their efforts in the military field (the recent emphasis has been on the build-up of conventional forces). This is a foreign policy role of considerable importance. So is a major policy pronouncement by the Secretary of Defense on U. S. strategy for use of its nuclear deterrent forces.[22] Mr. McNamara has also been closely identified with U. S. policy and involvement in Vietnam, much more so than Secretary of State Dean Rusk.

Office of International Security Affairs

The Secretary of Defense can look in a number of directions for staff support in carrying out his responsibilities in the field of foreign policy or, as it is sometimes called in the military establishment, international security affairs. ("International security affairs" implies an understandably narrower focus than "foreign policy".) The role of the Joint Chiefs of Staff and the Joint Staff has already been noted. A Department of Defense directive, however, establishes the Assistant Secretary of Defense (International Security Affairs) as "the principal staff assistant to the Secretary" in the field of international security.[23]

This Assistant Secretary heads an Office of International Security Affairs (ISA) with a combined civilian-military professional staff which in September 1964 numbered 176 (104 civilians, 72 military). The Assistant Secretary and his Office are the focal point for the development and coordination of "defense positions, policies, plans and procedures" on the full range of foreign policy problems in which the military establishment has an interest. The Assistant Secretary is also supposed to "coordinate relations between the Department of Defense and the Department of State in the field of his assigned responsibility," which means in practical terms that the Office of International Security Affairs is the authorized Defense channel for communicating and conducting foreign policy business with the Department of State.

This function first formally appeared in the Defense Department organization when a Special Assistant to the Secretary for International Security Affairs was appointed in December 1950. He was elevated to Assistant Secretary rank in 1953. The Office is organized along both regional and functional lines. There is at present a grand total of

[22] See, for example, Secretary Robert McNamara's commencement address at the University of Michigan on June 16, 1962, reported in the *New York Times*, June 17, 1962.

[23] Department of Defense Directive 5132.2, dated May 20, 1961, "Assistant Secretary of Defense (International Security Affairs)."

six Deputy Assistant Secretaries whose assigned responsibilities include various regional areas, policy planning, arms control and disarmament, and international logistics negotiations (that is, sales of U. S. military equipment to foreign nations). A military officer who has roughly equivalent status serves as Director of Military Assistance. (See Chart 3.)

Five regional "directorates" roughly parallel the geographic bureaus of the Department of State (except for a separate Sino-Soviet unit and the continued association of Africa with the Near East and South Asia in a single unit). The military and civilian officers in these regional staffs conduct a great deal of day-to-day business with their opposite numbers on the country desks and in the regional affairs offices in the State Department. Much of it involves the military assistance and training programs carried on by the United States in friendly countries around the world. Since the State Department establishes the policy guidelines for these programs and the military establishment actually supplies the materiel and the training, considerable daily exchange of views and detailed collaboration are called for.

The two sets of regional units are also likely to be jointly concerned with questions related to U. S. participation in regional security alliances like NATO and SEATO, continuing negotiations and arrangements involved in the stationing of United States forces in various foreign countries, the capabilities of foreign military forces and their possible role in certain military contingencies, and, indeed, any foreign policy situation or relationship that has present or future implications for the activities and responsibilities of the military establishment. In most of these cases, officers representing the Joint Staff will also be involved.

These problems are not the exclusive responsibility of the regional units of the Office of International Security Affairs. The Office also has functional units in such fields as foreign military rights, foreign economic affairs, arms control, and policy planning. At present, it has its own Policy Planning Staff. Linked to the Office of International Security Affairs is the Defense Representative for the North Atlantic and Mediterranean Areas (DEFREPNAMA), located in Paris. He serves also as defense adviser to the United States Mission to the Regional Organizations (USRO), which represents the United States in the North Atlantic Treaty Organization.

CHART 3. Office of the Assistant Secretary of Defense (International Security Affairs), September 1964

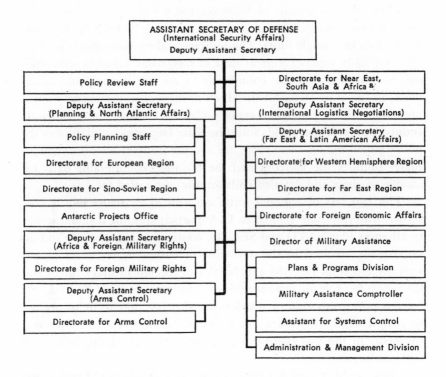

Source: OASD/ISA.
  a Reports to the Deputy Assistant Secretary on Near Eastern and South Asian matters; and to the Deputy Assistant Secretary (Africa & Foreign Military Rights) on African matters.

Another major responsibility of the Office of International Security Affairs is policy making, planning, and programming for the Military Assistance Program (MAP). The Assistant Secretary for International Security Affairs is charged to "act for the Secretary of Defense in military assistance matters and be responsible for all military assistance activities of the Department of Defense."[24]

In accordance with the recommendations of the President's Committee to Study the U. S. Military Assistance Program (the so-called Draper Committee after its chairman, William Draper), the Program was reorganized in 1959 and placed under a Director, who is responsible directly to the Assistant Secretary. The Committee thought that, at least initially, the Director should be a retired or active military officer, and this recommendation has so far been followed.

The Committee also recommended greater decentralization, with increased powers of direction, supervision, and coordination given to unified commands with relevant regional responsibilities, such as CINCPAC and CINCSO. This recommendation was also adopted. Detailed program guidance for the Military Assistance Advisory Groups (MAAG's) and other military aid missions in individual countries and detailed review and supervision of their country programs are now provided, on the basis of broader regional considerations, by the appropriate unified command overseas. Responsibility for basic policy and program guidance and for final decisions on country programs still rests with Washington policy officials.[25]

In performing its military assistance function, the Office of International Security Affairs operates within the framework of military advice provided by the Joint Chiefs of Staff about relevant military objectives and priorities and such basic questions as the relationship of

[24] Department of Defense Directive 5132.3, dated February 29, 1960, "Department of Defense Policy and Responsibilities Relating to the Military Assistance Program." This nine-page directive helps clarify the considerable organizational complexities of the military aid program, at least in its military establishment aspects.

[25] See the President's Committee to Study the United States Military Assistance Program, *The Organization and Administration of the Military Assistance Program* (June 3, 1959). This was the second interim report issued by the committee. Its final report, *Conclusions Concerning the Mutual Security Program* (Aug. 17, 1959) and, even more so, some of the special studies in the *Annexes* to the final report still provide useful, relevant reading for anyone interested in the military assistance program.

military aid programs to broader global security plans and strategic concepts. The Joint Chiefs also furnish nominations, based on recommendations by the services, for the Chiefs of the Military Assistance Advisory Groups. These must be approved by the Assistant Secretary for International Security Affairs. The three military services and the overseas commands actually conduct the operations of providing materiel, training, and other assistance to the recipient countries.

It has already been noted that officers from the regional staffs and from what is now called the Office of Defense Military Assistance (ODMA) in the Office of International Security Affairs work closely with their opposite numbers in the State Department, and with regional officials of the Agency for International Development, in carrying on the daily business of the aid program. They also work closely with the Program Coordination staff of the Administrator of the Agency for International Development, who is now responsible for coordinating the military and economic assistance programs both as operating activities and in their combined presentation to congressional committees.[26]

During the Eisenhower Administration, when the National Security Council structure was much more elaborate and active than it is at present, another major function of the Office of International Security Affairs was supporting and helping to staff Defense Department participation in the various units of the Council. In addition to coordinating the development of Defense policy positions and providing staff

[26] Section 622(c) of the Foreign Assistance Act of 1961 makes the Secretary of State responsible for integrating military as well as economic assistance programs with overall U. S. foreign policy. This responsibility is buttressed by at least two specific requirements: the Secretary must approve any new programs of military assistance and the dollar amounts of all ongoing country programs.

In November 1961 Secretary of State Rusk delegated this responsibility to the Administrator of the Agency for International Development, to be exercised in conjunction with interested geographic and other units of the State Department itself. The Administrator is supported in carrying out this function by a Military Assistance Division within his Program Coordination staff.

This is by no means a pro forma activity. No one questioned the impact of Mr. C. Douglas Dillon on the military assistance program when he performed this coordination function as Under Secretary of State in the last years of the Eisenhower Administration. The impact will obviously vary in terms of the energy, skills, and manpower brought to bear on the function by whoever is performing it on behalf of the Secretary of State.

assistance for the Secretary of Defense and the Deputy Secretary as members, respectively, of the National Security Council and the Operations Coordinating Board, the Assistant Secretary for International Security Affairs himself served as the Defense representative on the Planning Board.

The Office still provides staff support for the Secretary in his role as a statutory member of the National Security Council. The functions formally connected with the Council are far less time-consuming than they once were. The Office of International Security Affairs, however, continues to be the focal point within the military establishment for the development of policy positions and the implementation of policy decisions related to foreign policy. Its substantive responsibilities have not changed very much, even though policies may be decided upon in different forums and directives given different labels.

Joint Chiefs

ISA's role of foreign policy leadership in the military establishment has by no means put the Joint Staff or the individual service staffs out of the foreign policy business. The chairman of the JCS has a statutory role as adviser to the National Security Council and attends all its meetings. During the period when the Council had a Planning Board, the Joint Chiefs as well as the Secretary of Defense were represented on it. As the senior military officers of the government and principal military advisers to the President, the Joint Chiefs have a right of access to the President independent of the Secretary of Defense. They also have their own direct, continuing relationship with the Department of State, as noted in Chapter 5.

It is conceivable that if there is disagreement on certain matters, the advice of the Joint Chiefs might weigh more heavily with the President than that of the Secretary of Defense, and indeed rightfully so. This is, once again, a question of relationships among the top officials of the government, and there is no way to write into law some appropriate pattern and expect it to fix behavior.

At a minimum, it seems both inevitable and desirable that on any major foreign policy question with important operational military implications, the views of the Joint Chiefs of Staff will be sought and weighed carefully. The direct relationship of the Joint Chiefs with the unified and specified commands means that officers of the Joint Staff will be working daily on a great variety of problems with their military and civilian colleagues in the Office of International Security Affairs. While their present role in foreign policy is therefore a considerable one, it does seem fair to say that the Joint Chiefs no longer have the great influence on foreign policy generally attributed to them in the late 1940's and early 1950's.

Service Staffs

In spite of the growing size and expanding functions of the Office of the Secretary of Defense and the Joint Chiefs of Staff-Joint Staff complex, the individual service staffs are still quite large and active. Assignments to Office of the Secretary of Defense and Joint Staff positions continue to be made by the services themselves, although officers proposed for particular positions can be rejected. Furthermore, promotions and other aspects of career development remain essentially in the hands of the individual services.[27] In other words, the three military services are still powerful organizations in spite of the impressive Department of Defense superstructure that has been placed above them.

Each of the services has what amounts to an international security affairs unit of its own which works closely with planning and other staff units with related responsibilities within each service. The Army has its International and Policy Planning Division, under the Director for Strategic Plans and Policy. In recent years, some of the action officers on this staff have held Ph.D.'s in political science or history. The Air Force has an International Affairs Division. The Navy staff has a Politico-Military Policy Division headed by a rear admiral. Sometimes, an officer will serve for two years in the international

[27] Even here, it should be noted that the responsible civilian leaders do provide guidelines to military promotion boards that impose limits on the latter's freedom of choice. A notable example was the directive issued by Secretary of Defense Thomas Gates that established a tour of duty on a joint, combined, allied or OSD staff as a formal, qualifying requirement for promotion to flag or general rank. See Department of Defense Directive No. 1320.5, December 2, 1959, "Assignment to Duty with Joint, Combined, Allied and Office of the Secretary of Defense Staffs."

affairs unit of his service and then move on to a two-year tour in either the Joint Staff or the Office of International Security Affairs.[28]

These staffs are a focal point for the participation of the services in the foreign policy process; they provide analysis and advice to their service chiefs of staff and top civilian officials. The service chiefs of staff may bring these views to bear in the meetings of the Joint Chiefs of Staff, and the service secretaries in policy discussions with the Secretary or Deputy Secretary of Defense. When the National Security Council and its subsidiary units were more active, these staffs were responsible for developing or coordinating the policy positions of their services on the papers sent down to them by the Office of International Security Affairs. They still regularly provide service inputs on foreign policy-related matters to the Joint Staff.

Where one of the services has a specific interest at stake in the foreign policy field—for example, a major air or naval installation in a foreign country—it can be confidently assumed that officers from that service's staff will be involved in the development of policy views within the military establishment and may well participate in the discussions and negotiations with the Department of State. Although the Office of International Security Affairs is the formal channel for foreign policy communication with the State Department and the responsibilities of the Joint Staff inevitably bring its officers into contact with "the people on the other side of the river," there is also some continuing, direct contact between the service staffs and the Department of State. On relatively routine matters, where there are no larger Defense policy positions at stake, it is apparently acceptable for the service staff involved to deal directly with the State Department.

The situation of the Office of International Security Affairs within the Pentagon is, then, not without its difficulties. For most of the problems it deals with, one or more of four military staffs is bound to have at least overlapping functions and responsibilities. This is to say nothing of the other civilian-directed offices within the Office of the Secretary of Defense itself. ISA stands between the massive military bureaucracy on the one hand and the primary foreign policy agency, the Department of State, on the other. At times in the past, this has not been

[28] See *The Formulation and Administration of U. S. Foreign Policy*, pp. 167-68.

an enviable position. Some of the challenges to it are discussed in the final section of the chapter.

Related Military Activities

Given the wide-ranging military involvement in foreign affairs, the military establishment's various international security affairs staffs have no monopoly of participation in the processes of foreign policy development and execution. They have the major functional responsibility and presumably provide the overall leadership and policy guidance, but the responsibilities of many other military staff units bring them into the foreign policy business.

Even with the Secretary of Defense's policy control and the direction of combat forces by unified or specified commands, the services are still primarily responsible for training, manning, equipping, and logistically supporting these forces. The services supply the personnel for military assistance missions and advisory groups and procure and ship the materiel provided to other countries under the Military Assistance Program. The thousands of foreign military personnel trained each year in the United States under the Military Assistance Program with relatively few exceptions attend Army, Navy, Marine Corps, or Air Force schools.

The service staffs responsible for these activities are, legitimately and unavoidably, participants in foreign affairs. The same point can be made about the Office of the Secretary of Defense. The interrelations of military and foreign policy are so many and military personnel are engaged in so many activities relevant to foreign policy in so many parts of the world that all the major Defense offices find themselves involved to some extent in "international security affairs."

The Office of International Security Affairs has the major functional responsibility. In a sense, its coordinating and policy relationship to the other Defense units is similar to that of the State Department vis-à-vis other departments of the government whose responsibilities impinge on foreign affairs. Some of its problems are also similar. Other Defense offices do not always recognize that their activities and decisions have foreign policy implications. Sometimes, they resist such recognition.

Many examples of functions relevant to foreign policy can be mentioned. The work of the Assistant for Atomic Energy to the Secretary of Defense involves U. S. nuclear weapons positioned overseas, some earmarked for the forces of allied nations. The Assistant Secretary of Defense for Manpower and some of his staff are involved in the problems of training foreign military personnel in the United States. Although the Office of International Security Affairs has a unit of its own dealing with questions of foreign military rights and the status of U. S. forces and operating facilities abroad, there is also an Assistant General Counsel for International Affairs, who handles other treaty problems and questions of international law involving the Defense Department. He has also been involved in drafting foreign aid legislation.

The Assistant Secretary for Installations and Logistics is concerned with U. S. bases overseas as well as in the continental United States. The large-scale closings of such bases in 1964 and earlier were matters of considerable interest to the foreign governments as well as to the American state and city governments in whose territories the bases were located.

The two functional areas that probably have the greatest impact on the substance of military policy making and therefore affect U. S. foreign policy in a variety of obvious and subtle ways are research and development and budget preparation. Both reflect the larger trend in the Pentagon toward increasing centralization of decision-making power in the hands of the Secretary and his primarily civilian staffs in the Office of the Secretary of Defense.

RESEARCH AND DEVELOPMENT. As was indicated earlier in this chapter, the 1958 legislation placed the Secretary of Defense in a position to exercise firm control over military research and development and provided him with an organizational instrument of control by creating the new position of Director of Defense Research and Engineering. The latter ranks third in the Pentagon hierarchy, just below the Secretary and Deputy Secretary and senior to the Assistant Secretaries. His staff is organized primarily along functional lines, concerning itself with such problem areas as strategic weapons and air defense, although there are also units concerned with more traditional military and science-engineering fields like telecommunications, electronics, and ordnance. The Director can assign work to the Weapons Systems Evaluation Group (WSEG), originally set up as an instrumentality of the Joint Chiefs of Staff, and provides general direction to the Advanced Research Projects Agency.

The existence of the Advanced Research Projects Agency, with research funds independent of the three services, provides the Director of Defense Research and the Secretary of Defense with additional leverage on the direction of military research and development. ARPA is also the logical source of support for research by the military establishment on problems of arms control and disarmament. The primary role of the Secretary and the Director of Defense Research in this field, however, is still to coordinate and monitor the research and development activities of the individual services, and make the difficult choices in allocating limited resources among them. Most military research and development is carried on by the services, either in their own research facilities or, for the most part, by contract with business corporations, universities, and other outside organizations.

The machinery for research and development within the three services is quite complicated. One of the three civilian Assistant Secretaries in each military department is usually given responsibility for this area. There is usually a ranking civilian scientist as well. Within the military staffs, one of the Deputy Chiefs of Staff is charged with overall responsibility for research and development. There is, however, considerable variation among the services in how much research and development is carried on "in-house" and how particular fields of research and individual research projects are managed.

In other words, within the framework of policy and allocation of resources provided by the Secretary—including the difficult and sometimes dramatic choices that he must make with regard to particular programs (for example, the B-70 and the anti-missile missile)—the three services still play a most important role in determining what is and is not done in research and development. For example, Navy officials presumably make the first set of decisions regarding the allocation of Navy research and development funds among antisubmarine warfare, aircraft carrier development, and the nuclear submarine-Polaris missile weapon system. Similarly, the Army's research and development officers, working with the Chief of Staff and the Secretary of the Army, are likely to have a considerable influence on the original choices about dividing research and development money between improving combat infantry equipment and working on short-range ballistic missiles.

Changes will be introduced at succeeding levels of decision and review, but for the most part, with some dramatic exceptions, these are likely to take the form of modifications and, probably, reductions rather than radical changes of emphasis and distribution.

Military research and development significantly affects the military posture and, therefore, the foreign policy of the United States. There are even more direct international aspects and consequences of military "R and D" activities. One question that arises periodically is whether and under what conditions military technology can be made available to allied nations. The most dramatic examples are in the nuclear weapons field, but these are not the only ones. Since these questions are often seriously regarded by other governments, they become a matter of foreign policy as well as military policy. The same is true for the joint research and development activities carried on with certain allied nations. The agreement with the Federal Republic of Germany to develop the main battle tank of the 1970's on a joint basis had foreign as well as military policy consequences and implications. This international dimension in American military development activities is reflected in the presence of an International Programs staff, headed by an Assistant Director, within the organization of the Director of Defense Research and Engineering.

BUDGET PREPARATION. Aspects of the budgetary process have been commented on in Chapter 4.[29] As previously observed, the budgetary process provides one occasion for making major military policy choices. Since there are never sufficient resources available to meet all the demands, many of the difficult choices about the size, weapons, and functions of the armed forces must be confronted and made in the process of preparing the budget.

The budgetary process is inevitably political as well as analytical.

[29] There is some good discussion of the defense budget process in Ransom, *Can American Democracy Survive Cold War?*, Chaps. IV and V.

In both of these dimensions, it is difficult and troublesome. There can be no one right solution. The results depend, among other things, on the risks one is prepared to take, one's theory of strategy and deterrence, and one's assumptions about the future course of international politics—matters about which the most reasonable and knowledgeable of men may and do differ. There is certainly no budget that can fully satisfy all or even most of those affected by it. Nevertheless, particularly in view of the astronomic cost of the military establishment, the budgetary process is an appropriate as well as unavoidable vehicle for making tough choices about weapons systems, national military strategies, and allocation of service missions.

Costs and performance of competitive weapons systems can be compared—although the hypothetical or uncertain character of the assumptions that underly some of the figures used must always be kept in mind. Limited funds may force choices between functions, or between capabilities, or increments thereto. One point to be emphasized is that over the past fifteen or sixteen years the ability to do this kind of budgetary analysis has greatly improved. A Defense staff now conducts and generates studies that systematically analyze military requirements and problem areas as well as compare the cost-effectiveness of particular weapons systems. Detailed studies in such fields as airlift and sealift, ballistic missile defense, and antisubmarine warfare then provide the basis for more specific budgetary choices.

Until July 1965 Alain Enthoven, one of the most widely publicized of Mr. McNamara's bright young civilian experts on military affairs, was a Deputy Assistant Secretary of Defense (Comptroller) in charge of a systems analysis and special studies staff that had the reputation of being quite able and influential. The function was given even greater emphasis at that time with Mr. Enthoven's appointment as Assistant Secretary for Systems Analysis. Charles Hitch, Comptroller from 1961 to 1965, Enthoven, and their colleagues received considerable public and press attention as influential figures in Mr. McNamara's Pentagon; it should be remembered that the first Comptroller of the Defense Department, Wilfred J. McNeil, had a similar reputation during most of the more than ten years he served in the position.[30]

---

[30] See, for example, Charlotte Knight, "Mystery Man of the Pentagon," *Collier's*, Vol. 133 (Jan. 22, 1954), pp. 30-36. Also worth noting is Mr. McNeil's testimony before the first Jackson subcommittee. See *Organizing for National Security*, Vol. 1, Hearings, pp. 1057-92.

In light of this discussion, it is not surprising that one of the practical ways in which the Department of State's concern with military policy making is now being expressed is through the budget process. A State Department memorandum to the second Jackson subcommittee describes the innovation in these terms:

> One example of this relatively new politico-military role is the participation of the Department of State, for the past 3 years, in the Defense Department's annual planning and budget exercise. The Secretary of Defense has now made this a 5-year projection of strategy and force structure, which is reviewed annually. The relevant documents embody the Defense Department's plans for the future, and the force levels, worldwide force dispositions, and weapons systems development envisaged in them. The Department of State reviews and analyzes these plans and projections from the standpoint of their foreign policy implications and thus permits the Secretary of State to provide appropriate guidance in this field to the Secretary of Defense and advice to the President.[31]

Major Problems

The fundamental problems in the operation of the American military establishment are organizational, analytical, and political rather than ideological. Not only is meaningful civilian supremacy accepted in principle by military and civilians alike, but military officers are essentially willing to accept the actions and decisions that flow from it (however much they may deplore specific ones). The leadership role of the Department of State in foreign policy is accepted in the same spirit. Similarly, the State Department accepts military participation in foreign policy although it may have reservations about military performance in specific instances. On the military side, there is increasing acceptance of a legitimate State Department concern about military policy making. The problems that remain are difficult enough, but they are at least not at the level of constitutional principle, basic democratic values, or the fundamental division of departmental labors.

[31] "Memorandum on the Department of State's Politico-Military Organization and Staffing," in *Administration of National Security*, Hearings before the Subcommittee on National Security Staffing and Operations of the Senate Government Operations Committee, 88 Cong. 1 sess. (1963), Pt. 6, pp. 415-16. This memorandum appears as Appendix B of the present study.

Long-Term Organizational Trends

There are some long-term trends in the development of military establishment organization and decision making that seem essentially irreversible. The military establishment will continue to be faced by difficult choices among various broad national military strategies, the competing demands of a number of military functions, and competing weapons systems to perform individual military functions. There is the continuing dilemma of how much is enough—the weighing of costs against risks. Given the almost built-in competition for limited resources among the three services (and within each of them) and, indeed, given the difficulty of choice irrespective of interservice rivalry, the toughest and most important of these decisions will end up on the desk of the Secretary of Defense for final resolution short of the President. The major decision-making role of the Secretary did not begin with Mr. McNamara and will certainly not end with him.

It should not be assumed that all of his successors will define the job in precisely the same way or in fact be capable of doing it in the same way. It should not even be assumed that this would be desirable. Bernard Brodie puts it this way:

> . . . there seems to be little chance for institutionalizing the pervasive and searching kind of civilian control of the whole gamut of important military decisions that a very special kind of secretary with a most unusual array of assistants has undertaken. Most future secretaries will very likely not want to shoulder that kind of responsibility.[32]

Nevertheless, the responsibility for military decision that they will have to shoulder is, to say the least, formidable. The centralization of decision-making responsibilities, as has been indicated, rests on a more fundamental base than the energy and intellect of Mr. McNamara.

A future Secretary of Defense might rely heavily on one or more of his Assistant Secretaries for advice and for the making of many lesser, implementing decisions. The Director of Defense Research and Engineering or the Comptroller would be likely but not necessary choices

[32] Bernard Brodie, "The Scientific Strategists" (monograph of the Council for Atomic Age Studies, Columbia University, 1962), reprinted in *Administration of National Security, Selected Papers*, 87 Cong. 2 sess. (1962), p. 201.

for such a role. Seven or eight years ago, Colonel Kintner and his colleagues were arguing that the Secretary needed more substantial staff assistance attached to his own immediate office if he were not to be "captured" by his Assistant Secretaries.[33] Mr. McNamara's incumbency suggests that a certain kind of Secretary of Defense is capable of mustering the Assistant Secretaries of the Office of the Secretary of Defense effectively for his own purposes without the need for any substantial additional staffing of this kind. Of course, a successor might find such a device quite helpful.

On the other hand, some future Secretary of Defense might develop a particularly close working relationship with the chairman of the Joint Chiefs and look to the chairman and the Joint Staff as a primary source of decision-making advice. Even short of such a development, the chairman is likely to continue as the key figure in the Joint Chiefs of Staff structure. Assuming that he has the confidence of the President and the Secretary of Defense (and he will not last long if he does not), he will be looked to as an individual for professional military advice, whatever the views of the Joint Chiefs as a corporate body may be. This is not to say that where their views differ, his views will necessarily prevail over those of his JCS colleagues.

As the discussion in this chapter has made clear, however, it is highly unlikely that the Secretary will ever be able to satisfy all of his needs for integrating analysis and advice from the Joint Chiefs of Staff and the Joint Staff. Leaving aside detailed questions of size and structure, he will require continuing assistance from an OSD-type organization in making major decisions and supervising the operation of the military establishment.

Whatever the exact future role of the uniformed officer, the place of civilian experts and practitioners in the military business seems well-established and bound to continue. Indeed, as Professor Lyons suggests, one of the noteworthy developments of recent years has been the increasing professionalization of the political appointees as well as career civilians in the Defense Department.[34] Civilians have made im-

[33] Kintner, et al., Forging A New Sword, pp. 193-95.
[34] See Gene M. Lyons, "The New Civil-Military Relations," American Political Science Review, Vol. 55 (March 1961), pp. 53-63. This very useful essay has also been reprinted in Administration of National Security, Selected Papers, 87 Cong. 2 sess. (1962), pp. 102-16.

portant contributions to military strategic thinking, the development
of weapons systems, and techniques for increasing the rationality of
military decision-making. The increasing interest of civilian scholars,
research organizations, universities, learned journals, and the mass
media in military problems assures a steady supply of professional civilian talent in this field as well as the critical scrutiny of governmental military policy by knowledgeable outsiders.

At the same time, the military services have been quite concerned
about this development. The military educational system was already
turning out a considerable number of officers capable of dealing with
some of the distinctive politico-military and scientific-engineering
problems of the day; it can be confidently assumed that the pressures
of Mr. McNamara and his civilian experts will assure the increasing
emergence of military officers with the "civilian" training and skills
required for military decision making in the '60's and '70's.

It can also be assumed that military budgets, contracts, weapons
systems, and strategies will continue to stir controversy within the
Pentagon as well as outside and that the processes of resolution will in
large measure be "political," in both the general sense employed in
Chapter 2 and the narrower common usage. Given the nature of the
governmental system of the United States and the nature of the problems involved, this is probably inevitable.

The military establishment is a tough organization to bring under
the tight control of one man and one point of view. In terms of broadening military options and capabilities, this may have some desirable
consequences even though the process often seems so untidy and costly. With increased experience in dealing with these problems and a
larger supply of civilians and military better trained in analyzing
them, it should be possible to conduct the inevitable "political" battles over military decisions so that more light than heat is shed on the
questions to be resolved. Stronger staffs in the Office of the Secretary
of Defense should increase the pressure on the Joint Staff and the
military service staffs to improve the intellectual quality of their own
products.

One of the organizational consequences of increasing centralization
of decision-making power in the Secretary of Defense and the Joint
Chiefs of Staff, combined with the continued existence of three separate military services, is that at least five Pentagon staffs now deal

with most important military policies and problems. In addition to the staff of the responsible Assistant Secretary of Defense and the appropriate element within the Joint Staff, units of the Army, Navy, and Air Force are likely to be involved. Furthermore, there is often more than one unit in each of these staffs (and more than one Assistant Secretary of Defense) involved in any particular problem.

It is not implied that these five or more staffs and the component units within them perform completely duplicative functions; each has its distinctive role and responsibilities. There is often considerable overlap, however, in their interests and activities. It seems fair to say that this is not the system one would devise if starting from scratch. This comment undoubtedly applies to most government agencies. Nevertheless, the likelihood of footdragging and slowness of response and decision increases with such a structure.

Such a system can be made to face its tough problems and act vigorously and expeditiously, as Secretary McNamara has demonstrated. It does take notably strong leadership abilities to do so. From the perspective of the official who sits at the top of this structure, it is easy to understand why exceedingly difficult tasks are assigned with seemingly impossible deadlines. A tight deadline is one way of getting a quick response from this labyrinthine organization.

The need for a man of considerable stature and relevant background and experience as Secretary of Defense has been made amply clear. He needs a group of capable Assistant Secretaries who are in turn strongly staffed. The quality of the civilian personnel in OSD, both political and career, is crucial. OSD becomes something of an empty shell or, even worse, a major hindrance to effective military policy making if it is staffed by inexperienced, mediocre civilian personnel.

The widely-held view is that the quality of political and career civilians has improved in recent years. If indeed increasing numbers of civilians are becoming deeply interested in military affairs and being professionally trained in the field, this situation should continue to get better. It will be in marked contrast to the 1950's when it was often difficult to recruit able men to the political-level positions in the Defense Department and the three services and when the career civilian staffs were also regarded as far from adequate.

It should be remembered that career civilians are in a rather difficult position in the Pentagon since they are members of an organization principally staffed by other career services, the military. In some Pentagon offices, their prospects for career development and promotion are narrowly limited. This situation, too, has been improved in recent years, but some of the limitations and accompanying frustrations still prevail.

Military Participation in Foreign Policy Making

How do these general comments apply to the military role in foreign policy? The experience of the past few years has emphasized the importance of the distinction between civilian control over military policy making on the one hand and foreign policy leadership and direction of the military establishment's foreign affairs activities on the other. They are not the same; it is possible to have one without the other. From the point of view of foreign policy making, and from the organizational perspective of the Department of State, foreign policy considerations and requirements must enter into the making of military establishment decisions no matter who is in effective control of the Department of Defense.

This point has been illustrated clearly during the present period of policy dominance in the Pentagon by Secretary McNamara and certain key civilian aides. The requirement that their decisions reflect foreign policy desiderata and give due attention to foreign affairs implications is just as great, and sometimes as hard to accomplish, as if some military body like the Joint Chiefs of Staff were in fact the dominant policy influence in the Pentagon. Indeed, Mr. McNamara's energy and ability, as expressed in certain foreign policy-national security problem areas, have probably put more pressure on the State Department than would have been the case with a more conventional Secretary of Defense and Joint Chiefs of Staff.

There have even been occasions when the interests and concerns of the State Department seemed more compatible with those of one of the services than with the Secretary and Department of Defense. In sum, while meaningful civilian control of the military is undoubtedly a desirable state of affairs, it should not be confused or automatically identified with civilian leadership of the military establishment on those foreign policy and national security problems that concern them both.

In the immediate postwar period, there was considerable concern that the military establishment, and particularly its professional officer corps, was exercising too great an influence on American foreign policy and, furthermore, that this influence was bound to be baneful. While such views are still held in some quarters, most observers find the record of the past twenty years reassuring. Civilian foreign policy agencies and their personnel have been strengthened, civilian experts and professionals in military affairs have come increasingly to the fore and, finally, the armed forces themselves have developed a substantial cadre of officers with skill, experience, and sophistication in dealing with broader foreign policy and national security problems.

Beyond these fundamentals, there are continuing problems in the military establishment's organization for foreign policy. The key role of the Secretary of Defense in foreign policy making has already been made clear. If he is interested in active and effective performance of this role, he will probably prefer not to rely solely on the Joint Staff and the service staffs for advice and support and will therefore require a professional foreign affairs staff within OSD (the Office of the Secretary of Defense). This, of course, is the role of the Assistant Secretary of Defense for International Security Affairs and his staff. The position of the Office of International Security Affairs depends in the first instance, then, on how the Secretary of Defense defines his foreign policy role and where he looks within the Defense structure for his primary source of staff support. If he looks to ISA to perform this function and if this is made clear to the Joint Staff, the service staffs, and the other OSD units, and to the Department of State and the other foreign affairs agencies, there is no reason for any ambiguity about the organizational division of labor. The military staffs will look to ISA to provide leadership and guidance on foreign policy problems within the Pentagon. If the Secretary of Defense is inclined to look elsewhere for help or does not clearly define responsibilities in this field, the position of ISA is bound to be a difficult one.

If these responsibilities are in fact allocated to ISA, its essential problems become those of performance. The general comments about OSD units made above apply equally to ISA. Able civilians, preferably with some previous substantive experience in the national security field, are required for the political appointee positions. Able career civilians are also needed. The present career civilian complement numbers more than 50 percent of the total ISA professional staff. There has usually been a roughly 50-50 civilian-military split in ISA.

While proportions vary from unit to unit, ISA's mixture of political civilians, career civilians, and career military working side by side is typical of the Office of the Secretary of Defense.[35] While some argue that this dilutes or confuses the civilian control principle, this is an unnecessarily rigid and arbitrary interpretation. One way of broadening the horizons of the professional military officer is to assign him to work in a civilian-oriented staff. He may well make a similar contribution to the perspectives of his civilian colleagues.

ISA does face the problem of developing a career pattern for its nonpolitical civilian employees that will provide the opportunity for a varied, stimulating, and long-term work experience, with the possibility of tours abroad as well as in Washington. Otherwise, it is difficult to see how the necessary high quality of civilian staffing can be maintained on a continuing basis. Perhaps these ISA career civilians and foreign affairs personnel in other OSD units will have to be linked eventually to some broader, interagency foreign affairs personnel system.[36]

Another problem is whether the services will assign their best-trained and qualified officers to the Office of International Security Affairs or the Joint Staff, or, rather, retain them to do international security affairs work within their own individual service staffs.

In the past, there was some feeling that the latter was in fact the dominant pattern. However, as noted earlier in the chapter, one present pattern is to assign an officer for a couple of years to one of the service international security affairs staffs and then to make him available for a two-year tour in the Joint Staff, the Office of International Security Affairs, or perhaps as a participant in the State-Defense Officer Exchange Program. To put the matter crudely, the services are likely to be willing, not to say eager, to assign their ablest politico-mil-

---

[35] One notable exception is the General Counsel's office. (Most military officer-lawyers work in the Judge Advocate General staffs of the individual services.) There are also relatively few military officers on the staffs of the Comptroller and the Assistant Secretary of Defense for Installations and Logistics.

[36] See the discussion of this question in Chap. 11.

itary specialists to ISA if they view ISA as a key unit in the making of military establishment policy. If they do not, their motivation for making such assignments is certainly reduced.

From the point of view of the State Department, ISA serves a number of useful purposes. First and most obviously, it is a convenient central point of contact and coordination with the Defense Department on the host of problems that are of common concern to the two departments. ISA provides the State Department with a useful channel for dealing not only with the Joint Staff and the service staffs but also the other OSD staffs whose work impinges on the foreign policy field. On the other hand, with sensible and responsible bureaucratic handling, there is no reason why this channel has to be rigidly exclusive.

Furthermore, as the Defense Department unit closest to foreign policy problems and to the Department of State, ISA is in a position to reflect foreign policy views and guidance intramurally to other Pentagon units without always requiring the direct involvement of the State Department. This not only has the merit of economizing on the time and efforts of the State Department, but there is sometimes the additional advantage that ISA, with its more intimate knowledge of Pentagon views and organizational patterns and relationships, may deal more deftly and effectively with a particular problem.

One organizational change that used to be proposed from time to time a number of years ago was to abolish the Office of International Security Affairs and let the State Department deal directly with the Joint Staff and even the service staffs.[37] This proposal does not reflect an adequate sense of the organizational complexities involved and how difficult and challenging a job it would be for the State Department to provide detailed foreign policy leadership and guidance to the military establishment without the assistance of some intervening OSD unit like the Office of International Security Affairs.

This is not meant to derogate the importance of the Joint Chiefs of Staff and the Joint Staff in the foreign affairs activities of the military establishment. However, the Joint Chiefs, the Joint Staff, and the unified military commanders are likely to be most authoritative and effective in expressing views on operational problems—the disposition

[37] See *The Formulation and Administration of U. S. Foreign Policy*, pp. 89-91, where the idea was discussed though not adopted.

and use of forces, contingency planning, and the military implications and requirements of particular crisis situations.

For a foreign policy perspective on military policies and actions and the ability to reflect military views and concerns to the foreign policy agencies, the Secretary of Defense needs something like the Office of International Security Affairs. If he is conscious of this need and if ISA is well led and ably staffed, it can play an important role in the foreign policy process. This seems to be the case at present.

7

Economic, Information, and Cultural Agencies

MUCH THAT HAS BEEN SAID about relations between the State Department and the military establishment is applicable to the State Department's relations with the other major foreign affairs agencies. Their participation in the formulation and implementation of foreign policy is unquestionably legitimate and important. Organizational difficulties revolve around appropriate roles in the processes of policy making, arrangements for the coordination of related programs both at home and abroad and, perhaps most important and most difficult, the quality of performance in the field. This chapter is concerned with these problems as they arise in connection with foreign economic policies and programs and overseas information and cultural exchange.[1] Within this broad field, primary attention will be given to the cluster of agencies involved in the economic aid program, and to the United States Information Agency (USIA) and the State Department's Bureau of Educational and Cultural Affairs.

The economic aid and information agencies can be distinguished from other units in the foreign policy organization in a number of ways. They differ from the military establishment in that they are *wholly* foreign affairs organizations, carrying out United States policies and programs abroad, rather than national defense or national security

[1] The role of science and the "scientific" agencies is dealt with in Chap. 8. The "intelligence community" is discussed in Chap. 10. Field missions are treated separately in Chap. 9.

organizations whose activities have a wide range of foreign policy aspects and implications. Furthermore, in contrast to the Department of State, they are primarily program agencies, implementing policy through a variety of concrete activities and projects, either directed or carried out overseas, which are designed to produce social, economic, and political changes in the countries affected.

This contrast with the State Department is an imperfect one since the Department does have some limited program responsibilities—for example, the international exchange of persons program and other cultural exchange activities of the Bureau of Educational and Cultural Affairs—in addition to political and economic reporting, diplomatic representation and negotiation, and varied consular functions. And the economic aid and information agencies are necessarily interested in the formulation of policies, as well as in their detailed implementation. Nevertheless, this crude distinction is useful because it does have implications for the distinctive character and role of each of these organizations.

Perhaps it is worth repeating a point made earlier: the most fundamental questions regarding these programs are substantive—the framework of objectives and assumptions within which they are conceived, the quality of their detailed preparation and development, the amount of funds voted to support them and, finally, the skill, imagination, and devotion with which they are actually carried out. First-rate performance in all of these can probably transcend organizational inadequacies; appropriately coordinated organizational units cannot compensate for inadequate funds or personnel or fundamental errors in policy choice.

Bases for Evaluation

The organization of these agencies and their programs can be approached, for purposes of evaluation, in terms of two broad categories: external relationships and internal organization.

The relationship with the State Department is by far the most important of the external relations. Under the doctrine of State Department foreign policy leadership, the President looks to the Secretary and the Department of State as his primary source of advice on foreign policy problems and relies upon the Department to provide day-to-day direction to the other governmental agencies whose responsibilities bring them into the foreign policy field. From the point of view of the State Department, it is essential that these other agencies respond to State's leadership and carry out their foreign operations in a manner that supports official policies. Typical concerns of the other agencies, particularly those with major foreign affairs functions, are that their voices be heard in the formulation of the policies that they must help implement and that the State Department's policy leadership role not become a vehicle for extensive "kibitzing" of the details of their programs.

It has already been pointed out, in Chapter 5, that there is no set of organizational arrangements ideally designed and guaranteed to bring about this state of affairs. To state the principle is not to imply that some particular organizational solution automatically follows. Executive maneuverability is, of course, limited by the views and preferences of Congress and the kind of structure it establishes by statute. Much depends on the President. Much depends on the skills, personalities, and attitudes of the top officials of all the agencies involved, and the habits and patterns of communication and coordination that develop among these officials and among their subordinates at lower levels in the agencies.

In short, whatever the formal relationships established between the State Department and these other agencies, the actual results depend on the day-to-day working relations developed between the people in the State Department concerned with United States policy toward a particular country or region and the officials responsible for the related programs of economic aid, information, and educational and cultural exchange. Such close working relations are necessary whether these officials are under the formal authority of the Secretary of State or are members of an independent agency.

Granting the overall policy primacy of the State Department does not imply any exact role for other agencies in the processes of policy formulation and decision making. There are those, for example, who argue that the information, propaganda, or "strategic psychological operations" function should be represented with full membership in the National Security Council and even in the Cabinet.[2] This argument seems to assume that the "strategic-psychological" perspective on national security questions is not likely to be represented effectively by the Secretary of State, or anyone else whose attendance is normal or required by statute. On the basis of present organizational arrangements, such an assumption would presumably require the presence of the Director of the United States Information Agency. And, indeed, beginning in the last years of the Eisenhower Administration and continuing into the Kennedy Administration, he has regularly attended meetings of the National Security Council at the request of the President.

This raises a more general question. Programs in such fields as information and propaganda, economic aid, educational and cultural exchange, arms control and disarmament, and, perhaps in the not too distant future, the exploration of space, are highly relevant to certain major foreign policy and national security decisions. One way of attempting to assure adequate attention to a particular problem area or functional perspective is to bring one of its ranking governmental representatives into high policy councils. Clearly, this cannot be done with every claimant or importunate agency if discussion and decision making in these councils are not to become impossibly cumbersome. As suggested in Chapter 4, this would argue for a minimum of statutory prescription of membership on such bodies as the National Security Council and a maximum flexibility for the President in bringing into his highest councils those officials whose responsibilities and perspectives he regards as most significant. On the other hand, those who are convinced of the central importance of one or another of these functions might wish to assure its representation by fixing it in law.

Tensions, sensitivities, and ambiguities about the proper boundary lines between policy execution and program implementation are inevitable. State Department officers tend not only to scrutinize program details but, frequently, to argue about them with program officials because policies do take on more specific character and meaning through the quantities and emphases of particular programs. This is all the

---

[2] See the interesting discussion in Robert T. Holt and Robert W. van de Velde, *Strategic Psychological Operations and American Foreign Policy* (University of Chicago Press, 1960), Chap. IV.

more true when several lines of policy that are not completely compatible are applied to a particular situation.

It can therefore be assumed that the clearer and more precise the grant of authority to the Department of State for overall direction and control, the more extensive and detailed its scrutiny is likely to be. The reaction of the operating agencies is predictable: the State Department is trespassing into areas that are none of its concern and, furthermore, into areas where it can contribute no special knowledge or expertise and therefore can only add to waste, confusion, and delay.

This kind of conflict is not necessarily harmful. It certainly cannot be resolved by some precise, once-and-for-all drawing of boundary lines between the functions and the agencies that perform them. It should, however, be kept within reasonable bounds. This calls for forceful leadership at the top and a certain sense of responsibility, intellectual breadth, and sophistication at the working levels.

Before turning briefly to the question of personnel, one point relating to the organization of the economic aid program warrants some comment. In general, it means very little to say that organizational characteristics should reflect the nature of the program they are designed to implement. To be more specific, in the economic aid field it is now the official view that a country or region must be looked at as a whole, that an integrated, long-range program of development must be planned in full cooperation with the people being aided to make the most efficient, balanced use not only of United States assistance but that of other countries as well.

In his foreign aid message to the Congress on March 22, 1961, President Kennedy emphasized the importance of a carefully thought-through program tailored to meet the needs and the resource potential of each country, instead of a series of individual, unrelated projects within a country. Frequently in the past, it was suggested, development goals and projects had not been viewed and undertaken as integral steps in a long-range economic development program.[3]

What organizational implications can be drawn from this policy

[3] For the text of the Kennedy message, see the *New York Times*, March 23, 1961. It also appears in the *Department of State Bulletin*, April 10, 1961, pp. 507-14. There is no intention in this discussion to imply that the Kennedy Administration's approach to economic development aid represented a completely new and revolutionary departure. Inevitably, it was built on much that preceded it.

approach? It has been argued in this study that unification or federation of related programs is no sure cure for organizational ills. Thus, if economic aid responsibilities are shared by a number of agencies, this in itself should not be a cause for alarm. It seems important, however, that there be some single organizational locus where the long-range development needs of countries are examined on an overall basis and programs of economic aid planned accordingly. It may not be necessary that all the economic aid programs be brought together in one organization, but it certainly seems requisite that one agency have unambiguous responsibility for economic development planning and specific regional and country programming of aid in accordance with these plans, and also some authority to bring the other participating agencies into line with these plans and programs. It also seems logical that one agency and one official have operating responsibility for the economic aid programs in each country.

It is generally agreed that the geographic bureaus and country desks of the State Department are not equipped with either the technical and professional skills or the sheer numbers necessary to do this job. This means that while State can provide, hopefully, the overall policy framework and the coordination of major programs, another major unit will have to pull together the various program strands contributing to U.S. economic aid abroad.

Personnel

The information, cultural, and economic aid programs share some of the general difficulties that hamper other governmental agencies in the recruitment and retention of able personnel: an inability to recruit many of the brightest and most energetic young people in the society who are drawn to other pursuits; conflicts-of-interest problems among some who are willing to accept government positions; and the frustrations and irritations of a governmental bureaucracy operating within a democratic framework. These programs have, in addition, some special problems.

For one thing, many of the people carrying out overseas assignments under these programs face a particularly difficult, double challenge. They are often professionally trained and highly skilled specialists, brought in to perform or to teach others to perform very specific jobs. Furthermore, they are often exercising their special skills in the very midst of some alien society and culture (instead of at the more civilized and formalized periphery, which the central government and capital city usually represent), and are in a very real sense conscious agents of social and economic change. The cross-cultural empathy and understanding and diplomatic finesse that are called for in such situations are obvious, if hard to achieve. They have been remarked upon many times and emphasized to the point of caricature and gross over-simplification in *The Ugly American.*

Such combinations of first-rate professional skill with a willingness and ability to exercise these skills effectively in an alien culture, and often under difficult living conditions, have apparently been hard to come by—although the Peace Corps may be revealing hitherto untapped sources of talent in the society. Aside from engineers and agriculturalists of many descriptions, it has also, seemingly, been difficult to recruit able economists to work on economic planning and programming and to direct some of the aid missions abroad. An underlying theme in Mr. Kennedy's many speeches, messages, and legislative proposals dealing with foreign aid in 1961 was the need for a much higher quality of personnel than had been available to staff these programs in the past.

There are other problems. The dominant foreign affairs career service, the Foreign Service, has not traditionally concerned itself with the kinds of activities and programs represented by such fields as economic development, information, and cultural exchange and therefore has recruited relatively few people with relevant professional skills in these areas. This has necessitated the development of separate career "services" by the information and economic aid agencies, though with something of a temporary, *ad hoc* character about them.[4]

To some extent, short-term personnel assignments are inevitable. The needs of the countries being aided change over time, and different categories of expert help are called for. On the other hand, a corps of skilled and dedicated information and economic development officials

[4] The situation of most career Foreign Service Reserve officers of USIA changed in October 1964 with Department of State-USIA agreement to integrate them into the Foreign Service. See the discussion in Chap. 11.

cannot be built up solely on such a basis. In broad terms, the answer would seem to be a system that combines opportunity for long-term careers with sufficient flexibility to bring in needed categories of personnel for short-term assignments.

Organization for Economic Aid

The foreign aid and information fields have some general characteristics in common in their organizational histories. Both have been at one time or another independent agencies. Both have been semi-autonomous entities within the State Department. The various programs and activities that fall under each of these broad headings have never been brought together in a single agency. Since the end of World War II, the foreign aid activities of the United States have always been located in more than one agency and have at times been splintered among a half dozen or more. In lesser degree the same has been true of information and cultural activities.

There are important foreign economic policies and activities of the United States that do not fall in the aid category, and there is one important category of foreign aid, the Military Assistance Program, that does not fall in the economic category. While these activities will be noted briefly, the major concern of this discussion will be with the past and present U.S. organization for economic aid.[5]

A Note on Foreign Economic Policies

In viewing U.S. foreign economic policies, either organizationally or substantively, it is helpful to keep in mind the political setting in which these must operate. One of the difficulties in harmonizing foreign economic policies with other aspects of foreign policy is that external economic activities impinge directly on a wide range of specifically identifiable domestic interests that are likely to have vocal and often powerful political spokesmen.

Other actions of the United States in foreign affairs have domestic

[5] This section is adapted in part from H. Field Haviland, Jr. and Associates, *The Formulation and Administration of United States Foreign Policy* (Brookings Institution, 1960), pp. 61-65.

effects, but these tend to be cushioned somewhat by their broad impact. Taxes may increase, families may be faced with military service for their sons, and tensions may be heightened by world conditions. In economic matters, the impact is likely to be focused more narrowly and intensively. Economic aid to foreign agriculture may diminish the export markets of identifiable interest groups. The fostering of industrial development abroad may threaten the foreign and domestic markets of important American industries. Tariff concessions may result in heightened foreign competition for particular enterprises.

Specific constituencies affected are likely to carry great weight with the legislators who represent them. In addition to consequent congressional support and pressure, the domestic interests affected often have special relationships with one or more executive agencies, such as the Departments of Agriculture, Commerce, Interior, or Labor. These agencies have only a secondary concern in the broad direction of foreign policy but are vitally interested in the effects of foreign policies on the particular groups with which they are closely associated.

Such interests are legitimate and should (and presumably will) be taken into account in the formulation of national policy, in both the legislature and the executive branch. They do, in this sense, provide a limiting political framework within which foreign economic policies must be developed. The foreign aid program has two additional political handicaps: it has no such powerful domestic clientele to support it; and it is, compared to most other foreign and domestic programs, rather expensive.

From the organizational point of view, foreign economic problems can be divided into three broad categories: (1) the complex of activities that constitute foreign aid; (2) commercial policy problems and related issues of monetary and investment policy; and (3) transportation and communications problems. All three fields, particularly the first and second, are interdependent and interrelated; their successes and failures are correspondingly linked.

The aid field is the newest, most costly, and most complex in its organizational ramifications. Its pattern of organizational dispersal and splintering, however, is evident in other areas of economic policy. Agency actions are coordinated by numerous interdepartmental committees, and there are many lines of advisory opinion to the President. He is advised on Tariff Commission cases by the Trade Policy Committee under the chairmanship of the Department of Commerce, on restrictions of imports for national security reasons by the Director of the Office of Emergency Planning, on restriction of agricultural imports for price support reasons by the Secretary of Agriculture, and on international financial matters by the National Advisory Council on International Monetary and Financial Problems under the leadership of the Department of the Treasury. The functions of the National Advisory Council include the provision of guidance to the U.S. Executive Directors accredited to the International Bank for Reconstruction and Development, the International Monetary Fund, and the International Finance Corporation.

Under the Eisenhower Administration, there was also a Council on Foreign Economic Policy, headed by a presidential special assistant for foreign economic policy, concerned with trade and commodity problems. The Council could take cognizance of any foreign economic policy problem outside of the foreign aid field and make recommendations to the President. As part of his effort to reduce the number of such committees, President Kennedy abolished the Council and the special assistant's position when he took office and asked the Secretary of State to take responsibility for the coordinating and policy-making functions that it had been performing.

In accordance with the Trade Expansion Act of 1962, Mr. Kennedy did, however, establish at the presidential level the position of Special Representative for Trade Negotiations. The latter was to have broad responsibilities in this field, but his immediate task was to handle the negotiation of trade barrier reductions with the European Economic Community (the Common Market) which came to be known as the "Kennedy Round." In November 1962 President Kennedy appointed former Secretary of State Christian Herter to this position. The position and Mr. Herter's incumbency have continued under President Johnson.

The picture in aviation, shipping, and telecommunications is no less complicated than in the international trade and monetary fields. In international civil aviation, the Department of State plays a policy-making role, with advice from the Civil Aeronautics Board, the Federal Aviation Agency, and the Department of Commerce. In shipping and telecommunications, the role of the Department of State is a coordinating one.

The Bureau of Economic Affairs in the State Department is responsible for bringing foreign policy considerations to bear on most foreign economic problems outside of the foreign aid field. It does this in collaboration with the relevant geographic bureaus and other units in the Department. Where specialized international agencies like the Food and Agriculture Organization (FAO) or the World Health Organization (WHO) are involved, primary responsibility usually rests with the Bureau of International Organization Affairs.

Besides the Assistant Secretary of State who heads the Bureau of Economic Affairs, one of the two Under Secretaries of State usually has broad responsibilities in the economic policy area, providing a point of high-level attention and decision for these problems.

As in other fields where the Department of State provides foreign policy guidance to more specialized agencies and activities, the Bureau of Economic Affairs must have enough competence to understand the problems and specialized requirements of international financial and economic activities and, at the same time, to place these activities in the larger context of national and foreign policy.[6]

Aid Organization, 1945-1961

One of the most fundamental aspects of the postwar revolution in American foreign policy has been the massive use of governmentally administered economic programs, especially foreign aid, to serve the political objectives of the United States. Before the war, the normal assumption was that foreign, as well as domestic, economic relations belonged primarily in private hands and that governmental intervention in such matters was and could be of only peripheral significance.

Starting with the United Nations Relief and Rehabilitation Administration (UNRRA) effort in 1944, however, the United States began to act according to a new philosophy: that because the economic ills of other countries could have disastrous effects on the political as well as economic interests of this country, it was both desirable and feasible for the United States to intervene on a scale capable of producing significant improvements. This imperative has seemed increasingly

[6] On this topic as on many others, Arthur Macmahon's comments are still quite perceptive and valid. See *Administration in Foreign Affairs* (University of Alabama Press, 1953), pp. 173-77.

compelling as the plight of the less-developed countries became more serious and as the influence of various extremist elements, particularly the Communists, became more threatening. The extraordinary scale of the U.S. effort along these lines is indicated by the more than one hundred billion dollars of foreign aid that the United States has dispensed since 1945.[7]

The overall foreign aid program of the United States consists of a number of separate programs carried out by a variety of separate agencies. Most of these programs have their own legislative mandates and statutory bases; they serve a variety of purposes, not all of which are completely compatible or even oriented primarily to foreign policy objectives.

At present, military assistance is provided for in a separate section of the broader foreign assistance act. It is administered by the Department of Defense, and there have been continuing proposals that it become a line item within the Defense Department budget. So far, these efforts have not been successful, in large part because of congressional opposition.

Within the economic aid program itself, there are a number of categories of assistance. These include technical aid, long-term development loans and grants, the supply of equipment and goods in connection with particular programs, and short-term emergency or disaster grants.

Technical assistance is provided through the various activities of the Peace Corps as well as through the technical aid activities of the Agency for International Development (AID). Development loans may be "hard" or "soft" (to the extent that they are repayable in local currency); they may be made through the Agency for International Development (previously, through the Development Loan Fund) or through the Export-Import Bank, an independent institution; they

[7] Robert E. Asher estimates the net foreign grants and credits provided by the U.S. government from July 1945 through December 1960 at about $75 billion. At the same time, he emphasizes that specific foreign aid figures arrived at depend on the assumptions one makes (for example, whether U.S. contributions to international financial institutions are included, or how the value of U.S. military equipment or surplus agricultural commodities supplied to other nations is actually computed). See *Grants, Loans, and Local Currencies* (Brookings Institution. 1961), particularly Chap. 3.

may stem from the sale of surplus American agricultural commodities under the program established by Public Law 480. The picture is further complicated by the activities of such international agencies as the International Bank for Reconstruction and Development, the International Finance Corporation, and the International Development Association. The United States has been the major contributor of funds to these agencies and, correspondingly, has the strongest influence on their activities.

To put the present, complicated foreign aid structure in some perspective, it may be useful to sketch briefly its equally complicated history. Geographically, the program has been marked by a gradual shift from the early Marshall Plan days of massive aid to the highly developed industrial nations of Western Europe to the present emphasis on development assistance to the underdeveloped areas of Asia, Africa, the Middle East, and Latin America. In terms of aid categories, the Marshall Plan, or Economic Cooperation Act, beginning in 1948, poured billions of dollars of economic grant assistance into Europe. With the signing of the North Atlantic Treaty, the outbreak of the Korean War, the stationing of large American military contingents in Europe, and the rapid economic recovery of that continent, the emphasis of the program shifted rapidly to the provision of large-scale military assistance to the NATO nations of Western Europe and a number of key countries in the Far East.

In 1950 a modest program of technical assistance to the underdeveloped areas (Point Four) was inaugurated, but the emphasis on military assistance, and on economic assistance designed to shore up military allies, continued into the late 1950's. By 1955 assistance to Europe was almost exclusively military. In 1957 the establishment of the Development Loan Fund underscored a new trend in the foreign aid program: an emphasis on supporting economic development in the underdeveloped countries, and increasingly with loans rather than grants. Substantial programs of military and defense support assistance to some of the less developed countries continue,[8] but the present, growing empha-

---

[8] For example, in the foreign aid program proposed for fiscal year 1966, 72 percent of the $1.17 billion military assistance program was to go to eleven so-called "forward defense" countries—Greece, Turkey, Iran, Pakistan, India, Thailand, Laos, Vietnam, the Philippines, Taiwan, and Korea. All but 5 percent of the remainder

sis is on long-term loans and technical assistance for economic development.

It is possible in a brief account to note only the major organizational landmarks in the foreign aid program. The first major United States unit in the post-World War II period was the Economic Cooperation Administration, established in 1948 by Congress as a separate, independent agency. President Truman's Point Four program of technical assistance was implemented organizationally with the establishment in 1950 of the Technical Cooperation Administration as a semiautonomous unit loosely lodged within the State Department.

As the military assistance program began to expand rapidly, it was necessary to coordinate it with the economic aid program and with broader United States foreign policy. At first, an interdepartmental coordinating committee was set up, chaired by a State Department official. In 1951 the military and economic assistance programs were combined in a single statute, and a Director of this Mutual Security Program was established to provide the necessary coordination of programs. Operational responsibility for military assistance and training continued to rest with the Defense Department.

The Director for Mutual Security was made a presidential aide and placed organizationally in the Executive Office of the President. At the same time, the Economic Cooperation Administration was renamed the Mutual Security Agency and the Director for Mutual Security appointed its head. Thus, the latter wore two organizational hats, one as head of the economic aid program and the other as coordinator of the overall mutual security program.

One of the 1953 Eisenhower reorganization plans removed the Technical Cooperation Administration from the State Department, joined it with the Mutual Security Agency, and renamed the whole organization the Foreign Operations Administration. The Director, Foreign Operations Administration, was responsible for the overall coordination of the Mutual Security Program, but the Defense Department

---

was for programs in Latin America and Africa. Of the proposed program of $389 million for supporting assistance—"economic aid provided for security and stability purposes"—more than 80 percent was to go to Vietnam, Laos, Thailand, and Korea and 14 percent to Jordan and the Congo. See *Proposed Mutual Defense and Development Programs Fiscal Year 1966*, Summary Presentation to the Congress by AID and Department of Defense (Government Printing Office, 1965), pp. 194-99.

continued in operational control of military assistance and the Director was to look to the Secretary of State for foreign policy guidance.

In 1955, with large-scale economic aid to Europe coming to an end, the foreign aid agency was reduced to the status of an autonomous unit within the State Department. Once again a new name was provided, this time, the International Cooperation Administration. For most practical purposes it continued very much as before. In 1957, with the kind of disregard for consistency of organizational doctrine that has been typical of this program, a new and independent agency, the Development Loan Fund, was established in order to provide soft-currency loans to the underdeveloped countries. At about the same time, it was decided to place the responsibility for broad control and coordination of the Mutual Security Program squarely in the hands of the Secretary of State. He in turn delegated this responsibility to his Under Secretary of State for Economic Affairs, who developed a mutual security coordination staff within his own office, headed by a special assistant.

In the last years of the Eisenhower Administration, Under Secretary for Economic Affairs, C. Douglas Dillon, won a reputation in Washington as a vigorous (some thought too vigorous) policy leader and coordinator of the total Mutual Security Program. His ability to carry out these responsibilities in a concrete, meaningful way rested in part on the fact that, acting on behalf of the Secretary of State who was in turn acting on behalf of the President, he was responsible for the approval of specific money amounts of the military and economic assistance to be granted various countries as well as the initiation of programs in any additional countries.

Some officials in the International Cooperation Administration and in the Defense Department felt that Mr. Dillon was using this power as a means of interfering with their detailed implementation of programs, a matter presumably beyond his ken, but it seemed to be generally agreed in any event that Dillon was carrying out his responsibilities for policy control and coordination of the aid programs in a vigorous rather than *pro forma* manner.

The lineup of United States foreign aid agencies and activities at the time Mr. Kennedy took office in January 1961 looked, then, about as follows. The State Department was responsible for policy leadership and coordination. It performed this function through a mutual security coordination unit in the office of the Under Secretary of State for Economic Affairs. This unit also coordinated the preparation and pre-sentation of the Mutual Security Program to Congress by the various agencies involved.

Within the framework of the State Department's policy guidance and determination of the precise dollar value of country programs, the Department of Defense was responsible for the Military Assistance Pro-gram, which was submitted as one part of the total legislative "pack-age" for foreign aid. The Assistant Secretary of Defense for Interna-tional Security Affairs and a special unit in his office were (and are) responsible for policy and for detailed programming of assistance, with the Joint Chiefs of Staff providing military guidelines and the three services providing the military hardware and military personnel to staff training and advisory missions.

In January 1961 U. S. economic assistance abroad was being fur-nished by four agencies operating under four separate programs and legislative enactments: the International Cooperation Administration, the Development Loan Fund, the Export-Import Bank, and the De-partment of Agriculture.

The International Cooperation Administration provided aid, primarily in the form of grants, in three main categories: defense sup-port, that is, economic assistance to those countries where agreed mili-tary programs were deemed to create a special economic burden; spe-cial assistance, where loans were not feasible; and programs of techni-cal cooperation. These activities were designed to help attain certain economic goals in the recipient countries, after taking account of all other prospective sources of funds. The International Cooperation Ad-ministration was responsible for directing and staffing the United States Operations Missions (USOM's) abroad which actually carried out the programs of economic and technical assistance.

Established in 1957, the Development Loan Fund was made an in-dependent corporation in 1958, subject to the foreign policy guidance of the Secretary of State. As already indicated, the Fund was designed to provide long-term economic development loans to the underdevel-oped countries repayable, if need be, in local currency.

The Export-Import Bank was established in 1934 primarily to finance and facilitate American foreign trade. It is a completely independent agency, although it has always been reputed to have a good working relationship with the Department of State. Its preference has been, where possible, to extend loans or guarantees to private borrowers. Loans are repayable in U.S. dollars and are almost always tied to purchases of American-made goods. The Export-Import Bank's operations have thus tended to fall in the "hard" loan category and have limited usefulness in providing assistance to the underdeveloped countries.

The Agricultural Trade Development and Assistance Act (more popularly known as Public Law or PL 480), originally enacted in 1954, was designed, among other things, to encourage the disposal of American agricultural surpluses abroad. It does, however, provide that the foreign currencies accruing to the United States from these sales can be used for economic and military assistance purposes, and this program has in fact become a major component of U.S. assistance to many countries. (It should be remembered that these surpluses represent the result of substantial price-support programs for American agriculture by the federal government.)

In some recipient countries this agricultural surplus disposal program has overshadowed the more conventional economic assistance programs in magnitude of aid furnished. Through the end of 1964 agricultural commodities with an export market value of more than $13 billion had actually been shipped under this program. It is administered by the Department of Agriculture under the foreign policy guidance of the Department of State. However, since the Public Law 480 program is not budgeted as part of the foreign aid program, the policy control of the State Department is not likely to be as strong. There would seem to be built-in tensions in a program that is important in foreign affairs and yet is administered by a domestically-oriented agency to serve purposes that are in large part domestic.[9]

In addition to these American agencies, the United States has a strong, if not controlling, voice in the allocation of funds by various international agencies, notably the International Bank, the Interna-

[9] For a detailed description of this complex program, and a positive statement of its role as a foreign policy instrument, see *Food for Peace: 1964 Annual Report on Public Law 480,* H. Doc. No. 130, 89 Cong. 1 sess. (1965).

tional Monetary Fund, the International Finance Corporation, the Inter-American Development Bank, the International Development Association, and the United Nations Special Fund. To a lesser extent, the United States can influence decisions of the United Nations expanded program of technical assistance.

The Kennedy Changes

This was the foreign aid organization picture that confronted Mr. Kennedy when he took office in January 1961. In a special message to Congress on March 22, he indicated the general approach that he would take to both the substance and organization of the foreign aid program. His detailed legislative proposals to implement that approach were presented to Congress two months later. By that time, directors had already been appointed for both the International Cooperation Administration and the Development Loan Fund. In addition, in March 1961 a new program of technical assistance had been established by executive order and given organizational embodiment in the form of the Peace Corps. It enlisted young Americans to work on specific projects in those underdeveloped nations interested in their services. A director, R. Sargent Shriver, had been appointed at the same time.

On January 24, the President had also announced the establishment of the position of Director of the Food for Peace Program, to be located within the Executive Office. This new presidential aide was to be "responsible for the continuous supervision and coordination" of those portions of the Mutual Security Act of 1954, and the Agricultural Trade Development and Assistance Act already referred to, dealing with "the use of American agricultural commodities in furtherance of the foreign policy of the United States." The Department of Agriculture's responsibility for selecting and shipping the commodities was to continue, as was the State Department's role in providing foreign policy guidance. Thus, prior to submitting his specific proposals for reorganizing the foreign aid program, Mr. Kennedy had already appointed four officials with major responsibilities in this area.

The Foreign Assistance Act, approved by Congress in September 1961, provided for the establishment of the new Agency for International Development that President Kennedy had proposed in May.

This agency replaced the International Cooperation Administration and the Development Loan Fund, which were abolished. It is, formally, a semi-autonomous unit within the Department of State and is headed by an Administrator of Under Secretary rank, reporting directly to the Secretary of State and the President. The major organizational structure beneath him consists of four regional bureaus—for Latin America, the Far East, the Near East and South Asia, and Africa, headed by Assistant Administrators equal in rank to the geographical Assistant Secretaries of State, with whom they are supposed to work closely. The President stated in his letter accompanying the proposed legislation that economic development aid could no longer be viewed as merely a convenient tool for meeting short-run political objectives: "Development assistance, therefore, must—and shall—take its place as a full partner in the complex of foreign policy."[10]

The Peace Corps was not made a part of this new agency. It remained an autonomous agency within the State Department, with its Director having the rank of Assistant Secretary. The position and duties of the Director of the Food for Peace Program were also left unchanged. The status of the military assistance program similarly continued as before although the general orientation seemed to be to distinguish it more sharply from the economic development programs. Although the Secretary of State continued to have the overall responsibility for policy direction and coordination of the aid program, he in turn delegated this function to the AID Administrator.

Thus, under the Kennedy reorganization, the greater part of the foreign aid program is not only subject in principle to the policy leadership of the Secretary of State but is actually located organizationally within the Department. This does not guarantee that policy leadership and coordination will therefore be more effective. Indeed, although officials of the Agency for International Development work closely with their State Department colleagues, they continue to act in many ways like members of an independent agency. Furthermore, since the Secretary of State has delegated his overall aid coordinating responsibilities to the AID Administrator, the assistance programs—and particularly military assistance—have been placed organizationally at a somewhat further remove from the State Department, complicating

[10] For the full text of President Kennedy's letter, see *Department of State Bulletin*, Vol. 44 (June 19, 1961), pp. 977-79. The quotation appears on p. 978.

CHART 4. Agency for International Development, October 1965

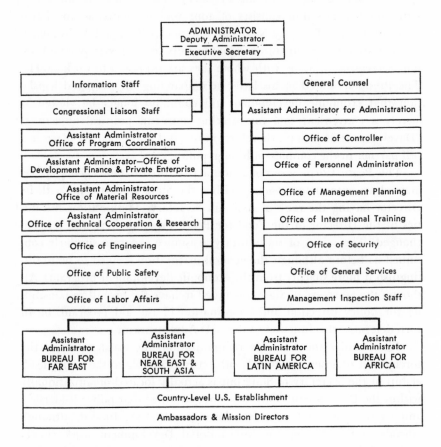

Source: Office of Management Planning, AID.

200

the Department's ability to bring foreign policy considerations directly to bear on foreign aid problems.

Leaving aside this question of "in and yet not of" the State Department, the past pattern of organizational dispersion of the aid program is still present to some extent. The Department of Agriculture continues its separate operation of the Public Law 480 program, although the Director of the Food for Peace Program was shifted from the Executive Office of the President to the Department of State in October 1965.[11] The Peace Corps is outside of AID and, although formally located within the State Department, is for most purposes independent.

Organizationally, AID differs somewhat from the predecessor International Cooperation Administration in the clear primacy its geographic units have in developing policy and detailed programs of country assistance. Previously, these units had been roughly on a par with the offices responsible for providing the various country programs and projects with the necessary technical services, personnel, and advice. The central role of the geographic units is expressed organizationally in the fact that they are now constituted as Bureaus; the technical staffs remain as Offices. The Assistant Administrators who head the four regional bureaus are supposed to play a leadership role in the aid field similar to that envisaged in current governmental doctrine for the five geographic Assistant Secretaries of State on broader foreign policy matters. (See Chart 4.)

The Agency for International Development was slow in getting started. The executive order that officially established its existence was not issued until early November 1961; in mid-1962 it was still in the throes of reorganizing and recruiting new personnel. By December 1962 the economic aid agency had its third Kennedy-appointed director.[12] In line with President Kennedy's evident feeling that previous personnel had been far from adequate, new people were brought in to fill many of the top positions in Washington and to direct many of the aid missions abroad. A very considerable effort was made to re-

[11] The Director, Food for Peace, was made Special Assistant (Food for Peace) to the Secretary of State with rank equivalent to an Assistant Secretary of State. Given the State Department's responsibility for foreign policy guidance of the activities carried on under Public Law 480, the change seemed designed to simplify organizational arrangements in this field and increase the effectiveness of the Department of State's role. For a report on this organizational change, see *Department of State News Letter*, No. 55 (November 1965), p. 19.

[12] David Bell succeeded Fowler Hamilton, who in turn had succeeded Henry Labouisse.

cruit first-rate executive talent from the business world and elsewhere.

Without defending the adequacy of the previous officials, some observers felt that too many new and relatively inexperienced people had been brought in too quickly. Since the Kennedy Administration had come into office with strong views about the economic development field, considerable presidential impatience and frustration were reportedly added to the burdens of a major reorganization and the rapid turnover of personnel. The much-discussed Alliance for Progress was perhaps the most notable victim of urgent presidential interest and eagerness for results combined with organizational growing pains and personnel changes. Its difficulties were further compounded by the need to develop a satisfactory division of labor and working relationship with the Bureau of Inter-American Affairs and other interested units in the State Department.

President Johnson indicated his own concern about the Alliance in his first major appointment in December 1963. Thomas Mann, a highly experienced, senior Foreign Service Officer, was simultaneously appointed Assistant Secretary of State for Inter-American Affairs, Coordinator of the Alliance for Progress (organizationally located in AID), and special assistant to the President for Latin American affairs!

The organizational troubles of AID have been compounded by rapidly spreading skepticism and downright hostility toward the aid program in Congress.[13] Unfortunately, this congressional dissatisfaction only increases the pressure on the executive to look for organizational solutions to what are essentially nonorganizational problems. Periodic major reorganizations and rapid personnel turnover seem to be hallmark characteristics of the aid program. While they may reflect in part the periodic changes in its purposes, assumptions, and methods, and continuing uncertainty about its long-term future, they have without a doubt taken their own toll. On balance, they may aggravate the difficulties of the program more than they ease them.

Organization for Information and Cultural Exchange

Although these two programs have had their share of controversy and detailed legislative and executive attention since the end of World

[13] See Chap. 3.

War II, their organizational history is far less complicated than that of the foreign aid program. They have been far less costly than foreign aid, their operations somewhat less complex, and, it seems fair to say, less central to the success of postwar U.S. foreign policy. Perhaps some crude order of magnitude is suggested by the fact that recent budgets of the United States Information Agency have been in the vicinity of $170 million a year while appropriations to the State Department for its educational and cultural exchange activities now exceed $50 million per year.[14]

There are some fairly clear-cut organizational patterns in the development of these two programs. Since the close of World War II, and even before, cultural and educational exchange activities have consistently been located within the Department of State, although their exact organizational locus has changed at least once. In 1945 the overseas information activities of the Office of War Information and the information activities of the Coordinator for Inter-American Affairs were transferred to the State Department, where they remained until an independent United States Information Agency was established by President Eisenhower in 1953. However, even before this shift to independent status, the information unit had gained increasing autonomy within the State Department and at the time of its separation from the Department had attained the status of a semi-autonomous International Information Administration.

A Brief Historical Sketch

From the time of the American Revolution to the present, the United States has employed propaganda and related information measures as instruments of war. Not until after the Second World War, however, was it determined that a governmental information service was needed to present the American case abroad during times of relative peace. Cultural exchanges and related programs have no such long history of governmental participation.

It was during the 1930's that the cultural activities of the European totalitarian powers provoked the nations of the Western Hemisphere into counteraction. One result was an inter-American treaty calling

---

[14] This section is adapted in part from the discussion in *The Formulation and Administration of U.S. Foreign Policy*, pp. 72-77.

for exchanges of intellectuals, musicians, artists, and other cultural figures among the various American nations. This resulted in the creation of a small staff in the Department of State to formulate programs and to link governmental and private efforts in this field. It is interesting, and not really surprising, to note that United States programs of cultural exchange and technical assistance had their beginnings in Latin America in the 1930's.

In 1948, the information and cultural programs were brought into close association, but not wholly merged, with the passage of the United States Information and Educational Exchange (or Smith-Mundt) Act. The resistance to total merger came largely from the educational and cultural constituencies who tended to associate information with grossly distorted propaganda. Thus, the legislation set up separate citizen advisory commissions for information and for cultural relations. Both functions reported to the Assistant Secretary of State for Public Affairs, but there was a sharp organizational division immediately below him. At the same time, there was recognition by many observers that the broad purposes of the two programs were closely intertwined and that there was need to see that they reinforced one another.

Much attention was also given to the division of responsibility between the governmental and private sectors. It was widely recognized that most of the task of representing the United States abroad, in both such "fast" media as radio and newspapers and such "slow" media as books, could and should be done by private enterprise. But studies of the performance and interests of private media demonstrated that they alone would not provide a "full and fair picture" of the United States, nor could they be counted on to publish abroad sufficient background about the activities of the government—including the texts of significant speeches and full descriptions of political action—to permit opinion leaders of other countries to form their views on the basis of comprehensive and prompt information.

Similarly, in the field of cultural activities, those concerned with the matter, both inside and outside the government, believed that the main job would have to be accomplished by nonofficial persons and institutions. There was recognition, however, that certain coordinating functions had to be performed by government and that the treaty commitments of the United States—to the Organization of American States and to the United Nations Educational, Scientific and Cultural Organization, for example—called for some governmental organization to provide staff and policy services that could neither be supplied by wholly nongovernmental agencies nor left to the geographic bureaus of the Department of State.

Prior to the passage of the Smith-Mundt Act in 1948, there was also some discussion of the proper location of the overseas information function within the government. Should it remain in the Department of State? Should it be in another executive department? Or should it be an independent agency? There was even a suggestion that it should be in the Federal Communications Commission. There was no parallel discussion of where the cultural program should be; the relation of that activity to treaty commitments suggested clearly that it should stay in the Department of State. The program was also relatively modest and not as politically sensitive a policy instrument as information and propaganda.

The decision in 1948 was to keep the information function in the State Department because of its close relation to foreign policy. It seemed inappropriate as a component of any other department or agency. It was deemed of insufficient size and stature to warrant establishment as an independent agency, and there was concern that independent status would make the function too prominent on the domestic scene—a constant target for public criticism. On the other hand, it could be argued that too close a relationship between foreign policy making and information and propaganda might at times prove embarrassing and even compromising for the former.

Assigning the information function to the State Department did create problems. The administrative system of the Department had been designed for purposes far different from those of information operations. It was difficult to meet the needs of flexibility, speed, and special handling of personnel and funds occasioned by the new service. In adjusting to this situation, the Department, as suggested above, encouraged increasing administrative autonomy for the information function. Just prior to the outbreak of the Korean War in 1950, an International Information Administration was created that helped to meet these special operational requirements.

Operational autonomy did not, however, mean policy autonomy.

Within the information unit, there were regional and overall policy and planning specialists who were to keep in close touch with the operators—the broadcasters and writers. The various geographic bureaus of the Department did the same. The operators, true to the custom of their profession, asserted a great deal of freedom in the practice of their trade. Nonetheless, close relations were established between some of the operators and relevant desk officers; in other cases, where the information function was less valued or less skillfully manipulated, relations were more abrasive.

As the government slowly readied itself for crisis and possible war after the Czechoslovakian coup of 1948, it became clear that there was more to the information function than was found in the Department of State. The military departments became interested. Their wartime and postwar occupation experiences had left them with extensive responsibilities for communication to Americans as well as to the nationals of other countries, and their facilities for such communication exceeded those available to the United States Information Service, the overseas arm of the information unit. It was also rediscovered that the mere presence and activities overseas of American troops and the civilians who accompanied them strongly affected relations between the United States and the foreign host countries.

At the same time, the extensive foreign aid activities then being carried out inevitably called for explanation and justification in the countries where aid was being provided. Thus, the Mutual Security Agency and its predecessors developed information services and staffs of their own.

For these and other reasons, efforts were initiated to examine the whole range of governmental actions that might affect the psychological climate abroad and to determine the optimum allocation of control and administration of information resources and people in times of peace, cold war, and war. The outcome was the creation in 1951 of the Psychological Strategy Board, which had as members a specially appointed chairman, plus the Under Secretary of State, the Deputy Secretary of Defense, the Director of the Central Intelligence Agency, and the Director of the Mutual Security Agency. Also attached to it were a small staff and a lower-level interdepartmental coordinating committee.

The Board was designed to plan governmentwide programs of communication, persuasion, and related action, and to see that these were executed in effective, coordinated fashion. The Board floundered, however, due to inexperience, ignorance of the probable impact of United States actions on countries abroad, and failure to set priorities and concentrate resources accordingly. It was abandoned by the Eisenhower Administration in 1953.

Two major actions in this field followed. One was the creation of the Operations Coordinating Board out of the ashes of the Psychological Strategy Board. The other was the issuance of Reorganization Plan No. 8 of July 1, 1953, which removed the International Information Administration from the Department of State, combined with it the information units of the Technical Cooperation Administration and the Mutual Security Agency, and created an independent United States Information Agency. Theoretically, the organizational rationale for this move was to free the Department of State from an operating function and thus strengthen its role as the primary agency for foreign policy making. A part of the motivation, however, appears to have been the desire to disengage from a perennial source of embarrassment. It was made clear in the reorganization plan that the new Information Agency should function within the ambit of foreign policy set by the Department of State.

While the overseas information program was subjected to considerable public and legislative scrutiny, particularly during the first years of the Eisenhower Administration, the basic organizational arrangements set forth in the 1953 plan have remained the same, continuing into the Kennedy and Johnson Administrations. There was one important organizational change in the cultural field in the last two years of Mr. Eisenhower's second term. The various cultural activities—international exchange of persons, including educational exchange, U. S. participation in the work of the United Nations Educational, Scientific and Cultural Organization, and the cultural programs carried on by means of the President's Special Fund—were removed from the Bureau of Public Affairs in the State Department and placed in a new office headed by a Foreign Service Officer serving as a special assistant to the Secretary of State himself. This office was later raised to bureau level, and there is now a Bureau of Educational and Cultural Affairs, headed by an Assistant Secretary of State.

The Information Agency, like the Agency for International De-

CHART 5. United States Information Agency, January 1963

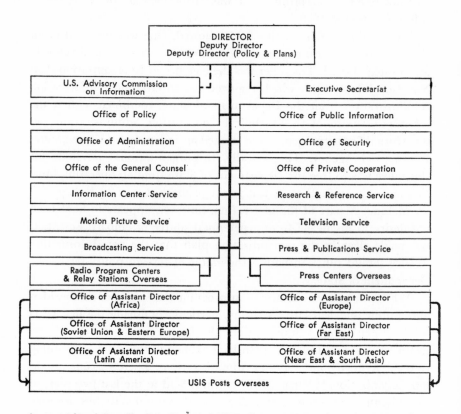

velopment, has both geographic units and technical services units in its domestic establishment. (See Chart 5.) The latter represent the various communications media—radio broadcasting (Voice of America), television, motion pictures, and newspapers and other publications. There are six regional offices, headed by Assistant Directors. Five parallel the geographic bureaus of the State Department—Africa, Europe, Latin America, Near East and South Asia, and Far East. The sixth deals with the Soviet Union and Eastern Europe. These regional Assistant Directors are responsible for information policies and programs in their areas, including the operations of the United States Information Service posts. They are the major link between the official policies developed in the State Department and their implementation abroad by the various information media.

Overlapping Functions and Responsibilities

The overseas information and cultural exchange programs are marked by the same overlapping and intermixing of organizational powers, responsibilities, and relationships that characterize the rest of the foreign policy organization. The Department of State has a Bureau of Public Affairs, headed by an Assistant Secretary, which is responsible for the Department's own news and information activities, including relations with the news media, press conferences, relations with various public groups concerned with foreign policy, and studies of domestic public and press opinion.

The Bureau of Public Affairs also provides foreign policy guidance for those governmental information functions carried on outside the Department, including those of the Information Agency. Furthermore, as noted in Chapter 5, officials of all government agencies are required by presidential directive to clear in advance with the Department of State any statements, speeches, articles, or books with foreign policy implications. The Bureau of Public Affairs coordinates this clearance process within the State Department. This directive is usually honored, though at times grudgingly. Of course, an official may not see or choose not to see foreign policy implications in his statement.

The public affairs function is decentralized in the Department through the presence of Public Affairs Advisers (sometimes with one or more assistants) on the staffs of each of the geographic bureaus and several of the functional bureaus (for example, Economic Affairs). These officials are "housed" with the geographic or functional units to which they are assigned but are also in close contact with their public affairs colleagues in the other bureaus as well as with Bureau of Public Affairs officers.

The United States Information Agency is linked to the units that formulate foreign policy, including the Department of State, in a number of ways. Indeed, it is widely stated in Washington that there is now a more satisfactory relationship between those who perform the information function and those who are responsible for foreign policy than existed when the former operated as a unit within the State Department. The practice of inviting the Director of the Information Agency to attend National Security Council meetings on a regular basis has already been mentioned. At present, the Director attends the regular morning staff meetings of the Secretary of State. He also sits on a number of important interdepartmental committees in addition to the National Security Council, including the Youth Committee and the Special Group (Counter-Insurgency). The Information Agency is also represented on regional foreign policy committees, like those for Latin America and Africa.

The high-level policy officials of the Information Agency have a well-established relationship with the Bureau of Public Affairs. In addition, Agency officials with regional policy responsibilities often are invited to attend the regular staff meetings of the corresponding geographic bureaus or offices in the State Department. Officials of both the USIA and the Department of State report that enough mutual respect and confidence have developed to allow considerable operating freedom for the Information Agency. It can thus take prompt action in line with known or predictable positions of the Department.

The organizational and personnel relationships of the cultural and information programs, both in Washington and in the field, also illustrate the pattern of overlap and intermixture. For example, the Director of the Information Agency is charged with overall coordination of the President's Special Fund, which supports United States participation in international trade fairs (actually carried out by the Department of Commerce) and such cultural activities as the sending of American artists, musicians, orchestras and theatrical productions overseas (a responsibility of State's Bureau of Educational and Cultural Affairs). While this authority is apparently largely *pro forma,* it puts the Director in a position of overall responsibility for programs actually carried out by the State and Commerce Departments.

Overseas, there are also some interesting examples. While the Bureau of Educational and Cultural Affairs has major responsibility for cultural exchange, the Information Agency runs one of the most important aspects of United States cultural relations with other nations, the United States Information Service libraries. In the overseas missions, the same official serves as head of the United States Information Service and as Public Affairs Officer (PAO) of the embassy. The Public Affairs Officers and their staffs are usually Foreign Service personnel recruited by and responsible to the United States Information Agency although they are at the same time under the general authority and control of the Ambassador. They are members of the Information Agency's personnel system and usually work for the Agency when rotated back to Washington.

In the smaller missions, the Public Affairs Officer may handle both the cultural and information activities carried on in his country. In most countries, however, he usually has a Cultural Affairs Officer (CAO) serving under him, and sometimes, in the larger countries, a separate Public Information Officer. While the Cultural Affairs Officers are for the most part Information Agency career officers, their work overseas is primarily on behalf of programs of the Bureau of Educational and Cultural Affairs.

The Information Agency does have a small staff that maintains close liaison with the Educational and Cultural Affairs Bureau. The latter's professional staff usually includes as many as thirty or more officers on detail to the Department of State from the Information Agency, as well as some Foreign Service Officers and a large number of Civil Service employees of the State Department. The second-ranking official of the Educational and Cultural Affairs unit during the first few years of its existence was a former deputy director of the Information Agency.

Information Agency officers are also regularly detailed to the public affairs staffs in the State Department. At any one time, there may be as many as ten or a dozen so assigned. Some of the State Department's own public affairs officers do have previous USIA work experience. There has also been some opportunity for Foreign Service Officers to serve a tour of duty with the Information Agency. Interchange in both directions, overseas as well as in Washington, is expected to increase with the integration of USIA career reserve officers into the regular Foreign Service.

The overseas information and cultural exchange programs provide a rather interesting microcosmic view of some of the more general problems and patterns that characterize the foreign policy organization. During the years in which the cultural and information activities have been pursued, now conjointly, now independently, and sometimes in uneasy liaison, the information activities have tended to overshadow the cultural efforts, at least in size of budgets and prominence of operations. In recent years, however, there has been a steady upswing in emphasis on cultural exchange. If this continues, it will be interesting to see what, if any, organizational adjustments are made to match the change in substantive emphasis.[15]

Major Problems

The present accepted official view is that economic development programs must be put on a long-term basis and that each country going through this process must be looked at as a whole, in terms of its own particular resources and needs, with its development planned and supported accordingly. This is one of the responsibilities of the Agency for International Development.[16] A related concern of the agency has been to refine the criteria in terms of which the United States provides economic assistance to various countries, including the point at which the countries assisted can move ahead on their own with little or no help from the United States.

[15] For an overview of the total U. S. governmental effort directed at "the minds of men," see the useful study prepared recently by the Legislative Reference Service of the Library of Congress for the Subcommittee on International Organizations and Movements of the House Foreign Affairs Committee, *The U.S. Ideological Effort: Government Agencies and Programs,* 88 Cong. 1 sess. (1964).

[16] The Agency's work in this field is discussed in greater detail in Chap. 10. The expanded research program of AID is noted in Chap. 8, and the organization of its field missions is discussed in Chap. 9.

The Administrator of the development agency has also assumed the responsibilities for overall control and guidance of the foreign aid or mutual security program previously performed on behalf of the Secretary of State by the Under Secretary of State for Economic Affairs. Thus, he has a combination of powers and responsibilities in the aid field that no official has had since military assistance and, then, technical and economic assistance to the underdeveloped areas, became important additions to and eventually replacements for the original program of economic assistance to Western Europe.

While the Agency for International Development is formally a part of the Department of State and its Administrator is responsible to the Secretary of State, a heavily burdened Secretary of State is unlikely to be in a position to exercise any more detailed control over him than over the formally independent Director of the United States Information Agency.

Basic to both policy agreement and effective direction at the top are close working relationships among the Secretary of State, the AID Administrator, and the Information Agency Director. Since the Secretary of State must look to these men for high-level policy advice in their particular fields and for the detailed implementation of programs in the spirit of policies agreed upon, anything but such relationships would seem to be intolerable from his point of view. On the other hand, if mutual confidence can be established, it can also be assumed that a very busy and harried Secretary will rely substantially on these men for the detailed performance in their own program areas.

The prescription for highest-level coordination of policies and programs is a relatively simple one, however difficult it may be to achieve in particular circumstances. Complications multiply as one moves down the hierarchy to the working-level officials, if only because of the numbers of people involved and because authority relationships are rather unclear, both formally and operationally. In the final resort, the Secretary of State is the boss in his relationship to the AID Administrator; State Department office directors and desk officers, however, do not have the same relationship to their opposite numbers in AID. There is one partial exception, which is discussed below.

Differences are bound to develop among the economic-development, politico-diplomatic, information, cultural, military, intelligence, and other officials concerned with United States policies and programs

within a particular country or region. These may be based on differing policy and program priorities, on differing agency or professional perspectives, on differing sets of data or differing interpretations,
on sensitivity about agency prerogatives, or on specific personality
conflicts. To some extent, the source is irrelevant. The question is how
to resolve these differences with minimum cost either in the quality of
work performed or in getting the job done.[17]

At this point, it may be appropriate to comment specifically on
working relationships between economic aid officials and their opposite numbers in the State Department geographic bureaus; these are
particularly important and sometimes particularly troublesome. The
differences in agency perspectives and concerns are such that the
difficulties are probably unavoidable, perhaps rightfully so.

In certain situations there seems to be an inevitable tension between short-term political objectives and long-range economic goals,
between political and military security and economic growth. How one
strikes the balance is a question about which honest and able men may
differ. As was suggested in a broader context in Chapter 5, these
differences do not always have to be settled in favor of the State Department or short-range political considerations. What may help in
their resolution is a clearer and deeper reciprocal understanding at all
organizational levels of the premises on which these differences are
based.

When the Department of State moved into the greatly expanded
quarters that had been added to the New State Department Building, much of the staff of the International Cooperation Administration
moved into the building from previously scattered locations in Washington. The top echelons of the Agency for International Development, the staffs of the four regional bureaus, and most of AID's other
operating units are now located in new, New State.

The physical contiguity provided by being housed in the same
rather massive building does not, however, seem to provide a sufficient
basis for furthering the desired understanding and closer working relations. At the time the Agency for International Development was
being established, thought was given to the notion of combining the

[17] Recent developments relevant to this problem are discussed in Chap. 9, particularly in the section titled "Supporting Organizational Arrangements in Washington."

geographic units of AID with their opposite numbers in State. Another less radical proposal was that they be located in the same or adjoining office suites while maintaining their separate organizational identities. This was referred to as a "back-to-back" arrangement. While nothing came of the proposal to combine units, the "back-to-back" concept was actually implemented in the case of the State Department's Bureau of Inter-American Affairs and the Agency for International Development's Latin American bureau (the Alliance for Progress staff).

In the spring of 1964, the geographic office units of these two bureaus were combined. A larger number of geographic offices were established, with each responsible for fewer countries. While most of the office directors were State Department Foreign Service Officers, some did come from AID. Where the ranking office personnel were from the State Department, AID officials were made deputy directors or, perhaps, assistant directors for economic development matters.[18]

It is too early to assess the results of this organizational innovation, prompted perhaps by the continuing eagerness of the U.S. government to show results in the Alliance for Progress. As formally delineated in an organization chart, it looks extremely clumsy and complicated. No doubt the same can be said about the previous arrangement of parallel but separate units in the two agencies.

Some who view long-term economic development assistance as a key tool of U. S. foreign policy in the less-developed countries have been concerned that the commitment to it may be smothered within such a combined organization. In this view, separate organizations are necessary to maintain the integrity and independence of the development perspective. I would argue that whatever happens to the Alliance for Progress over the next few years will not be an inevitable consequence of the new organizational arrangements, which represent one way to deal with the fact of very closely related responsibilities carried out by separate organizational units.

Clearly, organizational changes, no matter how daring, cannot assure the desired changes in perspective and depth of understanding. Whatever their precise organizational relationship to the Agency for International Development, State Department officials must be interested in and knowledgeable about the planning and programming

[18] For an account of these developments and a diagrammatic presentation of the new organization, see *Department of State News Letter*, No. 36 (April 1964), pp. 6-7.

of economic and technical assistance in the countries for which they have some responsibility. At the same time, development officials must be sensitive to noneconomic problems and to the urgencies of immediate political relations—while prepared to resist them if this seems appropriate.

This line of reasoning has implications for the staffing of some of the State Department desks and offices in Washington and the missions overseas. It suggests one area in which greater flexibility in the assignment of personnel and in career management systems might prove extremely useful: namely, detailing officers from the economic development agency to country desks in State and, similarly, assigning Foreign Service Officers to duty with economic development units either at home or in the field. The latter is already taking place; aside from the occasional lateral entry of aid officials into the Foreign Service, the first is not.

It should be acknowledged in conclusion that much of the foregoing discussion is generally applicable to relationships between the officials of other program agencies and State Department officers. Because of the critical role that economic and technical assistance often plays in U.S. policy toward the countries of the less developed world, the AID-State relationships seem particularly worthy of comment.

8

Science and Foreign Policy

THE TERM "SCIENCE" has a wide variety of usages and meanings. It refers to a general method by which reliable, verified knowledge about the world is systematically gathered and utilized. It may denote bodies of knowledge and fields of study that have been built up through use of this method, ranging from the well established natural sciences, the so-called "hard" sciences, to the still somewhat uncertain and suspect newcomers, the social sciences or "soft" sciences. In the more general and popular usage, reference to the natural, or more narrowly, the physical, sciences is usually intended.

The term may refer to the skills, attitudes, values, and perspectives supposedly developed in the practice of the scientific method or at least attributed to those who have demonstrated mastery in one of the scientific fields of knowledge. It may refer to the individuals who are practitioners in all or some of these fields, to their research facilities and organizations, or perhaps to some of their professional associations. Finally, "science" in a governmental context may be a label for those government agencies or subagency units whose functions and programs rest very largely on scientific research and development, like the Atomic Energy Commission or the National Aeronautics and Space Administration.

All of these usages of the term serve some purpose, and a number of them will be employed in this chapter. Hopefully, the particular connotation that is intended in each instance will be made clear. Since it is the swift rate of development in the physical sciences and their technological applications that have had and continue to have such

217

important implications in both the military and foreign policy fields, it is the physical sciences that will provide the major focus of attention.

Bases for Evaluation

The close relationship between the physical and other natural sciences, engineering, and mathematics on the one hand and national military capabilities on the other is widely recognized and reasonably well understood. The relationship of these fields to foreign policy problems, insofar as these are distinguished from military problems, is somewhat less obvious. Indeed, the connection was remote in the eyes of many until the past few years, when the complex questions of arms control and disarmament moved closer to the center of the world political stage. To the problems of arms control, however, can be added others: the opening efforts in the exploration of outer space, the challenges involved in the productive and imaginative application of Western science and technology to the needs of the underdeveloped countries, and the various programs for international scientific cooperation and for the exchange of scientific assistance and information, nonmilitary as well as military.[1] Clearly, the foreign policy organization needs scientific advice, and there are "scientific" agencies within the government with a role to play in foreign policy making.

It therefore becomes necessary to evaluate the performance of scientific advisers and "scientific" agencies in the foreign policy process. The relevant bases for judgment are familiar ones. First are the quality of the scientific personnel involved and the quality of the scientific advice offered, as these would be judged by their scientific peers. There are also the questions of the appropriate role for these individuals and agencies in the policy process, and what their relationship should be to the foreign affairs agencies, particularly the Department of State. Finally, since the functions, skills, and interests of a number of impor-

[1] The long-term nonmilitary aspects of "science and foreign policy" are very usefully surveyed in *Possible Nonmilitary Scientific Developments and their Potential Impact on Foreign Policy Problems of the United States*, Stanford Research Institute study for the Senate Committee on Foreign Relations, 86 Cong. 1 sess. (1959). See also the penetrating essay by Caryl P. Haskins, "Technology, Science and American Foreign Policy," *Foreign Affairs*, Vol. 40 (January 1962), pp. 224-43.

tant governmental agencies are involved, the reciprocal attitudes of the personnel of these organizations and their capacity to understand the special language and point of view of the others are particularly important.[2]

If a physical scientist is operating within the governmental structure as an administrative official with formal responsibilities for a set of policies, programs, and specific activities, his job is in general terms no different from that of any other governmental administrator, and he can be evaluated accordingly. However, when one moves into the realm of the scientist as expert and adviser, the problem of analysis tends to become cloudier. Fortunately, there are relevant guidelines that can be derived from the study of the role of the professional soldier in military and foreign policy making, a problem that has received considerable attention during the past fifteen or twenty years.[3]

An Appropriate Role for the Scientist and the Scientific Agencies

An official participating in the processes of foreign policy making in an expert, advisory capacity is presumably contributing certain special skills or bodies of information necessary to the foreign policy officials but not possessed by them. From the point of view of role definition, it makes no difference whether the expert is a member of an agency or comes from outside of it. The essential and often difficult problem is to be clear about the nature of his expertise and self-conscious about its boundaries, so that when he begins to advise on matters that lie beyond these boundaries his advice can be put into perspective.

This is not just an academic concern. In the complex questions of foreign policy or national security policy, it is quite important to recognize when the expert, whether he be a member of the Joint Chiefs of Staff or an outstanding physical scientist, is moving beyond his field of special skill and knowledge. His ideas in other fields may, indeed, be

[2] This choice of problems and criteria is selective. The broader relations of the scientific community and the government, with particular but not exclusive reference to military research and development, are brilliantly discussed in Don K. Price, *Government and Science* (New York University Press, 1954).

[3] See the discussion in Chap. 6.

quite worthwhile (or, on the other hand, worthless), but they are in any event entitled to no special deference as reflecting expert views.[4]

Nothing sinister is being implied here. It is not to be expected that able men, with great energy and strong views, are always going to be self-conscious about these boundary lines themselves and highly disciplined and circumspect about indicating when they sense they are moving across them. A staff study by the first Jackson subcommittee put it more bluntly:

> Scientists often have strong opinions about the morality or political utility of developments in the laboratory. They are not exempt from the human tendency to allow these beliefs to color their technical judgments, and to become ardent pleaders for special causes. A President needs as much sales resistance in science and technology as anywhere else.[5]

There is no neat organizational or other solution to this problem.

---

[4] The problem of expert knowledge is by no means as simple as these comments imply. While an extended analysis is not necessary for present purposes, a few basic points are worth noting. For one thing military and scientific "expertness" cannot and should not be blithely equated although some of their problems are roughly parallel. Some military expertness represents the seasoned judgment and experience of the professional but does not necessarily rest on a scientifically derived body of theory and principle. Other military views—for example, on the comparative effectiveness of weapons systems—may represent the result of considerable testing and research fully scientific in spirit and method.

On the other hand, some scientific theories and fields of knowledge are more tentative and less solidly based than others. There are also important scientific and technological questions on which distinguished scientists disagree, or on which they are frank to admit that they do not have reliable answers.

These uncertainties about the nature and extent of both military and scientific expertness underscore the need to keep both groups "honest" in their policy-making and policy-advising roles.

[5] "Science Organization and the President's Office," in *Organizing for National Security*, Vol. 3 (1961), Staff Reports and Recommendations submitted to the Senate Government Operations Committee by its Subcommittee on National Policy Machinery, p. 80. This seven-page document contains a great deal of useful commentary on both the substantive and organizational aspects of science in national security policy making. Its recommendation that the work of the President's Science Adviser be expanded into a full-fledged Office of Science and Technology was apparently the basis for that change, made by President Kennedy in the spring of 1962.

The hearings on "Science, Technology, and the Policy Process" in *ibid.*, Vol. 1, pp. 237-411, represent another very useful contribution to this problem by the Jackson subcommittee.

As was suggested a number of years ago with regard to the role of military "experts" in foreign policy making,[6] the following seem essential for a healthy situation: a self-consciousness about these roles and boundaries on the part of all concerned; a certain amount of discipline and self-restraint by the experts; and, finally, a solidly-based confidence on the part of the foreign policy makers which will encourage them to take issue and argue vigorously on matters where there is no well-established and generally accepted scientific evidence. Given the long experience with the military since the Second World War and given a world where with each succeeding day the solid bases of professional expertise in military, scientific, and other fields become increasingly shaky, this last requirement should now be less difficult to meet. Of course, it is easier to challenge the expert or realize that he has left his area of expertise behind if you have some reasonable grasp of the nature and substance of his expert knowledge.[7]

[6] See Burton M. Sapin and Richard C. Snyder, *The Role of the Military in American Foreign Policy* (Doubleday, 1954), particularly Chaps. IV and V.

[7] Robert Gilpin takes a somewhat different view of this problem in his study, *American Scientists and Nuclear Weapons Policy* (Princeton University Press, 1962). On p. 15, he comments that the "advice of experts to the policy-maker, including that of scientists, is seldom if ever solely technical. While the advice generally appears quite technical, careful analysis of its substance will reveal it to be political in nature." Furthermore, the higher the governmental level at which the advice is provided, the more this is likely to be the case. Gilpin feels that this is inevitable, however, and that it is impossible for the scientist-adviser to disentangle the technical and nontechnical (that is, political or normative) strands of the advice he is giving. He does agree that one of the fundamental difficulties in the nuclear weapons policy field has been a failure on the part of those involved— the scientists providing the advice, their interested scientific colleagues, and the responsible political officials receiving the advice—to recognize this intermixture of scientific truth and policy "wisdom."

In other words, Gilpin recognizes the problem posed here and some of its troublesome policy consequences but does not think it possible for the scientist-advisers, or their political clients, to differentiate clearly and precisely between the scientific and nonscientific elements in their advice. He does propose some remedial measures including conscious use of scientist-advisers with differing viewpoints on problems and a more widespread use of scientific advice throughout the government. He agrees that the government needs people who can bridge the intellectual gap between the scientists and the responsible political leaders and that scientist-advisers must become more self-conscious about the nature, limits, and possible burdens of the advisory role. For a more detailed presentation of Gilpin's views, see *American Scientists and Nuclear Weapons Policy*, particularly Chaps. I and X.

Among the scientific agencies, the activities of the Atomic Energy Commission (AEC) and the National Aeronautics and Space Administration (NASA) have the most important international aspects and implications. Outer space and its exploration are already subjects on the United Nations agenda. Tracking stations to follow the flights of the various space vehicles must be located in certain foreign countries; a number already are. These involve formal agreements with the host countries.[8]

Usually, foreign sensitivities are not as disturbed by these installations as by military bases, but this is not always the case. The granting of independence to Zanzibar by Great Britain and the violent overthrow of the government shortly thereafter, in early 1964, drew considerable attention to the presence of a Project Mercury tracking station on that faraway island. Indeed, the station was soon closed by the United States at the request of the new Zanzibar government.

The Atomic Energy Commission is involved in growing programs of exchange of information and provision of materials and equipment in the field of peaceful uses of the atom. There is in existence an International Atomic Energy Agency as well as EURATOM, the European Atomic Energy Community. There are international conferences and exhibitions on the peaceful uses of atomic energy. There is also the vital military side of the atom, which ranges all the way from exchange of information and provision of nuclear weapons to selected allies to international negotiations on various aspects of disarmament and arms control (which in turn run the gamut from nuclear test cessation to total disarmament).

These agencies have an important concern with certain foreign policy decisions and a legitimate role to play in the making and implementation of these decisions. As always, the difficult questions are those of precise delineation: what are the specific areas of legitimate concern and how extensive should policy-making participation be with regard to them? It has been suggested in the three previous chapters that it is difficult if not impossible to draw clear-cut boundaries between the con-

[8] For example, as of January 1965, there were U.S. stations in Australia, Bermuda, the Canary Islands, Canton Island, the Malagasy Republic, Mexico, Nigeria, and Spain in connection with the NASA manned flight program. For more details on NASA's international activities, see the summary pamphlet periodically prepared by its Office of International Affairs—National Aeronautics and Space Administration, *International Affairs*, January 1965.

cerns of the Department of State and those of the other foreign affairs agencies. On a smaller scale, the same can be said here.

AEC and NASA officials have been known to grumble about the constraints imposed upon some of their international activities by the requirement to clear these with the State Department or, at other times, to wait for the State Department to initiate action on them. On the other hand, responsible State Department officers occasionally bemoan the lack of foreign policy sophistication on the part of these agencies. Indeed, some have been heard to comment to the effect that scientists are far more difficult to deal with than the military.

If the State Department is to discharge its responsibility for foreign policy leadership, all official international activities of other governmental agencies must operate within the foreign policy guidelines it has established. This means little in the case of a branch office of the Veterans Administration in Paris, has some implications for the varied foreign activities of the Department of Health, Education and Welfare, and may mean a great deal in the international activities of the AEC and NASA. While such agencies as AEC and NASA must understand the broader ramifications of American foreign policy, and the relationship of their particular programs to it, the Department of State in turn must demonstrate a sensitivity to the particular needs and problems of these agencies in their international activities.

These organizational requirements carry with them some familiar implications for personnel. Briefly, at the many points in contemporary foreign policy where politico-diplomatic, scientific, and military factors intersect, there must be available to the agencies involved personnel well-trained and highly skilled in one of these areas and at the same time capable of grasping the essential viewpoints and perspectives of the others. These kinds of people are no doubt hard to come by, but this cannot be sufficient excuse for ignoring the need. Perhaps as scientific and engineering institutions like MIT and Carnegie Tech turn their attention to the expanding interrelations between science and politics, personnel with the necessary training and breadth will become increasingly available.[9]

[9] Since the end of World War II, these and other major scientific and engineering institutions have given increasing attention to the social sciences (and to the humanities as well). In addition to expanded teaching programs, they have sponsored substantial social science research units. Furthermore, MIT, as an example, now offers a doctorate in both economics and political science.

Present Organizational Arrangements

Although there is a long history of scientists working for the government and of government sponsorship of scientific research, dating back at least to the establishment of the land-grant colleges during the Civil War, physical scientists and mathematicians emerged as a vital asset in the furthering of governmental programs and a major force in governmental policy councils during the Second World War. Their major role during this war was in the military field, and this continues to be true today.

They have been heavily involved in the conception, development, and production of new weapons systems, and in the application of scientific, mathematical, and statistical methods and techniques to the analysis and solution of strategic and tactical military problems (what has come to be known as operations research). The close linking of the military with certain fields of science and engineering has a long historical tradition behind it. As manifested in the vital field of military research and development, the intimate collaboration of military establishments and contemporary science and technology explains much of the character of the present arms race and, with the ever-present possibility of new scientific breakthroughs, gives it much of its life-and-death quality.

The governmental machinery for military research and development is in itself a fascinating and complicated subject, worthy of at least a full-length volume. Its broad outlines have been sketched in Chapter 6. It cannot be ignored entirely here, both because its activities have major foreign policy implications and because it is likely to become involved in any substantial research efforts on the peaceful side of the military coin, the "arms control" side.[10]

[10] The military establishment is by far the nation's largest consumer and supporter of scientific and technological research and advice. While most of it is related to the development of weapons systems, there are probably few areas of physical and social science research, basic or applied, that have not been supported at one time or another by military funds. The range of organizations that carry on research for the military is almost as wide as the subjects covered. They include "in-house" facilities like the Army Signal Corps laboratories at Fort Monmouth, autonomous organizations supported primarily by military funds—illustrated most

Scientific Advice at the Presidential Level

At the end of May 1962 a Presidential reorganization plan went into effect that established an Office of Science and Technology within the Executive Office of the President. This new office was the outgrowth of developments that had begun in November 1957 with the appointment of Dr. James R. Killian, Jr., then president of Massachusetts Institute of Technology, as full-time science adviser to the President. The formal title given to Killian's position was Special Assistant to the President for Science and Technology although he was usually referred to as the Science Adviser.

Killian's appointment reflected the deep concern with the pace and quality of Soviet advances in science and technology so impressively dramatized by the launching of Sputnik. While some observers were skeptical about the arrival of yet another presidental staff aide, it was apparently felt that circumstances demanded that the President have available a source of scientific advice free from any narrower departmental connection or concern.

The structure of scientific advice at the presidential level was further bolstered at the same time by the establishment of a Science Advisory Committee reporting directly to the President and including the Science Adviser among its members. A Science Advisory Committee connected with the Office of Defense Mobilization had existed during the Truman Administration, but had fallen into disuse. In 1957, it was resuscitated and established in a much more central position as the President's Science Advisory Committee (PSAC). From the beginning, by the Committee's choice, the Science Adviser served as its chairman. The Committee is, as its name suggests, a part-time group although some of its seventeen nongovernmental members give a great deal of time to its work. They serve by request of the President and co-opt new members for the Committee as present members depart for one reason or another.

In March 1959 President Eisenhower established the Federal Coun-

---

notably by the Air Force-Rand Corporation relationship facilities run exclusively for the armed forces by universities or private business concerns, and, finally, research organizations and academic institutions doing contract work.

cil for Science and Technology. It is composed of the ranking officials, usually Assistant Secretaries, responsible for scientific research programs in the government agencies with major research activities. The Science Adviser was an ex officio member and, again, served as chairman. The Council's role is to provide an overview of the research programs being carried on by the various federal agencies, improve cooperation and coordination among the related ones, and try to identify important research areas that fall between departmental responsibilities and may therefore be neglected. Its effectiveness has been limited, both because it is an interdepartmental committee with no directive authority and because the departmental representatives have varied widely in ability and in their interest in the problem of monitoring and coordinating government scientific research programs.

Rounding out this picture of high-level scientific agencies is the National Science Foundation, established in 1950. It was not only supposed to support basic scientific research and scientific education but, as the Jackson subcommittee staff study notes, was "formally charged with larger responsibilities for developing national scientific policies and evaluating research programs of other agencies." The study goes on to say, reflecting a widely-held judgment, that the Foundation had been reluctant to carry out the latter set of responsibilities and that this gap was being filled—though not on a systematic, across-the-board basis—by the Science Adviser and his staff and the Science Advisory Committee.[11]

The Science Adviser was assisted in carrying out his important and widely varied duties by a small professional staff numbering fewer than a dozen. This staff also provided support for the Science Advisory Committee and its various subcommittees, special panels, and individual consultants, and for the Federal Council. The major fields of policy in which the Science Adviser and his staff were active included military research and development, the disarmament problem, and the vast range of nonmilitary and domestically-oriented scientific activities of the government supposedly under the surveillance of the Federal Council and the National Science Foundation.

To help meet its broad responsibilities, the Science Advisory Committee has a number of regular panels giving attention to certain key policy and scientific research areas. These may run the gamut from missiles and anti-missile defense to oceanography or the problems of

---

[11] "Science Organization and the President's Office," pp. 81 and 82.

international scientific cooperation. Outstanding scientific specialists who are not members of the Committee itself often serve on these panels. In addition, special panels are set up to deal with particular problems, and individual consultants may be called in to give advice in their own fields of very special expertise. While this rather untidy technique of consultation and co-optation has sometimes put a heavy strain on certain very able people who find themselves called upon repeatedly, it does enable the government to seek out, and usually get, first-rate scientific advice on particular problems.

In 1961 the Jackson subcommittee staff study, quoting an unidentified source, gave two concrete examples of the contribution of the Science Adviser, his staff, and the Committee:

> They have been a scientific fire brigade. Two examples: At the outset they helped fill a vacuum created by the lack of a sufficiently strong research and development staff within the Office of the Secretary of Defense, and they still concern themselves with a broad range of problems of military technology. They have also helped offset the failure of the Department of State to secure technical competence adequate for dealing with such problems as arms control, nuclear test cessation, international scientific cooperation, NATO technical problems, and the like.[12]

The Office of Science and Technology established by President Kennedy grew very naturally out of what had preceded it and represented an effort to strengthen and put on a more permanent basis the arrangements developed since 1957. The President's Science Advisory Committee and the Federal Council for Science and Technology were retained. The Office is headed by a Director, assisted by a Deputy Director. The Director has very much the same role as the Special Assistant, acting as personal adviser to the President and at the same time presiding over the modest machinery of scientific advice at the presidential level. The incumbent Special Assistant or Science Adviser, Dr. Jerome B. Wiesner, became the first Director of the Office. The new Office continues to have a very small staff, numbering sixteen or seventeen professionals at this writing.

The Deputy Director should help ease the burdens of a most difficult job and at the same time make available to the President another scientific perspective. More significantly, both the Director and Deputy Director are subject to Senate confirmation and available

[12] *Ibid.*

to testify before congressional committees. The Special Assistants, because they were solely personal aides to the President, were not able to give testimony or provide appropriate scientific advice to the Congress.

The Office of Science and Technology continues to perform the same basic functions: advising on the implications of scientific and technological developments for national policy, and on the impact of governmental policies and programs on scientific research; identifying fields of knowledge in need of expanded research effort; filling gaps in the scientific expertise available to certain agencies, like the State Department and the Arms Control and Disarmament Agency; and, finally, providing a major link between the federal government and the scientific and engineering communities. In addition, it has taken on the function of evaluating for the President (and the Bureau of the Budget, among others) the scientific research plans and programs of other government agencies. As was indicated above, the Science Adviser and his staff and the Science Advisory Committee were already performing this function in part even though it was formally a statutory responsibility of the National Science Foundation.

After more than a half-dozen years of operation under three Presidents and four Science Advisers,[13] it is generally agreed that this somewhat informal machinery of scientific advice at the presidential level has proved its worth. It has filled a vacuum by making available to the President, and certain other executive agencies, a source of highly respectable scientific advice completely divorced from departmental considerations or responsibilities.

"Science" in the Department of State

Since 1951 the Department of State has had a Science Adviser reporting directly to the Secretary. In September 1962 this official and his staff were transformed into the Office of International Science Affairs. In April 1965 this was renamed the Office of International Scientific and Technological Affairs.

A number of well-known physical scientists have held the position

[13] Dr. Killian was succeeded during the Eisenhower Administration by George Kistiakowsky, a Harvard University chemistry professor. Kistiakowsky was in turn followed at the start of the Kennedy Administration by Professor Jerome B. Wiesner of the Massachusetts Institute of Technology. Professor Donald Hornig of Princeton University succeeded Wiesner in January 1964.

of Science Adviser and, now, Director of the new office. From the beginning, a primary responsibility of this office has been the science attaché program, under which U.S. scientists are now serving at sixteen missions abroad as regular members of the embassy staff. (In a few cases, the attachés or their deputies are regular Foreign Service Officers with appropriate background for these positions.) These attachés provide a link to the foreign scientific community; they also make available to the U.S. diplomatic mission professional advice on scientific developments in the host country that may have foreign policy implications.[14]

The general orientation of the State Department's Science Adviser was toward the research activities of the scientific community, primarily the physical and biological sciences, and the various ways in which these affected and were affected by foreign policy. Thus, the Science Adviser's Office cooperated with the National Academy of Sciences in connection with the 1957-58 International Geophysical Year (IGY), facilitating those phases of the IGY program which required formal intergovernmental agreement. It was also actively involved in the Antarctic Treaty, signed in December 1959.[15]

The Science Adviser served as State Department observer on the Science Advisory Committee and the Federal Council for Science and Technology and was chairman of the Council's subcommittee on international science. The Director of the new science office also succeeded to these functions.

Until the spring of 1962 the Science Adviser's office had very little to do with the major problems stemming from the convergence of foreign policy, military policy, and scientific and technological advance—for example, arms control and disarmament, nuclear testing, nuclear-missile weaponry and the NATO alliance, the exploration and uses of outer space, or the peaceful uses of atomic energy. Most of these prob-

---

[14] A useful brief history of the Science Adviser's Office and the science attaché program is provided in *The Science Adviser of the Department of State,* Department of State Publication 7056 (Government Printing Office, 1960). As of March 31, 1965 there were science attaché positions in the U.S. missions to these European nations—France, Germany, Great Britain, Italy, Sweden, Switzerland, and the Soviet Union, plus the special mission to NATO; Brazil and Argentina in Latin America; Australia and Japan in the Far East; Israel and the United Arab Republic in the Near East; and India and Pakistan in South Asia.

[15] *Ibid.,* pp. 14 and 15.

lems were at one time or another the responsibility of a separate staff in the State Department, headed by a Special Assistant for Atomic Energy and Outer Space, who also reported directly to the Secretary.

From the end of Mr. Harold Stassen's tenure as Special Assistant to the President for Disarmament in February 1958 to the establishment of the United States Disarmament Administration as a semi-autonomous unit within the State Department in September 1960, the Special Assistant for Atomic Energy and Outer Space (with a slightly different title) and his staff were responsible for policy making and negotiating in the arms control and disarmament field. He had continuing policy responsibility for the foreign affairs aspects of the peaceful uses of atomic energy as well as its military applications and added the problem of outer space as this became a matter of foreign policy concern and negotiation.

In May 1962 the Office of the Special Assistant for Atomic Energy and Outer Space was abolished and its functions distributed to other units within the State Department. Functions connected with NATO and European regional affairs were assigned to the Bureau of European Affairs, those concerned with the military aspects of atomic energy and outer space to the Politico-Military Affairs staff attached to the Deputy Under Secretary for Political Affairs, and those dealing with certain international organization activities to the Bureau of International Organization Affairs.

Most interesting was the assignment of policy-making and coordinating responsibilities in the fields of peaceful uses of atomic energy and outer space to the Science Adviser. Coming soon after the strengthening of the machinery for scientific advice at the presidential level, it seemed an obvious effort to build up the role of the Science Adviser in the State Department. The latter had never played the kind of role vis-à-vis the Secretary and the rest of the Department that the President's Science Adviser has played for him and the Executive Office. For example, when the Special Assistant for Atomic Energy and Outer Space was responsible for the disarmament problem, he looked elsewhere for the scientific advice and analysis he needed—to the President's Science Adviser and Science Advisory Committee, among others. These new responsibilities provide an opportunity for what has now become the Office of International Scientific and Technological Affairs to enter into some of the main currents of foreign policy making and play a more vigorous and influential role in the Department.

The economic aid program has had from the beginning a strong technical assistance dimension. Even during the period of Marshall Plan aid to Western Europe, there was considerable interest in improving industrial productivity. Beginning with the Point Four program, this has been a fundamental part of aid to the underdeveloped countries. The rosters of the aid missions abroad run the gamut from highway and sanitary engineers and experts on automobile maintenance and diesel locomotives to entomologists, horticulturists, and advisers on community development.

The aid program has been criticized, however, for not making more imaginative use of the physical and social sciences *per se,* both in terms of illuminating the nature of the development or modernization process and of adapting available knowledge and methods more effectively to the needs of the countries being aided. In 1961 this kind of development research activity was proposed by the Kennedy Administration on the basis of the recommendations of a development assistance panel of the President's Science Advisory Committee and has now become a part of the program of the Agency for International Development. Within the Agency's Office of Technical Cooperation and Research, there is an Office of Research and Analysis headed by a Science Director.

The required research was described in the following terms in the summary of the Act for International Development for fiscal year 1962:

> The basic purpose of [the] research is to develop new techniques and tools to broaden the choices available to the decision makers.
> The three principal areas in which research will be undertaken are (a) techniques for developing both the human and natural resources of the less developed countries; (b) the adaptation of available technology to the conditions in those countries; and (c) the nature of the relationship between economic and social changes.
> . . . .
> Examples of research include explorations into better ways of improving such things as electric power facilities, transport, health, education, land redistribution, private investment, and personnel training in less developed countries.[16]

[16] *Highlights of President Kennedy's New Act for International Development,* Department of State Publication 7211 (Government Printing Office, 1961), pp. 35-36.

AEC and NASA

The role of the atom in contemporary world affairs explains the substantial involvement of the Atomic Energy Commission in decision making on certain aspects of foreign policy and military policy. As the uses and implications of atomic energy have become increasingly international in scope, the five-member Commission and its large professional staff have become increasingly involved in the national security policy arena.

The Commission is represented on the United States Intelligence Board, the ranking governmental body in the intelligence field. It is also a major participant in disarmament policy making. The chairman of the Commission sits on the Committee of Principals, the senior policy-making body in the arms control and disarmament field.

One of the Commission's Assistant General Managers is responsible for international activities; a Division of International Affairs helps perform this function. While this unit does play a general coordinating role in the foreign affairs field, all the international programs and activities of the Commission do not funnel through it. Technical divisions of the Commission's staff with international dimensions to their programs tend to deal directly with the Department of State and other foreign policy agencies. The Commissioners, as individuals or as a body, sometimes get directly involved in problems related to foreign policy.

As a governmental organization, the Atomic Energy Commission has some rather distinctive characteristics: the special and very close relationship with the powerful congressional Joint Committee on Atomic Energy; the relations between the five Commissioners with main offices in Washington, D.C., and the professional staff located twenty-five miles away in Germantown, Maryland (with visits by the Commissioners to Germantown something of a rarity); the relationships and division of labor among the Commissioners themselves; and, finally, the role of the President vis-à-vis the Commission and in the making of governmental policy in the atomic energy field. These characteristics can only be mentioned rather than explored. Obviously, they have implications for the nature of AEC's participation in the foreign policy process.

The major points of contact for the Commission within the State Department are provided by the Politico-Military Affairs staff attached to the Deputy Under Secretary for Political Affairs and the Office of International Scientific and Technological Affairs. In the Defense Department, a key figure is the Assistant to the Secretary of Defense for Atomic Energy. At the presidential level, members of the staffs of the Special Assistant for National Security Affairs and the Office of Science and Technology follow atomic energy problems.

As another reflection of its expanding role in international affairs, the Commission has begun to send its own scientific representatives abroad on regular assignments. There are now Atomic Energy Commission officials resident in Tokyo, London, Paris, and Buenos Aires. In addition, there are representatives in Brussels (seat of the European Atomic Energy Community), who are attached to the U.S. Mission to the European Communities, and in Vienna, as part of the U.S. Mission to the International Atomic Energy Agency. This program of AEC representation overseas is completely separate from the State Department's science attaché program.

The National Aeronautics and Space Administration has not yet started to send representatives abroad, but it also has been increasingly involved in international affairs. The idea of establishing a Space Council to help develop national policy in this field originated with Congress and was opposed by the executive. Despite this opposition, the Council was established in the National Aeronautics and Space Act of 1958, and Presidents Eisenhower and Kennedy both attempted to make use of it.

Its full name is the National Aeronautics and Space Council, and it is, at least formally, the ranking governmental policy-making body in the field of space exploration and space vehicles. Its statutory membership consists of the President, the Secretary of State, the Secretary of Defense, the Administrator of NASA, the Chairman of the Atomic Energy Commission, the Director of the National Science Foundation, the President of the National Academy of Sciences, plus two private citizens. This last requisite gives it a rather distinctive character as governmental policy bodies go. During the Eisenhower Administration, the President's Science Adviser sat in on the meetings of this Council although he is not a statutory member.

The Space Council had very little time to establish itself as a working body under the Eisenhower Administration. Given the interests and energy of his Vice President, Mr. Kennedy made an interesting adaptation. He asked Lyndon Johnson to assume the chairmanship of the Council. As a Senator, Johnson had evidenced a strong interest in defense and space matters. He had served on the Armed Services Committee, chaired its Preparedness Investigating Subcommittee, and chaired the new Aeronautical and Space Sciences Committee when it was established. Mr. Johnson was provided with office space in the Executive Office Building. A military affairs specialist with long service on Capitol Hill, including a considerable period as ranking aide to Senator Stuart Symington, was appointed executive secretary to the Council. It will be interesting to follow the development of the Space Council with Mr. Johnson as President.

The statutory members of the Council have followed the presidential lead and have usually been represented at Council meetings by ranking subordinates. At present, for example, the Deputy Under Secretary for Political Affairs represents the Department of State. While the Council would be a logical forum for the discussion of major foreign policy aspects of the use and exploration of outer space and of Space Administration activities that call for international negotiations or arrangements, it has apparently not yet assumed such a role in any continuing or effective fashion. Important decisions in this field tend to be made in other forums, often at *ad hoc* meetings of the principals involved.

The space agency itself has an Office of International Programs, attached directly to the Office of the Administrator, which deals on a day-to-day basis with NASA's international activities and with those officials with related responsibilities in the State Department and elsewhere. A number of the top officials of the Space Administration have been involved in aspects of foreign policy making. The Administrator himself is a member of the disarmament Committee of Principals. The Deputy Administrator has played a key role in some of the discussions and negotiations regarding outer space at the United Nations, including the limited agreement reached with the Soviet Union in December 1962 for cooperative efforts in space.[17]

[17] See the *New York Times,* Dec. 7, 1962.

Arms Control and Disarmament

However optimistic one may be, it is a little difficult to visualize a happy ending for the contemporary arms race if it continues along present lines. It is probably this simple truth that gives a continuing broad and powerful appeal to the notions of effective arms control and substantial disarmament, no matter how discouraging the prospects and how fundamental the obstacles. Even the fantastic arms bill of well over $100 billion a year to the nations of the world would apparently be acceptable if the road did not seem to point so clearly to eventual disaster.

Disarmament and arms control negotiations have gone through a number of phases since World War II, as have the governmental units and personnel responsible for them.[18] After the failure of the immediate postwar efforts for international control of atomic energy, the United States and its Western allies, and the Soviet Union as well, evidenced little serious interest in disarmament or arms control agreements until 1955. Changes in Soviet attitudes became evident as early as mid-1954 but were not translated into more concrete terms until early 1955. From the United States point of view, the modification of policy and approach is usually linked to the appointment of Harold Stassen as Special Assistant to the President for Disarmament in March 1955.

Governor Stassen's three-year tenure was stormy and eventful although, in the end, it produced no arms control agreements with the Soviets. Politically and organizationally, it was noteworthy for several reasons. While there were elements of ambiguity in his position, Stassen was given Cabinet rank. For the first time, the ranking disarmament official of the government not only had direct access to the President but also sat in the Cabinet. Stassen's staff was small by Washington standards—numbering fifty-two including both secretarial and

[18] Bernhard G. Bechhoefer has provided an authoritative account of the negotiations in the period 1946-60 and some useful comments on the relevant U.S. governmental machinery in *Postwar Negotiations for Arms Control* (Brookings Institution, 1961).

professional personnel[19]—but it was far larger than any previous group assigned to disarmament policy making and negotiation. Such groups had always consisted—literally—of a handful of people. Stassen also initiated a series of task force studies on inspection that represented the first full-scale effort in this field.

Thus, Mr. Stassen's operation represented the most energetic and sustained effort by the United States government up to that time in the disarmament field. Whether it could have accomplished any successful negotiation with the Soviet Union if it had had the full policy backing of the government is a moot question—but, as events proved, it did not have the backing. It is also arguable whether arms control or disarmament agreements with the Soviets at that point in time would have been desirable, but that particular argument must be left to others.

Stassen's eventual "denigration," to borrow Mr. Bechhoefer's term, represents an interesting case study of Eisenhower as president. Mr. Eisenhower had a strong personal commitment to the general notion of disarmament, but he had an even stronger commitment to the day-to-day foreign policy leadership and advice of John Foster Dulles. When the former, as concretely embodied in Stassen and his disarmament negotiations, clashed with the latter, Mr. Dulles was an easy winner. It should also be noted that Mr. Stassen found little support for his disarmament negotiation efforts in either the Defense Department or the Atomic Energy Commission.[20]

Stassen's failure has broader implications. Leaving aside the question of his political and other motivations, the clash of personalities, and the ambiguities of a position as Special Assistant to the President subject at the same time to the policy direction of the National Security Council and the Secretary of State, it is clear that no U.S. disarma-

---

[19] *Ibid.*, p. 261.

[20] For a discussion of Governor Stassen's tenure, see *ibid.*, pp. 241-439; the organizational arrangements are given particular attention on pp. 258-69 and 433-39. The "denigration" of Stassen, during the course of the negotiations in London in 1957, is discussed on pp. 403-13. See also Saville Davis, "Recent Policy Making in the United States Government," *Daedalus*, Vol. 89, No. 4 (Fall 1960), pp. 951-66. Mr. Davis has some interesting comments on Mr. Dulles' role. The volume of *Daedalus* cited—a special issue on arms control—is one of the best collections of material on arms control and disarmament problems in print and has been republished as a book, Donald G. Brennan (ed.), *Arms Control, Disarmament, and National Security* (Braziller, 1961).

ment organization, policy, or negotiation has any chance of success unless it has the strong backing of both the President and the Secretary of State. This is not to imply that such backing will always, or usually, be warranted but simply that nothing can be accomplished without it.

Given the nature of their national defense responsibilities, the views of the military establishment and the Atomic Energy Commission about major disarmament arrangements are almost bound to be skeptical, perhaps even downright hostile. The risks involved are also bound to arouse considerable anxiety and, probably, resistance in the Congress, if an agreement gets that far. Only a handful of legislators like Senator (now Vice President) Hubert Humphrey have given substantial attention and support to American governmental efforts in the arms control and disarmament field.[21]

Mr. Stassen's experience dramatizes a fundamental problem in the disarmament field. The need for strong presidential backing is a familiar requirement in the foreign policy process, but the substantive dilemmas of disarmament, and the political and governmental environment in which these must be faced, make it particularly important in this field.

After Mr. Stassen's departure, the responsibility for disarmament policy and negotiation was shifted to the Office of the Special Assistant to the Secretary of State for Disarmament and Atomic Energy (later, Atomic Energy and Outer Space). On September 9, 1960, the State Department announced the establishment of a United States Disarmament Administration within the Department "to develop and coordinate U.S. policies and activities in the field of arms limitation and control." The disarmament section of the Special Assistant's Office provided the hard core of this new organization; additional personnel were assigned to it from the State Department and elsewhere.

[21] This point is by no means invalidated by the overwhelming Senate approval of the limited nuclear test ban negotiated in August 1963. (The vote, on September 24, was 80 to 19.) For one thing, the agreement itself represented a quite limited kind of arms control, rather than actual reduction of armaments. Furthermore, it was generally assumed that cessation of all but underground tests would be to the overall advantage of the United States rather than the Soviet Union. Finally, it did seem technically possible to monitor continuing Soviet faithfulness to the agreement without on-site inspections within the Soviet Union itself.

In spite of these comforting limitations, there were still strong objections raised and dire predictions made by certain key scientists, ranking military officers (primarily Air Force), and influential legislators.

When President Kennedy took office, he appointed Mr. John J. McCloy as his special assistant for disarmament. While McCloy occupied offices in the quarters of the new Disarmament Administration—indeed, in the suite occupied by the Secretary of State before the latter moved into the new addition to the State Department building—and was considered for all practical purposes to be in charge, he never became its director. McCloy viewed his assignment as short-term, and after he submitted his recommendations and a new agency was established, he departed the scene. (There is no intention to imply that Mr. McCloy did not make a substantial contribution before his departure.)

On September 26, 1961, Mr. Kennedy signed the legislation that brought into being a new Arms Control and Disarmament Agency (ACDA). It grew out of the Disarmament Administration set up in the last months of the Eisenhower Administration and in that sense reflected the deep concern of both presidents with this problem and their desire to make a vigorous effort to do something about it. The Director of the new Agency was made principal adviser to both the Secretary of State and the President on arms control and disarmament matters.

At the same time, the legislation specified that in "carrying out his duties under this Act the Director shall, under the direction of the Secretary of State, have primary responsibility within the Government for arms control and disarmament matters . . ."[22] Within the framework of agreed policy, then, the Director and the Agency have primary responsibility. This includes carrying on the extensive international negotiations that have become a hallmark of the arms control and disarmament field.

To use the phrase of the present Director of ACDA, William C. Foster, the "primary device" for the interagency review and coordination of disarmament policy is, as indicated earlier in the chapter, the so-called Committee of Principals. Its recommendations are made to the President. This body was established in 1958 by President Eisenhower and includes in its membership—in addition to the Director of the Disarmament Agency—the Chairman of the Atomic Energy Commission and the Administrator of the Space Administration, already mentioned, and the Secretaries of State and Defense, the Chairman of the Joint Chiefs of Staff, the Directors of the U.S. Information Agency and

---

[22] *Arms Control and Disarmament Act,* Public Law 87-297, Sec. 22.

the Central Intelligence Agency, and the Presidential Special Assistants for National Security Affairs and Science and Technology. "Negotiations are never undertaken on an important measure until the Committee of Principals has been consulted."[23]

As presently organized, the Agency itself has a Deputy Director, appropriate staff units, and four operating bureaus. The International Relations Bureau is responsible for putting arms control problems into their larger international political setting and for the translation of policies into detailed bases for negotiation. The Science and Technology and Weapons Evaluation and Control Bureaus are, as their names suggest, responsible for bringing scientific and military data and perspectives to bear on arms control and disarmament problems. An Economics Bureau is concerned with the national and international economic implications of possible disarmament arrangements.

There are a number of points to be noted about this latest organizational manifestation of United States concern with the disarmament problem. In the legislation itself, in ACDA's budget and in its actual operations, there is a strong emphasis on research, covering a broad range of both the social and the physical sciences, much of it carried on by agencies outside the government. It indicates clear recognition that the problems of arms control and disarmament are likely to be around for a long time, that many of these problems are highly novel and complex, and that a long-range research program is one meaningful way of trying to grapple with them.

If close working relations with the State Department are a fundamental requirement for the Arms Control and Disarmament Agency, the latter has, at this writing, some built-in advantages. First of all, like the Agency for International Development, the Disarmament Agency is physically located within the State Department building. Indeed, the former fifth floor offices of the Secretary of State and his top aides are now divided between the ranking officials of these two agencies. A common roof by no means guarantees cooperation, but it should facilitate working relationships with the Politico-Military Affairs staff, the Office of International Scientific and Technological Affairs, and the various functional and geographic bureaus whose responsibilities intersect those of the Agency.

[23] *Third Annual Report of the United States Arms Control and Disarmament Agency*, H. Doc. No. 219, 88 Cong. 2 sess. (1964), p. 3.

In addition, a number of Foreign Service Officers and military officers have been assigned to ACDA. The first heads of the Bureau of International Relations and a Disarmament Advisory Staff were high-ranking Foreign Service Officers just back from ambassadorial assignments. A Navy vice admiral was made Assistant Director in charge of the Weapons Evaluation and Control Bureau. He has been succeeded by an Air Force lieutenant general.

Although small by Washington standards, the Arms Control and Disarmament Agency represents the most substantial unit yet established in this field. In December 1963, the Agency's professional staff numbered 126. In his third annual report to the Congress, Director Foster reported that the Agency's appropriation for fiscal year 1963 was $6,500,000, of which almost $4 million was for research.[24]

The United States organization for disarmament does not stop with the President, the arms control agency, the Committee of Principals, and the Department of State. The military establishment has an obvious and fundamental interest. Within the Defense Department, the Office of International Security Affairs has usually had policy responsibilities in the arms control and disarmament field. Since 1959 there has been a Deputy Assistant Secretary of Defense and supporting staff within that Office specifically charged with these responsibilities. Within the Joint Staff, a special staff works on arms control and disarmament problems.

The Atomic Energy Commission's interest in arms control, nuclear testing, and nuclear disarmament is as obvious as that of the military establishment. From the start, it has contributed both policy advice and relevant technical data. Responsibility for its participation has usually rested with a special staff outside its Division of International Affairs.

A discussion of the disarmament organization would be incomplete without further mention of the President's Special Assistant for Science and Technology and the Office he directs, and the President's Science Advisory Committee. Saville Davis argues that it was the appointment

[24] *Ibid.*, pp. 2-3. Since 1963, ACDA's staff has remained about the same size while its appropriations for contract research have been rising. For the fiscal year ending June 30, 1965, ACDA's total staff (clerical as well as professional) numbered 164, and its appropriation for contract research was approximately $5,400,000. See *The Budget of the United States Government for the Fiscal Year Ending June 30, 1966* (Government Printing Office, 1965), Appendix, p. 986.

of Dr. Killian as Science Adviser to the President and the establishment of the Science Advisory Committee in the fall of 1957 that began
to alter the balance of opinion and advice within the government
about the feasibility and desirability of arms control and disarmament
arrangements.

For the first time, the President and the Secretary of State were not
primarily dependent on the scientific advice of the Atomic Energy
Commission and the Defense Department, which have major interests
and responsibilities of their own at stake. The President's Science Adviser and Science Advisory Committee, and the disarmament panel established by the latter, provided the President and the State Department with independent scientific analyses and evaluations not tied to
departmental policies or responsibilities. Apparently, the weight of
these views and recommendations leaned in the direction of seriously
exploring and pursuing international agreements in this field. It was
reported that in the last couple of years of the Eisenhower Administration the line-up on disarmament policy issues was the Defense Department and Atomic Energy Commission on one side, and the State Department, the President's Special Assistant, and the Science Advisory
Committee on the other.[25]

Major Problems

Problems of organization and personnel in the field of disarmament
and arms control reflect broader problems of the foreign policy organization. The importance of the relationship with the Department of
State, and with the other major national security agencies, the key role
of the President, and the need for people whose skills and perspectives
straddle at least two major fields of competence—these are all familiar
themes.

[25] See Saville Davis, *op. cit.*, pp. 957-66. It is not implied that the new views
introduced by the Science Adviser and the Science Advisory Committee involved
a clear confrontation of scientific truth on the one hand and bureaucratic self-
interest, represented by the Defense Department and the Atomic Energy Commission,
on the other. As Gilpin's study makes quite clear, many of the physical scientists
have strong feelings and values as well as relevant knowledge in this field. Gilpin's
conclusion, as noted earlier, is that they have not been able to keep the two
completely separated in their advice on the development or the control of nuclear
weapons. See Robert Gilpin, *American Scientists and Nuclear Weapons Policy*,
cited above.

The establishment of the Arms Control and Disarmament Agency was preceded by considerable discussion about how the arms control and disarmament function could be most effectively organized within the government.[26] This interest was expressed primarily by those who felt that there could and should be more progress in this field and that the relevant governmental machinery should facilitate rather than hinder this progress.

It was generally agreed that the State Department was the logical choice to assume the disarmament function. In addition to its role of foreign policy leadership, it bore the primary responsibility for negotiations and day-to-day contacts with other nations. It also had some important handicaps, however. The Secretary of State was an extremely busy man, and he was unlikely to be in a position to give this policy area the sustained attention it was assumed to require. Furthermore, because the implications and ramifications of disarmament and arms control fall between the foreign policy responsibilities of the State Department and the national defense responsibilities of the military establishment and the Atomic Energy Commission, State could only be on a roughly equal footing with the latter on these questions. Policy making or negotiations with other nations, it was believed, could well bog down in major interdepartmental differences.

Finally, the State Department had practically no scientific capabilities of its own and apparently found it difficult to recruit even the handful of scientists it needed for the United States Disarmament Administration in 1960 and 1961. Only with the assistance of the President's Science Adviser and Science Advisory Committee could it even hope to cope with the great scientific capabilities of the Atomic Energy Commission and the Defense Department. Furthermore, it had been difficult to interest able Foreign Service Officers in this field and keep them in it very long if they were assigned to it.

The weight of this reasoning pointed toward an arms control and disarmament staff located at the presidential level, perhaps in the Ex-

[26] See the Davis article, *op. cit.*, and Bechhoefer, *op. cit.*, pp. 587-97. Senator Hubert Humphrey and the Subcommittee on Disarmament of the Senate Foreign Relations Committee that he chaired were quite interested in the subject. One expression of Humphrey's viewpoint is found in "Government Organization for Arms Control," *Daedalus, op. cit.*, pp. 967-83. Another widely-consulted source is the National Planning Association's Pamphlet No. 109, *Strengthening the Government for Arms Control* (1960).

ecutive Office of the President, with its head reporting directly to the President. Presumably, this would best enlist the President's interest and his backing. If there were significant disagreements within the government, there would be direct access to the President, and he would be in a position to push matters through to some sort of decisive resolution. If there were possibilities for progress in arms control or disarmament, at least they would not be smothered by the bureaucratic opposition.

All of this sounded fine—but what about the sad case of Harold Stassen? Apparently, a direct relationship to the President was no guarantor of organizational or policy effectiveness, and it did not solve the problem of who would actually take charge of the extensive negotiations that must inevitably accompany any major advances in this field.

The legislation establishing the Arms Control and Disarmament Agency dealt with these dilemmas in interesting fashion. The Director of the Agency was made principal disarmament adviser to both the President and the Secretary of State. At the same time, the Director and the Agency were given the responsibility for disarmament negotiations, under the direction of the Secretary of State. In formal terms, the Agency has a direct link to the President and at the same time a relationship with the Secretary of State which gives it the crucial negotiating responsibilities. Furthermore, the legislation enjoins the President to assure the necessary cooperation of the Arms Control Agency, the Defense Department, the Space Administration, the Atomic Energy Commission, and other interested government agencies and to resolve any differences that cannot be resolved through interagency consultation.[27]

It has been the publicly stated view of Presidents Eisenhower, Kennedy, and Johnson that the problems of arms control and disarmament are worth serious attention, no matter how slim the chances of making substantial progress. If this is so, the organization working on these problems needs the kind of backing that will enable it to explore in depth the relevant issues and the possibilities for effective and mutually advantageous arrangements with the Soviets and others. In short, it needs the active interest and support of the President.

Beyond that, one can prescribe close working relations with the

[27] *Arms Control and Disarmament Act,* Public Law 87-297, Sec. 35.

Secretary and the Department of State and with the Atomic Energy Commission and the military establishment. It may be more meaningful to suggest the basic premise on which those relations should rest: disarmament and arms control problems must be analyzed, assessed, and decided upon in the context of broader foreign and military policies. If international arms control and disarmament arrangements become increasingly desirable and likely, the organizations responsible for them will, therefore, have to move much closer to the mainstream of foreign and national security policy making.

The arms control field has often been quite active, particularly insofar as international negotiations are concerned. Because its efforts have not so far had major policy consequences, however, it has tended to be a somewhat remote and esoteric policy field. This cannot continue if and when the issues of arms control and disarmament become more central. They are not a self-contained set of problems; they represent one perspective and one line of attack on some of the basic international political problems of the day.

One risk that an arms control agency runs in the American governmental milieu is that it may be stifled by one or more of the major national security agencies, including the Department of State; the other is that a freewheeling approach to its mandate might ignore the legitimate policy objectives and concerns of these agencies. The lesson of Harold Stassen is that when the policy chips are down, the support of the Secretary of State as well as the President is required. The backing of the Secretary of Defense will not hurt either. There are those in Washington who believe that the present leadership of the Arms Control and Disarmament Agency has not fully absorbed the Stassen lesson and errs in the direction of freewheeling. On the other hand, their assessment may be that the alternative is lack of any movement at all in this field.

The kind of highly specialized and yet broadgauged personnel increasingly required by the foreign policy organization is well illustrated by the arms control and disarmament field. As Mr. Bechhoefer puts it:

> Arms control over the years has come to involve a wide variety of skills. It requires *expertise* in atomic energy and in military strategy and weapons systems, and also in political negotiations with the

Soviet Union, in international organization and, indeed, in the background and the ritual of the arms control negotiations themselves. The experts in a particular skill must also have some aptitude for comprehension of the remaining skills that enter into the successful conduct of an arms control negotiation.[28]

Highly specialized knowledge and training are called for, but so is the ability to think across traditional disciplinary, professional, and departmental boundaries. The physical as well as social sciences will increasingly become an important part of the business of foreign policy. There are already a fair number of scientists sophisticated and perceptive in matters political and diplomatic; given the opportunities available to many scientists, and their interest and motivations, it seems reasonable to assume that many more will be forthcoming.

It is equally important that a cadre of Foreign Service Officers and other foreign policy officials be available who are at least conversant with the concepts and methods of the physical sciences and some of their practical applications in such fields as space exploration, peaceful uses of atomic energy, and military research and development. This should facilitate communication and coordination with "scientific" agencies like the Space Administration and the Atomic Energy Commission and scientific staff units like the presidential Office of Science and Technology. It should also help the foreign policy officials to ask the scientists the right questions and not be overly deferential to assumed scientific expertise in areas where it really does not exist. A certain scientific sophistication on the part of the nonscientists is not merely a means of better understanding the scientists but also of "keeping them honest."[29]

Finally, this kind of cadre should strengthen the staffing of arms control units within the foreign policy organization. While new men and new ideas should always be welcome and are in fact absolutely essential in a frontier field like disarmament, the Foreign Service and the military services need solid personnel resources of their own to meet the requirements of arms control and disarmament organizations.

[28] Bechhoefer, *op. cit.*, p. 590. Emphasis in original.

[29] In this connection, one encouraging recent development was the establishment, beginning in January 1965, of a four-week seminar course at the Foreign Service Institute entitled "Science, Technology and Foreign Affairs." It is open to interested officials from other agencies as well as State Department officers.

9

Field Missions

For purposes of analysis, it is useful to distinguish between foreign policy formulation—the setting of goals and objectives and the choice of general lines of action—and foreign policy implementation—their translation into specific programs, actions, and operations. It should not be assumed, however, that these general functions are represented by separate and distinct organizational entities. Even the distinction between Washington and "the field" is much more complicated than a formulation-implementation dichotomy.

Responsible officials in Washington may make the major policy decisions, but one of their major sources of advice and information in doing so will be U.S. ambassadors, military force commanders, and other ranking officials and their staffs overseas. On the other hand, because policy takes on more precise meaning as it is translated into specific actions and into dollar amounts of programs, implementing actions and detailed programs are decided upon and supervised in Washington with at least as great care as major policy decisions. Many officials in Washington and in the field missions are concerned with the full range of decisions that affect their particular geographic or functional area of responsibility, from major policy choices to more or less routine actions.

In some cases, the detailed execution of policy may embody the most crucial choices of all. One example is Berlin, where a seemingly modest and innocuous incident on the autobahn or in the air corridors between the city and West Germany could signal or even trigger a world crisis of incalculable proportions. Here, the general lines of U.S.

246

policy are quite clear; the major decisions are taken in the tactical choices and maneuvers in day-to-day situations. It is not surprising, therefore, that this particular policy problem receives the continuing attention of top officials not only in this country but in the major Western European capitals.

Policy is implemented at home as well as in the field. Similarly, policy is sometimes developed in the field. Public statements or press briefings released in Washington are designed to influence the actions of foreign governments. Diplomatic representatives of those governments may be called in to discuss particular problems with the State Department while their U.S. opposite numbers abroad are making a similar démarche in the foreign capitals.

Modern transportation and communications contribute to this blurring of the distinction between the making and the carrying out of policy, with results no doubt unfortunate as well as helpful. Ambassadors can be, and often are, instructed in the minutest detail about what they should say tomorrow morning to the foreign minister. In addition, emissaries from Washington often go abroad to carry on particularly sensitive and important negotiations. Technical experts from Washington may, on the other hand, provide a field mission with highly specialized competence and knowledge not usefully located there on a full-time basis. To complete the circle, ambassadors and other senior officials overseas are brought back to Washington periodically on "consultations" so that field views and detailed knowledge of local situations can be fed into the processes of policy making and program planning.

Bases for Evaluation

If the activities of the foreign policy organization do not separate very neatly into policy-formulating and policy-implementing categories, what distinguishing functions can be ascribed to the field missions and what distinguishing requirements can be levied on them?

The policy advice of field missions cannot be determining because, among other reasons, they are not in a position to weigh the elements in their local situations against relevant considerations in other foreign countries and at home. The occupational hazard of the field mission in a foreign country is "localitis." One of the basic functions of agency headquarters in Washington is to put local problems and requirements, as interpreted by the U.S. field missions, into larger regional and worldwide policy contexts.

However, given an established framework of policy, field missions should be the authoritative reporters and interpreters of their local situations. They should be the fundamental sources of advice on: the detailed implications of policy for their particular country at any particular time; what is possible, impossible or inadvisable; the tactics of negotiation and approach; and what lies ahead and how this is likely to affect U.S. interests and objectives.

These are key inputs to the policy-making process. In some circumstances, they may just about determine the kind of decision that will be made. Going beyond this, even in the age of jet aircraft and almost instantaneous communication, there are situations in which events are moving so rapidly that it is simply not possible for Washington to direct U.S. responses by remote control on an hour-by-hour basis. Guided by policy instructions that are as clear and detailed as possible, the man on the scene must be given a certain tactical freedom and discretion. Success or failure for U.S. policy in the particular situation will rest to a very considerable extent on the skill and judgment with which he uses it.

There are many examples of such situations: the Congo from 1960 to the present;[1] South Vietnam in the months before the overthrow of the Diem regime in the fall of 1963 and since then; Laos any time in the last four or five years; a Latin American nation when the U.S. Ambassador learns that a military coup may be brewing or has to start dealing with a junta newly come to power. Perhaps it is gratuitous at this point to add that the notion of the contemporary U.S. representa-

[1] Edmund Gullion, U.S. Ambassador in the Congo (Leopoldville) from the summer of 1961 to early 1964, has reflected on the role of the Ambassador in a paper prepared for the second Jackson subcommittee. See "The American Diplomatist in Developing Countries," in *Administration of National Security*, Hearings before the Subcommittee on National Security Staffing and Operations of the Senate Government Operations Committee, 88 Cong. 1 sess. (1963), Pt. 7, pp. 471-88. Gullion notes that in the developing countries, whether he or Washington wishes it, the U.S. Ambassador "occasionally finds himself thrust into something like a pro-consular role" (p. 476).

tive overseas as little more than an errand-boy or messenger seems a rather gross exaggeration and oversimplification.[2]

It must be added that while the dependence of Washington on the field for interpretation of local situations is substantial, it is not and cannot be complete. Washington intelligence or policy staffs may interpret the information provided by the field differently from the way the field does. U.S. elements within a country may differ among themselves, or with nongovernmental sources like U.S. newspapermen assigned to the country. If the situation is important enough, Washington officials may go out to the area to have a look for themselves. Indeed, irrespective of differences of interpretation, in crisis situations policy officials at home are likely to exercise that prerogative.

Finally, in an international problem that involves two or more foreign countries—for example, the Ethiopian-Somali dispute over the Ogaden or Cambodia's difficulties with Thailand and South Vietnam— the U.S. missions to those countries may disagree about what is actually taking place as well as what the United States ought to do about it. It is up to Washington officials somehow to resolve both kinds of differences. With these important limitations, the understanding and interpreting of local situations is still a key function of the field.

U.S. policy implementation overseas, particularly in the less developed areas of the world, has at least two distinguishing characteristics. It is highly operational, and the operations must often be carried on across the barrier of deep-rooted cultural differences. In addition to the usual government-to-government relations, the United States is in many places actively and deeply involved in the socioeconomic and political-administrative life of these nations, participating and assisting in what are often fundamental processes of social change.

With all of Washington's help (and, field personnel would say, in-

[2] Ambassador Gullion puts it this way: ". . . despite the foreshortening of the diplomatist's world through modern transport and communications, the margins within which he plies his trade are still wide and the chief of any mission can still make or break the mission. No amount of instructions and visits from the Department can replace the exercise by an American representative abroad of independent judgment under field conditions. If anything, his policy responsibilities are wider than they were before the United States accepted the burden of world leadership a score or so years ago, and they are discharged under very unstandardized conditions in the new countries and in the so-called satellite zone." *Ibid.*, p. 481.

terference), this is essentially the field's job. It is in fact the essence of the field's job. However closely supervised from Washington, the field missions are still for most purposes most of the time the primary implementers of U.S. policy and purposes abroad. The critical questions are, first, how effectively the individual programs and functions are performed and, second, how systematically they are viewed, directed, and carried out in relation to one another and to a guiding set of U.S. objectives.

This field performance depends to a considerable extent on policy and program decisions, organizational arrangements and procedures, and personnel recruiting and assignment as determined in Washington. Also, relationships between agency representatives and programs in the field will reflect in part the way those relationships are viewed and developed at home. Within these at times quite confining limits, field performance is largely a function of the quality of the personnel doing the job.

As was suggested in Chapter 7, there are now two sets of requirements for effective personnel performance in the field: not only must a person have the necessary professional training and qualifications to do the job but, at least as important, he must have the ability to carry on his work across formidable cultural barriers. While this point is usually made with particular reference to technical personnel in the economic aid field, it applies to other field personnel as well—including the military and diplomats. This requirement is further discussed in Chapter 11.

Finally, effective performance in the field depends on the tying together of the various U.S. programs and activities in a particular country so that their relationships are recognized and exploited and all of them reflect U.S. policy purposes clearly and consistently. This is not just a problem in the less developed areas. In most countries, U.S. official representation is variegated enough to make this a meaningful requirement and concern. Many executive orders have been issued on this subject, many hopes have been expressed, and, indeed, many clichés uttered. The requirement is, nevertheless, a real one.

The congeries of agencies and people that represent the United States and carry out its policies abroad should have a keen awareness of related activities being carried on by their colleagues and a concern to increase their combined effectiveness; senior officials, including but by no means limited to the Ambassador, should recognize the desirability of cohesive and consistent implementation of U.S. policy objectives. The concept of the "Country Team" is an attempt to give dramatic expression to this requirement. It is complementary to the notion of the leadership role of the Ambassador.

It is relatively easy to establish these premises. It is a lot more difficult to translate them into appropriate organizational arrangements, planning and programming procedures, and personnel skills. There are no all-purpose organizational nostrums although, as will be seen, some ambassadors have shown a considerable ability to make the "Country Team" a working concept. Changes in agency programming procedures may prove helpful in some cases. In the end, much depends on the understanding, attitudes, and skills of agency mission chiefs and, most particularly, of the Ambassador.

Organization in the Field

There are considerable variation and diversity in the representation of the United States abroad. U.S. missions reflect the size and importance of the countries in which they are located, U.S. policies and purposes regarding them, and the nature and extent of the programs through which those policies are being implemented. It is not surprising, therefore, to find seventy-one officers in the political, economic, and consular sections of the U.S. Embassy in London, more than fifty in the equivalent units in Tokyo and, on the other hand, a complete staff of six in the U.S. Embassy in Bangui, Central African Republic [plus an officer from the Agency for International Development (AID) and another from the United States Information Agency (USIA)].[3]

Similarly, while there are few economic aid personnel in the Western European missions, the Agency for International Development staffs in those underdeveloped countries in which the United States has aid programs usually outnumber by far the staffs of the diplomatic

[3] The figure for the Embassy in London is drawn from Ambassador David Bruce's testimony before the Senate Subcommittee on National Security Staffing and Operations. See *Administration of National Security*, Hearings, Pt. 3, p. 236. The other figures are drawn from the *Foreign Service List*, January 1965, Department of State Publication 7802 (Government Printing Office, 1965). Unless otherwise indicated, this *List* is also the source for the other field mission statistics and data mentioned in the chapter.

missions. In Nigeria, the total embassy professional staff numbers less than thirty, including administrative personnel, while the AID mission has more than one hundred and fifty professionals.

In most countries, however small, agencies other than the Department of State are represented. A Civil Service Commission compilation as of June 30, 1964 showed that of somewhat more than 30,000 U.S. citizen civilians employed overseas by the federal government, the Department of State accounted for approximately 7,200. The Departments of Justice, Interior, Health, Education and Welfare, and the Federal Aviation Agency were represented as well as the Departments of Defense, Treasury, and Agriculture and the Atomic Energy Commission.[4]

While U.S. personnel carrying on primarily foreign affairs functions are under the general leadership and control of the Ambassador (with the exception of U.S. military field forces), the status of individual agency representatives and their precise relationship to the Ambassador and the Department of State vary considerably. For example, although their representatives are attached to the diplomatic mission, the Treasury and Agriculture Departments have foreign service personnel systems independent of the Foreign Service. On the other hand, even before agreement was reached to integrate most of its Career Reserve officers into the Foreign Service Officer Corps in the fall of 1964, the personnel system of the United States Information Agency was closely linked to the Foreign Service. Furthermore, the director of the United States Information Service in each country serves simultaneously as Public Affairs Officer of the embassy.[5]

Overseas labor and commercial functions are usually carried out by Foreign Service Officers on the basis of agreements between the Departments of Labor and Commerce and the State Department. Sometimes, members of those two departments are given overseas assignments with short-term appointments as Foreign Service Reserve officers, but more typically, Foreign Service Officers, chosen with some attention to the views of Labor and Commerce, perform these functions. Civil aviation is another specialized function taken care of within the Foreign Service itself.

[4] This compilation is included as App. C in the present study.
[5] The integration of USIA Foreign Service (Career) Reserve officers into the Foreign Service is discussed in Chap. 11.

There are also flexibility and variation in the way particular functions are organized and carried out. Although there are standard patterns, military assistance and training agreements and arrangements do vary from country to country. In Latin America, there has been a tradition of separate U.S. service training missions to the particular countries, with the host governments supplying the necessary administrative support. Only in the last few years has an effort been made to coordinate these separate service activities under a single, responsible U.S. military officer. The Military Assistance Advisory Groups (the MAAG's), established to administer the Military Assistance Program in other parts of the world, advise local military forces and supervise and train them in the use of the military equipment supplied; they have from the beginning, however, been headed by one military officer and been under the general direction of the Ambassador.

The overlap in functions between the economic sections of embassies and the economic aid missions is clear. While the latter's responsibilities are primarily programmatic and operational and the former's analytical and reportorial, both are concerned with the state of the local economy and those factors significantly affecting its pace and direction of development. This overlap is sometimes reflected in administrative adaptations and arrangements. In some cases, one man has served simultaneously as head of the embassy economic section (counselor of embassy for economic affairs, in diplomatic terminology) and director of the AID mission; in others, the embassy economic counselor has served as deputy director of the AID mission. Both arrangements, it should be noted, are exceptional rather than typical. Another recent variant has been to "delegate to the Ambassador the total authority and responsibility for administering the AID program in the country to which he was accredited."[6] Clearly, providing this overlap of personnel and responsibility does not guarantee the desired coordination; nor does its absence necessarily imply a failure of close working relations.

[6] See *The Ambassador and the Problem of Coordination,* a study by the Historical Studies Division of the Department of State for the Subcommittee on National Security Staffing and Operations, 88 Cong. 1 sess. (1963), p. 37. The study notes that this arrangement is being tried in countries where the size of the AID program did not warrant establishment of a separate mission. Aside from Algeria, the countries listed are all in sub-Saharan Africa.

The Role of the Ambassador

If there is diversity in the organization of field missions, there are also many standard and even traditional patterns and relationships. The Ambassador and the diplomatic mission still represent the essential core of official U.S. representation in any foreign nation. The Ambassador, by tradition as well as current governmental doctrine, is the President's personal representative in the country to which he is accredited and his emissary to its government. At the same time, the Ambassador's direct line of communication is to the Secretary of State rather than the President; the Department of State provides his administrative support and Washington "back-up," and his diplomatic mission is staffed primarily by Foreign Service Officers and other Foreign Service personnel. A further point to be noted is that in recent years, two-thirds or more of ambassadorial and chief of mission positions have been occupied by career Foreign Service Officers.

The proliferation of overseas programs conducted by agencies and personnel substantially or completely independent of the State Department brought into sharp focus this ambiguity of ambassadorial role. It might be said to have begun with the Marshall Plan program of economic aid to Western Europe, carried out by an independent Economic Cooperation Administration (ECA). Some ECA country mission chiefs acted with considerable independence of the local U.S. Ambassador and, because of the importance of their program, had more influence with the local government. Situations arose that were confusing and embarrassing to both the local government and the United States government.

It was generally agreed that the United States should speak with one authoritative voice, rather than several, in each foreign country. Furthermore, one man should be responsible for overseeing the conduct of all U.S. programs and activities in each foreign country and assuring their effectiveness and cohesion. The Ambassador was the logical candidate to provide this policy leadership and program coordination.

What has been going on, in essence, for the last dozen or so years, is an effort to clarify and strengthen this ambassadorial role and, closely related, to emphasize and give concrete meaning to the Ambassador's relationship to the President and his status as the President's representative in the field. President Eisenhower issued a number of directives designed to accomplish this purpose, but it seems fair to say that President Kennedy contributed even more substantially to this development, not only because of his oft-quoted personal letter of May 29, 1961 to all chiefs of mission but also because of his own considerable interest in the individuals appointed as chiefs of mission and his efforts to keep in personal contact with them.

The key paragraphs of Mr. Kennedy's letter of May 29, 1961 stated the following:

> In regard to your personal authority and responsibility, I shall count on you to oversee and coordinate all the activities of the United State Government in . . . .
>
> You are in charge of the entire United States Diplomatic Mission, and I shall expect you to supervise all of its operations. The Mission includes not only the personnel of the Department of State and the Foreign Service, but also the representatives of all other United States agencies which have programs of activities in . . . . I shall give you full support and backing in carrying out your assignment.
>
> Needless to say, the representatives of other agencies are expected to communicate directly with their offices here in Washington, and in the event of a decision by you in which they do not concur, they may ask to have the decision reviewed by a higher authority in Washington.
>
> However, it is their responsibility to keep you fully informed of their views and activities and to abide by your decisions unless in some particular instance you and they are notified to the contrary.
>
> If in your judgment individual members of the Mission are not functioning effectively, you should take whatever action you feel may be required, reporting the circumstances, of course, to the Department of State.
>
> In case the departure from . . . . of any individual member of the Mission is indicated in your judgment, I shall expect you to make the decision and see that it is carried into effect. Such instances I am confident will be rare.[7]

The letter made clear that the Ambassador's authority did not extend to military forces in the field; at the same time it enjoined close working relations between the Ambassador and the appropriate area

[7] The Kennedy letter and the other relevant official documentation on the role of the Ambassador, including the Eisenhower directives, are reprinted in full in *The Ambassador and the Problem of Coordination*. The Kennedy letter of May 29 appears on pp. 155-56.

military commander. It recognized the need for a single point of leadership and responsibility for U.S. country activities overseas while it acknowledged that the representatives of agencies other than the Department of State had the right to communicate directly with their own agency headquarters in Washington and the basic right to disagree with the Ambassador. Although these principles had been recognized in previous efforts to define ambassadorial authority, this letter is generally regarded as the strongest and most positive statement of the Ambassador's role and prerogatives.

The Ambassador's leadership and supervisory role in overseas missions is now generally accepted as doctrine, just as is the Department of State's leadership role in foreign policy formulation and implementation. In both instances, the key questions are more practical. In the case of ambassadorial leadership, these involve finding men with the necessary breadth of interest and competence and determining whether enough of them can be found in the career service; arming the Ambassador with the specific powers and the staff support necessary to make his leadership meaningful; and developing organizational devices both in the field and in Washington that assist him and at the same time leave room for the autonomy and initiative desirable in the individual operating programs.

Diplomatic Missions and Consulates

On January 1, 1965 the United States diplomatic establishment overseas included 111 embassies, 2 legations, 9 special missions, 66 consulates general, 85 consulates, and 5 special offices—a total of 278 posts. If one adds 18 consular agencies scattered around the world, the grand total is close to 300.[8]

The basic organizational structure of a U.S. Embassy is essentially

[8] The source for these data is the *Foreign Service List*, January 1965. The special missions include the diplomatic staff assigned to the U.S. military command in Berlin, and the U.S. missions to the United Nations, the Organization of American States, NATO, the European Economic Community, the International Atomic Energy Agency in Vienna, the International Civil Aviation Organization in Montreal, and the international agencies located in Geneva. Effective January 1, 1965 the U.S. mission to the Organization for Economic Cooperation and Development (OECD) was separated from the staff of the U.S. representative to NATO and now functions as an independent mission. Two of the five special offices are located in Brazil and Pakistan where there are, for present purposes, two capital cities.

the same around the world. (The organization of the U.S. Embassy in Japan is shown in Chart 6.) Unless the embassy is extremely small, at its head will be an executive section that includes the Ambassador and his Deputy Chief of Mission (whose diplomatic title may be Counselor of Embassy or, in the larger missions, Minister Counselor). In most cases, the embassy staff is divided into political, economic, consular, and administrative sections. This staff, particularly the political and economic sections, carries on the traditional diplomatic functions of representation, negotiation, and political and economic reporting.

It is the embassy staff that carries on most of the daily, continuing business with the local foreign office on those matters of common concern to the two governments. The range of the possible subject matter is enormous. Much depends on the nature of the relationship with the particular country. The U.S. Embassy in London has to be a kind of miniature Department of State because the British and American governments have substantially overlapping interests and concerns all over the world. The range of problems to be discussed with the Norwegian government, for example, is much more limited; this is even more true with one of the new nations of former French Equatorial Africa. Even here, the many important international issues dealt with or discussed in the forums of the United Nations require consultations with the United Nations delegations and foreign affairs ministries of literally all the member nations.

Embassies and local foreign offices exchange views and negotiate positions on major problems like the Congo, nuclear testing, Arab-Israeli relations, and East-West trade, but the same process also takes place for less world-shaking though by no means unimportant matters—the question of which nations should be elected to fill next year's vacancies on the United Nations Security Council, the detailed arrangements and conditions for the closing or opening of some American installation, or plans for a chief of state's visit to the other country.

In addition to negotiating and exchanging views on problems with the host government, the embassy staff is responsible for reporting on major developments within the country—significant political trends and personalities (and their implications for relations with the United States), economic, scientific and technological developments, and, it should not be forgotten, commercial trends and commercial opportu-

CHART 6. U.S. Embassy and U.S. Information Service: Tokyo, Japan, July 1, 1963 [a]

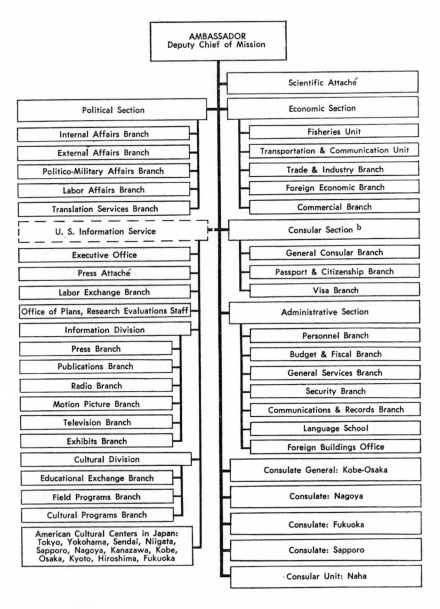

AMBASSADOR
Deputy Chief of Mission

Scientific Attaché

Political Section

Economic Section

Internal Affairs Branch

Fisheries Unit

External Affairs Branch

Transportation & Communication Unit

Politico-Military Affairs Branch

Trade & Industry Branch

Labor Affairs Branch

Foreign Economic Branch

Translation Services Branch

Commercial Branch

U. S. Information Service

Consular Section [b]

Executive Office

General Consular Branch

Press Attaché

Passport & Citizenship Branch

Labor Exchange Branch

Visa Branch

Office of Plans, Research Evaluations Staff

Administrative Section

Information Division

Personnel Branch

Press Branch

Budget & Fiscal Branch

Publications Branch

General Services Branch

Radio Branch

Security Branch

Motion Picture Branch

Communications & Records Branch

Television Branch

Language School

Exhibits Branch

Foreign Buildings Office

Cultural Division

Consulate General: Kobe-Osaka

Educational Exchange Branch

Consulate: Nagoya

Field Programs Branch

Cultural Programs Branch

Consulate: Fukuoka

American Cultural Centers in Japan: Tokyo, Yokohama, Sendai, Niigata, Sapporo, Nagoya, Kanazawa, Kobe, Osaka, Kyoto, Hiroshima, Fukuoka

Consulate: Sapporo

Consular Unit: Naha

Source: Adapted from **Administration of National Security,** Hearings, Part 3, p. 223.
  [a] Dotted lines indicate subordination for purposes of coordination within the Embassy of agencies representing branches of the U.S. government other than the Department of State.
  [b] Includes the Consulate General: Tokyo-Yokohama.

258

nities for U.S. business. In other words, the advent of new programs and new agencies has by no means eliminated the need for traditional diplomatic activities; they have created a much broader range of relations that has, in fact, increased the diplomatic workload and the variety and complexity of the problems to be dealt with.

Finally, it should be noted that the embassy staff provides the primary organizational assistance to the Ambassador in his role of field leadership, supervision, and coordination.

There is both functional and geographic specialization in field staffs, just as there is in Washington, although the degree of specialized responsibilities is limited by the much smaller size of the staffs. Officers in the political sections of large and medium-sized embassies, for example, follow developments in particular parts of the world where the local government is substantially involved. The U.S. Embassy in Paris undoubtedly has one or more officers following events in the former French areas of sub-Saharan Africa and others with responsibilities for North Africa, the Near East, and Southeast Asia. Most embassies now have one or more Foreign Service Officers following politico-military problems like military assistance, base rights, and even public discussions of military strategy within the host country. The science attachés are a part of the embassy staff, as are the civil aviation, commercial, and labor attachés.

The administrative section of the embassy usually provides administrative support (office space, supplies, communications, transportation, and budgetary and fiscal services) to the personnel of other agencies—like the United States Information Service and the military and agricultural attachés—as well as to the embassy staff itself. This would for the most part not include the larger military assistance and economic aid missions. The costs of any administrative services supplied by the Department of State are reimbursed.[9] Beginning several years ago at a number of selected posts in Africa, the State Department has been introducing a Consolidated Administrative and Management Organization (CAMO). These units not only service all elements at a post but also

[9] A recent estimate is that the Department of State serves about 120 agencies in this way and collects about $70 million a year in reimbursements. See the article by Verne B. Lewis, then Deputy Assistant Secretary of State for Budget and Finance, "New System Developed for Shared Administrative Costs," *Department of State News Letter*, No. 48 (April 1965), pp. 16-17.

draw staff from those agencies principally involved, usually AID and USIA in addition to the State Department.

Embassy consular sections and the consulates located in cities outside the capital carry on another set of traditional functions: protection of and assistance to Americans who are abroad for reasons of business or pleasure; issuance of visas to local citizens intending to visit, study in, or emigrate to the United States; and commercial reporting and assistance to American business activity.

Consulates also do their share of more basic political and economic reporting. They are in a position to report on and evaluate political attitudes and trends outside the capital city, which may be more significant than what can be observed in the capital itself. Furthermore, the major centers of industrial and other economic activity are often located outside the capital city. Thus, American consulates located in those cities—for example, Bombay, Calcutta, and Madras in India—are an essential source of economic and commercial as well as political reporting.

The British Crown Colony of Hong Kong is of considerable importance in the Far East for a number of reasons, primary among them its many connections with Communist China. The U.S. Consulate General in Hong Kong is a key listening-post in the effort to follow and assess developments on the Chinese mainland. Many of the key consulates-general in cities around the world have far larger staffs than the U.S. embassies located in the smaller European, Latin American, and African nations.

Military attachés represent another well-established element in U.S. overseas representation. As their attaché label suggests, these military officers are attached to the diplomatic mission itself. Their essential function is of an intelligence nature—gathering information about the capabilities and significant characteristics of the local military establishment. Within the U.S. defense establishment, they are viewed as one element in the military intelligence-gathering machinery.

In simpler days, it might have been said without hesitation that the military attachés did serve, or were available to serve, as military advisers to the Ambassador. With the proliferation of military activities overseas, however, this is often no longer the case. There are U.S. military assistance groups in many countries, often headed by officers of general or flag rank (who usually outrank the attachés). Furthermore, major U.S. field forces are located in some places, and ambassadors must be concerned to develop close working relations with their commanders and even the regional unified commanders to whom they report. There are also other Defense Department activities represented overseas. The net result of all of this, undoubtedly, has been to downgrade the role of the military attaché.[10]

In an effort to strengthen the attaché system, the Secretary of Defense approved the establishment, effective July 1, 1965, of a Defense Attaché System. "A single Defense attaché, appointed from the military services, will be designated in each foreign country to supervise and coordinate the work of all of the military attachés assigned to that country."[11] It is hoped that these Defense attachés will focus and economize effort within the attaché staffs and, in addition, provide a clearly defined point of contact and support for other U.S. officials abroad, including the Ambassador.

Officials representing the Treasury Department have been assigned to certain key posts overseas on a regular basis since 1939. These Treasury representatives or attachés have always been separate from and independent of the Foreign Service; they have their own legislative authorization. They are primarily concerned with financial and monetary developments in or affecting the host country, including its balance of payments, capital movements, and exchange rates and controls. At present, there are sixteen Treasury representatives attached to ten of the major missions abroad. Their financial analysis, reporting, and negotiating activities fall under the same general ambassadorial cognizance and direction as the other U.S. elements attached directly to the embassies.[12]

[10] The proliferation of Defense Department activities overseas, as might be inferred, raises some interesting questions of relationships within the military establishment as well as with the Ambassador and other U.S. field elements. See *Basic Issues*, Staff Report of the Subcommittee on National Security Staffing and Operations, 88 Cong. 1 sess. (1963) and Ambassador David Bruce's description of the situation in Great Britain in *Administration of National Security*, Hearings, Pt. 3, pp. 234-37.

[11] Solis Horwitz (Assistant Secretary of Defense for Administration), "Military Members of the Country Team," *Department of State Bulletin*, Vol. LIII (Aug. 16, 1965), p. 271.

[12] In connection with the work of the Committee on Foreign Affairs Personnel, headed by former Secretary of State Christian Herter, a series of monographs was prepared on various foreign affairs personnel topics. In one, Professor Robert E. Elder discusses the overseas activities of those federal agencies that are primarily oriented to domestic rather than foreign affairs. For his discussion of the Treasury

Agriculture representatives abroad have moved from independence of the Foreign Service, to amalgamation in it, to renewed independence. Since 1954 the Department of Agriculture has had its own Foreign Agricultural Service. At present, there are agricultural attachés serving in more than sixty foreign posts. Their assigned role is assistance to U.S. agriculture—by reporting on foreign agricultural developments and by helping promote expanded U.S. agricultural exports. The relatively new appearance abroad of Atomic Energy Commission "scientific representatives" was noted in Chapter 8.[13]

Information Programs

Three major programs account for most of the U.S. personnel carrying on foreign affairs activities abroad and for most of the funds expended: economic aid, military assistance and training, and information and cultural exchange. The staffing and, more particularly, the funds available to the last-named are quite modest compared to those of the first two.

Some note has already been made (in Chapter 7) of the overseas organization and activities of the United States Information Agency. The overseas operations of the Agency are referred to as the United States Information Service (USIS). In each country, these activities are headed by a Public Affairs Officer (PAO) with a separate Information Agency staff working under him. Most of this staff is located in the capital city, along with the U.S. Embassy, but there are often branch offices located in other major cities, headed by branch public affairs officers. In Japan, for example, there are branch units attached to consular offices in Fukuoka, Osaka, Kobe, Nagoya, Sapporo, and Yokohama as well as representation in several smaller Japanese cities. Given the role of the Information Service in disseminating information about American life and American policies and purposes, it seems appropriate to have its personnel located in major population centers throughout a country, rather than just in the capital city.

The Information Service carries out its functions through the pro-

representative program, see *Overseas Representation and Services for Federal Domestic Agencies* (Carnegie Endowment for International Peace, 1965), pp. 18-21. The report of the Herter Committee is discussed in detail in Chap. 11.

[13] See the comments on both the AEC representatives and the agricultural attachés in *ibid.*, pp. 12-18 and 21-24.

duction and distribution of books, magazines, pamphlets and other printed matter, motion pictures, and a variety of materials for radio and television broadcasting. It is responsible for the USIS libraries and helps run the binational centers that have been set up in many countries under joint local resident-American auspices to improve mutual understanding.

Through its cultural affairs officers, the Information Agency staff also provides for the administering overseas, on behalf of the Bureau of Educational and Cultural Affairs in the State Department, of the latter's programs of international exchange of persons and of cultural exchange. Included in the latter category is the appearance of American musical and theatrical artists and organizations in foreign countries. As has already been indicated, the Public Affairs Officer and his staff are closely linked to the Ambassador and embassy and serve as their public affairs and press advisers.

Economic Aid Programs

With the handful of exceptions noted earlier, country economic assistance programs are administered by a completely separate U.S. AID mission. Before the establishment of the Agency for International Development, these were known as USOM's (U.S. Operations Missions). Each AID mission is headed by a director, who may be an AID career official,[14] a political appointee or, in a few cases, a career Foreign Service Officer. The AID mission staff is usually located in the capital although its work takes it throughout a country. There are country situations that require AID representatives or even small field units to be formally located elsewhere. In the case of Brazil, which is exceptional, there are small AID staffs located in five cities outside Rio de Janeiro and quite a large one in the critical Northeast section of Brazil, in the city of Recife.

In most countries where there is an economic aid program, the AID mission has a larger staff than the embassy. The essential explanation is that present economic assistance programs are concentrated in the less developed countries and usually have a considerable technical as-

[14] While the Agency for International Development and its predecessor agencies have not been permitted by Congress to establish a regular career service of their own, the Agency does have officials recruited through the Civil Service and through the Foreign Service Reserve device who belong in the merit, career service category.

sistance dimension. This means a variety of specialists on the scene helping to strengthen local technical capabilities and train local technicians. This was much less necessary during Marshall Plan aid to Western Europe, and, consequently, those missions were much smaller than present ones, both in absolute terms and in relation to the dollar amounts of assistance being provided.[15]

Thus, AID missions are staffed to a very considerable extent with people whose skills range from care of livestock and well digging to highway building, agricultural commodity marketing, public health, education, and police administration. Often, these people are recruited from U.S. federal, state, and local agencies working in these fields. They are by background and training a very different group from the State Department's Foreign Service Officers or the career officers of the Information Agency.

This probably helps account for the frequent observation that working relations in the field between the embassy and the AID mission are by no means as good as embassy-USIS relationships. AID missions are to a very considerable degree approaching foreign policy problems at a different level and with a different focus than diplomats, who are primarily concerned with government-to-government relations. The Information Agency lies somewhere in-between in terms of its responsibilities, but it also has long-standing ties of personal and organizational association with the State Department. In any event, recognition of the kinds of functions performed by AID missions, particularly in the underdeveloped countries, helps explain why day-to-day working relations between economic aid and diplomatic staffs may not always be very close.

On the other hand, they must join at the level of program planning because the economic aid program usually represents a key element in U.S. relations with the local government. If the Ambassador and the AID mission director are operating in the spirit of the Kennedy letter of May 29, the concept and the details of the economic aid program

---

[15] John Lindeman provides some interesting comparisons in his essay, "Economic Representation Overseas," in Vincent M. Barnett, Jr. (ed.), *The Representation of the United States Abroad* (New York, 1956), p. 62. This collection of papers prepared for the Ninth American Assembly represents one of the most useful studies of the overseas projection of U.S. foreign policy. It has recently been revised and republished (Frederick A. Praeger, 1965).

developed and submitted to Washington should represent a joint effort and a consensus of views. In the normal order of things, it will be the subject of considerable discussion between the Ambassador and officials of the local government as well as between local officials and AID's Director.

While the detailed planning and programming of economic and technical assistance fall under the aegis of the AID mission, its work and interests meet those of the embassy economic and political sections, and the agricultural attachés in the basic political and economic analysis that presumably underlies any program of assistance. Reflecting particularly the earlier period of Marshall Plan assistance to Western Europe, John Lindeman wrote in 1956 that "our strongest and best economic representation overseas has been in countries where aid programs have placed special missions. Thus, the kind of representation required by our changed emphasis has come as a by-product of foreign aid."[16]

In his essay, Lindeman distinguishes between two quite different economic functions—the representational, and the operational and technical. Under the representational function, he includes government-to-government negotiation on economic problems and the economic reporting and analysis that provide the necessary underpinning for such efforts. Economic and technical assistance programs *per se* he characterizes as operational and technical, economic in consequences without necessarily requiring economists in quantity as staff.

Lindeman's conclusion that the economic aid programs have strengthened the economic capabilities of U.S. overseas missions seems to reflect primarily the Marshall Plan experience where, as he himself points out, there was much less of a requirement for a wide range of technical experts and much more need for economists. The AID missions, for the most part, make less of a contribution today to the overall economic analysis and negotiating capabilities of U.S. missions than their predecessor organizations did during the earlier period. Given the Department of State's continuing requirement—noted by Lindeman—for economists with negotiating and analytical skills, this suggests a weakness that is likely to impair the performance of both the representational and technical assistance functions.

[16] *Ibid.*, p. 54.

Military Field Forces and Military Assistance Programs

The U.S. military establishment is represented overseas in three major ways: by military field forces, by the military attachés, and by a variety of military assistance and training missions. Some attention has already been given in Chapter 6 to the chain of command between the Secretary of Defense and U.S. forces overseas and to the role of the regional unified commanders, both with regard to field forces and as regional coordinating points for the Military Assistance Program (MAP) between Washington and the country missions.

Relationships between the unified military commander responsible for a particular region of the world and the U.S. ambassadors serving in countries within that region can be quite important. One example is the U.S. commander (CINCSO) whose headquarters are located in the Panama Canal Zone and who is responsible for U.S. military activities in Central and South America. In recent years he has played an important role in U.S. military assistance programs for Latin America and in providing leadership to the U.S. military personnel carrying out those programs in the field. The usefulness of good working relations with the U.S. ambassadors in those countries is obvious.

These are relationships of equals. At least, neither ambassador nor military commander can be, short of extraordinary circumstances, formally subordinated to the other. Much therefore depends on the attitudes of the individuals involved and the personal rapport they can develop. It should be emphasized that these relationships are neither out of channels nor out of order.

Another key relationship in the field involves the U.S. Ambassador in a particular country and the commanding officer of the U.S. forces that may be stationed in that country.[17] The two have a great many common or overlapping problems. Both must be concerned with the attitudes and preferences of the host government and the citizenry of

---

[17] The testimony of the U.S. Ambassador to Japan, Edwin O. Reischauer, before the second Jackson subcommittee, is particularly revealing. See *Administration of National Security*, Hearings, Pt. 3, pp. 198-222. Reischauer's testimony also represents one of the most detailed and illuminating statements by a U.S. Ambassador regarding the concept and functioning of a "Country Team" overseas.

the country although their priorities and perspectives are likely to differ. Again, since neither can command the other, close, coopera-tive working relations are called for.

U.S. military assistance and training are provided to close to fifty na-tions under a variety of agreements and limiting conditions. They run the gamut from extensive provision of grant aid to limited sales of equipment to narrow, technical training; they vary considerably in organization, nomenclature, and size of mission.

The most common military assistance arrangement is the MAAG or Military Assistance Advisory Group. Within the MAAG, there are usu-ally separate Army, Navy, and Air Force sections, with one officer in overall command of the Group. In most cases, the MAAG's administer programs of U.S. military grant aid and work very closely with the armed forces of the local government in: developing and assessing the latter's military requirements; evaluating local requests for assistance; advising and assisting in training local forces to use the material sup-plied; and screening and recommending local candidates proposed for military training in the United States.

Until recently, as was noted above, the three U.S. military services sent separate training missions to Latin American countries. Close working relations tended to develop between the U.S. service missions and their local military counterparts, with the U.S. military missions thinking of themselves, perhaps, as performing a function on behalf of the local government. In the last few years, these arrangements have been modified with the introduction of a U.S. Military Group com-mander responsible for coordinating the activities of the separate ser-vice missions.

There are still other variations in military assistance arrangements. In some places, for reasons of local sensitivity or preference, there are U.S. military missions rather than MAAG's, with more narrowly defined functions and with primary emphasis on supply of limited cat-egories of equipment rather than on training local forces and assessing local military capabilities and deficiencies. In some countries, only one service may be represented in a mission.

Whatever the particular organizational arrangement, the head of the country military assistance mission is almost always a key figure in the "Country Team". Beyond their traditional functions of defense against internal as well as external threat, new nations and old nations alike tend to be concerned with their armed forces as part of the trappings and symbolism of national independence and prestige. In many countries, the status of these forces and of U.S. programs designed to assist them are likely to receive as urgent attention as social and economic development.

From the United States point of view, the planning and detailed programming of military aid usually represent one of the major topics of discussion and negotiation with the local government and, therefore, presumably require the detailed attention of the Ambassador, working closely with the military mission chief. In addition, military aid and economic development are linked in a number of ways. To oversimplify considerably, the resources of a country that are allocated to the armed forces cannot be devoted to economic development projects —although they may make a contribution to economic development.

There is, in any event, the question of a proper balance between U.S. military and economic assistance. Both should have as their point of departure the same basic analysis of the local economy and the same view of how military and economic development expenditures fit together in an overall country development concept. Military and economic aid programs converge in a very specific way in the field of civic action: the use of military units to carry out projects that contribute to broader social development, like building roads, constructing schools, and introducing public health and sanitary engineering measures. Military aid can help equip the military units while economic assistance may supply some of the materials needed for particular projects. It is difficult to see how any of this can be accomplished without considerable collaboration among embassy, AID mission, and military assistance mission staffs.

Finally, local military establishments play a highly significant role in the political life of many countries, even when they do not have direct control of the governments. This is a particularly widespread phenomenon in the underdeveloped countries, by no means limited to Latin America. This suggests a possible area of influence for military assistance missions that goes beyond the provision of material and advice on how to use it. This, too, calls for close working relations with the embassy diplomatic staff.

Missions to International Organizations

While the power and purposes of sovereign nation-states still represent the basic motivating forces of international politics, the past twenty years have seen a dramatic rise in the number of problems and issues channeled into international organizations for discussion, negotiation, and even active resolution. These organizations vary widely in membership, purposes, functions, and structure. (Chart 7 shows the agencies affiliated with the U.S. Embassy in Japan.)

Regional security organizations comprise one important category, with considerable variations among them. These range from what is undoubtedly the most ambitious and highly organized political and military security alliance of all time, the North Atlantic Treaty Organization, to much more dilute arrangements like SEATO (the Southeast Asia Treaty Organization) and CENTO (Central Treaty Organization), and the highly distinctive regional organization represented by OAS (the Organization of American States).

The United Nations and its immediate constituent units represent another category. There are also a variety of highly specialized, functional organizations ranging from those that call forth considerable national policy interest and sensitivity, like the International Labor Organization and the International Civil Aviation Organization, to those that usually excite little national policy concern, like the Universal Postal Union and the International Telecommunications Union. There are regional economic organizations set up under United Nations auspices and others outside the United Nations, like the Organization for Economic Cooperation and Development (OECD), originally established in Western Europe as the European counterpart organization for the Marshall Plan.

This is a very brief and incomplete listing of the various international and multilateral organizations of the day. The U.S. foreign policy organization must concern itself with the programs and policies of almost all of them, develop official U.S. views thereon, and participate in their continuing activities and their periodic meetings and conferences. In certain cases, this calls for special U.S. field missions whose sole task is participation in the activities of one or more international organizations.

CHART 7. U.S. Embassy and Affiliated Agencies: Tokyo, Japan, July 1, 1963 [a]

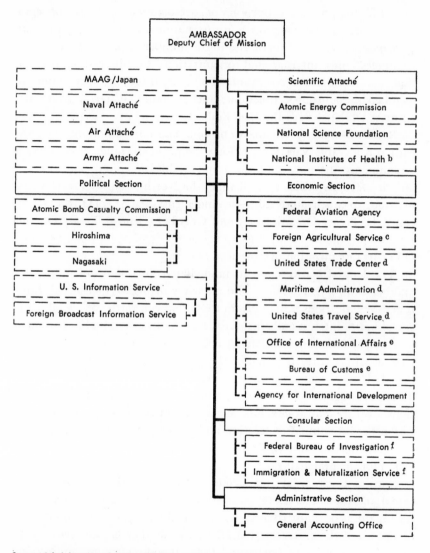

Source: **Administration of National Security,** Hearings, Part 3, p. 224.
  a Dotted lines indicate subordination for purposes of coordination within the Embassy of agencies representing branches of the U.S. government other than the Department of State.
  b A subunit of the Department of Health, Education, and Welfare.
  c A subunit of the Department of Agriculture.
  d A subunit of the Department of Commerce.
  e A subunit of the Department of the Treasury.
  f A subunit of the Department of Justice.

With regard to the universal membership organizations, the most important U.S. mission is the one to the United Nations (USUN in State Department terminology). In January 1965 its professional staff, not including military or administrative personnel, numbered approximately thirty. During particularly busy times of year, like the opening weeks of the General Assembly, this staff is supplemented with officers detailed on a temporary duty basis from the Department of State. They provide added manpower and the necessary specialized competence that may not be available within the mission staff.

USUN represents the United States in the deliberations of the United Nations Security Council, the General Assembly, the Economic and Social Council, and the Trusteeship Council—and in the corridors, lunchrooms and delegates' lounge where much of the politics of the United Nations takes place. The intensity and importance of this politicking are among the factors that make a full-time U.S. staff at the United Nations necessary despite the proximity of Washington.

The organs of the United Nations deal with many of the leading international issues of the day, often very actively. It can be assumed that votes are more likely to be influenced by informal discussions and negotiations outside the chambers than by the formal proceedings within. Furthermore, in places like the Near East, the Congo, Yemen, and Cyprus, the United Nations and its international secretariat and staff have been active participants in the handling of difficult international problems.

For many nations, particularly the new nations recently graduated from colonial status, the United Nations represents the major channel and opportunity for active participation in world affairs. Some of these nations have even been more interested in establishing a mission in New York than an embassy in Washington. Under these circumstances, full-time U.S. representation in New York is an unquestionable necessity. For the U.S. diplomats involved, there is a practical problem: although living and representational expenses in New York are far higher than they would be in most overseas posts, the additional allowances that would be provided overseas are not granted to the USUN staff.

Although New York is the seat of the United Nations, much international organization activity continues to be based in Geneva. There is a special U.S. mission in Geneva, completely separate from the Embassy in Bern; it is responsible for, among other things, U.S. participation in the General Agreement on Tariffs and Trade (GATT)—the nearest approximation to an international trade organization that now exists, the International Labor Organization (ILO), and the World Health Organization (WHO). This mission also provides a base for the U.S. representatives who have been involved for the past few years in the continuing disarmament negotiations in Geneva.[18]

The most important, by far, of the U.S. missions to regional organizations is located in Paris—the U.S. mission to the North Atlantic Treaty Organization. This is known as USRO and is a completely separate entity from the regular U.S. diplomatic mission to France. As noted above, there is now a separate U.S. mission to the Organization for Economic Cooperation and Development, including the latter's important Development Assistance Committee (DAC).

During the past fifteen years, the NATO organization has become elaborate indeed. Each nation has a permanent representative assigned to the policy-making body of NATO, the North Atlantic Council (NAC), which thus has a continuing existence and agenda going far beyond the semi-annual ministerial meetings of the Council attended by foreign ministers and, sometimes, defense and treasury ministers. The U.S. Ambassador who heads USRO is the permanent U.S. representative on the North Atlantic Council. The work of the Council is supported by an international staff on which there is a U.S. contingent. All of this is in addition to the complex military command and staff structure and field forces headed by the Supreme Allied Commander, Europe (SACEUR), who also has an international staff. Since the inception of NATO, SACEUR has been an American officer who also serves as the commander of U.S. forces in Europe.

In this highly complex NATO structure, fundamental questions of military strategy and detailed questions of military implementation in terms of force levels, budgetary allocations, weapons systems, and operational planning are intertwined with the broader problems of the political relationships among the member countries. Thus, in the North Atlantic Council and subsidiary bodies, problems in Franco-American relationships can and do find expression in a great variety of ways. To the extent that the NATO alliance is the keystone of U.S. policy

[18] See the account by Harold Kaplan, "The United States Mission at Geneva," *Department of State News Letter*, No. 38 (June 1964), pp. 22-24.

in Europe and that many of the problems in U.S.-European and intra-European relations manifest themselves in NATO bodies, USRO is a busy and important U.S. overseas mission.

The headquarters of the European Economic Community (the Common Market) and the European Atomic Energy Community (EURATOM) have been located in Brussels, which will remain the headquarters site when the executive bodies of the Common Market, EURATOM, and the European Coal and Steel Community are merged in 1966. Another special U.S. mission, USEC, reports on the activities of these organizations and carries on official American business with them. USEC has some Atomic Energy Commission representatives on its staff, as well as the usual Foreign Service personnel, to handle problems relating to atomic energy. Two or three officers of the mission are also located in Luxembourg because of the presence there of a number of European Community activities.[19]

The eighth special U.S. mission to international organizations is the U.S. Representative to the Organization of American States. Because the OAS has its headquarters in Washington, the U.S. representative has his office in the State Department, and his staff support is supplied by one of the regional offices of the Department's Bureau of Inter-American Affairs. U.S. relations with the headquarters of CENTO and SEATO are maintained by the regular U.S. embassies in Ankara and Bangkok.

In addition to the continuing involvement in the activities of international organizations reflected in these permanent missions, the United States participates officially each year in hundreds of regular and special international meetings and conferences dealing with subjects ranging from population control and the peaceful uses of atomic energy to international law of the seas and the international traffic in narcotics. In fiscal year 1964, there were 540 such meetings. A special staff in the Department of State's Bureau of International Organization Affairs, the Office of International Conferences, helps coordinate U.S. governmental preparation for attendance at these meetings.

Participation in international organizations demands both special

[19] For a more detailed description of USEC, see George M. Hellyer, "The U. S. Mission to the European Communities," *Department of State News Letter*, No. 46 (February 1965), pp. 24-25 ff.

competence in the tactics of operating in such settings and the necessary background and understanding of the substantive problems being dealt with. Within the State Department, the Bureau of International Organization Affairs has primary responsibility for supporting U.S. participation in the United Nations and the many specialized international organizations and agencies.

This Bureau serves as much more than a procedural guide and political adviser to the other elements of the foreign policy organization whose problems are being considered by international bodies. These international institutions tend to develop distinctive characteristics, traditions, problems, and even interests and policy attitudes of their own. These are likely to be reflected to some extent in the approach to problems and the policy views of the Bureau of International Organization Affairs. It is said, and probably with justice, that the Bureau's Office of United Nations Political Affairs (UNP), responsible for U.S. activities in the United Nations Security Council and General Assembly, is an organization of considerable policy influence within the State Department, making effective use of its crossroads position on matters being dealt with in these United Nations forums.

Inspection of Field Missions

One classic device for keeping organizations more alert and efficient is that of periodic inspections by some special outside staff. While inspection as a management tool is usually associated with the military, the major foreign policy agencies also have inspection staffs designed primarily to evaluate and strengthen their overseas activities.

The Foreign Service Inspection Corps, provided for in the Foreign Service Act of 1946, is responsible for the continuing scrutiny of U.S. diplomatic and consular posts. It is headed by an Inspector General and staffed by senior, experienced Foreign Service Officers. Their functions include evaluation of the performance of all U.S. personnel as well as the overall operation of the missions and the effectiveness of their accomplishment of American policy objectives. The statutory requirement is that each diplomatic and consular post be inspected at least once every two years.

In 1961 Congress provided for the establishment of an Inspector General of Foreign Assistance, reporting directly to the Secretary of State. The responsibilities of this Inspector General and his staff of

Foreign Service Officers and other personnel include all foreign assistance programs, but major attention is given to economic assistance programs. Finally, it should be noted that the United States Information Agency has a special staff that inspects its overseas units and operations.

Supporting Organizational Arrangements in Washington

In a sense, the entire foreign policy organization in Washington is supposed to support the activities of field missions, and vice versa. The country desk officers and their superiors in the geographic offices of the State Department, AID, USIA, and the Office of International Security Affairs in the Department of Defense handle most of the day-to-day bilateral problems and related communications with the field; they also inject the country viewpoint into larger multilateral or functional problems. Major policy and program decisions involving any single country, on the other hand, usually require the participation of higher echelons and other geographic and functional units.

One of the more noteworthy trends of the last ten or twelve years has been an effort to develop what might be called a Country Team perspective on country problems among the responsible agency staffs in Washington. Such a perspective would, generally speaking, serve the same purposes in Washington as in the field. The obstacles to its development in Washington are, however, much more substantial than in the field.

Within each individual country, the various U.S. missions and component elements are thrown into rather close contact with one another and with common problems. No matter how large some of these missions may be, they are still miniscule when compared to the massive and complex bureaucratic jungle that is Washington. Furthermore, in the foreign country, the Ambassador has been given a reasonably clear mandate of overall leadership and responsibility by the President— however difficult this may be to implement in particular situations. He is the President's personal representative.

In Washington, no one short of the President himself has this kind of power and responsibility.[20] The Ambassador and the other ranking

[20] The recent U.S. Ambassador to Brazil, Lincoln Gordon, summarizes the situation in these terms: "The reasons for relative simplicity in the field are the

officials representing the United States in some foreign country actually have a chance to make the Country Team concept more than an advertising slogan; often they succeed. Because of the sheer size and complexity of the foreign policy organization and the involvement of a number of major independent agencies, the integration of country policies and programs in Washington is much more difficult and frustrating, and far less successful.

In spite of these difficulties or perhaps because of them, there have been continuing efforts to improve country planning and programming within the national security organization. Under the Eisenhower Administration, as pointed out in Chapter 4, much of this effort took place within the National Security Council structure. Country policy papers were promulgated by the Council, and outline plans of operations—setting forth the various agency programs carried on in each country—were prepared in the machinery of the Operations Coordinating Board.

While the Kennedy Administration abolished most of this apparatus, it apparently concluded that at least some of the performed functions were necessary. Under Mr. Kennedy, country guideline and policy papers were produced on an interdepartmental basis, and an effort was made to link these policy and planning efforts more closely to their detailed action and program implications. Indeed, the Kennedy Administration seemed much more committed to the notion of effective country planning than had its predecessor.

In abolishing the Operations Coordinating Board and the elaborate structure of interdepartmental working groups that had grown up under it, Mr. Kennedy made clear that there were functions to be performed here—but in another way:

> I am today issuing an Executive Order abolishing the Operations Coordinating Board. This Board was used in the last Administration for work which we now plan to do in other ways. This action is

---

small numbers of people involved, their close contact with common problems, and the fact of integrated direction by the Ambassador. Except for the existence of ultimate Presidential authority in Washington, these conditions cannot be reproduced there."

See Ambassador (and Professor) Gordon's interesting memorandum submitted to the second Jackson subcommittee, "Organization and Coordination of Foreign Policy and Overseas Operations," in *Administration of National Security*, Hearings, Pt. 5, p. 374. In early 1966, Ambassador Gordon was appointed Assistant Secretary of State for Inter-American Affairs.

part of our program for strengthening the responsibility of the individual departments.

First, we will center responsibility for much of the Board's work in the Secretary of State. He expects to rely particularly on the Assistant Secretaries in charge of regional bureaus, and they in turn will consult closely with other departments and agencies. This will be our ordinary rule for continuing coordination of our work in relation to a country or area.

Second, insofar as the OCB—as a descendant of the old Psychological Strategy Board—was concerned with the impact of our actions on foreign opinion—our "image" abroad—we expect its work to be done in a number of ways: in my own office, in the State Department, under Mr. Murrow of USIA, and by all who are concerned with the spirit and meaning of our actions in foreign policy. We believe that appropriate coordination can be assured here without extensive formal machinery.

Third, insofar as the OCB served as an instrument for ensuring action at the President's direction, we plan to continue its work by maintaining direct communication with the responsible agencies, so that everyone will know what I have decided, while I in turn keep fully informed of the actions taken to carry out decisions. We of course expect that the policy of the White House will be the policy of the Executive Branch as a whole, and we shall take such steps as are needed to ensure this result.

I expect that the senior officials who served as formal members of OCB will still keep in close and informal touch with each other on problems of common interest. Mr. Bromley Smith, who has been the Executive Officer of the OCB, will continue to work with my Special Assistant, Mr. McGeorge Bundy, in following up on White House decisions in the area of national security. In these varied ways we intend that the net result shall be a strengthening of the process by which our policies are effectively coordinated and carried out, throughout the Executive Branch.[21]

The abolition of the Operations Coordinating Board reflected the Kennedy Administration's general organizational philosophy of increased reliance on the line departments and a much more direct relationship between them and the President. In the field of foreign policy,

[21] Statement by President Kennedy on February 19, 1961, accompanying his executive order abolishing the Operations Coordinating Board. The statement and the executive order are reprinted in *Administration of National Security, Selected Papers,* 87 Cong. 2 sess. (1962), pp. 3-4.

It is interesting to note that while abolishing the formal structure, Mr. Kennedy retained as one of his national security aides the highly experienced career official who had for several years been quite actively involved in its functioning.

as has been made amply clear in earlier chapters, this meant particular reliance on the Secretary and the Department of State for leadership and coordination. Since in almost all cases the Operations Coordinating Board working groups that did the staff level work on the country operations plans were chaired by their State Department members, the fundamental nature of the problem had not really changed. Under either arrangement, it was up to the Department of State to provide leadership and direction. Interestingly enough, the membership of the new Senior Interdepartmental Group, established in March 1966 (see Chapter 5, footnote 29), was almost identical to that of the Operations Coordinating Board. Furthermore, considerable emphasis was placed on the role of the geographic Assistant Secretaries of State and the supporting, lower-level interdepartmental groups they would head.[22]

In testimony before the Senate Subcommittee on National Security Staffing and Operations in November 1963, the senior State Department administrative official, William J. Crockett, suggested some of the steps the Department had taken to strengthen country planning and programming in Washington. Beyond observing that there was an increased recognition throughout the State Department of what was required if its leadership role were to be effectively performed, he noted the establishment of "regional interagency policy committees chaired by the regional assistant secretaries." Two have been established so far, for Latin America and Africa. While they are called policy committees, they are concerned to a very considerable degree with specific programs and current problems.

Mr. Crockett also reported on the current version of country policy papers, the "national policy papers, covering U.S. operations in a number of critical countries," prepared under the leadership of the Department's Policy Planning Council. They represent an attempt to tie U.S. objectives and policies more closely together with the necessary implementing actions and programs, a "marrying" of the policy paper and the operations plan:

> The national policy papers differ in several significant respects from previous policy planning exercises. They are intended to be operational plans governing all U.S. programs in a given country; they contain depth analyses of the social, political, economic, and mili-

[22] See *New York Times*, March 5, 1966.

tary forces operating within the country; they assess the tools and techniques the United States has available to change or channel developments within the country, and finally they express in concrete terms goals and objectives of U.S. action.

As a further effort to strengthen the connection between Washington-promulgated policy and operations in the field, the State Department is now introducing for the first time what it calls a comprehensive country programming system. This is discussed in the final section of the chapter.[23]

It was pointed out in Chapter 4 and has been demonstrated again in this chapter that while the approach to foreign policy making generated by the Kennedy Administration was more flexible than its predecessor's and did not force the agencies into one particular organizational mold, it by no means brought an end to interagency committees or to the preparation of papers. One of the committees established by the Kennedy Administration, the Special Group (Counter-Insurgency), reflected its deep concern about the vulnerability of the underdeveloped countries to Communist infiltration, subversion, and open insurgency, and the urgent need to strengthen the ability of these societies to defend themselves against the threat. It was assumed that this was as much a matter of socioeconomic and political development as of strengthening local police and military forces.

The membership of this Group was and is high level. It was chaired originally by General Maxwell Taylor when he was military assistant to the President and, later, by the senior State Department representative, an Under Secretary of State, who still has that role. The Attorney General is a member, as are the Deputy Secretary of Defense, the Director of the Central Intelligence Agency, the chairman of the Joint Chiefs of Staff, the Director of the Information Agency, and the Administrator of the Agency for International Development.

For those countries threatened by Communist-led or Communist-exploited subversion or insurgency, the Special Group (Counter-Insurgency) has been concerned that all relevant U.S. programs and activities contribute most effectively to the strengthening of internal security

[23] One of the major themes running through Mr. Crockett's testimony is the particular difficulties that stand in the way of State Department foreign policy leadership in Washington, and of a Country Team approach to country problems in Washington. See *Administration of National Security*, Hearings, Pt. 4, pp. 272-319, particularly pp. 286-90 and 317-18.

and stability and the diminution of the Communist threat. In effect, the Group has been insisting on a Country Team approach to this particular problem. Thus, both in Washington and the field, country programs have been examined critically and systematically from the point of view of internal defense or of countering an active Communist insurgency. The Group has attempted to identify program gaps or inadequacies as well as bureaucratic bottlenecks and, because of the high level of its membership, has presumably been in a position to do something about them.[24]

In sum, there are increasingly ambitious efforts to develop country planning and programming on an interagency basis in Washington. If the Department of State is in fact to exercise foreign policy leadership, this is one of the areas in which it will have to be more effective. Organizational experimentation will no doubt continue in this area as in others; once again, there are no simple, short-cut answers. It also seems true that the development of a Country Team approach will always be more difficult and less satisfactory in Washington than in the field.

Major Problems

Improving the effectiveness of U.S. foreign policy overseas has two fundamental aspects: strengthening the operations of the separate agencies, and tying them together into an integrated, mutually reinforcing expression of the purposes and concerns of the United States government. Attention will be focussed in this section on the latter requirement.

In good part, its fulfillment must rest on a particular way of looking at situations and problems, not just in terms of a single agency or program perspective but rather from the overall point of view of U.S. objectives and policies in the country. (It goes without saying that country problems must in turn be viewed in the larger context of regional and even global policies and requirements.) It should not be implied that some extraordinary degree of wisdom or insight is neces-

[24] One useful description of the activities of the Special Group (Counter-Insurgency) is William Beecher's article, "U.S. Effort to Counter Red Insurgency Guided by Little-Known Group," in the *Wall Street Journal,* June 27, 1963.

sary to develop such a point of view. It is simply that people grow accustomed to looking at the world from the vantage point of their particular responsibilities and activities. It is practical and necessary. It is even compatible with the broader perspective being suggested.

However, a country's problems simply do not break down along the lines of U.S. agency jurisdictions and activities. For example, as was suggested earlier, military and economic assistance programs are interrelated in a number of ways. They can work at cross-purposes or, on the other hand, they may even serve to reinforce one another. The activities of the agricultural attaché in stimulating the import of American agricultural products by the host country may bear directly on the efforts of technical assistance personnel of the Agency for International Development to improve local agricultural productivity or variety of product.

The need to see and act upon the significant relationships between activities carried on by different agencies does not apply only to some of the newer programs. It is quite relevant to a classic activity—the gathering and interpretation of intelligence. Information that is often quite closely related is gathered and interpreted regularly by embassy political and economic sections, by military attachés, intelligence personnel, consulate officers, and a variety of other persons—for example, science, agricultural and Treasury attachés. There are others as well—particularly members of military assistance and economic aid missions —who have opportunities to gather useful information even though this is not one of their assigned functions.

For the most part, the vast streams of data gathered by these units are assembled, collated, and interpreted by the Washington intelligence community. No doubt, this is an appropriate division of labor. It does seem, nevertheless, that intelligence collection and interpretation overseas could be much more systematically organized and related than they are at present. This would probably reveal both unnecessary duplication and important gaps of information. No elaborate reorganization seems required. It is primarily a matter of recognizing common problems and interests across the lines of established agency functions and responsibilities.

The recognition that agency programs and jurisdictions straddle most country problems does not guarantee agreed interagency solutions, but it should make possible an interagency approach to them. Some of the obstacles to such an approach in Washington have been noted above. In the field, the burden rests on the staffs and the chiefs of all the agencies represented, but, it seems generally agreed, the fundamental challenge is to the attitudes and abilities of the Ambassador or Chief of Mission. If he understands what is required in order to oversee, integrate, and coordinate the activities of the Country Team—and if he is capable of doing these things—the task can probably be accomplished. This seems to be the view of many recent and present U.S. ambassadors.

In other words, while the task of Country Team leadership is formidable and the characteristics of the ideal modern Ambassador suggest a superman,[25] the job can be accomplished by a capable and motivated, if not ordinary, human being. A practical question from the point of view of the Foreign Service, which at present fills more than two-thirds of ambassadorial positions, is whether it has or is developing the kind of officers that can meet these requirements for ambassadorial breadth and leadership. The same question can be directed at the career staffs of the Information Agency and the Agency for International Development since it can be assumed that, increasingly, they will be looked to for candidates for ambassadorial positions.

A further factor to be noted, particularly from the viewpoint of the career services, is the role of the Deputy Chief of Mission (the DCM, as he is called in the Foreign Service), who will almost always be a career officer. While the precise nature of the DCM's job will vary in terms of his relationship with the Ambassador and the precise division of labor arranged between the two, he must serve as the Ambassador's alter ego on occasion even if the latter does not regularly use him in that way. In the Ambassador's absence, the DCM does take charge of the mission (and thus becomes, in diplomatic parlance, the chargé). Ideally then, he too should have this across-the-board interest in U.S. programs and activities, including the many conducted outside the diplomatic mission proper, and a concern for their unified direction. Viewed in these terms, the DCM position should be the training and proving ground

[25] In his memorandum cited earlier, Ambassador Gullion humorously suggests the following ideal characteristics for the Chief of Mission: "a forceful executive, a creative thinker, a brilliant reporter, a topnotch economist, a wily negotiator, an expert at military affairs, a skillful propagandist, a versatile linguist, and an unusually attractive personality." See *Administration of National Security*, Hearings, Pt. 7, p. 474.

for future ambassadors drawn from the career ranks. (This is now the general State Department and Foreign Service concept of these positions.)

The Ambassador's need for a broad governmental perspective and point of view may be particularly difficult for a Foreign Service Officer ambassador to adjust to and accept. Lincoln Gordon states the need in these terms:

> The basic point is that the Ambassador must himself feel that he serves the Government as a whole, and not only the special interests of the Department of State, and that he convey this attitude to all his officers who share the coordinating task. He must have a positive interest in the operating programs as well as in the more traditional duties of diplomacy, and this sense of broad concern must likewise be conveyed to his subordinates.[26]

Beyond this broad perspective, the Ambassador and the DCM, in some suitable combination of skills and interests, must be capable of giving detailed direction to the varied elements present in their mission. A number of years ago, some observers were laying great stress on the concept of the "executive Ambassador", arguing that in the area of foreign operations, the effective Ambassador must have not only diplomatic but executive qualities of the first order.[27] While this probably overstated both what is necessary or feasible, the requirement for increased interest and ability in directing large operations is now generally accepted by the foreign affairs career services. A variety of efforts, including special courses, are being undertaken to strengthen the management skills of newly-appointed and potential ambassadors and DCM's.

There is no standard or accepted set of procedures through which the Ambassador is supposed to supply leadership and direction to his Country Team elements. There are even a variety of usages of the term "Country Team." In some missions, it is conceived of as dealing only with military-security problems and includes in its limited membership, as in Japan,[28] the commander of U.S. field forces in the country as

[26] See *ibid.*, Pt. 5, p. 367.

[27] See *The Operational Aspects of United States Foreign Policy,* Study by the Maxwell Graduate School of Syracuse University for the Senate Foreign Relations Committee, 86 Cong. 1 sess. (1959), p. 56.

[28] See the testimony of U.S. Ambassador to Japan Edwin O. Reischauer before the second Jackson subcommittee, *Administration of National Security,* Hearings, Pt. 3, pp. 199-201.

well as the MAAG chief. In others, it is focussed on military assistance problems or on economic and military aid problems. While it has these more specific usages in overseas missions, the term is increasingly used in the literature on the subject to suggest the Ambassador's leadership of the full range of U.S. foreign policy activities carried on in a country and the responsiveness of the various U.S. elements to his direction and control.

As the ambassadorial testimony and memoranda presented to the second Jackson subcommittee suggest, one standard device for giving direction to the Country Team is staff meetings. In one way or another, ambassadors meet on a regular basis with AID mission directors, MAAG chiefs, and U.S. field commanders where appropriate, as well as with embassy section chiefs, Public Affairs Officers, and military, agricultural, and Treasury attachés.[29]

It is usually assumed that the Ambassador needs some staff support within the embassy itself if he is to carry out his leadership role effectively, particularly as it relates to programs like economic and military assistance, which are often quite complicated. A staff study prepared for the second Jackson committee reported:

> Partly in order to deal with these [military] representatives and with an area military commander, if any, a new politico-military post has been established in many missions. This officer, usually a career foreign service officer with some special training, assists the ambassador with the coordination of political and military activities. In some cases he serves as the executive secretary of the country team.[30]

[29] The question of how ambassadors give direction to the various U.S. elements within their countries, and the problems that arise in doing so effectively, were given considerable attention by the second Jackson subcommittee. A number of past and present U.S. Ambassadors testified or submitted statements. Included among them, in addition to those already mentioned, were retired career Ambassadors Ellis O. Briggs, H. Freeman Matthews, Livingston T. Merchant, and George F. Kennan and present Ambassadors Samuel D. Berger, Foy D. Kohler, and David K. E. Bruce.

Former Ambassador Briggs has elaborated his critical views on the present functioning and operations of American diplomacy at home and abroad in *Farewell to Foggy Bottom* (McKay, 1964).

[30] *Administration of National Security*, "Basic Issues," Subcommittee Staff Report, 88 Cong. 1 sess. (1963), p. 15. Ambassador Samuel Berger indicated in his memorandum prepared for the subcommittee that sometimes the special assistant takes the form of someone responsible for aid matters, both military and economic. See *Administration of National Security*, Hearings, Pt. 3, pp. 265-66.

On the other hand, Ambassador Lincoln Gordon vigorously dissented. While

The precise nature of an Ambassador's staff needs in this area will depend on the importance of assistance programs or of military security problems in U.S. relations with the host government, the depth of the Ambassador's previous background and present interest in these questions, and the nature of his relationships with the men heading the relevant programs. As has been said about the Department of State, the Ambassador must strike the appropriate balance between overly detailed supervision of these programs and the kind of superficial acquaintance and approval that in effect leaves the significant choices to others. There is no reason why a special assistant who strengthens the Ambassador's ability to keep abreast of such programs without being drowned in their details must, as Ambassador Gordon implies, necessarily stand between him and the program chiefs.

A new tool that is designed to facilitate the Ambassador's understanding and control of the various agency and program components under his general direction is the comprehensive country programming system referred to above. It was developed by the Department of State's management staff, was introduced in a few field missions in 1963, and is now in the process of being installed at a larger number of overseas missions. It is designed to summarize in one document, for the first time, the various U.S. foreign affairs components present in a particular country, the objectives and lines of action they are pursuing, the activities in which they are engaged and the techniques they use, the resources they are expending (in both dollar and manpower terms), and their plans over a three-year period .

Since the activities of all agencies are broken down into standard categories, this system should make it possible to determine the total U.S. resources being expended to accomplish a particular purpose, rather than simply AID, Defense Department, or State Department funds. Furthermore, it should identify unnecessary overlapping, or even contradictions, in programs. It should also make possible a com-

---

agreeing that in any large embassy, an Ambassador and DCM will be greatly helped by a middle-level staff assistant, he saw no more reason for the latter "to be an intermediary between the Ambassador and the AID mission director or MAAG chief than for him to be an intermediary between the Ambassador and the political counselor. The mission directors should be considered as much a part of the Ambassador's staff as are the Embassy section heads." See *Administration of National Security*, Hearings, Pt. 5, p. 370.

parison of resources being devoted to various purposes, both within any one country or among a number of countries.

It is not implied that this system represents a panacea, a device for assuring effective Country Team operations painlessly. As a matter of fact, it is at this writing still very much in the experimental stage, an interesting innovation. At a minimum, it should provide an Ambassador with a complete, organized, and systematic overview of the foreign affairs activities carried on by the U.S. government in his country. More ambitiously, it may provide a device for clarifying choices among programs and activities within a country as well as between countries.[31]

In conclusion, it should be said again that while staff assistance and management tools can be helpful, the essential factor is the Ambassador's view of the job and his ability to implement this view. An effective Ambassador can cope with the separate agencies, their separate budgeting and programming cycles, and even their independent legislative status. Sometimes, the separate personnel assignment systems will produce added difficulties by bringing uncongenial personalities into close working relations, although an effort is increasingly made to get informal if not formal clearance from the Department of State for the mission chiefs assigned by other agencies.

In spite of these problems, it is not easy to short-circuit the Ambassador—if he takes his role of Country Team leadership seriously.[32] One of the first questions that will be asked in Washington about any proposed military aid, economic development, information, cultural exchange, agricultural surplus disposal or other program is whether it has been approved by the Ambassador. If the Ambassador sees his role in the same terms as those set forth in the presidential letter of May 29 and has the personal competence and staff support necessary to play it effectively, his chances of doing so are good indeed.

[31] For a more detailed presentation of this system, see *The Comprehensive Country Programming System,* prepared by the Management Planning Staff, Office of the Deputy Under Secretary for Administration, Department of State, March 1964.

[32] Donald Wilson, then Deputy Director of the Information Agency, stressed this point vis-à-vis USIA's overseas programs in his letter to Senator Henry Jackson. See *Administration of National Security,* Hearings, Pt. 6, p. 433.

10

Intelligence, Planning, and Policy Analysis

THE PRECEDING CHAPTERS of this study have been primarily concerned with the organizational machinery and relationships through which foreign policy is developed and implemented and day-to-day problems met and resolved. Little has been said about what might be referred to as the analytical or intellectual dimension of foreign policy making. This involves the characteristic processes of thought and analysis that take place within the foreign policy organization and their written embodiments in the form of policy papers, intelligence estimates, plans, programs, and the like. This chapter is an attempt to identify some of the intellectual requirements of foreign policy making and their organizational implications. The focus is on the analytical and organizational underpinnings for the making of decisions, rather than on the actual processes of making final choices.

A few basic points should be made about the framework of policy that guides these activities. To start with a truism, societal values and fundamental national interests and purposes—particularly as these are translated into more specific goals and objectives—give direction, energy, and will to foreign policy. They set the fundamental courses of policy. At the same time, the most difficult decisions, often, are those of detailed implementation. There may be broad and solid consensus on values and objectives but strong disagreement on the programs most likely to accomplish them.

This suggests that the clarifying and specifying of goals and objectives are an important part of the policy-making process. Since objectives are likely to conflict as they are made more specific and since few are likely in any event to be fully achieved, it is necessary to be as clear as possible on the precise states of affairs that policies are designed to produce.

Bases for Evaluation

There are many similarities between the pursuit of reliable knowledge by the foreign policy organization and by the academic scholar or university research group. Both are handicapped by the difficulty of obtaining important categories of relevant data—or their sheer inaccessibility, by the often subtle cultural presuppositions that even the best of observers bring to the scrutiny of societies other than their own, and by the relatively modest state of development that still characterizes the theories and research methods of the social sciences. Even more fundamentally, both are handicapped because many of the situations they would like to understand better, and make projections into the future about, are highly complex and not susceptible to simple causative explanation or prediction.

To calculate the behavior of the Russian or the Chinese Communist leadership; to understand the political dynamics of countries like Brazil, Turkey, Algeria, Burma, or France; to project major political and socioeconomic developments over the next five years, or even the next twelve months, in Africa south of the Sahara; to anticipate the broad political and military consequences of space exploration; or, perhaps even more difficult, to predict what the volatile leaders in some of the underdeveloped countries are going to do the day after tomorrow—these are intellectual tasks to challenge the best-trained and most highly skilled observers, whether in the bureaucracy or on the campus.

It might be added that each of these environments has its advantages. The government has or should have a superior capacity to gather data about most current international problems and situations while the presumably less hurried and harried atmosphere of the university should make for more deeply probing and systematic studies. This would seem to provide the basis for a natural division of labor between the two, although it does not always work out that way in practice.

There is at least one essential and significant difference between the scholar and the policy official: the policy official *must act* on the basis of what he knows or thinks he knows. In some instances, this means that he must act in full awareness that his knowledge is quite inadequate. This is not to imply that the scholar's knowledge is not useful or does not provide a basis for action. Sometimes, the scholar's knowledge is so relevant to the policy maker's problem that the latter calls upon him for policy advice and recommendations. The point is that the policy maker is *required* to act, that his approach to the knowledge available to him must be instrumental, and what he knows does serve as a direct basis for his actions.

Intellectual Requirements

Whether the work of the foreign policy organization is viewed as problem solving or decision making, whether the focus is policy formulation or its implementation, several broad categories of intellectual product and performance are called for. The terms commonly applied to them are *intelligence, policy analysis,* and *planning.* While there are sometimes separate organizational units designated to perform each of these functions, sometimes there are not. The distinction between the organizations and the intellectual functions is important and should be kept clearly in mind. Relevant skills and abilities exist throughout the foreign policy organization, and, therefore, useful intelligence and planning papers may well be produced by units other than the designated intelligence and planning staffs.

INTELLIGENCE. Within the framework of established policy objectives, the foreign policy official's first requirement is for the most accurate possible picture of the international environment in which he must pursue these objectives. This is far more easily said than done. Providing this "picture" is the special though not exclusive bailiwick of intelligence organizations. Some of what is needed falls in the category of straightforward factual data—biographic sketches of key foreign leaders, production and foreign trade statistics for other countries, or current military data like Soviet monthly production of intercontinental ballistic missiles—although, as the last example makes clear, these are not always easy to get.

The more important and difficult intelligence work, however, falls in the general category of selecting, analyzing, interpreting and attaching relevance to the available data. This involves not only understanding and evaluating the present but, more important and difficult, attempting in some degree to predict or anticipate the future. One aspect of such efforts, the warning function, is particularly important in wartime. Learning the date of a critical event, like a planned enemy attack, and confusing the enemy about one's own plans are of the utmost importance. Because this part of the intelligence job often involves covert activities, it is the one most frequently dramatized. There is probably still too much of a tendency—kept alive by wartime memory—to look at contemporary intelligence in terms of this "detective-work" warning function. While this is still very much a part of the contemporary intelligence responsibility, it does not represent the major interpretive effort for foreign policy purposes.

Foreign policy intelligence estimates are concerned with much broader and more complex sets of phenomena and problems: political and economic trends in key developed and underdeveloped countries, policy motivation and likely policy choices of the leadership groups in these countries, and likely developments in such world trouble spots as Berlin, the Horn of Africa, Yemen, the Near East, and Vietnam.

These estimates may vary from a quick "reading" on the political orientation of a military junta that has just taken power in Latin America to a longer-term look at the prospects for East Africa or Communist China. Whatever the urgency of the request being responded to and the time frame of the estimate itself, these are predictions about the future. However guarded or even hedged, they represent challenging intellectual enterprises, difficult to do well, subject to strong differences of view, only verifiable as events actually unfold and, therefore, probably the most easily ignored or rejected of intelligence staff products.

POLICY ANALYSIS. The intellectual function that has been labelled policy analysis is performed by a relatively large number of people in the foreign policy organization. In contrast to intelligence and planning, it is usually not carried on by a specially-designated organizational unit;

it is an important activity of many senior- and middle-level officials in the operating bureaus and policy staffs of the Department of State. The problems on which it is brought to bear range from those with relatively narrow and modest implications to the much smaller number that are of momentous importance. The organizational levels at which policy analysis takes place, and by whom, vary accordingly.

The policy analyst must attempt to define the external situation with which he is dealing (with the help of intelligence estimates, if he wishes), examine its implications for relevant U.S. policy objectives, develop and evaluate alternative courses of action for dealing with the situation,[1] and, then, depending upon his location in the hierarchy, either recommend or decide upon that course of action that seems to offer best net advantage to the interests and objectives of the United States. In the process, priorities must be established among relevant objectives, possible short-term consequences and longer-range implications weighed against one another, incomplete information discounted, and significant differences in relevant intelligence analyses resolved. This is tough, demanding intellectual work, and the ability to do it well must be spread rather widely throughout the foreign policy organization.

To round out the picture, a choice finally has to be made among the courses of action available. Even lack of choice and action represents a choice of sorts. Decisions will usually be followed in turn by actions of one kind or another, and, eventually, it can be assumed that feedback from these actions will produce new occasions for decision and perhaps even adjustment or major change in previous decisions.

This is a familiar formulation: clarification of objectives; definition of external situations; identification of problems; development and assessment of alternative courses of action; and, finally, the making of decisions. A number of points should be made about this formulation. First of all, this brief sketch is a highly simplified version of what is likely to be taking place, a model of rational decision making rather

[1] Sometimes the facts are clearly established, and what is called for is a new and imaginative way of dealing with an old, familiar problem. W. W. Rostow suggests that "one major form of intellectual contribution to public policy" is in the redefining of problems, in expanding the range of alternatives perceived to be open, and posing new questions. He comments that "the definition of alternatives in a rapidly changing field for action is, in itself, a powerful creative act. . . ." See W. W. Rostow, *The United States in the World Arena* (Harper, 1960), pp. 490-98.

than an exact replica of the policy-making world. That world is likely to be characterized as much by hurried analyses, snap decisions, and "crash" programs as by logical analysis and intellectual rigor.

At the same time, it is easy for one to forget, in setting forth in abstract terms the intellectual ingredients of decision making, how much of a difference these elements can make in specific situations. The way a situation is defined, a problem formulated, a framework or theory for dealing with it conceptualized, can have significant policy consequences.

An obvious example is whether a native movement is conceived of as a group of "agrarian reformers" or "fervent nationalists" on the one hand, or as Moscow- or Peking-line Communists on the other. Somewhat less obviously, the theory of economic development that guides the policies and programs of the U.S. economic aid agency can make a great deal of difference in the likelihood of success or failure. To be more specific, a program of economic aid that ignores certain fundamental social and political characteristics and limitations may very well fall on its face.

Finally, it should be emphasized once again that while this discussion has been couched in terms of the individual analyst, these analytical processes are usually carried on collaboratively by a number, sometimes a considerable number, of officials representing a variety of bureaucratic interests and intellectual and policy perspectives.[2]

PLANNING. The term planning has been applied to a considerable range of activities and the organizations that carry them on. Common to all of them is an effort to look ahead in some systematic way, to anticipate future developments and problems, and then to prepare to deal with them, if necessary, by adjustments in present policies and programs.[3] This kind of activity is carried on both by separate plan-

[2] Little systematic research attention has been directed to these processes of foreign policy analysis or "problem solving." For one such effort, focused on a geographic office in the Department of State, see Dean G. Pruitt, *Problem Solving in the Department of State* (The Social Science Foundation and Department of International Relations, University of Denver, Monograph Series in World Affairs, No. 2, 1964-65).

[3] Mr. Rostow, recent Chairman of the State Department's Policy Planning Council, comments: "The planner does not face a choice between long-run and short-run interests: he must combine them." See W. W. Rostow, "The Planning of Foreign Policy," in E. A. J. Johnson (ed.), *The Dimensions of Diplomacy* (Johns Hopkins Press, 1964), pp. 41-55.

ning staffs and by personnel elsewhere in the governmental structure.[4] It can be usefully differentiated from policy analysis to the extent that it is concerned with future rather than current problems.

Among the foreign policy and national security agencies, the military establishment without a doubt has a planning perspective and planning activities built most substantially into its normal functioning. Indeed, a standard military complaint about the civilian agencies, and particularly about the Department of State, is that they do not do enough planning and, furthermore, that this inadequacy is a handicap to the military establishment in its own planning efforts.

The nature of military responsibilities and functions makes planning of a quite detailed and precise nature both necessary and at the same time feasible. Even military operations of rather limited scope, like the dispatch of forces to Lebanon in July of 1958, may involve marshalling large numbers of men, weapons and other equipment, and supplying and supporting them in some remote corner of the globe for a perhaps indefinite period of time. Given the range and variety of military contingencies that may face the United States at any time in almost any part of the world, it is not possible to have either plans or capabilities to meet all of these contingencies, nor even to have plans in the files that will anticipate all the essential elements of situations as they actually arise.

Given the complex nature of military operations, something is better than nothing. To have planned in advance what specific forces one is prepared to commit to a particular situation and the detailed logistics of their support could make the difference between success and failure. The difficulties and uncertainties involved in contingency planning multiply as one broadens the scope of the planning effort.

The nation's military capabilities two, three, and five years in the future will rest to a considerable extent on present decisions about weapons systems development and procurement, the size and structure

---

[4] George Allen Morgan, a Foreign Service Officer with considerable planning experience, talks about planning in these terms: "Planning is thinking ahead with a view to action. It is thus an organic ingredient in the whole process of conducting foreign affairs, not the monopoly of a cloistered few. Indeed, most planning, and some of the weightiest, is neither so labelled nor done by planners so called." See his article, "Planning in Foreign Affairs: The State of the Art," *Foreign Affairs*, Vol. 39 (January 1961), p. 271. The article is a thoughtful, almost philosophical, essay on the subject.

of the forces, their positioning at home and abroad, and the translation of these decisions into detailed programs and budgets. These decisions, in turn, presumably rest in part on projections into the future of present trends in world politics as well as in scientific and engineering research.

These complex burdens of the defense establishment have been discussed in more detail in Chapter 6. What should be noted here is that while military planning has its share of uncertainties and dilemmas, it does have some "hard" empirical bases to work from in making its plans and projections and developing its programs: for example, the size, composition, and disposition of forces; the nature and characteristics of weapons systems; the military capabilities of potential enemies and allies; the physical and socioeconomic geography of possible target or operating areas.

In comparison, the foreign policy planner is operating on a much more slippery, "softer" footing in making his own projections into the future. When it is also remembered that, at least traditionally, foreign affairs has had very little of an operational character about it, it is easy to understand why planning has tended to be a much less familiar and valued activity in the foreign policy organization than in the military. It seems fair to say that this situation is now in process of changing.

Planning was defined earlier as thinking ahead systematically and in depth about some problem or situation with a view to doing something about it in the present. It might be asked how far ahead the thinking has to be, and in how much depth, to rate as planning. Obviously, there is no magic point where the look into the future suddenly becomes planning. All policy analysis involves some projecting of present trends and circumstances into the future.

It is primarily a matter of posture and perspective, an assumption that detailed and systematic thinking ahead promises enough practical policy payoffs to warrant substantial investments of bureaucratic time and effort. There are differences of view about this basic point; there are also strong differences about how far ahead, in any event, it is worthwhile to project one's analysis. In practical organizational terms, the daily pressure of events on the line, operating official leaves him relatively few moments for this kind of perspective. That is one of the reasons why separate planning units tend to get established.

Several kinds of foreign policy planning can be distinguished, and they parallel in a rough way the varieties of military planning. Foreign policy planners may find it useful to do some contingency planning. For example: what is likely to happen, and what courses of action would be open to the United States, if the key leader of some friendly foreign nation suddenly departs from the scene, or fighting flares again in the Near East between the Arabs and the Israelis, or an indigenous Communist-dominated political movement takes over a key country in Latin America?

As with the military, it is not possible to plan for all possible contingencies and, furthermore, even if one that has been anticipated does arise, it is bound to develop somewhat differently from what was anticipated. Even if it is a carbon copy of the scenario that is locked up in the planning staff's safe and the best course of action available to the U.S. government has been identified in advance, it still remains to be seen whether the unfolding of events will favor the interests of the United States.

Since contingency planning must be selective, it does involve some ability to identify possible future developments with particularly significant implications for U.S. interests, situations where advance planning may substantially improve this country's ability to respond effectively to the event and even exploit it to its own advantage. Since the best that is possible through such intellectual exercises is partial preparation for the future, it also becomes useful to recognize the rough limits beyond which anticipation of the future in detail can serve no useful policy purpose. The rising interest in and experimentation with gaming and simulating military and politico-military problems make available another set of techniques that may be helpful in contingency planning. In the process of "playing" through a particular contingency situation in advance of its occurrence, and perhaps doing so several times with differing sequences of events assumed, possible dimensions may be illuminated for the planner that would not otherwise have been.

The military establishment has the difficult job of translating national purposes and objectives into a national strategy and translating that strategy into forces-in-being ready to do a wide variety of jobs in a wide variety of places. In an era of far-reaching foreign policies backed by substantial and highly varied foreign programs, the foreign policy organization has an almost equally difficult set of responsibilities. The cost and the numbers of people employed here are considerably less than in the military, but the problems of operating in a hundred-odd foreign societies and attempting to influence in some degree events and decisions within them more than rival the complexities of weapons research and development. Thus, the foreign policy organization also has a requirement for what might be called program planning.

Franklin Lindsay defines it this way:

> Program planning is the process by which policy objectives are translated into action programs of the scope, magnitude and timing required for their realization. Because today's policies require massive applications of manpower, money and facilities—and because it takes time to bring these assets into being—we must increasingly *anticipate* the needs posed by our objectives.[5]

This kind of planning has two major dimensions. It involves projecting into the future major political and socioeconomic developments in the foreign countries with which one is dealing. This is particularly relevant to development efforts in the underdeveloped nations and U.S. assistance to them. If the host country has its own development plan, the U.S. government must not only understand it in all its details but must also be able to assess it and estimate the likelihood of its accomplishment. Where the host government does not have a development plan, or perhaps even the capability to prepare one, the United States may have to provide one if its own development assistance is to accomplish any results.

Along with its concern for the program planning of other nations, as Mr. Lindsay indicates, the United States should be programming its own requirements in money, material, and personnel skills. The budgetary process makes some of this an absolute necessity, but critics like Mr. Lindsay feel that this is far from sufficient. The budgetary process in the federal government requires programming only a year, perhaps two, in advance. Furthermore, it does not assure that the agencies concerned are doing the personnel planning, and the in-depth analyses of other societies, which should underpin the program and project descriptions and the financial estimates required for budgeting purposes.

Program planning, in effect, is aimed at the more effective implementation of policy. What George Morgan calls "long-range planning"

---

[5] Franklin A. Lindsay, "Program Planning: The Missing Element," *Foreign Affairs*, Vol. 39 (January 1961), p. 280. Italics in the original.

is designed to strengthen the formulation of policy. An underlying question about any such efforts is, as was suggested above, how far into the future one's analyses can be usefully projected. Again, this is essentially a matter of judgment rather than a fixed point rationally calculated. As Mr. Morgan reminds us, what the planner should be looking for is not a detailed blueprint of the future but insights that might prove helpful in coping more effectively with present and upcoming policy problems.

Morgan notes three general varieties of long-range planning. The first is plumbing the socio-political implications of significant developments in science and engineering, military technology, and in the economic structure and situation of societies. These provide some hard bases for the riskier social and political projections. One example is the question of the spread of nuclear technology and its possible military as well as peaceful implications. As with most other planning efforts, this is or should be a combination of the most difficult kind of intelligence estimate with the most sophisticated policy analysis.

The second general type of long-range planning is the analysis of present trends and forces that are likely to affect some important area of policy. The North Atlantic Treaty Organization and the role and purposes of the United States in it have been the subject of a number of such studies both inside and outside the government. The same can be said for the Alliance for Progress, the Common Market and its impact on world trading patterns, and the question of a strategic nuclear deterrent for Western Europe.

Finally, there is the grand strategy or overall policy framework that guides foreign and defense policies.[6] During the last decade or so, the United States has had a basic national security policy document which presumably provides this kind of broad framework and guidance. It combines a statement of U.S. interests and objectives with a projection and analysis of major trends in world affairs and then sets forth a national strategy designed to maximize the accomplishment of U.S. purposes. This is truly planning on an ambitious scale, which perhaps explains why such an effort tends to be viewed skeptically by some.

If such a document is too specific and detailed, it is likely to go on endlessly, need almost continuing revision, stir almost continuing con-

---

[6] George A. Morgan's comments on long-range planning are to be found in the article cited earlier, pp. 275-78.

troversy within the government, and still not provide authoritative guidance on all the matters with which it deals. If it is general, it is likely to be dismissed as too vague to be meaningful. If this type of long-range planning is to be of any use at all, it must somehow steer a path between these two extremes.

It should be kept in mind that much of the benefit to be derived from the preparation of such a document comes from the very process of developing and drafting it, which includes the reconciliation of differences of view that emerge within as well as among the responsible government agencies. The clarification of problems and the identification of key policy issues for resolution that take place in the process are probably at least as important as their formal statement in the final document produced. At the same time, such a document can be quite useful in setting forth the official position on certain basic policy issues —for example, under what conditions nuclear weapons will be employed in support of certain U.S. policy interests.

The interrelations of foreign policy and military policy were suggested in Chapter 6; these apply as much to planning as to current operations. Foreign policy objectives and assumptions about the international scene should be built into all military planning efforts, whether for the overall size and structure of the military establishment or for some specific contingency. Similarly, foreign policy planning should rest on reliable, detailed knowledge of what the military forces of the United States and any other nations that may be involved are capable of doing in any given situation. There is no point in the foreign policy planners projecting a show of force if the U.S. military establishment does not have the ability to send a force to the scene. On the other hand, there is no point in military planners either explicitly or implicitly making certain political assessments or assumptions if the experts of the foreign policy organization feel that these have no basis in current reality.

Two further points should be made about the intellectual or analytical aspects of foreign policy making. First, it should not be assumed that these activities are always carried on with quite the self-consciousness implied in this discussion. Given the growing complexity of the problems to be dealt with and the number of individual and agency perspectives brought to bear upon them, the trend of events is nevertheless in this direction.

It should also be stressed once again that these intellectual operations can, at best, serve only to narrow and clarify the problems of choice faced by responsible policy officials, particularly when major policy decisions are involved.[7] The relevant intelligence will inevitably be incomplete, there will be conflicting interpretations of the present and estimates of the future, and there will be a variety of possibly relevant U.S. interests and objectives that must be sorted out and put in some sort of priority order. Experts may disagree, as may the heads of great government departments or important units within these departments. Domestic political considerations may have to be taken into account, including the views of a handful of extremely influential senators and congressmen.

In sum, the best efforts of the policy analysts, planners, and intelligence specialists can greatly facilitate the work of the high-level foreign policy maker but cannot relieve him of the burden of painful choices and dilemmas. These tough decisions in the end are probably based as much on subtleties of judgment as on systematic research and rational analysis.

Organizational Implications

While there are specifically designated organizational units carrying on at least two of the intellectual functions, namely, intelligence and planning, it must be kept in mind that both can be performed by any official in the policy-making structure. Thus, the Assistant Secretary heading one of the geographic bureaus in the State Department may rely on his own subordinates for intelligence estimates and completely ignore those of the Bureau of Intelligence and Research. If he wishes, the policy maker can even be his own planning staff or his own interpreter of information. He may rely on his own personal reading of a situation. Since foreign policy planning is a much less well-defined and well-established function than intelligence, this is even more likely to be the case when a planning perspective and input are called for.

Given this lack of neat compartmentalization in the intellectual labors of the foreign policy organization, there is little point in trying to

[7] See the essay by Max Millikan, "Inquiry and Policy: The Relation of Knowledge to Action," in Daniel Lerner (ed.), *The Human Meaning of Social Sciences* (Meridian Books, 1959), pp. 158-80.

specify organizational arrangements and relationships in great detail. In the past, a good deal of discussion has revolved around the question of whether planning and intelligence units should be separately organized or be a part of operating line units. Starting with the reasonable premise that both intelligence and systematic "thinking ahead" are closely related to present actions and operations, it is possible to conclude that these functions should be performed within the same organizational unit as the latter.

On the other hand, it seems likely that the urgencies of current operations will sweep all available hands, including the intelligence analysts and the planners, into the business of the moment. In addition to the likelihood that the planning and intelligence types would get little time to perform their distinctive intellectual tasks, there is the further concern that intelligence estimates and planning studies, not necessarily by conscious direction but by the very nature of the close association, would tend to reflect and support present policies rather than provide an independent perspective and check on them.

Thus, the premise that intelligence and planning are closely related to current decision making does not provide a clear-cut answer to the question of organizational arrangements. The fundamental problem is how to maintain the integrity of the intellectual function while at the same time assuring the necessary close link with the decision-making and problem-solving activities it is supposed to facilitate and support. It is likely to be difficult to maintain this integrity within an operating unit. On the other hand, it may be difficult to maintain it even when intelligence and planning are separately organized. Intelligence specialists and policy planners are far from immune to the lure of the immediate and the operational.

An organizational division of labor cannot guarantee effective intellectual performance. What may help is a widespread understanding within the foreign policy organization about the requirements of rational policy making, a self-conscious and self-critical approach to the decision-making process and, ideally, some concern about how the various organizational units can best contribute to it.

On balance, there is something to be said for the separately organized intelligence unit, on the assumption that it is more likely to provide to responsible policy officials estimates of international situations independent of those developed by the line organizations dealing with those situations. Often the two estimates will coincide; sometimes, they will disagree. This is one way of building into the organization a check against any one set of interpretations of the state of the world remaining too long unchallenged by policy officials. It may be one of the major contributions of intelligence agencies to the foreign policy process.

Similarly, given the time pressures on operating officials, the best way of assuring that someone in the organization is looking ahead on a systematic basis is to make this his primary responsibility, and to reinforce the distinction by establishing a separate organization to perform the function. The separate organization cannot guarantee this result; it just makes it somewhat more likely.

This is the way the actual organizational decisions have gone. The foreign policy and national security organizations are characterized by separate planning and intelligence units. The size and resources of the Central Intelligence Agency, symbolized by its massive new headquarters in Langley, Virginia, provide impressive evidence of the triumph of "separate and equal" in the intelligence field. The existence of Central Intelligence adds, in fact, another complication to this analysis. Not only are there separate intelligence units within most of the major national security agencies, but there is, in addition, a separate intelligence agency on a par with these other agencies. Effective working relationships between intelligence units and the policy-formulating and policy-implementing organizations that are their customers must develop across as well as within agency lines.

The fundamental organizational question remains the clarity with which organizational roles are defined and responsibilities divided and the extent to which these assignments are mutually agreed upon and understood. These in turn rest in good part on the conception of policy making and its intellectual or analytical requirements held by both the top leadership of the foreign policy agencies and the substantial body of their career servants. There is no reason to assume a rigidly fixed state of affairs. For example, effective performance by intelligence or planning units may help change people's minds about the nature of relevant analytical needs and where in the organization these are likely to be satisfied.

Differences in Basic Intellectual Training and Assumptions

We return, then, to a number of basic themes. Organizational performance reflects the interaction of the formal organizational structure and the individuals who man it. How the latter define and interpret the structure, and operate within it, will determine its detailed functioning.

With regard to the intellectual capabilities of the organization, it is appropriate to ask whether particular attitudes, sets of assumptions, or views of the world dominate among its personnel and if they do, whether this in turn can be attributed to a common set of career experiences in the organization or to particular types of people recruited into the organization. Thus, for example, if an organization continues over time to recruit people with certain kinds of background and training to the exclusion of others, the intellectual performance of the organization may change very little even though its formal organizational arrangements have at the same time been radically altered. The first hypothesis is illustrated by the popular notion of a "military mind," or a "Foreign Service mind."[8] Even if recruitment patterns do begin to change, it may take considerable time before previously dominant viewpoints are significantly altered. New recruits may continue to be provided with the organization's standard doctrine on the usefulness of planning, the intelligence-policy relationship, or how one goes about solving a policy problem.

However derived and maintained, such underlying attitudes, concepts, and views of the world have a considerable bearing on the intellectual performance of the foreign policy organization. While it may not strike others this way, this is somewhat reassuring to the outside researcher interested in the processes of contemporary foreign policy making. The student of foreign policy making must operate with at least one fundamental handicap: the intellectual materials of the foreign policy organization, the papers and documents that are the grist of the policy mill, are for the most part security-classified and thus normally not available to him. He is not in a position to judge for himself the intellectual quality of the foreign policy organization's work by direct examination of its present or recent intellectual products.

[8] See the discussion in Chaps. 2 and 6.

There are a number of ways, however, in which he can get at the intellectual skills, attitudes, and frames of reference that help determine this quality. Memoirs and other writings by officials retired from public office or government service may be useful. Systematic interviewing of former officials is another possibility. Aside from the detailed documentation officially published twenty-five years after the event (as in the State Department's *Foreign Relations of the United States* series), certain critical or much debated policies sometimes call forth official White Papers or extensive congressional investigations which result in the availability of substantial bodies of official materials far sooner than the keepers of the archives would normally release them.

Former or present officials of the foreign policy organization can comment on intellectual skills and training without compromising classified data about substantive policy problems. Similarly, the outside scholar can himself probe attitudes and assumptions by interviewing operating officials in the various national security agencies. Interestingly enough, very little of this kind of research has been directed at the foreign policy organization. One of the exceptions is the study that Roger Hilsman did more than ten years ago on the prevalent doctrine among policy and intelligence officials regarding the role of intelligence in foreign policy making.[9]

The study was based primarily on a series of interviews with intelligence and policy officials in the Executive Office of the President, the Central Intelligence Agency, and the Department of State. In brief summary, Hilsman found that for most of these officials, whether they were working in intelligence or policy, the realms of knowledge (that is, intelligence) and action (that is, policy) were essentially separate and could be kept separate: "facts were facts." The intelligence specialist gathered and organized the facts and presented them to the policy official, who then used them as he saw fit in making and carrying out decisions.

This may be a useful way of defending an organizational division of labor, but, as Hilsman suggested, it represents a rather crude and unsophisticated theory of knowledge. Without embarking on an elaborate philosophical discussion, it can be premised that it is impossible to describe the totality of a particular situation or event and that no ana-

[9] See Roger Hilsman, *Strategic Intelligence and National Decisions* (Free Press of Glencoe, 1956).

lytical observer is in any case interested in so doing. Furthermore, facts do not "speak for themselves." They must be selected, related to other facts, interpreted, given meaning.

Put in terms of the foreign policy process, the inevitable selectivity of the intelligence analyst is useful to the policy official only to the extent that it is focused on problems of concern to the latter. Thus, the realms of intelligence analysis and policy making are far from separate, intellectually speaking. They are intimately related, and this should be reflected in their organizational relationships.

It is not necessary to accept the specific organizational implications that Hilsman drew from his analysis. More relevant for present purposes is the fact that Hilsman's work was never followed up by other scholars. Thus, it is difficult to judge the applicability of his findings to present attitudes in the "intelligence community" and among those who are its clients. It seems reasonable to assume that Hilsman tried to implement his own philosophy during his tenure of approximately two years, from 1961 to 1963, as Director of Intelligence and Research in the State Department.

Reference was made above to the question of the kinds of intellectual skills typically recruited into the foreign policy and national security agencies, and the apparent consequences of such recruiting. This, too, has received relatively little systematic study. For example, the academic background and training of Foreign Service Officers typically have been and continue to be in history, political science, and law (with an increasing trend in recent years toward economics) rather than in the behavioral and the natural sciences. This pattern can probably be explained in terms of the kinds of interests that lead people into the Foreign Service and, also, the kinds of knowledge that make it possible to pass the Foreign Service Officer examinations.

What can be hypothesized about the consequences? For example, the behavioral sciences—psychology, sociology, anthropology—have been notably more oriented to explicit theory and conceptualization and to more precise and systematic research methods than history, law, and political science. If one assumes that, all other things being equal, such training will make for more rigor and depth of analysis and provide tools for the more systematic study and understanding of social and political behavior, it would have to be concluded that the relative scarcity in the Foreign Service of personnel so trained is unfortunate.

It certainly means that the Department of State is not in a position to tap the knowledge and theories of these major fields of study directly through the backgrounds of its own personnel. The same general point can be made about the scarcity of people with considerable undergraduate and even graduate training in the natural sciences.[10]

There is amazingly little evidence on dominant intellectual orientations within the foreign policy organization and even less to explain how these may have developed and what their policy and organizational implications might be. These would seem to be data worth having.[11]

Organizational Machinery for Intelligence and Planning

Since what has been defined as policy analysis has no separate and distinct organizational base, this section will be devoted to a brief description of planning and intelligence units.

The Intelligence Community

The present U.S. organization for national security intelligence has been described at length elsewhere.[12] Some summary comments must suffice here. The key unit is the Central Intelligence Agency (CIA). Its size and its role have expanded greatly since its original establishment in the National Security Act of 1947. It is responsible for the overall coordination and integration of the efforts of the various departmental intelligence units working in the fields of national security and foreign

[10] An experienced Foreign Service Officer, approaching this question of professional training from a somewhat different point of view, argues very strongly for cultural anthropology, the behavioral sciences (in which he does include political science), and the comparative study of value systems as part of the core curriculum for the "new diplomat." See Robert Rossow, "The Professionalization of the New Diplomacy," World Politics, Vol. 14 (July 1962), pp. 561-75. Rossow sees the "new diplomacy," defined as the facilitation of crosscultural communications and operations, as having a far wider area of application than the traditional field of government-to-government relations.

[11] Personnel research needs are discussed at greater length in Chap. 11.

[12] See Harry Howe Ransom, Central Intelligence and National Security (Harvard University Press, 1958). Also relevant is Ransom's Can American Democracy Survive Cold War?, Chaps. VI and VII.

policy. However, it does much more. It is assumed to have the primary responsibility for covert U.S. intelligence activities abroad as well as for certain covert U.S. operations. In the latter category, published accounts of the preparation of Cuban exile forces for the Bay of Pigs landing in the spring of 1961 ascribe a key role to the Agency. The same is true for a more successful venture—the overthrow in 1954 of the Communist-oriented Arbenz regime in Guatemala.

It also carries on a great deal of independent intelligence research work. At one time, it may have been primarily a central coordinating, interpreting, and disseminating agency, with departmental intelligence units doing most of the substantive work. However, that time is past; the CIA does a great deal of its own research and analysis and has governmentwide responsibility for certain particularly sensitive and significant problem areas.

Substantial intelligence activities are carried on elsewhere in the government, and the various departmental intelligence units are still quite large and active. The functions of the Federal Bureau of Investigation are primarily domestic. There is the supersecret National Security Agency, a large and growing organization presumably responsible for worldwide communications, including the important cryptographic function; this agency has apparently taken on in Washington some of the hush-hush atmosphere and reputation formerly the hallmark of CIA.

In the summer of 1961, a joint Defense Intelligence Agency (DIA) was established. It was designed to tie together more closely the separate intelligence efforts of the three services and to strengthen the capacity of the military establishment to provide overall military intelligence assessments. Each of the military services continues to carry on a wide range of intelligence activities through intelligence organizations in Washington and elsewhere and through the military attachés assigned as members of U.S. missions in countries around the world.

The Department of State, as already noted, has a large Bureau of Intelligence and Research, which went through a difficult transitional period as a result of the major personnel changes introduced by the Wriston reforms but now seems to be finding qualified Foreign Service Officers as well as civil servants to man its key positions.

All of these agencies taken together, plus the Atomic Energy Commission, are referred to as the "intelligence community." While this sounds suspiciously like an advertising label, it reflects the fact that the intelligence units of these agencies, in addition to carrying on their own intra-agency activities, work closely together in a number of important interdepartmental intelligence enterprises. In these activities, the Central Intelligence Agency is the unquestioned leader. In statutory terms, it is directly responsible to the National Security Council. Its Director sits as one of the statutory advisers on the Council and was a member of the Operations Coordinating Board during the latter's existence. The Director of Central Intelligence also sits as chairman of the U.S. Intelligence Board (USIB), formerly the Intelligence Advisory Committee, which is the highest-level interdepartmental intelligence unit in the government and has the final word on the important National Intelligence Estimates.

These National Intelligence Estimates (or NIE's as they are called in the government) represent the intelligence community's agreed analysis and interpretation of the relevant facts and likely future developments with regard to some particular geographic area or functional problem, or some crisis situation that has suddenly arisen. These estimates may emerge from the usual periodic intelligence review of a question; on the other hand, they may be generated by the U.S. Intelligence Board or by the query of some high official (even the President or the National Security Council itself).

The estimates may be called for as part of an effort to reappraise U.S. policy in a particular country or area, to look ahead and anticipate likely future developments. In this case, it may take a number of months to produce the estimate. Some examples have been given earlier in the chapter. Others might be: Chinese Communist policy in Asia in light of the Sino-Soviet split; present and anticipated Soviet anti-missile missile development and capabilities; the present and likely future state of affairs in Indonesia, Algeria, or Japan, to name just a few. The estimates may also be called for in response to some immediate crisis: Suez in 1956; Lebanon in 1958; or the Chinese move into Korea in the winter of 1950-51. Under such circumstances, the estimates may be forthcoming in a matter of days or even hours.

The original draft for these estimates is usually prepared by an interdepartmental working group consisting primarily of representatives from the Department of State, the Defense Intelligence Agency, and the three military services, and chaired by a CIA representative. Pre-

sumably these are working-level officials expert in the particular problem or area under consideration. The key role in guiding these draft
estimates through the working groups and then putting them into final
shape for presentation to the U.S. Intelligence Board is played by the
Board of National Estimates.

This little-known group within the Central Intelligence Agency is
one of the most important in the entire intelligence field. The Board
consists of fifteen to twenty experienced and senior intelligence officers
supported by a small professional staff; their function is the supervision, editing, and final preparation of the National Intelligence Estimates. Their work is highly regarded in many quarters, but it is obviously impossible for the outside observer to appraise it.

The National Intelligence Surveys represent another major product
of the intelligence community. They are encyclopedic compendia dealing individually with most of the countries of the world and covering a
broad range of topics, from political structure and processes and military capabilities to transportation and communications networks and
availability of natural resources. Different parts of the surveys are assigned to member agencies in terms of their special knowledge and
skills, with Central Intelligence responsible for final editing and approval. These surveys are periodically reviewed and updated, sometimes every year; frequency of revision varies with the importance of
the country and the pace of change within it.

Little has been said in this discussion about the overseas activities
of the intelligence community. Brief comment on two major problem
areas must suffice. First, as was pointed out in Chapter 9, the fact that
many U.S. elements report on developments overseas produces a real
need for coordinating their intelligence-gathering activities. The present division of labor represents neither a rational nor an economic use
of intelligence resources.

It has been widely reported in published accounts that elements in
the intelligence community are responsible for carrying on or supporting covert operations abroad designed to accomplish particular U.S.
foreign policy objectives. These activities are said to go beyond espio-
nage and to be of such a nature that knowledge of U.S. involvement
would be damaging to its interests. For present purposes, it is enough
to stress that any such operations as may take place require the same
policy guidance and monitoring as the overt foreign affairs activities

and programs of the U.S. government. The organizational means for implementing this requirement may be different, but the requirement itself is, in principle, the same.

Planning Units

It has already been made clear that planning, as defined, can be accomplished just about anywhere in the national security organization—and often is. Even when the initiative for a particular project comes from the planning staff, the contributions of line or operational units are likely to be sought. Requirements for providing such assistance may even be levied on them.

To generalize further, planning activities have expanded considerably in the last few years, and current operational problems are probably more commonly viewed from what might be called a planning perspective than would have been the case five years ago. A number of factors help explain this increasing orientation toward thinking ahead systematically with a view to present action.

The long-term character of the international situation that faces the United States suggests that *ad hoc* responses to crises and challenges are neither adequate nor reassuring. Such responses probably add to the cost of maintaining its national security, a factor not to be ignored; they become increasingly less acceptable as the United States grows more experienced in the business of international politics and more assured in the playing of its own role. Finally, they represent a mighty challenge to the scientific-rationalistic orientation of the American culture and character, which refuses to admit that even the complexities of contemporary international affairs cannot be more fully understood and anticipated and thus at least partially controlled and manipulated.

Perhaps this explanation is unnecessarily elaborate. Certainly it should not be implied that this change represents anything more than a developing trend. Particularly among the civilian foreign policy agencies, planning efforts are still very much at the experimental stage, with a variety of formats and techniques being explored. About many problems that concern the foreign policy maker, the reliable knowledge and predictive power that can be contributed by the social sciences and others are relatively modest (although it should be added that even this modest body of knowledge has not been fully drawn on by the foreign policy agencies). Nevertheless, planning as a posture and as an activity is becoming increasingly important in the intellectual activities of national security agencies.

Under present arrangements, the President's national security affairs staff is not in a position to carry on policy planning of its own. Even under the more elaborate National Security Council structure and staffing of the Eisenhower Administration, the attached staffs were primarily concerned with the operation of the Security Council machinery. In both cases, the primary planning role of the presidential staffs and the National Security Council has been to focus and occasionally to prod the efforts of the line departments.

The National Security Council policy papers, as they were prepared before the Kennedy Administration, were an effort to anticipate future lines of development and set appropriate present courses of policy. The basic national security policy paper set forth the framework of guiding assumptions, objectives, and policies in terms of which more immediate decisions could presumably be taken. The operations plans prepared under the aegis of the Operations Coordination Board were a form of program planning—or at least a statement of present, ongoing programs, usually on a country basis. While the Kennedy Administration dropped almost all of these formats, it encouraged its own varieties of studies, planning exercises, and basic policy and program documents.

It should be noted that planning efforts directly or indirectly related to foreign policy are carried on or sponsored by other units within the Executive Office of the President. As indicated in Chapter 8, the Office of Science and Technology has a broad interest in the military and foreign policy implications of scientific research and development. Before its formal change in status in 1962, this presidential staff played a role in strengthening the scientific capabilities of the Defense and State Departments and in supporting the establishment of a strengthened Arms Control and Disarmament Agency. The Office of Science and Technology and the President's Science Advisory Committee together with its various subsidiary scientific advisory panels continue to play an important role in drawing governmental attention to scientific fields being ignored or critical questions going unanswered.

The Office of Emergency Planning in the Executive Office, along with the Office of Civil Defense—now a part of the Defense Department—are the major responsible units attempting to plan, in terms of possible domestic consequences and requirements, for the variety of critical contingencies the nation may face, from a major natural disaster to the ultimate disaster of thermonuclear war.

The Bureau of the Budget, through its legislative clearance and budget preparation responsibilities, probably has the key role in coordinating program planning on a governmentwide basis. As budgetary problems mesh with broader considerations relating to the state of the economy, its concerns are closely related to those of the Council of Economic Advisers and, from a somewhat different perspective, those of the Treasury Department.

Most substantive planning continues to be done in the departments. Both the Kennedy and Johnson Administrations have strongly emphasized departmental planning responsibilities. Furthermore, certain major foreign policy documents, like the national policy papers, are now given final authoritative approval by the Secretary of State rather than the President.

After experimenting with a number of formats, the various foreign policy agencies, under the leadership of the State Department's Policy Planning Council, have been developing a series of "national policy papers" that embody U.S. policy toward particular foreign nations. As was noted in Chapter 9, these are distinguished from earlier efforts of this kind by the more detailed analysis of country situations and by the linking of U.S. objectives and policies with specific agency operations and programs in these countries.[13]

The work of the Department of State's Policy Planning Council has been described in some detail in Chapter 5. In addition to its own efforts, the Council and its members encourage and support planning efforts elsewhere in the Department and participate and sometimes provide leadership for a variety of interdepartmental planning efforts.

There is usually a designated point of contact with the Council within each of the operating bureaus in the State Department. Some of the Department's geographic and functional bureaus have relatively senior officers serving as "planning advisers." How much planning these officials actually engage in will vary from person to person and time to time. It is easy, and tempting, to use such a person—with no

[13] See the excerpts in Chap. 9 from the testimony of William J. Crockett, Deputy Under Secretary of State for Administration, before the second Jackson subcommittee.

well-defined area of responsibility—as a kind of roving special assistant and added organizational resource. This may well leave little time for anything that could reasonably be labelled planning.

The present focus of the economic aid program on development of the underdeveloped countries suggests a considerable need for long-range planning, both within the recipient countries and within the U.S. government, as well as for the program planning necessary to translate long-term strategies into year-by-year U.S. assistance. In its current organizational set-up, the Agency for International Development has an Office of Programming and Planning in each of its four geographic bureaus. The programming units are concerned with the detailed decisions and massive paperwork involved in translating foreign aid appropriations into approved country programs and projects. Their work is further complicated by the frequent readjustments and reprogramming called for as regional aid priorities are modified and funds reallocated for one reason or another.

The planning units are responsible for the longer-range view and projections. One effort now being pushed within the Agency for International Development is the formulation of a series of long-range country assistance studies. These are designed to put U.S. assistance on a more systematic basis, linked to an overall concept of a country's development and related strategic factors. Presumably, this is intended to minimize *ad hoc* responses to the political pressures of the moment and a resultant congeries of individual projects sometimes bearing little relation to one another and not reflecting any guiding development strategy.

There are obvious difficulties in the way of such an approach. Many of the countries being assisted do not have the indigenous planning and administrative capabilities that are an important if not essential counterpart of any U.S. planning efforts. Furthermore, there will continue to be significant uncertainties about the funds that Congress will appropriate for this purpose, and there will also continue to be situations where U.S. assistance will be provided to countries for reasons—often put in the broad category "political"—which have little to do with their economic needs, capabilities, or relationship to some overall concept or plan. Nevertheless, if long-term socioeconomic development is the guiding purpose of the economic aid program, and if the United States must provide a good deal of the planning in many of the countries being assisted, it seems quite appropriate for the Agency for International Development to be thinking in terms of long-range assistance strategies and to have organizational units charged with planning for their regions of responsibility.

Since the field of arms control and disarmament represents for the most part future possibilities and hopes, at least at present writing, much of the work of the Arms Control and Disarmament Agency is oriented to studies, research, and projections into the future. From its original establishment in 1961, its ranking officials have emphasized their interest in the assistance of outside scholars and research organizations and have contracted for a substantial number of outside studies. For a time, the Agency also had a special policy planning staff of three senior officials, the Disarmament Advisory Committee, which has now been abolished.

The range and variety of military planning activities were mentioned earlier in the chapter. From the foreign policy viewpoint, the most important of these are carried on by the military staffs and the Office of the Secretary of Defense in Washington and by the unified and specified commands in the field.

Two developments in military planning since World War II are particularly noteworthy. The first is the steadily increasing use of scientific theories and methods of analysis—borrowing particularly from the physical sciences and statistics—and the computers which so strikingly enhance the utility of these theories and methods. Perhaps an inevitable concomitant of the first has been the increasing role of civilian personnel in many of these analytical efforts of the military establishment, both directly on the government payroll and in the growing corps of satellite and independent research organizations, individual consultants, and public advisory panels that provide assistance to the Defense Department.

Secretary McNamara's distinctive contribution has been to put these massive intellectual resources to work on those problems he felt warranted priority attention and on which he planned to take action. To repeat a general point made in Chapter 6, Mr. McNamara's energy, keenness, and clear sense of direction have fashioned an effective organizational instrument from resources that were to a considerable extent already present. One important addition was the Directorate for Systems Analysis established in 1961 under the Defense Comptroller and headed by former RAND analyst Alain Enthoven. Also, the small Policy Planning Staff that had existed in the Office of International Security Affairs was expanded and another RAND alumnus, Henry Rowen, appointed as Deputy Assistant Secretary of Defense to head it.

It was pointed out above that there is in fact a U.S. "intelligence community" in the sense that departmental intelligence organizations do engage in joint enterprises and do produce estimates and surveys that represent their agreed views on particular subjects. If the intelligence community is the basis of comparison, there are only the modest beginnings of a U.S. "planning community," and much of it is a development of the last few years.

A good part of the explanation lies in the fact that the planning function is by no means as well-defined as intelligence and that what has been called planning here is carried out by a number of units within particular agencies to serve a wide variety of organizational purposes. Even where the substantive relationship between agency planning activities has been rather clear, it has not typically been reflected in organizational coordination. This is now beginning to change.

The State and Defense Departments do engage in some coordinated contingency planning. The Berlin situation provides one excellent example. Long-range planning for the Military Assistance Program involves the Agency for International Development as well as the State and Defense Departments. The State Department is beginning to play a limited role with regard to military establishment budget and force planning.

The problems of social, economic, and political development in the less developed countries are also beginning to get the concerted attention of planners in the Agency for International Development and the United States Information Agency as well as in the State and Defense Departments. Whatever the specific results to date of these efforts at coordinated planning, it can be said with assurance that the desirability of such planning is gaining rapidly increasing recognition within the foreign policy organization.

Assistance from Nongovernmental Sources

If the national security policy maker is not satisfied with the intellectual resources available to him within the governmental bureaucracy, he does not have to settle for them—provided he can afford outside assistance and advice. One of the hallmark characteristics of the post-World War II period has been the burgeoning of research organizations located outside the formal governmental structure though largely supported by government contracts. The military services, understandably, led the way in establishing or supporting these organizations. The challenge of a highly dynamic and highly competitive (both among the services themselves and vis-à-vis the Soviet Union) weapons technology, the fantastically varied and complex functions the military services are called upon to perform, the consequent dependence on frontier developments in the physical sciences and engineering, and—not to be ignored—the very substantial funds available to them for research and development purposes, help explain this development.

Organizational variety has been the theme. The services set up semi-autonomous research corporations either solely or primarily dependent on them for funds. The outstanding example in this category is the Air Force-supported RAND Corporation. The Army did have an Operations Research Office run for it under contract by Johns Hopkins University; this has been succeeded by the Research Analysis Corporation. The Massachusetts Institute of Technology runs the Operations Evaluation Group under contract for the Navy. These are the best-known examples of what might be termed "satellite" research organizations. Each of the services has a number that would fall in this category.

Another noteworthy phenomenon has been the appearance of the large research organization run by a university but more or less completely separated from its teaching and other research activities. Examples are MIT's Lincoln Laboratories and the Jet Propulsion Laboratory of the California Institute of Technology. Here again, the major customer has been the military establishment (although the Atomic Energy Commission and the National Aeronautics and Space Administration have also figured prominently), and the work has been primarily in the physical sciences and engineering. Regarding the last point, one of the trends of recent years has been the increasing attention—and financial support—given by the military establishment to social and behavioral science research.

The Institute for Defense Analyses represents another organizational variation. Originally incorporated as a nonprofit organization by a number of major universities, its essential purpose was to make available to the military establishment scientific and technical talent that would be difficult or impossible to recruit through the usual civil service procedures at going civil service salary scales. Thus, much of the scientific work of the Weapons Systems Evaluation Group of the Joint Chiefs of Staff has actually been done by a division administratively a part of the Institute for Defense Analyses.

The Institute has since branched out and broadened its activities. It does social as well as physical science research. In addition to the research it carries on for the Advanced Research Projects Agency (ARPA), the Office of International Security Affairs, and other units within the Office of the Secretary of Defense, it has in recent years started to do contract work for the Department of State, the Arms Control and Disarmament Agency, and the Agency for International Development.

The civilian national security agencies have in general increased their use of outside research resources. One practical limitation has been the availability of funds. In both the economic development and arms control fields, however, the relevant 1961 legislation laid particular emphasis on research, and much larger research funds have been voted to the Arms Control and Disarmament Agency and the Agency for International Development since then.[14] The State Department has extremely limited funds, counted in tens of thousands rather than in millions of dollars, available to contract for outside research assistance.[15] It has probably the least resources for such purposes of all the agencies with foreign affairs programs and responsibilities. It does not have any particular outside organization to call on for such assistance. This was one of the reasons that the proposal for establishing a National Academy of Foreign Affairs, which was made in early 1963, included a research center as one of the Academy's major units.[16]

---

[14] For example, the research and analysis program of the Agency for International Development for fiscal year 1965 amounted to $12 million. See *Proposed Mutual Defense and Development Programs Fiscal Year 1966,* Summary Presentation to the Congress by AID and the Department of Defense (Government Printing Office, 1965), p. 192. As noted in Chap. 8, more than half the ACDA budget has been allocated to research; for fiscal year 1965 ACDA had more than $5 million available for research.

[15] In fiscal year 1965, $125,000 was appropriated to the State Department for this purpose.

[16] This ambitious advanced training and research center was proposed by a presi-

It should be noted that the Department of State has traditionally had a reputation, and not without some justification, of a lack of interest in outside research assistance. Defenders of such a point of view tend to emphasize the differences between military and foreign policy problems and point out that while many dimensions of the former lend themselves to scientific, quantitative analysis, the most important foreign policy decisions involve matters of policy judgment and of highly current intelligence information—in both of which it is assumed that the Department is likely to be better equipped than any outside research or consulting organization. However, foreign policy decisions also rest, or should rest, on analyses of relevant aspects of the international scene. Here, in some instances, outside research organizations should be able to strengthen what internal staffs have to offer.[17]

The new varieties of government-supported and government-sponsored research organizations—semi-attached, semi-detached, and com-

---

dential advisory panel headed by Dr. James Perkins, now president of Cornell University. The text of the Perkins panel's report and recommendations appears in the *Department of State News Letter*, No. 21 (January 1963), pp. 6 ff. The National Foreign Affairs College proposed by the Herter Committee (of which Dr. Perkins was a member) was quite similar to the Academy; the major difference was the Academy's proposed emphasis on research as well as training. See Committee on Foreign Affairs Personnel, *Personnel for the New Diplomacy*, pp. 105-11.

In addition to the research center, the proposed Academy was to be distinguished from the present Foreign Service Institute by improved facilities, expanded course offerings, and a fully interdepartmental basis of operation. Hearings held on the proposal in the spring of 1963 by the Senate Foreign Relations Committee revealed some congressional reservations about it. Beyond continuing State Department efforts to strengthen the Foreign Service Institute, nothing has developed from the Academy idea.

[17] Whatever outside research the State Department itself may sponsor, it does have an interest in the foreign affairs research supported by other national security agencies to the extent that such research affects U.S. relations with other nations. This can happen, for example, when the research is actually carried on in a foreign country. Partly as a result of an embarrassing incident in Chile in connection with a research project supported by the Army Department, President Johnson in August 1965 charged the Secretary of State with reviewing all foreign areas research projects that other national security agencies proposed to support and assuring that none were undertaken that would adversely affect U.S. foreign relations. The Department of State took steps to implement this directive by establishing a Foreign Affairs Research Council as its review mechanism (see *Department of State News Letter*, No. 53 (September 1965), p. 20). The State Department's approach to this new responsibility was set forth in a speech by Thomas L. Hughes, Director of the Department's Bureau of Intelligence and Research, reported in *ibid.*, No. 55 (November 1965), pp. 14 ff.

pletely private, on campuses and off—by no means exhaust the picture of outside assistance available to government agencies. Individuals continue to act as consultants and carry out research projects for the Department of State and other national security agencies.

International relations research centers at schools like the Massachusetts Institute of Technology and Princeton are also research contractors. Indeed, if the funds are available, there is no fundamental stumbling-block to the foreign policy organization's calling on any of the intellectual resources of the country to help it do its job. There are a great variety of ways in which this can be done, and of possible relationships between the bureaucracy and the world outside.[18]

Major Problems

There are fundamental characteristics of the American political and governmental system that stand in the way of rational foreign policy analysis and decision making. Some of these were discussed in Chapter 2. In brief, the substantive difficulties of the mid-twentieth century are considerably compounded by the burdens and requirements of the separation of powers and executive-congressional relations, the number and variety of agencies in the national security business, and the relatively high turnover of career officials as well as political appointees.

The intellectual processes of foreign policy making reflect this organizational and political milieu. Who does what in particular situations or with regard to particular problem areas depends to a very considerable extent on the attitudes, skills, and experience of the key officials involved. Thus, while the aspects of policy making that have been labelled planning, policy analysis, and intelligence (in its estimating and anticipating dimensions) are closely related, it seems pointless to try to identify some ideal organizational relationship among them. The system is much too pluralistic, loosely disciplined, and intricately criss-crossed with lines of authority and communication for that. Much

---

[18] For a useful effort to canvass these relationships systematically, see Chadwick F. Alger, "The External Bureaucracy in United States Foreign Affairs," *Administrative Science Quarterly*, Vol. 7 (June 1962), pp. 50-78. A survey, somewhat critical in tone, of some of the major "outside" organizations that provide research and advice to the military establishment is to be found in Edward L. Katzenbach, Jr., "Ideas: A New Defense Industry," *The Reporter*, Vol. 24 (March 2, 1961), pp. 17-21.

more important are the general level and quality of intellectual skills within or available to the foreign policy organization and the effectiveness with which these are mustered and brought to bear on problems by the top leadership.

Intelligence-Policy-Planning Relationships

There always seems to be more work to do in the foreign policy organization than there are hands to do it. E. Northcote Parkinson might say that this is too kind, or naive, an observation, that the work is simply expanding to keep the many hands busy. Be this as it may, Parkinson would probably agree with a second point: first-rate work is always at a premium. Thus, even the ablest office director in a State Department geographic bureau does not have the time to be his own intelligence analyst and planning adviser on all the many problems he must cope with in the course of a month or a year. Even if he has spent considerable time in the country or countries for which he is responsible and is at least as knowledgeable about them as his intelligence colleagues, he is simply not going to have the time to do the more detailed study of a particular situation that his intelligence counterpart or the broader intelligence community is, hopefully, working on. Similarly, he may wish that he could sit down for several weeks and do a planning paper on developments in a key country over the next year, and their implications for U.S. policy, but he often does not have the time.

In other words, the organizational division of labor makes a rough kind of sense. Where there are mutual respect and good working relationships, the intellectual efforts of the individuals involved will tend to be reinforcing and mutually helpful. Where there are not respect and rapport, there will probably be duplication, frustration, and less adequate intellectual performance.

Even here, some organizational realities should be kept in mind. The fact that a particular intelligence office in the Department of State has poor working relations with its geographic bureau counterpart by no means eliminates its possible usefulness and effectiveness. Through the Director of Intelligence and Research, who attends the morning staff meetings of the Secretary of State and who may be called on in other circumstances for his analysis of some critical problem, this intel-

ligence office has an opportunity to bring its views before the most senior officials of the State Department. Through its participation in the
national intelligence estimating process of the interdepartmental "intelligence community," its influence may have an even wider ambit—
the heads of other agencies, the National Security Council, and the
President.

Planning staffs represent a flexible organizational resource. The
kind of work they are asked to do depends very much on the concerns
and the intellectual orientation of their immediate bosses and the senior officials to whom the latter in turn are ultimately responsible. This
point has already been made with regard to the Policy Planning Council of the State Department, which has from its inception been attached directly to the office of the Secretary. It is said that the Planning Staff worked more closely with the Secretary of State and had a
more central role in policy formulation during Mr. Acheson's tenure of
office than that of Mr. Dulles.[19] Critics believed that it did less long-
range planning under both men than would have been desirable.

As the concept and the processes of planning become increasingly
accepted and institutionalized in the State Department and in the foreign policy organization more generally, it must be assumed that the
nature and extent of the planning carried on will depend less on the
personal preferences of the Secretary. The effectiveness of planning
efforts—in terms of policy and operational consequences—will continue
to depend in large measure on the sympathetic understanding and support of the Secretary and his senior colleagues in the Department,
which—to complete the circle—are likely to reflect the responsiveness of
the planners to the latter's needs and purposes.

Members of the Policy Planning Council and planning officers in
the geographic bureaus are interested consumers of the estimates and
more substantial studies of the Bureau of Intelligence and Research
and the wider intelligence community. This is a quite natural relationship. Analytically speaking, solid intelligence estimates of the future
are the necessary foundation of any worthwhile policy planning. Organizationally speaking, intelligence and planning units are both a step
removed from current operating responsibilities.

As has already been indicated, relationships between intelligence

[19] See Robert E. Elder, *The Policy Machine: The Department of State and American Foreign Policy* (Syracuse University Press, 1960), pp. 85-87.

offices and line bureaus in the State Department vary widely. The Wriston program, under which many civil servant-intelligence specialists were brought into the Foreign Service,[20] is usually viewed as the turning-point in explaining the present weaknesses and strengths of the Bureau of Intelligence and Research (INR).

Some observers feel that the losses in expertise suffered as "Wristonized" civil servant specialists were rotated overseas and replaced by less specialized Foreign Service Officers have been at the least counterbalanced by the improved working relationships that now exist with Foreign Service Officers manning many of the intelligence as well as policy desks. Others argue that one major justification for a separate intelligence organization is precisely to keep the policy officials honest, to provide a source of information and analysis independent of the policy officials; they question whether this is as likely to be the case with Foreign Service Officers filling both sets of positions.

This last point rests on a doubtful assumption, as anyone will testify who has seen Foreign Service Officers representing the various geographic bureaus struggle over policies involving their particular countries or regions. Furthermore, while civil servants who "Wristonized" tended to be replaced by Foreign Service Officers, many of their colleagues did not go into the Foreign Service and remain in INR to this day. In addition, the intelligence specialists who did become Foreign Service Officers have begun to return from overseas tours of duty, and some of them have been assigned in Washington to the intelligence bureau. There are even some new civil servant specialists being recruited into the bureau.[21] In other words, whatever the present assets and liabilities of intelligence-policy relationships within the Department of State, the explanation is much more complicated than the consequences of the Wriston program, far-reaching as these were.

Because some of the State Department's difficulties in this field seem intrinsic to the intellectual and organizational relationships

[20] See Chap. 5.
[21] Recent statistical data indicate that of 197 officer-level positions in intelligence and research, 136 were filled by Civil Service personnel and the remainder by Foreign Service. In the last few years, there has been a tendency to hire specialists through Civil Service when the necessary expertness has not been available within the Foreign Service. For the statistical tables, see the *Manpower Profile: Departmental and Foreign Service*, published by the Office of Personnel, Department of State, July 1964, pp. 16 and 17.

involved, it can be assumed that they are shared by other agencies. A central intelligence organization, like the Central Intelligence Agency, has in some ways even greater difficulties. Its primary function is to service departments and officials outside of its own organization. Thus, top foreign policy officials and middle-level functionaries alike are put in a position of accepting and acting upon information and analyses developed to a large extent outside their own agencies.

It seems a reasonable hypothesis that many officials are likely to feel uncomfortable about this and find it quite difficult to do. To stake major questions of policy and program on anonymous intellectual products that come from outside one's own organization seems likely to arouse considerable anxiety and reluctance. There are undoubtedly difficulties even in the case of one's own department. If, for example, the Secretary of State is making use of an analysis of Egyptian politics prepared in the State Department intelligence bureau, he is not likely to know its author; he does, however, know and work closely with the Director of the intelligence bureau, who is one of his senior subordinates, and can hold him accountable for the quality of specific efforts as well as overall bureau performance.[22]

In the many instances where there is general agreement on some matter within the intelligence community, this particular dilemma is not likely to arise. When it does, it can be hypothesized that the departmental official is more likely to accept the views of his departmental intelligence organization than those of CIA. This by no means represents a complete loss for CIA. By statutory prescription, its Director sits as adviser to the National Security Council and, on this basis alone, has direct access to the President and the National Security Council. Furthermore, the key role of the Agency in the national intelligence estimating process assures it of a substantial impact on most

---

[22] A highly experienced senior intelligence official, Allan Evans, reports the following distinction between departmental and central intelligence products: "Departmental intelligence, they say, through its closer association with operations, more easily sticks to earth and remains aware of obstacles and the variety of unpredictables—of the facts of life, in short—but is also susceptible to the besetting complacency of operators who tend to feel that their operations must be going right. Central intelligence, on the other hand, is alleged to keep a sharper alert, to be keener at detecting ominous potentials, but to suffer a liability to see more ghosts and goblins than exist." See his review article, "Intelligence and Policy Formation," *World Politics*, Vol. 12 (October 1959), p. 87.

of what is produced. Its influential position is further supported by its intelligence coordinating role, its important and highly sensitive intelligence-gathering responsibilities and even more sensitive operational assignments, and the very substantial resources of men and money made available to it.[23]

The Quality of Intellectual Performance

The institutional impediments to first-rate intellectual performance in the foreign policy organization have already been made quite clear. The kinds of skills and abilities required have been touched on briefly in the present chapter and in earlier ones and are set forth in greater detail in Chapter 11.

To one who has, successively, observed the process of foreign policy making from afar, talked at length to those involved in it, and finally become a participant himself, the general intellectual quality of the people and what they produce via the spoken and written word is impressive. This is not to imply that everyone is first-rate and everything they do and say articulate, brilliant, and wise. But the general level of performance is high. Keenly analytical papers and studies are written and instructions sent to field missions as a matter of daily routine. Perhaps this is what is particularly impressive: a high order of intelligence under continuing, daily pressure to perform, to "put out."

There is not the leisure of academia. The work must be done every day, and to have done it extremely well one day brings no relief from next day's pressure. The foreign policy organization not only performs impressively on the most complicated and challenging of problems, and acts on the basis of this intellectual product, but must carry on this performance as a matter of course, as a matter of daily routine, with precious little time for the recharging of batteries. Of course, this continuing pressure has its disadvantages and imposes limitations. Problems often cannot be given the exploration in depth that they warrant.

[23] The existence and operations of the Central Intelligence Agency raise problems even more fundamental than its relationship to the making of foreign policy. The question of the nature and extent of congressional surveillance of the Agency's covert activities represents, probably in its sharpest form, the more general problem discussed in Chap. 3 of the compatibility of the requisites of representative democracy with those of mid-twentieth century international relations.

One must settle for good, quick responses rather than excellent ones produced in more measured fashion.

Clearly, in the bureaucratic setting, more than good intellectual work is called for. It must be combined with the patience, persistence, energy, and occasional toughness required to operate effectively in such a setting. The complicated and extremely cumbersome governmental system that has been described in these pages in a sense only works at all because many very capable people devote their considerable talents and energies to overcoming its built-in inertia and making it work in spite of itself.

The Use and Utility of Outside Assistance

The essential problem in the use of nongovernmental assistance is an extension of the internal problem already discussed at length. It can make a contribution only to the extent that officials responsible for formulating and implementing policy recognize a need for such assistance, arrange to obtain it, and then take it into account as they make their decisions. If ignored, outside studies, like internal planning papers or intelligence estimates, are obviously useless for policy purposes, no matter how impressive their intellectual quality.

Depending on the situation and the precise nature of his arrangements with the government, the outside contractor or adviser may as an alternative try to get his views before the public or Congress. Similarly, the planner and the intelligence analyst have other organizational channels open to them if their views are ignored by the policy official. Nevertheless, in terms of a sensible division of labor, the preferable arrangement is one in which intelligence analyst, planner, and outside consultant are providing intellectual materials to the policy official that he does not have the time, and perhaps the necessary skills and background, to develop himself. In those circumstances, they are adding to the relevant knowledge and analyses available to him as he makes decisions of varying degrees of urgency and significance.

Just as there are problems of analysis, understanding, or extended forethought more appropriately dealt with by the "intelligence community" or the planners than by operating units, there are questions that an outside person or organization may be better equipped to study and advise on. Some may call for more extended, detailed, and systematic investigation than is practically possible within the bureaucracy. Others may demand special kinds of expertness or detailed knowledge, available in sufficient array only at certain private research centers or universities. Others may profit from study with the more sophisticated research methods and theories that are the distinguishing hallmarks of first-rate universities and their staffs.

Looking at this relationship from the point of view of the foreign policy official, he should, ideally, have a pretty sophisticated awareness of what he doesn't know and would like to know, and how particular outside agencies or persons can fill these gaps of knowledge or understanding. There is no particular magic to outside assistance and advice although these may, unfortunately, have status-symbol appeal to the uncertain bureaucrat. On problems that involve access to substantial quantities of classified data and where seasoned policy judgment has a great deal to do with the answer arrived at, the outside advisory group or research organization may be of little real use, unless it is policy legitimation rather than policy assistance that is in fact sought.

If the government official must be self-conscious about his intellectual needs and how best to meet them, the outsider needs an equal degree of self-consciousness about what he has to offer. Is he in a position to contribute ideas, techniques of analysis, or bodies of theory and data not readily available to the governmental organization? Or is he essentially going to provide alternative policy views to the policy officials who have hired him? This outsider-insider relationship parallels in a number of ways the intragovernmental relationships that have been considered in this chapter. It calls for the same intellectual self-consciousness, the same mutual respect and rapport, and the same agreed understanding of the nature of policy analysis and what each can best contribute to it.

Such relationships do not develop overnight. Important elements of the foreign policy organization, including the Department of State, have had relatively limited experience with outside assistance. If resort to such assistance increases, as is likely, it seems reasonable to expect some experimentation and some learning—with high hopes disappointed and skepticism confirmed as well as useful working relationships developed.

In these circumstances, it seems premature to establish one institution as a major source of outside assistance for the Department of State and the other foreign policy agencies. This is particularly true when there are already in existence a score or more university research centers and private research organizations doing highly relevant, first-rate work. From this point of view, the research center aspect of the proposed National Academy of Foreign Affairs seemed to many the most questionable, even though its proponents did not intend for it any exclusive or all-encompassing role. The whole question of what kind of outside assistance the Department of State and the other foreign affairs agencies need is new enough to suggest the desirability of moving slowly and developing experience before becoming committed to a major institution.

The same general point can be made about some of the proposals in the waning years of the Eisenhower Administration for autonomous but quasi-governmental research organizations linked in some way to the Executive Office of the President.[24] It is not always possible to recruit top-notch personnel for such organizations. After all, the pool of talent in this field is rather limited; any new organization must compete to some extent with well-established and prestigious research institutions. Furthermore, intellectual needs will vary from one administration, or one President or Secretary of State, to another.

In this regard, it may be further hypothesized that those agencies and officials that seem most in need of outside help, from the outside observer's point of view, will be precisely those least interested in it and unable or unwilling to do much with that made available to them.

The Role of the Top Leadership

The complexities of the American system demand a great deal of its ranking officials. How effectively the system works depends to a considerable extent on their organizational, intellectual, and leadership skills. The strengths of those in charge must compensate for some of the inadequacies of the system.

Their role is critical for two fundamental reasons: they must make

[24] See, for example, Roger Hilsman, "Planning for National Security: A Proposal," *Bulletin of the Atomic Scientists,* Vol. XVI (March 1960), pp. 93-97. Some of the organizational possibilities are noted and evaluated in H. Field Haviland, Jr. and Associates, *The Formulation and Administration of United States Foreign Policy,* A Report for the Committee on Foreign Relations of the United States Senate (Brookings Institution, 1960), pp. 102-05.

the key decisions; and, furthermore, the way they run the foreign policy organization and the leadership they provide it set its tone and style. On the first point, to summarize an earlier discussion, the top departmental officials should not be thought of as primarily the ratifiers of the work done by their subordinates. While they must rely to a considerable extent on staff analyses and recommendations, on the questions they define as important they usually make the critical choices.

The leaders have considerable choice about how to bring organizational resources to bear on problems and which decision-making patterns and procedures to employ. These choices will be influenced in turn by their knowledge of the intellectual resources available to them within their organizations and their notions about how the foreign policy business should ideally be conducted.

From the point of view of the more effective intellectual performance of the foreign policy organization, senior officials should be aware of the pool of intellectual skills and talents available to them and should pay serious attention to the manner in which the organization performs its intellectual work; they should enter into this intellectual activity short of the point at which its finished products are passed up to them.

In a general way, this same prescription was applied to the President in Chapter 4. It may be protested that not only the President but, equally, the Secretary of State and other senior officials simply do not have the time for this kind of effort and interest, theoretically commendable though it may be. Perhaps this is the case. If it is, the intellectual efforts of the foreign policy organization will not get the leadership or sense of direction they require, and they are bound to suffer in the process.

11

Personnel

IT IS OFTEN SAID that good people are more important to the effective functioning of the foreign policy organization—or to any organization for that matter—than good organizational machinery. Unfortunately, in both cases the "good" qualities tend to be left undefined. As this study has shown, there are considerable uncertainty and disagreement about what governmental machinery could cope most effectively with the foreign policy problems of the United States. Perhaps the skills, attitudes, knowledge, and experience that *people* need to deal with these problems can more easily be defined. This, in any event, is one major purpose of this chapter.

With regard to the question of "good people" versus "good organization," the primarily organizational analysis of the preceding ten chapters does suggest one basic point. The American governmental system is characterized by continuing organizational change—major additions or innovations as well as minor tinkering—and a rather high turnover of career as well as political personnel. The effects of the latter are sharpened by the normal personnel rotation built into the military and foreign service systems. Given these characteristics, it seems essential that appropriately skilled career personnel (and a pool of similarly skilled outsiders to draw on for political appointments) be available in depth to man the foreign policy organization, no matter what its structure of the moment.

If there is a sufficiently large corps of people with the right knowledge and training, who "know their way around Washington," they can carry on the substantive business of foreign policy no matter what the organizational peculiarities of the moment. In that sense, the search for good people should have some priority over the concern for good organization. The organizational analyst's retort is that since the likelihood of either attracting enough good people or developing rational organizational arrangements is equally low, it is important to keep working at both; each, furthermore, will tend to reinforce the other.

Present Personnel Patterns

The Herter Committee compares the foreign affairs personnel systems of the United States to a "patchwork quilt," where "new and hasty improvisations mix uneasily with old and well-established practices."[1] This is not unjust. A brief summary description of the systems suggests an almost masochistic complexity and confusion. At the same time, it is well to remember that some of these apparent monstrosities have their rationale or at least historical explanation, that the ingenuity of man does enable the system to function, and that its very ambiguities and overlappings have been employed to serve useful purposes, for example, to recruit into the organization able people who might not otherwise have been available.

Personnel of the major foreign affairs agencies fall into three broad categories: Civil Service employees; a number of special career services separated either completely or to some degree from the Civil Service and its rules and regulations; and, finally, the broad range of "polit-

[1] The Committee on Foreign Affairs Personnel, *Personnel for the New Diplomacy* (Carnegie Endowment for International Peace, December 1962), p. 20. Chap. III of this report provides a useful summary of these personnel systems.

The work of this Committee, chaired by former Secretary of State Christian Herter, has been referred to in earlier chapters, and is discussed in detail later in this chapter. One of the useful byproducts of the Committee's efforts is a series of monographs originally prepared for it and then published for wider use by the Carnegie Endowment, which sponsored the entire undertaking by the Committee. The first five of these monographs were published in 1965; the sixth was multilithed for limited distribution. 1. Arthur G. Jones, *The Evolution of Personnel Systems for U. S. Foreign Affairs: A History of Reform Efforts;* 2. Robert E. Elder, *Overseas Representation and Services for Federal Domestic Agencies;* 3. John E. Harr, *The Development of Careers in the Foreign Service;* 4. John E. Harr, *The Anatomy of the Foreign Service—A Statistical Profile;* 5. Regis Walther, *Orientations and Behavioral Styles of Foreign Service Officers;* and 6. Frances Fielder and Godfrey Harris, *The Quest for Foreign Affairs Officers—Their Recruitment and Selection.*

ical" or "noncareer" officials who are recruited outside competitive career service channels, whether subject to Senate confirmation or not.

It is not possible to differentiate Civil Service employees in detail since they comprise the bulk of civilians employed by the United States government. The most important of the special career services are the Foreign Service and the three military services. The employees of the Central Intelligence Agency have a personnel system separate from, though similar to, the Civil Service. Political or noncareer appointees have as little homogeneity as these other groups. Two major categories are those positions subject to Senate confirmation and the wide range of ES or Excepted Schedule positions, including some of a "confidential or policy-determining character."[2]

Foreign Service and Civil Service

By the terms of the Foreign Service Act of 1946, the Foreign Service consists of three major groups: Foreign Service Officers (FSO's); Foreign Service Reserve officers (FSR's); and Foreign Service Staff (FSS). The Foreign Service Officers represent the principal professional staff of the Foreign Service and the Department of State. The Reserve category was provided to enable the Department and the Foreign Service to recruit for limited-duration tours of duty specialists and experts not available within the regular Officer Corps. Since the nature of this expertise was not spelled out, the Reserve officer category provides the State Department with a certain flexibility in meeting its personnel needs. As we shall see, this category also provides the basis under which personnel of the economic aid program are sent on overseas assignments; in the case of the United States Information Agency, it has not only served this purpose but also, until quite recently, provided a device for giving quasi-career status to its foreign service officers.

Foreign Service Staff officers and personnel represent essentially the clerical and technical personnel of the Foreign Service—for example, the code clerks, secretaries, couriers, and technical communications specialists. The Staff Corps serves primarily at overseas posts. Finally, the Foreign Service makes considerable use of local, non-American per-

---

[2] They are "excepted" in the sense that they are not subject to the usual Civil Service employment regulations.

sonnel, primarily though not exclusively in routine jobs in missions and consulates abroad.

The Foreign Service, under its own Director General, once had something of an autonomous, self-contained character vis-à-vis the rest of the State Department and even the Secretary of State. Although the position of Director General still exists, the Foreign Service is now clearly and unequivocally under the control of the Secretary and the senior officials of the State Department. This is made quite clear in the present, amended version of the Foreign Service Act of 1946.[3]

All three categories of United States Foreign Service personnel are represented in United States diplomatic missions and consulates abroad, which they staff. In the Department of State in Washington, a considerable number of Civil Service employees work alongside the Foreign Service personnel. This does raise problems of management and morale because the two systems differ in some important respects. The key difference is that in the Foreign Service rank is in the man, while the Civil Service system attaches rank, and pay, to the position actually held.

Each Foreign Service Officer belongs to a class. (There are ten classes or ranks, running from Class 8 at the bottom through 1 and then topped by the ranks of career minister and career ambassador.) He is evaluated and ranked annually on a comparative basis with the other members of his class, and promoted or not according to his standing. Since his rank and pay attach to him as a person, the system has considerable flexibility in moving him from position to position. A good personnel system tries to match the man to the appropriate job, but the man neither loses his rank if assigned to a position classified at a lower level nor gains if he is doing work above his level. In all of these ways, the Foreign Service is similar to the military services.

It is, on the other hand, markedly different from the Civil Service. In the latter system, rank and pay depend on the position actually occupied by the employee. (The Civil Service has 18 grades, ranging from 1 at the bottom to the so-called supergrades, 16, 17, and 18, at the top.) In the Civil Service, one is promoted only by being moved into a job

---

[3] The major portions of this Act are excerpted in Barnes and Morgan, *The Foreign Service of the United States* (Government Printing Office, 1961), App. 19, pp. 378-406.

with a higher classification or by having one's present job reclassified at a higher level. Thus, a bright and able young man in the Civil Service may move up quite rapidly as positions classified at higher grades are offered to him. The promotion of Foreign Service Officers depends on a more systematic, formalized review and evaluation process.

Since rank and status in the Civil Service are attached to the position actually occupied, it is far more difficult from the administrative point of view to move and rotate employees or send them on training assignments of any length. It is also almost impossible to remove them from their positions against their will short of such exceptional circumstances as a general reduction-in-force or incompetence charges and proceedings that are usually quite complicated and drawn-out. Even if a position is abolished, Civil Service regulations are such that another position appropriate to his skills (though not necessarily at the same rank) must usually be found for its occupant.

This points up another important difference between the Foreign Service and the Civil Service. It is not widely known, but the Foreign Service applies a system of "selection-out" to its officers. It provides that Foreign Service Officers who remain in one class for a certain number of years without promotion or who are identified by the annual selection (that is, promotion) boards as "substandard" in terms of the performance requirements of their class are subject to separation from the Service. While it is not possible to describe the system in detail, in recent years it has resulted in the annual forced retirement or resignation of two or three percent of the total Officer Corps. Furthermore, the selection-out is based, at least in principle, not on incompetence but simply on being below a certain standard of competence. The selection boards are composed primarily of senior Foreign Service Officers, but each board has a public member who is a full voting participant in its deliberatons. In addition, there are representatives of two or three of the other agencies with foreign responsibilities.

Finally, the Foreign and Civil Service systems also have somewhat different pay scales, markedly different retirement systems, distinctive provisions for in-service training and career development, and different bases and methods of recruitment.

The Department of State

The Department of State, then, is a somewhat unsystematic mixture of the three Foreign Service categories, Civil Service employees, and noncareer appointees of both the Senate-confirmation and Excepted Schedule varieties. (See Tables 1 and 2 for a detailed statistical breakdown.) These various personnel groupings are by no means compartmentalized in terms of organizational assignment although the Civil Service professionals do tend to be concentrated in such functional bureaus as Administration, Intelligence and Research, and Economic Affairs with very few to be found in the five geographic bureaus. The latter are the primary preserve of the Foreign Service Officers.

Under the implementation of the Wriston committee recommendations in 1954, all officer positions within the Department and overseas

> which were primarily concerned with (1) foreign affairs or (2) the executive management of or administrative responsibility for the overseas operations of the Department and the Foreign Service, for which there was interchangeability between the United States and abroad, were to be designated as Foreign Service Officer positions.[4]

Further experience under this program resulted in the "de-designation" of some positions on the grounds of the substance of the work performed and, also, in terms of the need either for continuity on the job or for very special skills and training not easily available even within an expanded Foreign Service.

Civil servants were permitted to remain in "designated" positions they already occupied, and some did. Furthermore, the system of designations was never so rigid that it was impossible to fill a designated position with a Civil Service employee if the personnel need could not easily be met from within the Foreign Service. The designation system was finally abandoned in 1962.

The essential point is that the effort under the Wriston program to draw a reasonably clear distinction between Foreign Service and Civil

[4] Quoted from a report prepared by the Department of State for the Senate Foreign Relations Committee and transmitted by Deputy Under Secretary for Administration Loy Henderson. This authoritative discussion of the designation of positions within the Department for occupancy by Foreign Service Officers appears in *Administration of the Department of State,* 86 Cong. 2 sess. (1960), pp. 1-40.

TABLE 1. *All Employees of the Department of State, June 30, 1965*

Category of Employment	All Areas		United States		Overseas	
	Number	Percentage of Total	Number	Percentage of Total	Number	Percentage of Total
U.S. citizens:						
Foreign Service	9,518[a]	*38.9*	2,304	*30.8*	7,214	*42.5*
Civil Service	5,166	*21.1*	5,166[b]	*69.2*	—	—
Total U.S. citizens	14,684	*60.0*	7,470	*100.0*	7,214	*42.5*
Foreign nationals	9,770	*40.0*	—	—	9,770[c]	*57.5*
Total employees	24,454	*100.0*	7,470	*100.0*	16,984	*100.0*

Source: Department of State.
[a] Includes 28 noncareer Chiefs of Mission and 25 intermittent employees.
[b] Includes (1) officials serving in unclassified positions such as Assistant Secretaries, (2) Excepted Schedule employees, (3) contract employees, (4) Wage Board employees, (5) employees assigned to the United Nations in New York City, and (6) employees of the International Boundary and Water Commission.
[c] Includes 196 intermittent employees.

TABLE 2. *Foreign Service Employees of the Department of State, June 30, 1965*

Category	Total		United States		Overseas	
	Number	Percentage of Total	Number	Percentage of Total	Number	Percentage of Total
Chiefs of Mission	111	*1.2*	—	—	111	*1.5*
Noncareer	28	—	—	—	28	—
Foreign Service Officers	83				83	
Foreign Service Officers	3,537[a]	*37.2*	1,196	*51.9*	2,341	*32.5*
Foreign Service Reserve officers	1,365	*14.3*	535	*23.2*	830	*11.5*
Foreign Service Staff officers and employees	4,505	*47.3*	573	*24.9*	3,932	*54.5*
Total	9,518	*100.0*	2,304	*100.0*	7,214	*100.0*

Source: Department of State.
[a] Excludes Foreign Service Officers serving as Chiefs of Mission.

Service positions within the State Department was by no means a complete success, and the distinction has grown progressively more fuzzy in the years since 1954. At the same time, it continues to be established policy to fill substantive positions with Foreign Service Officers if at all possible.

The top levels of the Department's hierarchy include the varying shades of political appointees, Foreign Service Officers, others appointed into the Reserve category, and high-ranking Civil Service employees, including some in the supergrade range. Some Assistant and Under Secretaries are political appointees; others are high-ranking Foreign Service Officers. There are even cases of successful civil servants moving up to the "political" level, like the recent Deputy Under Secretary of State for Administration, Roger Jones, a career administrator who was successively an Assistant Director of the Bureau of the Budget and Chairman of the Civil Service Commission before moving into the State Department position.

Other Foreign Affairs Agencies

The picture that has been drawn of State Department personnel arrangements applies in a general way to the other major foreign affairs agencies. As was noted in Chapter 6, most of the major units in the Office of the Secretary of Defense (OSD) of the Department of Defense include political appointee civilians and career civil servants as well as career military officers. Civil servants and military officers work side by side in the Office of International Security Affairs, with the present proportions roughly three civilians for every two military.

Both the United States Information Agency (USIA) and the Agency for International Development (AID) are permitted to make Foreign Service Reserve and Staff appointments under authority granted by the Foreign Service Act of 1946. Neither has been authorized by Congress to establish a permanent career service. Like the Department of State, both agencies are characterized by the numerical predominance of Civil Service employees in their Washington operations. However, the proportions are much more striking: in both cases, Foreign Service employees are a small minority, comprising about ten or fifteen percent of the personnel employed in the United States. (See Tables 3 and 5.) This means, among other things, that there are relatively few Washing-

TABLE 3. *Full-Time Employees of the United States*
Information Agency, November 30, 1965

Category of Employment	All Areas		United States		Overseas	
	Number	Percentage of Total	Number	Percentage of Total	Number	Percentage of Total
U. S. Citizens						
Foreign Service	1,812ᵃ	15.9	367	11.3	1,445	17.7
Civil Service	2,874	25.2	2,874ᵇ	88.7	—	—
Total U. S. citizens	4,686	41.1	3,241	100.0	1,445	17.7
Foreign nationals	6,714	58.9	—	—	6,714	82.3
Total employees	11,400	100.0	3,241	100.0	8,159	100.0

Source: United States Information Agency.
ᵃ Includes 32 State Department Foreign Service Officers assigned to USIA. Excludes 56 Career Reserve officers, 19 Limited Reserve officers, and 3 Staff employees on reimbursable detail to other agencies.
ᵇ Includes Wage Board employees and presidential appointees.

ton positions available for Information Agency and Agency for International Development personnel who have completed overseas assignments. It also raises the problem of too wide a gap between a "home service" primarily Civil Service in character and an "overseas service" in a somewhat anomalous Foreign Service Reserve status.

The Information Agency has been eager to establish its own career service but has so far been unable to obtain congressional authorization. This led to an interesting innovation—establishment of a Career Reserve category. On the basis of administrative action in July 1960, the Agency divided its Foreign Service Reserve officers into two categories, Career Reserve and Limited Reserve. The former included those officers who would be in a career foreign service corps if there were one; the latter were the more usual limited duration appointees. Since the law does allow two five-year appointments for Reserve officers and the possibility of further renewals beyond that ten-year period, the Information Agency had a certain period of grace available to it during which time it hoped to get some permanent basis for its foreign service personnel.

Meanwhile, it quite consciously modeled its Career Reserve after the Foreign Service Officer Corps. There were the same eight classes

TABLE 4. *Foreign Service Employees of the United States Information Agency, November 30, 1965*[a]

Category	Total		United States		Overseas	
	Number	Percentage of Total	Number	Percentage of Total	Number	Percentage of Total
Foreign Service Officers	15[b]	0.8	—	—	15	1.0
Foreign Service Career Reserve officers	883[c]	47.5	218	51.4	665	46.4
Foreign Service Limited Reserve officers	492	26.5	94	22.2	398	27.8
Foreign Service Staff	468	25.2	112	26.4	356	24.8
Total	1,858	100.0	424	100.0	1,434	100.0

Source: United States Information Agency.

[a] Excludes 32 State Department Foreign Service Officers assigned to USIA. Includes 78 Foreign Service employees on reimbursable detail to other agencies.

[b] These are junior Foreign Service Officers appointed by the President and confirmed by the Senate.

[c] The President has nominated most Career Reserve officers for appointment to the Foreign Service Officer Corps, but, at this writing, they have not yet been confirmed by the Senate (see note 26).

without the ranks of career minister and career ambassador, which are not open to any Reserve officers. Career Reserve officers were ranked and promoted by annual promotion panels, on which there was State Department representation. The procedures for recruitment of junior officers, and the examinations given them, were almost identical with those of the Foreign Service.[5] In effect, the Information Agency was carefully preparing its credentials for a permanent career service either parallel with or linked to the Foreign Service.

This process of patient preparation was finally rewarded in October 1964 when President Johnson announced an agreement between Secretary of State Dean Rusk and Information Agency Director Carl T. Rowan, under which most of USIA's Career Reserve officers would be integrated into the Foreign Service Officer Corps. The step was taken by administrative agreement and action rather than formal legislative authorization. In April 1965 the lists of Foreign Service Officer promo-

[5] In March 1964 the Information Agency and the Department of State began to give exactly the same general examination, at the same time and places, to their junior foreign service officer candidates. See the announcement in the *Department of State News Letter*, No. 33 (January 1964), p. 28.

TABLE 5. *Full-Time Employees of the Agency for International Development, June 25, 1965*[a]

Category of Employment	All Areas		United States		Overseas	
	Number	Percent-age of Total	Number	Percent-age of Total	Number	Percent-age of Total
U. S. citizens						
Foreign Service	4,012	26.9	473	15.1	3,539	30.0
Civil Service	2,662	17.8	2,662	84.9	—	—
Total U. S. citizens	6,674	44.7	3,135	100.0	3,539	30.0
Foreign nationals	8,244	55.3	—	—	8,244	70.0
Total employees	14,918	100.0	3,135	100.0	11,783	100.0

Source: Agency for International Development.

[a] Excludes 634 employees of other federal agencies assigned to AID, 2,769 U.S. national contract employees, 2,255 foreign national contract employees, and 180 part-time employees and consultants. Includes Wage Board and Excepted Schedule employees, and presidential appointees.

tions sent to the Senate for approval by President Johnson included 760 USIA Career Reserve officers selected for integration into the Foreign Service.[6]

Under the new arrangement, USIA's Foreign Service Officers will continue to serve as employees of that Agency, under the control of its Director, although greater interchange of officers between the State Department and the Information Agency is planned. The new FSO's will be administratively designated as Foreign Information Officers. They will be treated in all ways as members of the regular Foreign Service, including retirement provisions, promotions, and application of the system of selection-out mentioned above. Joint recruitment of junior officers will continue.

The Rusk-Rowan agreement does not affect the status of USIA's Civil Service, Foreign Service Staff, and Limited Reserve personnel. Those Career Reserve officers not accepted for regular Foreign Service appointments have the option of reverting to Limited Reserve status.[7]

The situation of the economic aid agency, whatever its label of the

[6] The USIA nominations were not acted on in the first session of the 89th Congress. In January 1966 the President submitted a slightly smaller list of 723 USIA Career Reserve officers for Senate approval.

[7] For the more detailed account of these developments, see the *Department of State News Letter,* No. 42 (October 1964), pp. 3-5.

TABLE 6. *Foreign Service Employees of the Agency for International Development, June 25, 1965*

Category	Total		United States		Overseas	
	Number	Percent-age of Total	Num-ber	Percent-age of Total	Number	Percent-age of Total
Foreign Service Reserve	3,370	*84.0*	417	*88.2*	2,953	*83.4*
Foreign Service Staff	642	*16.0*	56	*11.8*	586	*16.6*
Total	4,012	*100.0*	473	*100.0*	3,539	*100.0*

Source: Agency for International Development.

moment, has differed somewhat from that of the Information Agency. For one thing, since the inception of the Marshall Plan in 1948, Congress has tended to view economic aid as an essentially temporary program with a terminal date in sight; obviously, such a program does not require a permanent career staff. Furthermore, the personnel needs of the economic aid program have differed from those of both the Information Agency and the Department of State, particularly the latter.

Given the great variety of projects that the aid agency has helped supervise or carry out abroad, it has needed a much greater proportion of mature people already trained as professionals in their fields. Given the changing nature of these projects, many of these people could be or should be recruited and employed on a relatively short-term basis, for one or perhaps two overseas assignments. According to the Herter report, "AID hires relatively few junior professionals through competitive nationwide examinations."[8] At the same time, the Herter report goes on to emphasize the need for a core of long-term career personnel even within the economic aid agency.[9]

As with most new government programs, the Peace Corps has recruited its staff (as distinct from the Volunteers) from a variety of sources—Civil Service employees, political appointees and Foreign Service Officers detailed to the Corps for duty. The Foreign Service Reserve officer category has been used for Peace Corps representatives who are assigned to the various countries with Peace Corps contingents to supervise the latter's activities. Similarly, the Disarmament Agency includes political and Excepted Schedule appointments, Civil Service

[8] *Personnel for the New Diplomacy,* p. 26.
[9] *Ibid.* This recommendation is discussed below.

employees, and both military and Foreign Service officers on detail from their respective agencies.

These arrangements for the professional staffing of the foreign policy agencies seem unnecessarily disorderly and confused. A rather thorough overhauling and rationalization of the system are probably called for. Certainly the American personnel systems do not have the closed, highly disciplined, highly integrated, lifetime career character of the classic contrasting example, the British civil service.

At the same time, it should be kept in mind that the very fluidity and looseness of the American system have their advantages. The availability of several personnel services means that the range of choice open to the administrator in filling particular positions may be wider. In certain circumstances, this may be a considerable advantage if the official doing the recruiting is capable of exploiting it. The clumsiness and disorder of American personnel arrangements may also make possible the generation of greater imagination and intellectual creativity by, if need be, the conscious recruitment of these qualities into the system.

Bases for Evaluation

Since 1945 the personnel arrangements and requirements of the Department of State and the Foreign Service have been reviewed and evaluated by a series of outside groups and committees. The distinguished committee chaired by former Secretary of State Christian Herter was the latest of these advisory bodies.[10] It defined its assignment in

[10] The Foreign Service Act of 1946, the report of the Hoover Commission in 1949, the report of the Secretary's Advisory Committee on Personnel in 1950 (the Rowe-Ramspeck-DeCourcy Committee), the report of the Secretary of State's Public Committee on Personnel in 1954 (the Wriston Report), and the report of the Herter Committee at the end of 1962 are probably the major landmarks in the postwar concern with U. S. foreign affairs personnel. The major studies since 1945 are summarized briefly in *Personnel for the New Diplomacy*, pp. 142-45.

The process of intragovernmental discussion and negotiation that resulted in the Foreign Service Act of 1946 is set forth in the case study of that title in Harold Stein (ed.), *Public Administration and Policy Development* (Harcourt, Brace and Co., 1952), pp. 661-737. The Wriston Report, *Toward a Stronger Foreign Service* (Government Printing Office, 1954), was cited in Chapter 5. The report of the Secretary's Advisory Committee on Personnel was titled *An Improved Personnel System for the Conduct of Foreign Affairs* (1950).

broader terms than its predecessors, including within its focus the Information Agency and the Agency for International Development as well as the State Department. Some critics argue that it should have gone farther and dealt with the career civilians of the Department of Defense and perhaps the military, and even probed the personnel practices and problems of the Central Intelligence Agency.

Whatever its limitations and shortcomings, and some of these will be discussed below, the report of the Committee on Foreign Affairs Personnel is in many ways a turning-point study. This is not because most of its conclusions and recommendations have any startling originality. The Committee recognized its intellectual kinship with earlier advisory groups and the fact that "many of its basic conclusions and recommendations" were "essentially similar" to theirs.[11] Furthermore, as is often the case, many of its views reflected ideas being widely discussed within the bureaucracy itself and, in some cases, measures already going into effect.

The essential contribution of the Herter Committee has been to set forth the fundamental facts of life in the foreign affairs personnel field and to identify the major personnel problems that flow from the present international position of the United States. It is possible to take exception to some of the recommended changes in personnel policies, programs, and organizational machinery that the committee has derived from its more basic analysis.[12] The basic analysis seems essentially sound, however, and it is therefore incumbent on those who quarrel with the committee's detailed recommendations to come up with better answers to those problems the committee grappled with.

Some Basic Assumptions and Requirements

What is this basic analysis and the implications that emerge from it?[13] First of all, as the discussion in the preceding ten chapters has made amply clear, the functions and responsibilities of the foreign pol-

[11] See the comment on p. 142 of *Personnel for the New Diplomacy*.

[12] For example, I am quite skeptical about the proposal for an Executive Under Secretary of State, whom the Committee regards as an essential organizational instrument for implementation of its proposed reforms. See the discussion in *ibid.*, pp. 9-18.

[13] What follows is my interpretation, for which the Committee on Foreign Affairs Personnel cannot be held responsible.

icy organization reflect not only the worldwide interests of the United States but, equally, a depth and intensity of concern with internal developments in almost every country in the world. This kind of posture toward foreign affairs has not only brought into being new programs and the need for a much wider range of skills and specialties but has also substantially affected the kinds of problems faced and the kinds of skills required to perform the traditional diplomatic and military functions.

These are rather basic and unexceptionable premises. What are some of their implications? For one thing, they suggest that the generalist-specialist dichotomy in terms of which the problems of foreign affairs personnel have tended to be posed is—as suggested in Chapter 5 —the grossest oversimplification; its usefulness as a tool of analysis is dubious. Whether within the Foreign Service or outside it, the more fundamental challenge is to identify as precisely as possible the kinds of skills and competences called for and then try to determine how such talents can best be recruited, developed, and retained within the foreign policy organization.

It also seems clear that appropriate recognition and formal status must be given to those people outside the Foreign Service Officer Corps who are professionally engaged in foreign affairs work that includes some proportion of overseas duty. The career personnel of the United States Information Agency have now been given regularized career status. However one defines the appropriate cadre of officers within the economic aid agency to be given permanent career status, there is clearly the need for such a core group. Whether this group should also be integrated into a further expanded Foreign Service or become a separate member of a "family of compatible foreign affairs services" (in the phrase of the Herter Committee) is, in principle, not of great significance. The proposed arrangement for the Information Agency officers combines inclusion in the Foreign Service personnel system with agency autonomy in the control and use of its personnel.

This would still leave a variety of people outside the "family"— members of the Foreign Agricultural Service, Treasury Department attachés, representatives of the Atomic Energy Commission serving in a number of foreign capitals, Defense Department civilians (for example, from the Office of International Security Affairs) who occasionally get overseas assignments, and Peace Corps representatives. Presumably, if the Herter Committee concept were accepted and implemented, it would be quite easy to bring such personnel under a "foreign affairs services" umbrella.

A more difficult question, and one with a long history in the Department of State, is the relationship between home-based Civil Service employees and Foreign Service personnel in several of these agencies. As we have seen, the Department of State tried to deal with this problem in its implementation of the Wriston recommendations, but with far from complete success. Since approximately eighty-five and ninety percent of the U.S.-based employees of the aid agency and the Information Agency, respectively, are Civil Service, as noted above, this poses an even more fundamental problem for them.

It is not possible, and probably not necessary, to recapitulate the lengthy argumentation that has swirled around this question during the last fifteen or twenty years. Much of it can be found in the reports cited at the beginning of this section. It is not going to be possible to come up with a solution equally satisfactory or even equally equitable to all concerned. However, a number of factors argue strongly for an arrangement that would unify all the personnel within the Department of State and within the Agency for International Development and the Information Agency under single personnel systems. Many of these people, whether Civil Service or Foreign Service, work together on common or related problems. Furthermore, it is unquestionable that most officials professionally involved in foreign affairs would benefit by some overseas experience. Perhaps equally important, the Secretary of State and the heads of the aid and information agencies need maximum flexibility and discretion in mustering the personnel resources available to them.[14]

The relationships between home and foreign services, and between

[14] The comments and recommendations of the Herter Committee on this question seem quite reasonable. See *Personnel for the New Diplomacy*, pp. 30-36.

In early 1965 Congressman Wayne Hays introduced legislation, supported by the Johnson Administration, providing for the incorporation of Civil Service employees working in foreign affairs into an expanded Foreign Service personnel system. For a detailed discussion and analysis of this bill, see *Department of State News Letter*, No. 49 (May 1965), pp. 2-22. An amended version of the Hays bill, which limited its applicability to State, USIA, and AID and further permitted present Civil Service employees to retain their jobs even if they did not transfer to the Foreign Service, was passed by the House of Representatives in September 1965. For its details, see *Department of State News Letter*, No. 53 (September 1965), pp. 2-11.

professionals serving overseas for the aid and information agencies and the regular Foreign Service Officer Corps, are in essence questions of framework, of the broad shape and structure that a foreign affairs personnel system should have. Whatever the specific character of the answers devised, there are even more difficult problems to be dealt with within the framework. It is not enough to say that contemporary foreign policy requires a broad range of highly diversified and specialized skills. A personnel system must be developed that can identify these specialties and give appropriate recognition to them in the processes of recruitment, assignment, career development, training, evaluation of performance, and promotion.

This requirement bears particularly heavily on the Foreign Service, both because it still represents the largest body of professional foreign affairs personnel and because the generalist notion still lingers on as a concept and an ideal—that any good man can do just about any job in the Service—even if its practical significance diminishes with each passing day.

FUNCTIONAL DIFFERENTIATION. It must be conceded that the detailed implementation of this general requirement represents a difficult, ticklish task. If the specialized nature of the functions to be performed and of the personnel required to perform them is to be built into the personnel system, this presumably means that both positions and people have to be functionally differentiated. Positions are already classified, although even the specialists in this field would agree that these position classifications reveal much less about the skills required to fill them effectively than would be desirable.

The functional differentiation of personnel raises many difficulties of its own. I have never seen a proposed functional breakdown for the Foreign Service that seemed fully satisfactory. When these functional categories are applied to the processes of assignment and promotion, they seem even less satisfactory. The Herter Committee made functional differentiation one of the bases of its own recommendations, proposing that every officer be identified with what it termed a "career line" and that most officers have some exposure to at least one career line aside from their primary one. The committee mentioned the following as examples of "functional career lines in the foreign affairs agencies": "administrative, economic, political, consular, and public affairs; international organization affairs; cultural affairs; research and intelligence; public health; agriculture; radio; press and publications." It went on to indicate that in addition to the functional lines, "there should be an executive career line for persons occupying or qualified to occupy high executive posts."[15]

The functional categories illustratively supplied by the Herter Committee reveal quite clearly the problems of this kind of differentiation of personnel. If one tries to move beyond such a general list and develop more specific categories, there is the risk of introducing too much rigidity into the system, of confining officers to narrower molds than they would prefer and, on the other hand, making particular jobs more difficult to fill because their requirements have been overdefined. Furthermore, even the most carefully and sensibly developed system of functional differentiation will not be able to take into account the special combinations of personal qualities, skills, and previous experience that may be necessary or highly desirable in filling particular jobs at particular times. These become increasingly necessary for the jobs closer to the top of the organizational hierarchy.

Perhaps all that functional categories can provide is general guidelines, with their usefulness depending in large part on the abilities of the people who man the personnel machinery. If examiners and recruiters are made aware of detailed personnel requirements and can tailor their activities accordingly, if career development staffs can determine individual career preferences and at the same time alert personnel to the needs of the system, and if individual preferences and the needs of the system can be equitably and effectively meshed in the assignment process, rather broad functional categories may provide a sufficient basis for building personnel specialization into the foreign affairs personnel systems.

PROFESSIONAL PERSONNEL MACHINERY. The last point can be more positively stated. Given the much larger numbers of people now involved and the much greater diversity of skills required, the foreign policy organization must have full-time, thoroughly professional, and adequately staffed and supported personnel units. It is said that at one time in the

---

[15] *Personnel for the New Diplomacy*, pp. 84-85.

not too distant past, everyone knew almost everyone else in the Foreign Service. This could well have been true as recently as 1939, when the Officer Corps numbered only 712.[16] In such a system, it was possible, whether or not desirable, for assignments and other aspects of the personnel process to be handled on a highly individualized and not very formal basis.

With a Foreign Service Officers Corps that today numbers more than 3,600, it seems preferable to have organizational machinery that deals with these same personnel problems on a professional, systematic, and reasonably objective basis. It should be added that the numbers involved are, relatively speaking, still small enough and the requirements of the positions being filled particularized enough that a completely routinized and mechanized system is neither necessary nor desirable. Furthermore, bureaucratic habits being what they are, the introduction of such a system would be strongly resisted, particularly for personnel assignments. Individuals still tend to seek and to be sought for particular positions within the foreign policy organization.

There has already been noteworthy progress in the direction of strengthening personnel staffs, particularly in the Department of State, but the personnel function does tend to be skimpily treated in the allocation of funds and of first-rate people. It also does not get the kind of serious, continuing attention of top-level officials that is warranted. There is, here, a kind of built-in handicap. While senior officials may become quite concerned about some immediate staffing problem, it is more difficult, and understandably so, to enlist their interest and support with regard to longer-term personnel problems and programs. For these harried people, the problems and consequences of the moment have a greater urgency than plans or problems whose fruition is years away. It may not be a desirable state of affairs, but it seems unavoidable.

THE NEED FOR PERSONNEL RESEARCH. Perhaps this preoccupation with the current and the immediate explains the woeful lack of personnel research undertaken or supported by the foreign affairs agencies. As the Herter Committee points out, "The military services and private busi-

[16] In July 1939 this number was increased by the incorporation of 114 foreign service personnel from the Commerce and Agriculture Departments into the Corps. See Barnes and Morgan, op. cit., pp. 231 and 365.

ness have long recognized the value of professional research in human relations and in personnel management."[17] In the case of the State Department, perhaps this lack of interest reflects a more general lack of contact, noted in Chapter 10, with the behavioral social sciences like psychology and sociology as distinct from history, law, political science, and economics. In any event, if the Department and the other foreign affairs agencies are to move their personnel programs to a more professional and systematic basis, a substantially expanded personnel research program would seem to be one of the necessary ingredients.

While I am under no illusion that social science research will produce neat, simple solutions to extremely complicated questions, nevertheless the data such research could obtain should provide a somewhat firmer basis for action than the impressions and unquestioned assumptions that often guide personnel programs at present. As a senior personnel official once remarked, many of the present programs are based essentially on faith. Americans believe deeply in education, and, therefore, expanded programs of in-service training and advanced university training for foreign affairs personnel must be a good thing. No doubt they are, but it would be impossible to find research data that compare different types of educational experience and the benefits derived from each or that attempt to validate the training in terms of the purposes it is ostensibly designed to serve (if anyone has explicitly set forth the latter).

Perhaps one of the underlying reasons for the cool and skeptical reception of the proposed National Academy of Foreign Affairs in 1963 by Congress, the press, and the bureaucracy itself was that a fundamental need for this kind of institution was not persuasively demonstrated.[18] This may be difficult to do when there are not readily available either well-defined manpower requirements or agreed notions about what combinations of previous education and experience, work-

---

[17] *Personnel for the New Diplomacy*, p. 128. The committee's final recommendation was for an expanded program of personnel research (pp. 127-29).

[18] The proposed Academy, described briefly in Chap. 10, note 16, was not acted on by Congress. For a critical view of the proposal, and some reservations about what in-service training can accomplish, see former Secretary of State Dean Acheson's letter of July 29, 1963 to Senator J. William Fulbright, in *Administration of National Security*, Hearings before the Subcommittee on National Security Staffing and Operations of the Senate Government Operations Committee, 88 Cong. 1 sess. (1963), Pt. 5, pp. 378-83.

ing assignments, and in-service training will produce the kinds of foreign affairs officers the country needs.

The same comment can be made about the question of increased
lateral-entry recruiting versus continued reliance on recruiting primarily at the bottom. Perhaps some of the skills and specialties increasingly
required by the foreign affairs agencies, including the State Department, can be more economically and efficiently recruited from mature
professionals in their thirties. Perhaps not. The point is that little reliable evidence is available to help guide decisions on this kind of
difficult personnel policy question.

The rather fundamental question of the validity of the whole examination process for junior Foreign Service Officers has just begun—
in the last few years—to receive systematic attention. In part this has
resulted from a concern to make the Foreign Service as representative
of American society as possible (including, specifically, the problem of
recruiting Negroes for the Foreign Service), and from the work of the
Herter Committee and its staff.[19] There is the even more basic question
of what concepts, explicit or implicit, about the kinds of people needed
for the service now guide recruitment and examination processes, and
whether these concepts best meet its needs.

Another related question about which there are little systematic
data was raised in a narrower context in Chapter 10—the impact of
typical Foreign Service experiences and assignments on the values,
skills, and attitudes of Foreign Service Officers. If there are deepseated
values and mores within the Foreign Service which have a substantial
effect on most of the officers in the Service (and on the kind of junior
officers that they in turn select), improved in-service training and other
broadening experiences may have only a marginal impact. On the
other hand, if the major changes of the past decade or two are altering
the character of the Foreign Service as a social system, agonizing reap-
praisals may be unnecessary and somewhat irrelevant. What would be
extremely helpful, but do not really exist, are sociological and social-
psychological analyses of the Foreign Service.[20]

[19] It was recently announced that the examination and selection processes for
Foreign Service Officers would be studied by a group headed by Professor Kenneth
Clark of the City College of New York. Professor Clark, a psychologist, was a member of the Herter Committee. See *Department of State News Letter*, No. 50 (June
1965), p. 28.

[20] In addition to the discussion in Chap. 10, see the section on "intellectual

Finally, there is general agreement on one major need of all the foreign affairs personnel systems—the development and refinement of their manpower requirements, and some organizational unit that will be responsible for keeping these requirements current. It is not possible in the present study to perform this task for the foreign affairs agencies, but the section that follows does attempt to suggest some of the important kinds of people that the new diplomacy and the new foreign policy require.

What Kinds of People Are Needed?

This is not a systematic, all-inclusive canvass. It makes no effort to identify detailed categories of specialists but, rather, some broad and

---

creativity in a bureaucracy" in Chap. 2. The hypothesis about a "Foreign Service mind" parallels the older notion of a "military mind." The latter question has received somewhat more systematic attention, and Professor Morris Janowitz has attempted a sociological analysis of the American military officer along the general lines suggested for the Foreign Service. See *The Professional Soldier* (Free Press of Glencoe, 1960).

One of the first efforts to apply social-psychological research techniques and concepts to the Foreign Service is reflected in the previously-cited monograph prepared by Regis Walther for the Herter Committee. In this monograph, Foreign Service Officers are compared with other professional groupings, and certain behavioral characteristics are identified which seem to make for success in passing the Foreign Service examinations and in the Service itself.

Another Herter Committee monograph (Harr, *The Anatomy of the Foreign Service—A Statistical Profile*) provides the most detailed and systematic data available about the Foreign Service Officers Corps with regard to its methods of entry, educational background, functional fields, and language proficiency.

While there is considerable raw material for research purposes, including the memoirs and biographies of American diplomats, the only systematic studies of the social background of Foreign Service Officers are those by Professor James L. McCamy. See *The Administration of American Foreign Affairs* (Alfred A. Knopf, 1950), Chap. 9, and, with Alessandro Corradini, "The People of the State Department and the Foreign Service," *American Political Science Review*, Vol. 48 (December 1954), pp. 1067-82. More recently, McCamy has provided some rather crude analyses of the educational background and work experience of FSO's, FSR's and senior Civil Service officers listed in *The Biographic Register*, published annually by the State Department. This Register includes, in addition to State Department employees, officials who work in USIA, AID, the Foreign Agricultural Service, the Arms Control and Disarmament Agency, and the Peace Corps. For the results of McCamy's analysis, see *Conduct of the New Diplomacy* (Harper & Row, 1964), Chap. 14.

basic requirements. The focus is on career personnel although most of the skills and talents identified are assumed to be necessary for non-career officials doing similar work or bearing related responsibilities.

THE "NEW DIPLOMAT." As noted in Chapters 5 and 9, the traditional diplomatic and consular functions of the Foreign Service—negotiation, political and economic reporting, representation, citizen protection, commercial reporting, and promotion of American business abroad—have by no means disappeared from the contemporary scene. Indeed, they are carried on in much more difficult and unfamiliar local settings in many more remote areas of the globe. Because an increasingly significant proportion of overseas contacts must move across major cultural barriers, the problems of communication and understanding grow ever more difficult.

One thoughtful Foreign Service Officer has been sufficiently impressed with these problems to feel that they warranted some redefinition of the role and skills of the diplomat and the training and experience required to perform them effectively. From his point of view, the new diplomacy involves not merely the addition of new functions but the redefinition and rejuvenation of the old ones.[21] Rossow sees the new diplomacy in terms of the ability to communicate, and negotiate, across the cultural barriers that separate the states of European origin from most of the rest of the world. He suggests an educational preparation for this profession somewhat at variance with the more standard emphasis on political science, economics, and history. His emphasis would be on cultural anthropology, linguistics, comparative social analysis, and comparative philosophical systems.

Rossow is not alone in his emphasis on comparative social and cultural analysis as one of the requisite skills for the new diplomat. In the training of area specialists inside and outside the government, it has become increasingly recognized that it takes more than facility in the language or languages of an area and even a solid knowledge of its past history to produce capable analysts of contemporary situations and problems. An extensive exposure to the concepts and methods of the behavioral sciences is probably equally necessary. The importance of linguistic skill cannot be questioned, and this is one area where the

___

[21] See Robert Rossow's stimulating essay, "The Professionalization of the New Diplomacy," *World Politics,* Vol. 14 (July 1962), pp. 561-75.

Foreign Service and the State Department and, to a somewhat lesser extent, the other foreign affairs agencies have made considerable progress in the last ten years.[22]

Not only are the local settings more challenging in the cultural sense, but there is more to be done. The Herter Committee and others may exaggerate the differences between the passivity of traditional American diplomatic activities abroad and the action-orientation of the present, but it cannot be denied that there are differences.[23] The diplomat has many more matters to talk about with officials of the local government and a much more varied kit of tools at his disposal to try to influence their actions. It should not be forgotten that influencing the actions of other governments in directions viewed as desirable by one's own government has always been viewed as the basic diplomatic function. What have changed are the instruments available to the diplomat and the range of decisions he is trying to affect (and effect).

This means, among other things, that his range of acquaintance and interest in the country where he is serving must be far wider than was once necessary in most places. Furthermore, while he is not directly charged with most of the new foreign affairs programs, he must understand in considerable detail what they are designed to accomplish and how they operate. The implications of all of this for the effective performance of U. S. ambassadors, whatever their previous background, have been discussed at length in Chapter 9.

The Foreign Service Officer Corps has traditionally had the reputation of looking down its nose at the administrative tasks connected with its work. For those primarily interested in the substance of international relations, this is an understandable attitude. With the increasing numbers of American programs and personnel overseas, and the State Department's role in providing administrative support to many of them, heavy administrative burdens overseas have been added to the workload of the Foreign Service. It is clear that the Foreign Service must add specialized skills in management, budgeting, and personnel administration to its expanding set of specialist requirements. The same general point also applies to the other foreign affairs agencies, notably AID and the Information Agency.

[22] There are more detailed comments in Chap. 5.
[23] See the comments in *Personnel for the New Diplomacy*, pp. 6 and 49.

An option has been added to the Foreign Service written examinations designed to attract young officers primarily interested in the administrative as distinct from the substantive work of foreign policy. Given the substantive foreign affairs interests that have in the past attracted people to the Foreign Service, it is too early to tell how successful this device will be.

A further complication in the life of the contemporary diplomat is the fact that, today, very few situations or problems can be dealt with strictly in bilateral terms or channels. Third-country, fourth-country, nth-country considerations enter into most of the questions about which any two nations are in communication. Often in dealing with particular governments, the United States is trying to influence policies and attitudes toward third countries almost as much as toward itself.

This dimension of contemporary international politics is highlighted by the increasing importance of multilateral forums and organizations in carrying on the business of interstate relations. Those that probably provide the greatest challenge to effective U. S. foreign affairs staffing are the major organs of the United Nations—the Security Council, the General Assembly, the Economic and Social Council—more generally, the whole complex of diplomatic activities in United Nations/ New York.

There are a number of elements that contribute to this judgment, but from the point of view of the skills and relevant experience of the career diplomat, two basic problems can be noted. First of all, the United Nations has much of the atmosphere of a legislative body—one with quite a few political parties, weak party discipline and shifting coalitions, much "politicking" in the corridors and the lounges, exchanging of favors and logrolling of votes, and both temporary and more stable voting blocs. Not all of this is attractive or desirable in its consequences. Nevertheless, if the United States is to be effective in this particular institutional setting, its mission at the United Nations and the special mission maintained at Geneva should be manned by officers who feel at home in this atmosphere and can operate effectively in it.

While these political skills and the skills of diplomacy are not mutually exclusive, they are not necessarily identical. With the growing importance of these international forums, the Department of State and the other foreign affairs agencies should identify officers with the appropriate skills and encourage at least some of them to specialize in this field. In the case of the Department of State, the Bureau of International Organization Affairs provides a bureaucratic base in Washington for such officers.

The major political organs of the United Nations are not the only challenging international institutions in which Foreign Service Officers must operate. Important international social, economic, and technical-scientific policies are decided on at the periodic meetings and in the continuing work of the specialized agencies of the United Nations. From a foreign policy viewpoint, the concern is that the various American governmental agencies, primarily domestic in orientation, who are often the leading spokesmen and participants for the United States in these specialized agencies, may have neither the capability nor, in some cases, the motivation to represent the broad national interests of the United States. Nor do they always get the necessary policy guidance from the Department of State. This is a case of definition and fulfillment of organizational responsibilities and of having the appropriately skilled and motivated personnel available to carry them out.

CROSS-DEPARTMENTAL SKILLS AND PERSPECTIVES. One theme of this study is that all important foreign policy problems are interdepartmental in nature. The departments involved need people who can work effectively across departmental, professional, and disciplinary boundaries. Some of these major "intersections" demanding cross-departmental and cross-disciplinary skills and perspectives have already been identified. Chapters 5 and 6 discussed the need for Foreign Service Officers, military officers, and civil servants with politico-military interests and skills. Chapter 8 noted the rapidly increasing importance of scientific and technological developments for both the peaceful and military dimensions of foreign policy and international politics; this should be matched by the presence of foreign affairs officials, military officers, scientists, and scientific administrators with some depth of understanding of the relevant activities and responsibilities of the others.

A more familiar theme is that the battle for the minds of men cannot be the exclusive preserve of any one agency or group. Organizational division of labor requires that special public affairs, information, and cultural exchange units be established, but the requisite insights and sensitivities should be much more widely spread through the foreign policy organization.

The same can be said for the broad range of foreign economic policies and problems, from the relatively nonpolitical questions of technical assistance or cooperation through international agencies to the highly political issues of international trade policy and economic aid. It is interesting to note the return to the old English term, political economy, as a way of emphasizing the interdependence of the two realms in the development of policy at home and its successful implementation overseas.

In sum, in the age of the foreign policy specialist, there is a considerable requirement for men capable of straddling two or more fields or professional perspectives and adding balanced understanding and perspective of their own. They might be thought of as specialists in integrating the work of more narrow specialists. To confuse the issue completely, perhaps they could be called generalist-specialists! One assumption of the present study is that the functioning of the foreign policy organization will improve substantially as increasing numbers of people become available within it who can think and work effectively across departmental and professional boundaries.

FORMULATING NATIONAL SECURITY POLICY. There is a more specific, related requirement—for officers capable of contributing effectively to the policy-making processes by which major national security and foreign policy decisions are shaped. Daily, weekly, monthly—sometimes from hour to hour—the responsible officials of the government must make critical and difficult decisions that involve all or many of the factors mentioned earlier, and many of the responsible departments and agencies. The career officials and the political officials who participate in the formulation of these decisions must not only have the ability to understand and weigh a variety of specialized and partial perspectives and sources of advice but also—and perhaps this is just another way of saying the same thing—they must be able to place these considerations in a broader national policy framework. They must be sensitive to relevant considerations in the domestic political scene, to the likely reactions of friends and allies abroad, and to the relationship of the policy question under consideration to other interests and concerns of the United States.

Some would argue that the analytical skills and policy judgment required to do this kind of job effectively are not easily developed or widely available within the foreign policy-national security machinery of the government.[24] They are certainly not going to be produced by taking a three-month course at the Foreign Service Institute, or even a year at Harvard. But such an approach to the problems of the day— whether these involve Cuba, Laos, a nuclear test ban treaty, strategic nuclear weapons for Europe, what to do about the ruling government in South Vietnam, or the remaining white settler and white colonial governments in Southern Africa—is required of the President and the Secretaries of State and Defense and their top aides. It is obvious that those who work for these men must also be capable of thinking and operating effectively in the same terms.[25]

It is difficult to evaluate the judgment that present career staffing for these positions is inadequate. There is really little "hard" evidence to go on. Perhaps the growing body of Foreign Service Officers, military men, civil servants, and noncareer officials with cross-departmental and cross-disciplinary experience and training will provide a sufficient pool from which to fill these positions adequately. On the other hand, a more explicit, determined effort may be required.

I would be inclined to agree that the national security policy business does make some distinctive demands on the officials responsible for important decisions and those who work for them; this therefore

[24] One thoughtful participant-observer has made available to the author a private paper that takes this position. His view is that those who man the "national security policy machinery" do need a special kind of competence, that so far these positions have been filled on a rather unsystematic basis, that very little is known about the performance of the Foreign Service Officers, military officers, civil servants, and political appointees who have filled these positions, and that the government is doing relatively little to improve this state of affairs. Among other things, he proposes some research projects designed to refine the scanty knowledge in this field.

[25] It may be useful to suggest some of the organizational units where the kind of perspective and skills we are talking about would be particularly applicable: the President's Special Assistant for National Security Affairs and those who work for him; the Director of the Office of Science and Technology and at least a few of his aides; some in the International and Military Divisions of the Bureau of the Budget; the Policy Planning Council, the Politico-Military Affairs staff, and the regional offices of the Bureau of European Affairs in the Department of State; the Office of International Security Affairs, and elements of the Joint Staff and the Comptroller's office in the Department of Defense; the Program Coordination staff in the Agency for International Development; and the Office of National Estimates in the Central Intelligence Agency.

This is a partial list. Not everyone in the offices mentioned either has or needs this kind of approach; certainly, other persons and governmental units in other agencies could be added to the list.

represents another distinctive skill category that must be taken into account by the various personnel systems.[26]

What is required of career officials in the national security policy field is also called for at the highest political levels of the government, if at a somewhat broader and more general level. The President, the Secretary of State, and the Secretary of Defense, among others, must be able to grasp essential facts and analyses in all of these fields, query their experts and advisers with intelligence and understanding, recognize in a general way the limits of the expertise of their experts, and be willing to make judgments where their advisers strongly disagree or where there is no solid, reliable basis of information on which to rest a decision. To say that this is asking a great deal of these men is simply to say in another way what everyone readily acknowledges.

Major Problems

The personnel requirements of the foreign policy organization include able noncareer as well as career officials. In this concluding section, some attention will be given to the former although the primary focus will be, as it has been throughout, on the career services.

Some general comments apply to both. A basic question is why one should work for the federal government in the first place. For many, there are no enterprises in the private sector of the society that can even come close to the national security activities of the government in the complexity of the problems, their high importance in the affairs of men, and the consequent challenge, stimulation, and possibility for personal dedication to larger goals.

On the other hand, government service by no means rates among the most prestigious of American occupations. There are also far greater pecuniary rewards to be found outside the government—particularly

---

[26] In my view, one of the shortcomings of the Herter Committee report was that it directed almost all of its attention to the requirements for personnel overseas. Furthermore, this was an implicit rather than explicit focussing of attention. Not only were the requirements for policy-making and policy-analyzing positions in Washington ignored, but as a consequence the equally difficult problem of the compatibility of the skills and attitudes necessary overseas with those called for in Washington was not faced.

at upper levels where the governmental pay scale tends to flatten out. For the bright and imaginative, there are organizational milieus freer and more flexible than the federal bureaucracy. For the sensitive and thinskinned, Congress and the representatives of the mass media can be sharp and severe, even hostile, critics. The net result is not disastrous. It must simply be recognized that the federal government faces some important initial handicaps in attempting to recruit first-rate talent into its service.

Recruiting and Retaining Able Noncareer Appointees

It has been made clear throughout this study that the politically responsible officials at the top of the various foreign affairs agencies have an absolutely essential role to play in giving these agencies leadership, energy, and direction. Let no one think that these men are the mere echoes of their career staff. With at least the top three levels (Secretary, Under Secretary, Assistant Secretary) in most agencies politically appointed and no American equivalent for the British system of Permanent Under Secretaries (ranking civil servants who act in effect as chiefs of staff to the political heads of government ministries), the requirements for relevant ability and background are substantial.

Some of the obstacles to the recruiting of men for such positions—particularly at the second, third, and fourth levels—have already been mentioned. The relatively low pay, long hours, and exposure to public criticism and attack discourage many. The understandable concern that a political appointee not be tempted to advance his personal or business interests while in the public service has, as translated into the conflict-of-interest laws, imposed some rather rigid requirements, and even financial disabilities, on the prospective political appointee.

During the Truman and Eisenhower Administrations, there was growing concern about the quality of political appointees recruited, the brief duration of their Washington tours, and the consequent high rate of turnover. The problem was particularly marked in the military establishment, where the average "tenure of top civilian officials" was estimated by one source at about eighteen months.[27] There was some improvement in the situation during the Kennedy Administration,

[27] See William R. Kintner, et al., Forging a New Sword (Harper, 1958), p. 71.

with relatively few departures from the ranks of either Cabinet members or their Under and Assistant Secretary subordinates. Some of the underlying problems were highlighted in the course of President Johnson's effort to get a federal pay bill passed in the spring and summer of 1964. The bill was aimed particularly at raising Cabinet, sub-Cabinet, and senior grade civil servant salaries. Debate about it was accompanied by the widely-publicized departure of some key subordinate officials from government service.

The organizational and policy-making role of politically-appointed officials, and those noncareer aides who work closely with them, is of unquestionable significance. If strenuous efforts to strengthen the career services are necessary, a similar drive for excellence among noncareer officials seems appropriate. Furthermore, since the latter, by the very nature of the system, are recruited from highly diverse sources and have quite varied backgrounds of education, training, and previous experience, it is all the more desirable that considerable thought and effort be given to their recruitment and to improving the quality of those willing to serve.[28]

Traditionally, recruiting people for the political positions in the foreign policy-national security organization, and for the federal government in general, has tended to be rather haphazard and unsystematic. It has been viewed, for the most part, as a function of the political parties and an aspect of party politics. In recent years, however, this pattern has begun to change. General Eisenhower enlisted the aid of Mr. John Corson, a distinguished figure in the field of public administration, and the Brookings Institution in drawing up rosters of able men to fill major positions in his administration. Mr. Kennedy's efforts were apparently even more extensive and systematic. He had the assistance of Mr. Clark Clifford, a former official of the Truman Administration, as well as Brookings, and also put to work on the problem a task force of some of his own immediate aides.[29]

---

[28] This was one of the problems that the first Jackson subcommittee looked into in some detail. See *Organizing for National Security*, Hearings before the Subcommittee on National Policy Machinery of the Senate Government Operations Committee, 86 Cong. 2 sess. (1960), Vol. 1, pp. 413-558; and Vol. 3, Staff Reports and Recommendations, "The Private Citizen and the National Service," pp. 59-71.

[29] See the interesting account by Adam Yarmolinsky, "The Kennedy Talent Hunt," *The Reporter*, Vol. 24 (June 8, 1961), pp. 22-25.

There seems to be a growing feeling that where very able men can be found who are willing to serve in national security positions, the criteria of strong party identification and loyalty, or even of party membership, should not be heavily weighed. Neither Secretary of State Rusk nor Secretary of Defense McNamara was identified as a strong Democrat. If anything, Mr. McNamara probably qualified as an independent leaning toward Republican. There was no doubt about the Republican background of Mr. Kennedy's Secretary of the Treasury, Douglas Dillon, who had served the Eisenhower Administration successively as Ambassador to France, Under Secretary of State for Economic Affairs, and ranking Under Secretary of State.

These moves were not without precedent. During World War II and the period that followed, a number of Republicans held a series of high positions under the Roosevelt and Truman Administrations. Again, this was particularly true in the national security field, in the persons of men like Stimson, Lovett, and McCloy. In spite of the pressures on behalf of the party faithful after twenty years out of office, General Eisenhower turned to certain well-known Democrats, like David Bruce, to fill positions in the foreign policy field.

Assuming that men able and willing to fill political-level positions in the foreign policy and national security fields are not plentiful, the question becomes how best to identify and recruit them. It does not seem farfetched to suggest that it would be desirable for the two major parties to build up and maintain informal rosters of such men. These may very well exist. There is no reason why each new administration must go through these processes of identification and recruitment without being able to benefit by the previous experiences of its own party. Furthermore, conscious efforts should be made to bring back those who have already had some useful governmental experience and to go beyond the handful of very well known names.

One has the impression that bringing first-rate talent into key national security posts is becoming good politics, even if some of the talent has no strong party identification or is from the other party. Indeed, those inclined to the view that partisan differences are significant and should be emphasized rather than blurred tend to deplore this trend toward appointing nonpartisan "experts" or "technicians" to politically responsible executive positions.

As part of its broad interest in this problem, the Brookings Institution has developed a series of programs designed to expose business executives, labor union officials, and members of the professions to government problems and operations. One such program enables young executives to spend a period of time in Washington working for an agency of the federal government. Aside from developing a deeper interest in and understanding of governmental problems, the working experience should provide useful background and preparation for the outsider who may be recruited for a government position at some later stage in his career.[30]

All of these developments should help produce a corps of men able and experienced in some significant sector of the foreign policy-national security field, and willing to serve from time to time in the government. Over time, the number of such men who are available to serve should also grow—if systematic efforts are made to keep them identified and to bring them back into the government periodically.

Strengthening the Career Services

Perhaps in a book so problem-oriented, it may be excusable to suggest that time will take care of some of the personnel problems of the foreign policy organization. It is inevitable that some of the Foreign Service Officers, military officers, and civil servants recruited twenty or more years ago should be out of tune with present problems and requirements. They were educated in and trained for a rather different age.

Younger officers, weaned as it were on these problems, exposed to the new programs, the new diplomacy, and the new nations in the course of their regular assignments and duties, should not find them particularly strange or difficult to adjust to. One who learns the foreign policy trade in a system that takes for granted the interdepartmental nature of its problems, who deals as a matter of course with the

---

[30] Two Brookings studies quite relevant to the present discussion are: Marver H. Bernstein, *The Job of the Federal Executive* (Brookings Institution, 1958); and Paul T. David and Ross Pollock, *Executives for Government* (Brookings Institution, 1957). The *Annual Reports* of the Institution describe its Advanced Study Program which has among its responsibilities the programs for business executives, labor leaders, and others in private life.

Pentagon and with the military aspects of foreign relations or with the details of economic and technical assistance programs in the country for which he is responsible, should not have to be formally educated to the acceptance and understanding of these things. They are likely to become a part of his definition of the job. In other words, the fact that much of the training in the foreign affairs field, as elsewhere, is on-the-job training has advantages as well as drawbacks.

It might even be hypothesized that, over time, a more action- and program-oriented diplomacy and Foreign Service will increasingly attract to its ranks young officers with this kind of orientation. This is not to suggest any crude dichotomy between the man of thought and the man of action. However, it is clear that the mere analysis of foreign situations and problems is not enough; the "new diplomat," be he in the Foreign Service, USIA, or AID, must be interested in and capable of effective action in such situations. It will be interesting to see how many Peace Corps Volunteers and young officers coming out of the military services join the foreign affairs agencies and how successful they turn out to be.

Of course, it is neither prudent nor realistic to rely completely on the natural unfolding of events. There have in fact been some substantial accomplishments in the personnel field during the past five or six years. All the problems discussed in this chapter, and by the Herter Committee, have been the subject of detailed examination within the government in recent years. The foreign affairs agencies have also been actively engaged since the issuance of the Herter report in implementing many of its recommendations.

Often, it is much easier to identify the problem and even the general shape of its solution than to develop a detailed answer, and a legislative proposal, that is acceptable to all the interested bureaucratic parties and legislative committees. For example, even if it were agreed by the responsible agency personnel officials that all foreign affairs personnel should be removed from Civil Service status and made a part of a "family of compatible foreign affairs services," this would represent only one short step in the long and difficult process of public policy making. Another perhaps longer step was taken with the introduction of the legislation by Congressman Wayne Hays noted above.[31]

[31] See note 14.

Even without the benefit of legislative mandate and direction, the administrative and personnel officials of the various foreign affairs agencies recognize their many common problems and the practical desirability of working closely together. There has been a great deal of collaboration in connection with the implementation of the Herter recommendations. The closer links between the personnel programs of the Department of State and the United States Information Agency have already been noted. The two agencies have also adopted the same performance rating procedures and forms, with AID using a basically similar approach. The three agencies have also begun more systematic efforts to pool their executive talent, and this should lead to increasing numbers of interagency assignments in Washington and in the field.[32]

The Foreign Service Institute, although still primarily a Department of State training institution, is increasingly providing services to the other foreign affairs agencies, particularly in the language and area-training fields. While it has its share of inadequacies, and critics, the Institute has shown notable improvement in recent years. In the field of language training and research, it has become something of a leader, particularly in some of the more exotic tongues of Asia and sub-Saharan Africa.

The Institute now offers three major courses for Foreign Service Officers: an orientation course for all beginning junior FSO's (the classes include the junior USIA officers); a twelve-week course for officers in midcareer; and, finally, a nine-month course for senior officers, roughly equivalent in concept to the senior war college courses of the military. Some Institute staff members regard its Senior Seminar as superior to the war college courses. Students include military officers and foreign affairs officials of other civilian agencies as well as State Department civil servants and Foreign Service Officers.

The Department of State now has a Junior Officers Program to supervise these officers until they receive their first promotion. They are on probationary status and are rotated through two or three different interne-type positions during this period. This phase ends with either their promotion or separation from the Service.

[32] See the story in the *Department of State News Letter,* No. 32 (December 1963), p. 40.

The Department has also established a new career management program. In essence, it is an attempt to link the assignment process more directly with career development planning and counselling.[33] This program and the Junior Officers Program reflect the increasingly self-conscious attention now being given to the personnel needs and problems of the foreign policy organization.

The notion that actual working experience in another agency can help develop the effectiveness of officers operating in a world of interdepartmental problems has won wide acceptance within the foreign policy organization. According to a report prepared by the Department of State for the Senate Subcommittee on National Security Staffing and Operations, there were in February 1964:

> 130 [Foreign Service] officers detailed in Washington to 12 agencies as follows: ACDA, 26; AID, 23; Commerce, 31; Defense, 18; HEW, 1; Labor, 2; NASA, 2; Peace Corps, 10; USIA, 5; White House, 5; Treasury 6; and Interior, 1.

> An additional 30 officers are detailed overseas to: USIA, 8; AID, 20; U.S. Army Map Service, 1; and Peace Corps, 1.[34]

It was further pointed out that this program, while authorized in the Foreign Service Act of 1946, had increased substantially in numbers and in agencies involved during the last five years. Defense, USIA, and Treasury officials also serve in the Department of State, and officials of the Commerce and Labor Departments are assigned overseas as labor and commercial attachés, with Foreign Service Reserve officer status.

The State-Defense Officer Exchange Program, begun in January 1961, at the close of the Eisenhower Administration, is but one of a number of personnel programs that link the two departments. Under the Exchange Program, approximately a dozen officers of each agency are at any one time serving two-year tours of duty with the other, not as observers but in regular working positions. In addition, there is a completely separate arrangement under which several officers from the State Department's Operations Center and from the National Military Command Center serve with the other unit. It is generally agreed that

[33] See *ibid.*, pp. 36-39.
[34] See *ibid.*, No. 34 (February 1964), p. 25. The paper, prepared for the second Jackson subcommittee, appears in *Administration of National Security*, Hearings, Pt. 6, pp. 439-40.

the Exchange Program has been highly successful, in terms of the quality of personnel assigned, the performance and loyalty of the exchangees to their "new" agency, and the improvement in working relations between the two departments.[35]

Separate from this Program is the assignment of senior Foreign Service Officers as Political Advisers (POLAD's) to major military commands. These officers work for the military commanders. They are not in the State Department chain of command. There are at present eight such positions: at the Atlantic, Pacific, European, and Southern (Canal Zone) Commands; the Strategic Air Command; Strike Command; the Military Air Transport Service; and U.S. High Commissioner, Ryukyus.

There are State Department faculty members and students at the five U.S. war colleges and the Armed Forces Staff College. (Officials of other civilian agencies also attend the National War College and the Industrial College of the Armed Forces.) A quite recent development is the assignment of Foreign Service Officers to the faculties of the Air Force, Naval, and Military Academies. There are military officers attending various courses at the Foreign Service Institute, including the nine-month Senior Seminar.

Thus, the critical importance of politico-military problems that overlap and indeed transcend the responsibilities of the State and Defense Departments is being matched to a considerable extent by personnel programs that should enlarge the pool of appropriately skilled talent available in both agencies and strengthen the personal as well as organizational links between the two.[36]

The training of foreign affairs personnel has expanded considerably in fields other than politico-military affairs. The broadening activities of the Foreign Service Institute have already been noted. Foreign Service Officers and other foreign affairs personnel are also detailed to universities for work in economics, management, and area studies. While there is no doubt that the military services have led the way

[35] See the reports on the exchange program provided to the second Jackson subcommittee by Secretary of State Rusk and Secretary of Defense McNamara in *ibid.*, Pt. 9, pp. 597-600.

[36] For a more detailed discussion of some of these points, see App. B of the present study, "Memorandum on the Department of State's Politico-Military Organization and Staffing" submitted by the Department to the Subcommittee on National Security Staffing and Operations.

among the national security agencies in their systematic and foresight-
ed provision of in-service training to their officers, the foreign affairs
agencies, and particularly the Department of State, have made rapid
strides of their own in recent years.

The services deserve particular credit for having recognized the
importance of political, diplomatic and economic factors in dealing
with military problems and having developed training programs in response to this requirement soon after World War II, not only in their
own war colleges but also by detailing officers for extended study at civilian universities. While detailed implementation has not always been
as impressive as the general concept, for example at the war colleges,
the overall achievement has been notable.[37]

Finally, the great expansion of the research and training activities
of American universities in the many fields related to foreign affairs
should be noted. In addition to the regular work of political science
departments in such fields as international politics, international law,
and U.S. foreign policy, major centers of international relations research have been developed at a number of American universities.
Greatly increased attention has been devoted to the underdeveloped
countries, and a number of highly specialized area studies programs
have been introduced. Furthermore, as was pointed out in Chapter 6,
there has been a great burst of academic interest in defense studies,
military problems and policies, and, more broadly, in what has been
labeled national security policy.[38]

The development of these many programs has a double-edged significance for the career services of the foreign affairs agencies. The programs should provide an excellent source of well-trained personnel for
these agencies and, in the process, ease some of the pressures for extensive in-service training of personnel. Where in-service training is still required, they provide specialized resources that are in some instances
not attainable by government institutions.

On the other hand, the existence of these academic research and
training centers promises an increasing supply of persons with relevant

[37] A major study of the total military educational system is John W. Masland
and Laurence I. Radway, *Soldiers and Scholars* (Princeton University Press, 1957).

[38] A survey of these activities is provided in the recent study by Professors
Gene M. Lyons and Louis Morton of Dartmouth College, *Schools for Strategy,
Education and Research in National Secuirty Affairs* (Frederick A. Praeger, 1965).

foreign affairs skills outside the foreign policy organization—working for the universities and their affiliated research centers, for the new breed of private research corporations, and in the business world proper. If the career services cannot meet the challenges set forth earlier in the chapter, it is reasonable to assume that political administrations with critical problems that need effective handling will look elsewhere for the kind of people they think they need—and they may very well find them. The federal personnel systems are flexible enough to make it possible to bring in personnel from the outside as required, particularly in response to the needs of a President and his administration.

From a broad national or governmental perspective, this may be a desirable state of affairs. It does enable the foreign policy organization to capitalize on the career mobility that characterizes some sectors of American life today, with certain people changing jobs relatively easily among government agencies, the major foundations, the universities, the private and quasi-public research corporations, and a variety of business activities. There are many links among these "worlds," and without much difficulty they draw on one another for information, advice, and personnel.

This does open up a pool of talented people for government service. It also provides channels out of government service as well as access to it. It represents, in a sense, the kind of flexibility and creativity that a free society is supposed to possess, and whose absence is frequently bemoaned. At the same time, it represents an added if subtle pressure on the career services. If they cannot do the varied jobs demanded by contemporary circumstances, alternative sources of personnel supply do exist.

12

Conclusion

THE CHARACTER OF NATIONS, as of individuals, is often marked by contradictory traits and tendencies. If Americans are wont to assume as self-evident the superiority of their society and form of government over all others and, on occasion, to proclaim this superiority far and wide, they are also extremely critical of their shortcomings and inclined to think that these could be quickly remedied if sufficient public attention were drawn to them. In many ways, these last-mentioned qualities are charming and attractive and a source of strength to the society. On the other hand, they do tend to stimulate the fruitless pursuit of perfection and the search for grand designs where less all-encompassing efforts at improvement would be more productive.

Understandably, American foreign policy has received a great deal of this kind of treatment over the past twenty years. By no means all of those who are dissatisfied with the wisdom, foresight, or effectiveness of that policy, or some particular aspect of it, explain its deficiencies in organizational terms. Some critics are either not interested in organizational arrangements or are convinced that these are of little consequence apart from the particular individuals who fill important positions within the organization.

However, the foreign policy organization has not lacked for critics, including those who despair so deeply of the viability of the present structure that they believe nothing less than a thorough overhaul could save the day. As the reader will no doubt have observed by this point, I am not of this school of worrisome observers and eager reformers.

The underlying themes of this study reflect a more tempered view. The political and governmental milieu in which the foreign policy organization is enmeshed imposes fundamental limitations on how it spends its time and does its work; there are "built-in" inefficiencies in the American system. These limitations cannot be overcome by instituting some dramatic reform in the structure, like a super-Secretary and super-Department of State, or five operating deputies to the President. More useful organizational improvement is likely to be accomplished by the identification and satisfaction of specific functional requirements. There have been some notable accomplishments along these lines, and one is tempted to conclude that the American government has done a rather remarkable job of mustering intellectual and organizational resources to meet its foreign policy problems in the two decades since it assumed the burdens of what has become a Pax Americana.

Fundamental Limitations

The most fundamental limits on American foreign policy are imposed by the international environment. While it is a lesson that Americans find particularly hard to learn and that must therefore be relearned from time to time, situations outside the boundaries of the United States are often not responsive to even its highest purposes and best efforts, and sometimes the application of substantial American resources will have only the most marginal effect on them. In other words, international politics is from the start a competition in which the United States cannot win all the games and is likely to lose quite a few.

The American political system imposes some limitations of its own which are almost as resistant to rational American calculation and manipulation as the international setting. The separation of powers in general and the characteristics of the United States Congress in particular impose a whole series of requirements on the executive branch which absorb a substantial proportion of its working time each year. The role of the President and the manner of his election practically assure a complete turnover of the top leadership levels of the executive branch every four or eight years, and a fair amount of turnover is likely in between as well.

The foreign policy concerns of the American people, be they noble or selfish, sophisticated or simpleminded, are thrust at the foreign policy organization from a number of directions—from the President himself, from a variety of congressional sources, from mass media that are energetic, aggressive, and fully confident that their role in the system is a key one, from interest groups and organizations, and from all the individuals willing to write a letter or pay a visit. In brief, American foreign policy is very much a part of American politics. Gaining and maintaining public understanding and support is another important demand on the time and energies of the organization.

Presidents are bound to change every four or eight years. With them, they bring an almost completely new top management, extending down from heads of departments to under and assistant secretaries, the usual covey of special assistants and other personal aides, and officials even farther down in the hierarchy. The backgrounds of those appointed, and the reasons for their appointment, vary widely. It would be highly exceptional, to say the least, for a group of four or five key men to be appointed to one particular department who have had considerable previous experience working together. The complementary qualities, more broadly, of those appointed to a particular department can be at best one among a number of factors considered (and hardly likely to be the most important). All of these characteristics suggest significant limitations on the continuity and consistency of styles of work, substantive interests, and managerial abilities among the ranking officers of the executive branch from the President on down.

Given the nature of the American presidential system, the fundamentals just described seem unlikely to change. Furthermore, they have a significant impact on the tone, style, and substance of the work throughout the foreign policy organization. If those who play such a key role in the functioning of the executive branch, and the foreign policy machinery, are relative "short-timers," this does not bode well for the permanent success of organizational grand designs that ignore this fact.

In sum, the separation of powers, the particular manner in which Congress is organized and functions, the intense and all-encompassing character of American political processes (from which foreign policy is not exempt) and, finally, the directing energy that the President must give the federal government combined with the relatively fleeting period of service that he and his associates usually provide, all impose fundamental limitations on how well the United States foreign policy organization can perform. Its processes are bound to be somewhat cumbersome and its organizational structure too sprawling and proliferated. It must meet many requirements and fulfill many needs that are intrinsic to the internal rather than the international political setting. If this is a valid view, such limitations are not likely to be overcome by drastic organizational surgery.

Possible Directions for Improvement

The First Secretary concept might have worked well with General Eisenhower as President and John Foster Dulles as his First Secretary, although whoever was Secretary of State under Dulles might have given the latter some anxious moments, sitting, as he would, closer to the daily actions that both express and help mold foreign policy. Certainly, both Presidents John Kennedy and Lyndon Johnson would have had little use for the office as originally conceived and would probably have returned the First Secretary to the kind of role played by the Special Assistant for National Security Affairs, if they kept the position at all. I would be inclined to take the same skeptical view of the long-term usefulness of the five operating deputies for the President proposed by Professor McCamy.[1]

McCamy has also proposed bringing all the full-time, nonmilitary activities of the federal government in the foreign policy field into the Department of State. In addition to the United States Information Agency, an obvious choice, McCamy includes, among others, the international affairs units in the Departments of Commerce, Labor, Agri-

---

[1] See James L. McCamy, *Conduct of the New Diplomacy* (Harper & Row, 1964), Chap. 10. As McCamy himself admits (p. 56), he has not written a deep analysis of the foreign policy organization. In his desire to encourage what he regards as some badly needed major reforms, he has oversimplified present patterns and problems as well as what would be required to effectuate his proposed reforms and what these could reasonably be expected to accomplish.

culture, and the Treasury, and the Atomic Energy Commission and the National Aeronautics and Space Administration. This proposal must either be interpreted as exaggerating to make a basic point or dismissed as ignoring the integral role such units play in the work of their own agencies—and to the advantage of the State Department. They connect their own domestically-oriented departments, which have responsibilities involving them in important international activities, and the Department of State, which must provide foreign policy guidance for these activities. At their best, these international affairs staffs provide, for their agencies, a central point of liaison for the State Department and an "in-house" source of foreign policy advice.[2]

The more restrained version of McCamy's idea has usually been expressed in terms of a Secretary of Foreign Affairs (sometimes he is even allowed to retain the traditional title of Secretary of State), who would have direct control of what is now the Department of State, the Information Agency, the Agency for International Development, and related economic aid activities. As was pointed out earlier in the study, the Secretary of State already has formal authority over two of the three and, apparently, good working relations with the third. Much more relevant to integrated American foreign policies and programs are the view the President and the Secretary take of the latter's role, the Secretary's effectiveness as foreign policy leader, and the supporting skills found in the working staff of the State Department.

If grand designs and oft-repeated nostrums are not the answer, how does one go about trying to improve the performance of the foreign policy organization? Certainly the present study leaves no doubt that there are plenty of problems in the organizational and personnel fields and that they deserve serious and continuing attention. What tests should be applied to proposals for organizational improvement? How does one distinguish between the organizational renovation or innovation that will in fact meet a need, and the change whose very implementation may cause more difficulties and abrasions than any long-term advantages it may offer?

In Chapter 1, a number of possible bases for evaluating the usefulness of organizational change were suggested. An obvious one is em-

---

[2] Arthur MacMahon emphasized the useful role these units could play in their own departments in his study of a dozen years ago. See *Administration in Foreign Affairs* (University of Alabama Press, 1953) pp. 177-83.

ployment of the most up-to-date equipment and technology applicable to the work being done. The communications equipment and capabilities of the foreign policy organization (if the military are excepted) have fallen far short of that. The same can be said about the most economical and efficient storage and retrieval of information. Fantastic quantities and varieties of information and intelligence arrive at, depart from, and are distributed every day within the State Department, the Central Intelligence Agency, and the other component agencies of the foreign policy organization. They are in a sense the lifeblood of the organization. The State Department, for one, has not done very well in this field of "information management" and is just now taking steps to remedy the situation.

Can one go any farther than technical innovation, with which few will quarrel? New fields of activity and new relationships among traditional fields continue to emerge in the foreign policy realm. This study has devoted considerable attention to the politico-military, politico-scientific, and politico-economic "intersections" of foreign policy making. They produce requirements for new organizational units and new personnel perspectives. Even here, it should be emphasized that a new organizational unit may languish on the vine if responsible officials do not understand or are not interested in the function it is supposed to perform. This is true of the relatively new Politico-Military Affairs staff in the State Department, so far judged a success. Admittedly, this may also be true of a well-established organizational unit. Without top-level interest and support, its effectiveness is likely to diminish unless it has an autonomous status, granted by statute or otherwise, that does not require such support.

Sometimes the organizational analyst can identify a fundamental functional problem that lies at the very heart of the system. These are often more easily studied than remedied. One example that has begun to receive considerable attention inside the government is what is called "crisis management."

The United States government has faced a number of situations in the last fifteen years where the stakes were extremely high, and rapid decisions, entailing major national commitments and risks, were called for. The decision to send U.S. Marines into the Dominican Republic in the spring of 1965 is only the most recent example of crisis decision making. Among the most crucial in the postwar period were the decisions in October 1962 directed to the presence of Soviet missiles in Cuba. Other obvious examples include Korea (1950), Suez and Hungary (1956), and Lebanon (1958).

Each time such a crisis has arisen, it has seemed as if United States decision making were being handled on an essentially *ad hoc* basis, with the President gathering his key aides around him and making the necessary decisions with their advice. Many of the highest officials of the government have worked full-time on the crises as long as these lasted. There has been a sense of procedures developed along the way and labors divided on a quite unsystematic basis. Would it be possible to develop standard procedures for responding to such an event? It is certainly possible to have communications and other facilities available to expedite both the necessary predecisional activities and the operational implementation of whatever decisions are reached. Much has already been accomplished in this regard.

It might further be asked whether there are organizational devices or techniques for assuring that some senior officials continue to give attention to other major problems around the world while the crisis goes on. There is also the matter of ensuring that those officials with relevant responsibilities and, even more important, with scarce and expert knowledge, get into the decision-making processes. These are some of the problems involved in more effective "crisis management."

The ultimate in national security crisis would be an actual or ominously impending strategic nuclear attack on the United States. Where should the President's command post be, what officials should be at his side (and at theirs), what facilities and decision-making resources do they need, what command-and-control arrangements and alternative command authorities should exist? The government has done quite a bit of thinking and preparation regarding tnis ultimate test of crisis. Serious attention has only more recently begun to be given to the much more likely occurrences that have periodically tested the U.S. governmental system.

Perhaps a social scientist may be forgiven for remarking that the foreign policy organization, particularly the Department of State, does not make sufficient use of the social sciences in either its organizational or substantive work. This would be especially true of the more behaviorally- and scientifically-oriented of the social sciences. As was noted in Chapter 11, the processes of recruiting, training and retaining personnel, and inventorying manpower needs, are not supported by either very sophisticated psychological knowledge or systematic research. There are only a handful of sociologists, anthropologists, and social psychologists scattered through the foreign policy staffs.

Furthermore, the foreign policy organization does very little to learn organizationally and operationally from past experience. The Department of State's Historical Office publishes volumes setting forth official accounts of United States foreign policy and its development, but there is no equivalent organization critically and analytically recording such experiences as the nonmilitary operations in Vietnam since 1954, the activities of United States missions in the Congo since 1960, or the operations of United States aid missions in fifty or sixty countries around the world since the inception of the Marshall Plan. Put bluntly and not too oversimply, the foreign policy organization has at present little ability to learn systematically from its own experiences. This strikes me as a functional requirement calling for some sort of organizational response.

Some Notable Accomplishments

A complete cataloguing of the units contained in the foreign policy organization—and their functions, responsibilities and interrelationships—would provide a description most difficult to grasp or accept. This often leads the outside observer, be he journalist, academician or congressman, to conclude that the system simply cannot work, or should not be working. In fact, it does work. Indeed, with regard to most of the matters with which it is charged, it works reasonably effectively and expeditiously. Most large organizations give something of the impression of overwhelming complexity to the outsider. Once on the inside, the newcomer who is reasonably intelligent begins to "learn the ropes," to find out who does what and where, and before long he is able to thread his way through the intricacies of the organizational maze and get his particular job done.

It must be admitted that the challenges represented by the foreign policy organization in this regard are considerable, but they are by no means insurmountable. People quickly identify those in their own agency and elsewhere who are clearly involved in the same business and must therefore be dealt with. If a particular matter is urgent, people can be reached quickly and their views ascertained quickly. In other words, we do well not to forget what human ingenuity, resourcefulness, and motivation can accomplish. If the foreign policy organization has more people and more agencies and subagency units than ideally it needs, this makes it more difficult, but not impossible, to get the job done. This is particularly true if the people at the top have clear views about what they consider important and what they want done.

There is more to be said about the accomplishments of the foreign policy organization than the rather negative tribute that its people manage to transcend the obstacles imposed upon them. The preceding chapters have indicated the number of new programs, new agencies, new perspectives, and new categories of personnel skills that have been made a part of American foreign policy and its organizational apparatus since World War II. Both overseas and in Washington, these new additions have become increasingly integrated into the foreign policy organization. Their practitioners have learned how to harness their efforts with the wide range of related activities throughout the government, and those with a much longer history of experience in the foreign policy business have increasingly accepted and even seized upon the newer tools of statecraft.

Within the foreign policy organization, there is broad acceptance of the involvement of many governmental agencies in the foreign relations of the United States government and, along with it, of the need for authoritative foreign policy guidance to be provided these agencies by the Department of State. The relationships involved are never going to be ideal, that is, equally satisfactory to all concerned. There will be faults and errors, unfortunate actions marked by good intentions and others not so burdened. However, there is greatly increased reciprocal understanding of what is required in these relationships and why.

Without denigrating other important organizational overlaps and interfaces, the most crucial one continues to be the vast range of interdependent activities and responsibilities that go under the brief heading of State-Defense relations. Here, it seems to be the almost unanimous opinion of experienced officials in both agencies that State-Defense relations have improved dramatically in the last five or so years and are far better then they have ever been. They are characterized by a greatly sharpened awareness on "both sides of the river" of the problems and requirements of the other, of the nature of each department's business, and how one can facilitate the other's work without necessarily abdicating its own responsibilities. Relationships and interactions are continuing and informal, and take place at every organizational level. Each agency is deeply involved in the business of the other.

This improved state of affairs has been facilitated by such programs as the State-Defense exchange of officers and the sending of Foreign Service and military officer personnel to the schools of the other. But these personnel and training programs do not represent the complete explanation. Joint planning and joint study efforts are increasingly encouraged. These range from planning for short-term politico-military contingencies to long-range planning exercises.

State Department review of Defense's Five-Year Force Structure and Budget document, by which the Secretary of Defense presents the annual military budget to the President and Congress, is a little heralded but major development. How much is made of it depends on the abilities and interests of senior officials of the two departments and the responsible staffs. By this involvement, the State Department does have an opportunity to bring a foreign policy perspective to bear on major military policy decisions whose foreign policy implications are often equally important, to learn of future developments in military technology in time to plan for possible consequences in foreign affairs, and, in turn, to provide the military establishment with foreign policy views and advice on these matters.

In sum, the two departments are, increasingly, focussing on what are recognized as common problems. For those who feel that the integrity of the two functions, foreign policy and military policy, can be maintained only by a reasonably clear-cut separation of the two agencies and their activities, this may seem like an unfortunate development. To those who, like the author, are convinced that American military and foreign policies require organizational relations that reflect their intimate linkage in the realities of international politics, it is highly encouraging. One somewhat troublesome question is whether the new patterns have become sufficiently institutionalized or sufficiently integrated into the perspectives and working habits of the professional staffs involved to survive the departure of the group of officials in both agencies, at both political and career levels, who have done so much to encourage this development and who are still largely on the scene.

While energetic and purposeful officials have learned to cut through the bureaucratic undergrowth, Washington remains something of an organizational jungle. As was pointed out in Chapter 9, the possibilities for interagency integration and coordination are much greater in the field missions, which at their worst are only a microcosm of the Washington scene. The requirement for some equivalent of presidential leadership for the various United States elements represented in almost every foreign country has been recognized for more than a decade. Ambassadors were the obvious choice to fill this leadership role.

What has taken place in recent years is a more energetic effort to give meaning and substance to that role—by defining ambassadorial authority more clearly and strengthening it, by providing ambassadors with a variety of organizational tools to help them do their job, and by picking ambassadors much more carefully. In Washington, this concern with a more unified approach to U.S. relations with particular foreign countries has been reinforced by agency and interagency efforts at longer-range planning and more integrated programming of U.S. activities directed to these countries. While these developments will not solve all the problems of policy implementation overseas, they do represent major achievements in increasing United States effectiveness abroad.

Much of what has been said translates into the attitudes, training, skills, and experience of the people who man the foreign policy organization. The past twenty-five years have been marked by a many-fold increase in their numbers and by sharp changes in the kinds of talents and interests they bring to their work. In part because of the sheer nature of the work, there is a much larger proportion of operational, action-oriented types. One also senses throughout the structure, even in the more tradition-based if not tradition-bound Foreign Service, a greater maturity and professionalism in handling the kinds of problems that tend to typify the contemporary international scene—crises, need for quick responses, use of a variety of instruments of policy, with military force or the capabilities of the military establishment present in the background if not the foreground of many situations.

As was suggested in Chapter 11, many of the officials in the present foreign policy organization have grown up, as it were, coping with such situations as part of their normal working pattern. With greater experience, they have become increasingly assured and confident in handling them. Thus, the combination of the toughening and maturing provided in the pressure-cooker of actual experience and the self-critical American posture (commented on at the beginning of this chapter) have brought into being a corps of personnel capable of handling contemporary foreign policy problems with the same professional assurance that the traditional diplomat brought to bear on his narrower range of problems and responsibilities in simpler days.

Another of Professor McCamy's proposals is for the establishment of what he calls a Policy Corps.[3] As he puts it, there is more to the formulation of foreign policy than "answering the mail," that is, responding to the cables coming from U.S. missions abroad. He emphasizes the need for people in the foreign policy organization skilled at what I have called policy analysis and policy planning, at extracting from the interplay of American objectives and international situations those short-term and longer-term courses of action that seem most likely, in balance, to advance the national interest. These efforts must be initiatory as well as responsive, creative and imaginative as well as simply keenly analytical within an established framework, capable of taking the longer view as well as meeting the immediate need.

The need is clear, but I question whether the proposed Policy Corps represents the most realistic means of satisfying it. There are quite a few people with such policy skills located within the foreign policy organization. If ranking officials recognize the need for such skills and demand the assignment of people so endowed to their units, personnel staffs are quite capable of identifying and assigning them. If the foreign policy organization lacks a sufficient number, there are many people with similar talents to be found on the staffs of univer-

---

[3] See the discussion in McCamy, *op. cit.,* pp. 256-66.

sities, private research organizations, and the like. The additional gain to be derived from formally establishing a Policy Corps seems to me at best incremental, and the concept has the potential for a kind of rigidity that could prove more damaging than the rather casual arrangements that now exist for identifying and employing such people.

One of the reassuring elements that leads one to question the desirability of a formal Policy Corps is the availability of substantial resources of intellectual talent outside the governmental organization for foreign policy. One of the true wonders of the age has been, to borrow the phrase of some colleagues, the American "intellectual response to the cold war." The quantity and quality of serious attention devoted to the problems of national security policy, foreign policy, and military policy by this society over the past twenty years are nothing short of amazing.

This can be explained in part by the tremendous wealth of the country. An acerb view would be that there is so much wealth that some of it even overflows into intellectual pursuits. A more balanced view would be that a great deal of public and private monies have been devoted to examination of the international problems of the day. In some cases, it is even fair to say that the resources available for this kind of effort exceed the results that can now be produced.

There is more than sheer wealth at work here. In part, it is the pragmatic, problem-oriented character of the society, reinforced by the self-critical sense and concern for self-improvement alluded to above. Whatever the exact explanation, the results have been impressive. Problems of national security, foreign policy, and the changing nature of the external world have come under the detailed scrutiny of university research centers, private research organizations of both the nonprofit and for-profit variety, and a variety of research units more or less directly connected with the military establishment.

While research has tended to get most of the attention of these new units, education and training have not been completely neglected. New fields of study have been opened for those following academic and scholarly pursuits, training to meet some of the new needs of the national security and foreign policy organizations has been provided for those interested in government careers and, finally, professional military personnel and civilians already in the national security business

have increasingly been given the opportunity to broaden their horizons or, if you will, to get "re-tooled" to meet more effectively the demands of the "new diplomacy."

In addition, the channels of communication and personal acquaintance, and of personnel recruitment, among government agencies,
academia, the private research organizations, private business, and the
foundations have widened notably. There is considerable circulation of
people among these various sectors of the society, and it is very
definitely on the upswing. This means that in practice as well as in
theory, there is a much larger cadre of skilled talent for the foreign
policy organization to draw on than the people immediately available
within the government.

This is a tremendous source of strength for the foreign policy machinery of the United States, and for the American position in the
world. Americans are quick to bemoan the limitations imposed upon
their country's foreign policy by the nature of its government and
politics and by flaws in the American national character. They would
do well to recognize and take pride in the strengths of the society and
how these, too, are reflected in its international efforts. I am prepared
to give the United States high marks for its overall international performance during the past twenty years, and I am inclined to think that
history will share this view.

APPENDIXES

APPENDIX A

The Flow of Policy Making in the Department of State[1]

NOTE: *Time has left its mark on Mr. Ogburn's essay as on all else. Consulate General Brazzaville is now American Embassy Brazzaville; the fifth floor location of the Secretary of State and his top aides in New State has become the seventh floor in new New State; Dependent Area Affairs are no longer dealt with by a separate office in the Bureau of International Organization Affairs; but Africa does have a separate office to analyze its problems in the Bureau of Intelligence and Research. These are minor changes. Mr. Ogburn's essay still captures brilliantly some of the typical decision-making patterns and activities of the Department of State. (BMS)*

The Department of State is an organism that is constantly responding to a vast assortment of stimuli. A new Soviet threat to Berlin, a forthcoming conference of Foreign Ministers of the Organization of American States, a request from Poland for credit, a solicitation for support of a candidacy for the Presidency of the United Nations General Assembly, a plea from an ambassador that the head of the government to which he is accredited be invited to visit the United States officially, a refusal by another government to permit the duty-free importation of some official supplies for a U.S. consulate, a request from the White House for comment on the foreign affairs section of a major presidential address, an earthquake in the Aegean creating hardships which it appears the U.S. Navy might be able to alleviate, a request for a speaker from a foreign policy association in California, a transmittal slip from a Member of Congress asking for information with which to reply to a letter from a constituent protesting discriminatory actions against his business by a foreign government, letters from citizens both supporting and deploring the policy of nonrecognition of Communist China, a continuing inquiry by a press correspondent who has got wind of a top secret telegram from Embassy Bonn on

[1] By Charlton Ogburn, Jr., in H. Field Haviland, Jr. and Associates, *The Formulation and Administration of United States Foreign Policy*, a Report for the Committee on Foreign Relations of the United States Senate (Brookings Institution, 1960), pp. 172-77.

the subject of German rearmament and is determined to find out what is in it, a demand by a Protestant church group that the Department take steps to prevent harassment of their coreligionists in a foreign country, a request by a delegation of a federation of women's clubs for a briefing on southeast Asia and suggestions as to how its members might be useful in their planned tour of the area, a request from Consulate General Brazzaville for a revision of cost-of-living allowances, a visit by a commission of inquiry into the operations of U.S. foreign aid programs, a notification from the staff of the National Security Council that a revision of the National Security Council paper on dependent areas is due, a telegram from a U.S. embassy in the Near East declaring that last night's flareups make a visit by the Assistant Secretary for Near Eastern and South Asian Affairs, now in mid-Atlantic, inopportune at the moment, a warning by a European Foreign Minister of the consequences should the United States fail to support his nation's position in the Security Council, and a counterwarning by an African representative at the United Nations of the consequences should the United States do so—this is a sample of the requirements made of the Department of State in a typical day. Of course it does not include the oceans of informational reports that come into the Department by telegram and air pouch or the countless periodicals from all parts of the world that arrive by sea.

What is required to begin with is that the flow be routed into the right channels. This does not apply to press correspondents and foreign embassy officials; they usually know where to go without being directed. For the rest, almost every piece of business—every requirement or opportunity for action—comes within the Department's ken first as a piece of paper. These pieces of paper—telegrams, dispatches (or "despatches," as the Department prefers to call them), letters—must be gotten as speedily as possible into the hands of the officers who will have to do something about them or whose jobs require that they know about them.

The telegram and mail branches of the Division of Communication Services, a part of the Bureau of Administration, receive the incoming material and, after decoding and reproducing the telegrams, indicate on each communication the distribution it should receive among the bureaus or equivalent components of the Department. If, in the case of a letter or a dispatch, there are not enough copies to go around, the recipients are listed one after another and receive it consecutively, the original going first to the bureau responsible for taking whatever action the document requires. With telegrams, the deliveries are simultaneous. Several score copies of a telegram may be run off. A yellow copy, called the action copy, like the original of a dispatch or letter, goes to the bureau responsible for taking any necessary action; white copies go to all others interested.

A telegram (No. 1029, let us say) from a major U.S. embassy in Western Europe reports the warning of the Foreign Minister of X country that a grave strain would be imposed on relations between X and the United States should the latter fail to vote with X on a sensitive colonial issue in the United Nations General Assembly. Such a telegram would have a wide distribution. The action copy would go to the Bureau of European Affairs. The action copy of a telegram to the same purpose from the U.S. delegation to the United Nations in New York, quoting the X delegation, would go to the Bureau of International Organization Affairs. This is a matter of convention.

Information copies of a telegram of such importance would go to all officers in the higher echelons—the Secretary of State (via the executive secretariat), the Under Secretaries, the Deputy Under Secretaries, the counselor. They would also go the Policy Planning Staff, to the Bureau of African Affairs because of the involvement of certain territories within its jurisdiction, to the Bureau of Far Eastern Affairs and the Bureau of Near Eastern and South Asian Affairs because the telegram concerns the incendiary question of European peoples' ruling non-European peoples, and of course to the Bureau of Intelligence and Research. Other copies would go to the Department of Defense and the Central Intelligence Agency. The executive secretariat would doubtless make certain that the Secretary would see the telegram. In addition, its staff would include a condensation in the secret daily summary, a slim compendium distributed in the Department on a need-to-know basis. If classified top secret, it would be included in the top secret daily staff summary, or black book, which goes only to Assistant Secretary-level officials and higher.

In the bureaus, incoming material is received by the message centers. There a further and more refined distribution would be made of telegram 1029. Copies would go to the Office of the Assistant Secretary (the so-called front office), to the United Nations adviser, to the public affairs adviser (since the United States is going to be in for trouble with public opinion in either one part of the world or the other), and to whatever geographic office or offices may seem to have the major interest. In the Bureau of International Organization Affairs, this would be the Office of United Nations Political and Security Affairs. Another copy, however, might go to the Office of Dependent Area Affairs.

In the Bureau of European Affairs, the yellow action copy of the telegram goes to the Office of Western European Affairs and thence to the X country desk, where it is the first thing to greet the desk officer's eye in the morning. As it happens, the desk officer was out the evening before at an official function where he discussed at length with the first secretary of the X embassy the desirability of avoiding any extremes of action in the United Nations over the territory in question. In the front office of the Bureau, the staff assistant has entered in his records the salient details of the problem the Bureau is charged with and has passed the telegram on to the Assistant Secretary.

The following scenes are now enacted:

The X country desk officer crosses the hall to the office of his superior, the officer-in-charge, and the two together repair to the office of the Director of the Office of Western European Affairs. The three officers put in a call to the

Assistant Secretary for European Affairs and tell his secretary that they would like as early an appointment as possible.

The Director of the Office of United Nations Political and Security Affairs (UNP) telephones the Director of the Office of Western European Affairs (WE). He says he assumes WE will be drafting an instruction to the U.S. embassy in X to try to dissuade the Foreign Office from its course, and that UNP would like to be in on it. He adds that they had thought of getting the U.S. delegation to the United Nations (US Del) to present this view to the X mission in New York but that there seemed to be no point in doing so since the latter would already be advising its government to take account of world opinion.

After the Secretary's morning staff conference, where the matter is discussed briefly, a conference is held in the Office of the Assistant Secretary for European Affairs to decide on a line to take with the X government. The X desk officer is designated to prepare the first draft of a telegram embodying it. The draft is reviewed and modified by his officer-in-charge and the Office Director for Western European Affairs.

The telegram instructs the U.S. embassy in X to make clear to the X government our fear that its projected course of action "will only play into hands of extremists and dishearten and undermine position elements friendly to West" and suggests that the X government emphasize its policy to take account of the legitimate aspirations of the indigenous population of the territory in order to improve the atmosphere for consideration of the problem by the General Assembly. The Assistant Secretary, after scrutinizing and approving the telegram, finds it necessary only to add the Bureau of Near Eastern and South Asian Affairs to the clearances. Those already listed for clearance are the Deputy Under Secretary for Political Affairs, the Bureau of International Organization Affairs, and the Bureau of African Affairs. He says it can be left to the Deputy Under Secretary for Political Affairs to sign the telegram; he does not see that the telegram need go higher.

It remains for the drafting officer to circulate the telegram for approval by those marked for clearance. In the Bureau of African Affairs the telegram is termed extremely gentle to the X government but is initialed as it stands. The Office of United Nations Political and Security Affairs (UNP) wishes to remind X that the United States, setting an example of its adherence to the principle of affording the widest latitude to the General Assembly, had even accepted on occasion the inscription of an item on the agenda accusing the United States of aggression. The X desk officer states, however, that WE would not favor such an addition, which might only further antagonize the X government. Thereupon, UNP, yielding on this point, requests deletion of a phrase in the telegram seeming to place the United States behind the X contention that the question is not appropriate for discussion in the United Nations. The drafter of the telegram telephones the Director of the Office of

Western European Affairs who authorizes the deletion, having decided that he can do so on his own without referring the question to his superior, the Assistant Secretary.

With that, the Director of the Office of United Nations Political and Security Affairs initials the telegram for his Bureau, and the X desk officer "hand carries" the telegram (in the departmental phrase), with telegram 1029 attached, to the Office of the Deputy Under Secretary for Political Affairs and leaves it with his secretary. At 6 o'clock he is informed by telephone that the Deputy Under Secretary has signed the telegram (that is, signed the Secretary's name with his own initials beneath) without comment. The desk officer goes to the fifth floor, retrieves it, and takes it to the correspondence review staff of the executive secretariat, where the telegram is examined for intelligibility, completion of clearances, conformity with departmental practices, etc., before being sped to the Telegram Branch for enciphering and transmission.

The next morning, all officers of the Department participating in the framing of the telegram receive copies of it hectographed on pink outgoing telegram forms. The telegram, bearing the transmission time of 8:16 p.m., has entered history as the Department's No. 736 to the embassy in X. The X desk officer writes "telegram sent," with the date, in the space indicated by a rubber stamp on the yellow copy of the original telegram 1029, and the staff assistant in the front office makes an equivalent notation in his records. The yellow copy is then sent on to the central files, whence in time it will probably be consigned to the National Archives. Only the white copies may be kept in the Bureau's files.

In this case, however, no one is under any illusion that the matter has been disposed of. Scarcely 24 hours later comes a new telegram 1035 from the embassy in X reporting that, while the X government may possibly make some concessions, it will certainly wage an all-out fight against inscription of the item and will expect the United States to exert itself to marshal all the negative votes possible. The question is, what position will the United States in fact take and how much effort will it make to win adherents for its position? No one supposes for a moment that this explosive question can be decided on the bureau level. Only the Secretary can do so—as the Secretary himself unhappily realizes.

At the end of a staff meeting on Berlin, the Secretary turns to the Assistant Secretary for Policy Planning and asks him to give some thought within the next few days to the alternatives open on the question. The official addressed sets the wheels in motion at once. A meeting is called for the next morning. Attending are: the Assistant Secretary for Policy Planning himself and several members of his staff (including the European and African specialists), the Director of the Office of United Nations Political and Security Affairs, the Western European officer-in-charge, the X desk officer, a member of the policy guidance and coordination staff of the Bureau of Public Affairs, and two intelligence specialists, namely, the Director of the Office of Research and Analysis for Western Europe and the Director of the Office of Research and Analysis for the Near East, South Asia, and Africa.

The discussion explores all ramifications of the issues involved and is generally detached and dispassionate. The object of the meeting it to help clarify the issues so that the Policy Planning Staff may be sure all relevant considerations are taken into account in the staff paper it will prepare for the Secretary.

The Secretary is in a difficult position. The President's views on what course of action to take are somewhat different from his. The Congress is also of divided view, with some Members impressed by the irresistible force of nationalism among dependent peoples, others by the essential role of X in NATO and European defense. The ambassadors of some countries pull him one way, others another. One of the Nation's leading newspapers editorially counsels "restraint, understanding and vision." At the staff meeting he calls to arrive at a decision, the Secretary perceives that his subordinates are as deeply divided as he feared. He takes counsel with each—the Assistant Secretaries for Policy Planning, European Affairs, African Affairs, and Near Eastern and South Asian Affairs. At the end he sums up and announces his decision. Thereupon the following things happen:

The Assistant Secretaries take the news back to their bureaus.

An urgent telegram is sent to the U.S. Embassy in X reporting the decision.

Telegrams are sent to embassies in important capitals around the world instructing the ambassador to go to the Foreign Office and present the U.S. case in persuasive terms.

A similar telegram is sent to the U.S. delegation in New York for its use in talks with the delegations of other United Nations members.

Conferences attended by representatives of the geographic bureaus concerned, of the Bureau of Public Affairs, and of the U.S. Information Agency, are held. Afterward, the representatives of the U.S. Information Agency return to their headquarters to draft guidances to the U.S. Information Service establishments all over the world. Such guidances tell how news of the U.S. decision is to be played when it breaks.

The more important the problem, the more the upper levels of the Department become involved. In a crisis—one brought about, say, by the overthrow of A, a Western-oriented government in the Middle East—the Secretary himself will take over. However, the bulk of the Department's business is carried on, of necessity, by the lower ranking officers. Even when a crisis receives the Secretary's personal, day-to-day direction, the desk officer and the officer-in-charge are always at hand to provide the detailed information only specialists possess, while in the intelligence bureau, country analysts and branch chiefs will be putting in 10-hour days and 6- or 7-day weeks. Generally, moreover, the crisis will have been preceded by a good deal of work on the part of lower level officials.

In the case suggested, it was apparent for some time that all was not well in A. The U.S. Embassy in A was aware of growing discontent with the regime through its indirect contacts with opposition political elements, from information from Cairo, from evidences of tension, from clandestine publications. Additional straws in the wind were supplied by the public affairs officer in A both to the embassy and to the U.S. Information Agency because of his special contacts among professional groups. On the strength of these reports and of dispatches from American foreign correspondents in the area, and equipped with analyses from the Bureau of Intelligence and Research, all pointing in the same direction, the desk officer at a staff meeting of the Office of Near Eastern Affairs imparts his disquiet. He is directed to prepare a memorandum which, if convincing in its presentation, the Office Director undertakes to put before the Assistant Secretary.

What the desk officer has in mind will require national action, so what he drafts takes the form of a memorandum to the Secretary. It embodies a statement of the problem, the actions recommended, a review of the facts bearing upon the problem, and a conclusion. At the end are listed the symbols of the offices of the Department from which concurrences must be sought. Backing up the memorandum will be supporting documents, especially telegrams from the embassy, each identified by a tab. The mass fills a third of an in-box.

The problem is defined as that of strengthening the present pro-Western regime of A. By way of recommendation, the desk officer is especially sensitive to the problems and needs of the country for which he is responsible. He calls for more detachment of the United States from A's rival, B, expediting U.S. arms deliveries to A and the supply of certain recoilless rifles and jet fighter planes the A government has been requesting, support for A's membership in various United Nations agencies, a Presidential invitation to the Prime Minister of A to visit the United States. Much of what the memorandum recommends has to be fought out in the Bureau and even in the Office since it conflicts with the claims of countries (and the desk officers responsible for them) in the same jurisdiction. While neither the Office Director nor the Assistant Secretary doubts that support of B is a handicap in the region, they consider that a proposal for a radical departure would simply doom the memorandum by preventing anyone from taking it seriously.

As it finally leaves the Bureau with the Assistant Secretary's signature, the memorandum is considerably revised, and further change awaits it. The Department of Defense cannot provide the desired recoilless rifles and jet fighters. The Bureau of International Organization Affairs cannot offer any undertakings at this stage with respect to the question of membership in United Nations agencies. The Deputy Under Secretary for Political Affairs rules out a request of the President to invite the A Prime Minister for an official visit because the number of those invited is already too large.

Among recommendations in memorandums to the Secretary, as among salmon battling their way upstream to the spawning grounds, mortality is heavy. Almost everywhere in the world, things are far from satisfactory, but the United States cannot be doing everything everywhere at the same time. And A, far from seeming to cry out for attention, looks like the one Middle Eastern country about which it is not necessary to worry.

Then the uprising occurs in A. Early in the morning, the officer-in-charge of A and one other country is awakened by the ringing of the telephone. In a flash, before his feet have touched the floor, he has visualized every conceivable disaster that could have befallen his area and has picked the overthrow of the monarchy in C as the most likely. Or did the security people find a top secret document under his desk?

On the telephone, the watch officer at the Department tells him that a "Niact" (a night action telegram, which means "Get this one read immediately even if you have to rout someone out of bed") is coming off the machine and it looks serious—he had better come down. En route, the officer-in-charge turns on his car radio and picks up a news broadcast, but nothing is said about A. Uncle Sam has beaten the press agencies.

At the Department, he finds the telegram wholly decoded and reads the hectograph master. There is revolution in A. The top leadership has been either murdered or banished. The officer in charge could legitimately awaken the Assistant Secretary, but for the moment it seems there is nothing that can be done, so he decides to hold off until 6 a.m. and then call the Office Director and put it up to him. He does, however, call the A desk officer and tell him to get on his way. To share his vigil beside the watch officer's window there is a representative of the executive secretariat, who will have the telegram ready for the Secretary to read immediately on his arrival. In the Bureau of Intelligence and Research—it being now after 4 o'clock—the morning briefers have arrived to go over the night's take and write up items of importance, with analyses, for the Director's use in briefing the Secretary's morning staff conference. The briefer for the Office of Research and Analysis for the Near East, South Asia and Africa—a GS-11 specialist on India—takes one look at the Niact on A and gets on the telephone to the A analyst.

By the time the Secretary has stepped from his black limousine and headed for the private elevator a good deal has happened. In the Bureau of Near Eastern and South Asian Affairs, everyone concerned with A from the Assistant Secretary down, and including the officer-in-charge of Baghdad Pact and Southeast Asia Treaty Organization affairs and the special assistant who serves as a policy and planning adviser, has been in conference for an hour laying out the tasks requiring immediate attention. Two more Niacts have come in from A, one reporting that so far no Americans are known to have been injured but offering little assurance with respect to the future. The Assistant Secretary has already put in a call to the Director of Intelligence Research to ask that all possible information on the new leader of A and his connections be marshaled and that the Central Intelligence Agency be informed of the need. For the rest, the following represent the Assistant Secretary's conception of what should be done first:

1. The Department of Defense must be apprised of the Department of State's anxiety and be requested to have transport planes in readiness at nearby fields for the evacuation of Americans if necessary in accordance with prearranged plans. There must be consultation on what instruments are available if American lives have to be protected by force.

2. The U.S. embassy in C, a friendly neighbor of A's to which the Niacts have been repeated, will be heard from at any moment, and the Special Assistant for Mutual Security Coordination in the Office of the Under Secretary for Economic Affairs and, also, the Office of International Security Affairs in the Department of Defense will have to be alerted to the possibility of emergency military assistance for C.

3. Anything in the pipeline for A should be held up. The Special Assistant for Mutual Security Coordination must be advised of this.

4. The possibility of a demonstration by the U.S. 6th Fleet in support of C's independence and integrity will have to be discussed with the Department of Defense.

5. A crash national intelligence estimate will be requested of the Central Intelligence Agency, provided the Agency does not consider the situation too fluid for a formal estimate to be useful.

6. The public affairs adviser will get in touch with the Bureau of Public Affairs, the departmental spokesman and the U.S. Information Agency to agree on the kind of face the United States will put on the affair.

7. The B Ambassador will probably have to be called in and apprised of the critical need for his government's acquiescence in overflights of B for the purpose of getting supplies to C. The B and C desk officers had better get busy immediately on a draft telegram to embassy B (repeat to C) setting forth the case the ambassador should make urgently to the B Foreign Office.

At 9:12, anticipating that he will be called to accompany the Secretary to the White House, the Assistant Secretary instructs his secretary to cancel all his appointments for the day, including one with the dentist but excepting his appointment with the C ambassador. ("Mr. Ambassador, you may assure His Majesty that my Government remains fully determined to support the sovereignty and territorial integrity of his nation.")

At 9:14, 1 minute before the scheduled commencement of the staff meeting, the Assistant Secretary joins his colleagues in the Secretary's anteroom, prepared to hear the estimate of the Director of Intelligence and Research and to give his own appraisal and submit his plan of action.

Memorandum on the Department of State's Politico-Military Organization and Staffing*

Organization

The Department of State has substantially strengthened its capabilities in the politico-military field during the past 3 years. The Secretary and the other senior officials of the Department have been provided with centralized staff support and functional expertise for dealing with the increasingly wide range of international problems that involve military factors and considerations. At the same time, the geographical and functional bureaus of the Department have strengthened their own staffing and sharpened their own interests in this field.

The Deputy Under Secretary of State for Political Affairs is the senior departmental official with primary staff responsibility for poltico-military affairs. He is the focal point for the Department's dealings with the Department of Defense. In May 1961, to assist him in this area, a Politico-Military Affairs staff headed by a Deputy Assistant Secretary of State for Politico-Military Affairs (G/PM) was established as a part of the office of the Deputy Under Secretary. As Secretary Rusk characterized the function in his testimony before the Senate Subcommittee on National Policy Machinery in August 1961, the Politico-Military Affairs staff is to—

assist the supervisory level of the State Department in the management and conduct all the Department's relations with the Department of Defense, including the Military Establishment. It is intended to provide leadership on such matters within the State Department, and thereby enable it to fulfill more effectively its role of providing timely political guidance to other governmental agencies on politico-military matters.[1]

The requirement for G/PM and the nature of its role have been stated more recently in the following terms:

* *Administration of National Security*, Hearings before the Subcommittee on National Security Staffing and Operations of the Government Operations Committee, 88 Cong. 1 Sess. (1963), pp. 413-19. This memorandum was prepared in the Office of the Honorable U. Alexis Johnson, Deputy Under Secretary of State for Political Affairs.

[1] *Organizing for National Security*, Hearings before the Subcommittee on National Policy Machinery of the Senate Government Operations Committee, 87 Cong. 1 sess. (1961), p. 1282.

Operating in such a setting, the Department needed a unit that could look at politico-military problems on a worldwide basis, assure that regional variations and interrelations had been taken into account, and provide a central point of focus and coordination, as required for the politico-military activities being carried on by the geographical bureaus of the Department. Such a unit would not replace regional politico-military staffs but rather strengthen and tie together their related activities.

There was also a requirement for some State Department unit to review the total U.S. defense effort and the major lines of policy being pursued by the Defense Department in terms of their overall foreign policy implications, and to bring these implications to the attention of the Defense Department where appropriate. In a situation where so many important problems involved the State and Defense Departments, it was also felt that it would be convenient to have one obvious point of contact within the Department well known to all elements of the Department of Defense.[2]

The Deputy Assistant Secretary for Politico-Military Affairs has organized his staff along three major lines of activity. An operations group deals with those military problems that have immediate action consequences or foreign policy implications or foreign policy actions that have military implications and therefore demand coordination and close collaboration with the Defense Department on a current basis. A combined plicy staff is concerned with politico-military problems of a policy, planning, and strategic nature. Military aspects of atomic energy and aerospace represent another major area of responsibility. The Deputy Assistant Secretary also has a Special Assistant for Soviet Bloc Politico-Military Affairs. In addition, G/PM has policy guidance and coordinating responsibilities for the Department of State in the fields of emergency preparedness and foreign disaster relief.

On July 1, 1963, the Office of Munitions Control was transferred from the Bureau of Economic Affairs to the jurisdiction of the Deputy Assistant Secretary. The responsibilities of this Office in the licensing of military sales to foreign countries and in monitoring exchange of military information with them are closely related to the activities of the Politico-Military Affairs staff, and this closer relationship seemed desirable.

While the presence of a special staff provides the management/supervisory level of the Department, for the first time, with substantial staff support on politico-military problems, the Deputy Assistant Secretary and his staff by no means represent the totality of the State Department's capabilities in this field. The Department has been involved in politico-military affairs since the end of World War II. Each of the Assistant Secretaries heading the geographical bureaus has officers or staffs charged with full-time responsibilities in this field, and there are, furthermore, few desk officers in these bureaus who do not at one time or another deal with questions of military assistance and training, base rights, overflights of U.S. military aircraft, and visits of U.S. military units or personnel.

[2] "The Politico-Military Affairs Staff: Its Organization and Its Duties," Department of State Newsletter, No. 30 (October 1963), p. 24. This article provides a detailed description of the organization and functioning of G/PM.

In March 1962, as part of an effort to strengthen the Department in the field of Atlantic Community affairs, the position of Deputy Assistant Secretary was established with that responsibility, and the Office of Regional Affairs (RA) in the Bureau of European Affairs was divided into two units, an Office of Atlantic Political-Economic Affairs (RPE) and an Office of Atlantic Political-Military Affairs (RPM). The latter office provides the primary organizational support in the Department of State for U.S. participation in the North Atlantic Treaty Organization. The complex organizational structure of NATO and the intimate interrelations of political and military-strategic problems that characterize its functioning make RPM an extremely busy and important office. The staff of RPM has a close working relationship with G/PM.

In the Inter-American, Near Eastern and South Asian, Far Eastern, and African Affairs Bureaus, there are regional offices that deal with problems that cut across country and subregional lines. Each of these offices has a number of officers who devote all or most of their time to such problems as regional security arrangements, military assistance, threats of Communist-inspired insurgency, and related internal security matters.

The Policy Planning Council has a long-standing interest in politico-military problems. In the period before 1961, when the National Security Council machinery was more elaborate than it is at present, the Policy Planning Staff (as it was then called) played a primary role in backstopping the Department of State's participation in the work of the Council. The Planning Council continues to be actively engaged in politico-military problems as an aspect of its long-term planning in the foreign policy field, and its members work with G/PM officers on the politico-military facets of their planning tasks.

In other words, while the Department of State has a number of units to meet a variety of politico-military needs and requirements, these units do not work in isolation from one another. With the support of the Politico-Military Affairs staff, the Deputy Under Secretary coordinates and provides leadership to the politico-military efforts of the geographical and functional bureaus and the Policy Planning Council and works closely with the Arms Control and Disarmament Agency and relevant geographical and functional units in the Agency for International Development. In addition to the usual working contacts, G/PM officers meet formally once a week with representatives of the politico-military staffs of the Department's geographical bureaus.

A significant portion of the day-to-day politico-military work of the Department is still done in the several regional bureaus. G/PM's significance lies in the fact that it has provided to the component units of the Department of State a central point of functional expertise, leadership, and coordination in this field.

Functions

These expanded organizational capabilities have enabled the Department of State to provide clearer guidance and more effective policy direction to those military programs and activities that help implement U.S. foreign policy, for example, stationing of U.S. forces abroad and other military operations overseas, military-strategic planning, and military assistance, training, and equipment sales. At least as noteworthy has been the increasing recognition within the Department that the overall military posture and capabilities of the United States significantly affect the strength and flexibility of its foreign policy and, therefore, that the Department of State must concern itself in a serious and continuing fashion with the military policy decisions that determine what those capabilities will be. The central position of the Deputy Under Secretary of State for Political Affairs, supported by the Politico-Military Affairs staff, has enabled him to provide active and positive leadership in these efforts and to mobilize the full politico-military resources of the Department for these purposes.

One example of this relatively new politico-military role is the participation of the Department of State, for the past 3 years, in the Defense Department's annual planning and budget exercise. The Secretary of Defense has now made this a 5-year projection of strategy and force structure, which is reviewed annually. The relevant documents embody the Defense Department's plans for the future, and the force levels, worldwide force dispositions, and weapons systems development envisaged in them. The Department of State reviews and analyzes these plans and projections from the standpoint of their foreign policy implications and thus permits the Secretary of State to provide appropriate guidance in this field to the Secretary of Defense and advice to the President.

Another field of military activity with which the Department of State now concerns itself on a systematic, continuing basis is deployment of U.S. forces overseas. Because of the relationship between the stationing of large numbers of U.S. troops abroad and the balance-of-payments problem, this has become a particularly sensitive issue during the past year. It is further complicated by the continuing changes in military technology that require or make possible adjustments in the positioning of U.S. forces as between foreign and U.S. bases.

Any redeployments of U.S. forces from oversea bases, or deployments to them, that represent more than the normal rotation of units or individuals are now reviewed as a matter of course by the Department of State to assess likely foreign policy implications. Special interagency coordinating mechanisms have been established, under the chairmanship of the Deputy Assistant Secretary for Politico-Military Affairs, to assure effective governmental attention to this complicated problem area. Within the Department of State, G/PM has worked closely with the geographical bureaus whose areas would be affected by proposed redeployments of forces.

There has also been greatly increased collaboration with the Defense Department on a broad range of military contingency planning efforts, special studies, and joint task forces. Major politico-strategic problems in Europe and elsewhere have been the subject of joint review. The Berlin task force is probably the best example of joint contingency planning, but there are others. Cuba and Vietnam have also been approached on an interagency task force basis.

The Cuban crisis of October 1962, and the detailed implementation of the Nassau agreements after December 1962, were marked by the closest State-Defense collaboration in policy development, planning, and execution. In the case of the Nassau agreements, special interagency machinery was established under Department of State chairmanship, with the Deputy Assistant Secretary for Politico-Military Affairs heading the effort, for coordination of the detailed and complicated activities involved in translating those agreements into national action. Other areas of the Department played an extensive part in this effort, including the Bureau of European Affairs and the Policy Planning Council.

The Department of State has been active in dealing with politico-military problems at both the nuclear and insurgency-subversion ends of the military spectrum. Under the leadership of the Deputy Under Secretary for Political Affairs and his G/PM staff, the Department has attempted to put the problem of Communist subversion and insurgency in its broader political and socio-economic context, to develop increased recognition among the U.S. agencies involved that Communist inspired or supported insurgency is not only or even primarily a military problem, and to translate that recognition into appropriate policies and programs.

The interdepartmental group that drafted the present U.S. policy doctrine on this subject was chaired by a G/PM officer. The Deputy Under Secretary served from its inception as a member and for a time as chairman for the high-level Special Group (Counter-Insurgency). He in turn has been succeeded by the Under Secretary for Political Affairs. The Deputy Under Secretary also served as Chairman of the Interagency Committee on Police Programs that led to a substantial reorganization and strengthening of that effort.

These examples represent major developments and improvements. They are only a very small sample of the wide range of activities carried on by the Department in relation to and collaboration with the Department of Defense.

Personnel Improvements in Washington and Overseas

The strengthening of the Department of State's organizational arrangements in the politico-military field has been accompanied by a planned program to build up within the Department a cadre of officers skilled and experienced in politico-military affairs. The Deputy Under Secretary, the Deputy Assistant Secretary and the G/PM staff have worked very closely with the administrative and personnel organizations of the Department in these efforts.

A number of personnel training and assignment programs are contributing to the result. Among the most important are: the State-Defense officer exchange program initiated at the end of 1960; assignment of State Department personnel to war colleges and other military training institutions as students, faculty, and liaison officers, the political advisers assigned to major U.S. military commands; and the special politico-military Foreign Service officer positions established and being established at many of our oversea missions. All of these are long-term programs, designed to produce an adequate corps of Foreign Service officers and State Department civil servants with politico-military training and operational experience.

Since 1946, more than 425 State Department officers have attended the five U.S. war colleges and the Armed Forces Staff College and equivalent foreign and international defense colleges. In the current 1963-64 school year, there are 15 Foreign Service officers in attendance at the National War College, 3 at the Industrial College of the Armed Forces, 3 at the Army War College, 3 at the Naval War College, 2 at the Air War College, and 2 at the Armed Forces Staff College. In addition, there are Foreign Service officers attending the Imperial Defence College in London, the Canadian National Defence College, and the NATO Defense College.

There are State Department faculty members at the five U.S. war colleges and the Armed Forces Staff College, a Foreign Service officer on the faculty of the U.S. Air Force Academy and a Foreign Service officer attached as State Department adviser to the U.S. Army Special Warfare Center at Fort Bragg, N.C. Agreement has also been reached for a Foreign Service officer to join the faculty of the U.S. Naval Academy beginning in the summer of 1964. It might also be noted that military officers attend courses at the Foreign Service Institute, including the senior seminar which is the Foreign Service Institute equivalent of a senior war college course and the interdepartmental seminar on problems of development and internal defense.

The State-Defense officer exchange program initiated in December 1960 is now entering its second round. Most of the State and Defense Department officials who participated in the initial 2-year tours of duty as exchange officers have now completed these tours and returned to their own agencies. It is generally agreed that the program, to this point, has been an outstanding success, and it seems well-established as a long-term arrangement. At this writing, 21 State Department officers are either on duty in the Pentagon or have completed a tour there; the total of military officers and Defense Department civilians in this category is 19. The State Department has attempted to monitor the program very carefully, in terms of the quality of personnel sent to the Defense Department, the positions opened up to the Defense exchange officers, and the follow-on assignments provided to returning State Department exchangees. The Deputy Under Secretary, the Politico-Military Affairs Staff acting on his behalf, and the personnel office of the Department have worked closely together on this problem.

G/PM has provided a "home away from home" for the State Department officials assigned as faculty members at the war colleges and as political advisers (POLADS) to major military commanders. A POLAD is defined as—

a Foreign Service officer who has been assigned to the staff of a U.S. unified or specified military commander on the basis of formal agreement between the Departments of State and Defense and who is responsible solely to the commander.

* * * * * * *

The POLAD is not an institutional representative of the Department of State nor is he a Department of State liaison officer serving with the command.

The function of the POLAD is to advise and consult with the commander on political, politico-military and economic matters affecting the commander's theater of operations. In performing this function, he provides a specialized expertise and source of information to the commander in the same way as any other special staff officer.[3]

There are at present eight designated positions as POLAD's, all filled by senior Foreign Service officers. They are located at the following military commands: European Command; Pacific Command; Atlantic Command; Southern Command (Canal Zone); Strategic Air Command; Strike Command; Military Air Transport Service; and U.S. High Commissioner, Ryukyus.

The Department has been actively engaged in strengthening the POLAD program. The goal has been to upgrade qualitatively the personnel assigned to these jobs by selecting, through an exhaustive review process, officers with the stature, background, and experience which would enable them to function effectively as senior advisers to key commanders.

The POLAD's represent one effort to strengthen politico-military collaboration and staffing in the field. In overseas diplomatic missions where there are important military problems confronting the ambassador, Foreign Service officers with the necessary politico-military background and experience are now being assigned to political sections or as special assistants and advisers to the ambassadors in this field. There are considerable variations in title, job description, and actual functioning, but the essential purpose is to strengthen the ambassador's ability to integrate effectively the military aspects of country team activities. In one recent case, a Foreign Service officer who had just completed a 2-year tour in the Joint Staff of the Joint Chiefs of Staff under the exchange program was sent to a key post in southeast Asia as politico-military special assistant to the ambassador. It is anticipated that this will be an increasingly typical assignment pattern, following up an exchange position in the Defense Department with some closely related oversea or Washington assignment. Along somewhat similar lines, a senior Foreign Service officer who had been on the G/PM staff has been transferred to Embassy London as counselor for politico-military affairs.

Another device that is being experimented with as a means of improving

[3] "POLAD's Role With the Military," Department of State Newsletter, No. 31 (November 1963), pp. 7 and 30.

communication and understanding about major politicio-military problems between Washington and oversea missions is the regional conference of embassy politico-military officials and responsible State and Defense officials from Washington. The first of these conferences—a 3-day session involving embassy politico-military officers and POLAD's in Europe and devoted to a broad but intensive review of existing and anticipated politico-military problems affecting the U.S. Government—took place in Paris in October 1962. It proved highly successful. A similar politico-military conference will be held in Europe sometime early in 1964 and in the Far East sometime later in the year. Thought is also being given to holding such conferences in other regional areas, depending upon the availability of funds.

The Future

It should not be inferred that the Department of State has perfected its organization and skills for these difficult and challenging politico-military tasks, or that the State and Defense Departments have developed a fully satisfactory basis for their multiple and complex relationships. It is clear that the range of foreign policy problems and relations with foreign nations affected in one way or another by military decisions and activities is broadening rather than narrowing. The Department of State's politico-military competence must, as consequence, continue to be strengthened. The personnel programs noted above do provide the basis for keeping abreast of this substantial and expanding challenge.

In order to discharge its leadership and coordinating responsibilities in the foreign policy field, the Department of State should be in a position to formulate specific policy guidance within which the Department of Defense can develop its detailed military programs as well as to advise the Defense Department on the foreign policy implications of proposed military policies and actions. This implies substantial, continuing involvement with military policies and problems and increasing ability to analyze and assess them in broader national policy terms. It also implies increased organizational and personnel resources devoted to this area, and continuing experimentation with the most effective institutional arrangements for doing the job.

Index

Acheson, Dean, 25*n*, 50*n*, 73, 102*n*, 106, 113, 320, 347*n*
Adams, Sherman, 78, 94
Administrative skills, need for, 351-52
Advanced Research Projects Agency (ARPA), 149, 168, 316
Aeronautical and Space Sciences, Senate Committee on, 43
Africa: Aid to, 193, 253*n;* diplomatic missions, 251, 257, 259; policy committee, 89, 210, 278; problems in, 19, 288, 290, 355
Agency for International Development (AID): Administrator, 162, 213, 279; foreign policy making, 20, 93; functions, 51, 162, 192, 212-13; organization, 119; overseas missions, 263-65, 284; personnel, 134, 251-53, 263, 281-82, 335-43, 351, 355*n*, 363; planning in, 312-14; relations with State, 22, 102, 108, 130-31, 213-16, 362, 371; research, 231, 316
Agreements, international, 102, 124, 222, 229
Agricultural Trade Development and Assistance Act, 197, 198, 201
Agriculture, Department of: Attachés, 44, 134, 252, 262, 265, 346*n;* Foreign Agricultural Service, 262, 342; foreign aid, 196-98, 201; foreign policy interests, 189-90; international affairs units, 370-71; relations with State, 16, 18, 103, 122
Agriculture Committees (congressional), 44
Aid programs. *See* Economic aid programs; Foreign aid
Air Force, 144-45, 164-65, 175; Academy, 166, 364; overseas missions, 267; RAND

Corp., 314, 315; research in, 168
Alger, Chadwick F., 318*n*
Alliance for Progress, 202, 215, 297
Ambassadors, 103, 134, 246-61, 264-68, 275, 282-86, 351, 377
American "character," 11, 23-24, 32*n*, 367, 379-80
Anderson, Dillon, 85
Antarctic Treaty, 229
Appropriations, congressional function, 37-38, 40-43, 45, 63
Armed Forces Staff College, 364
Armed Services Committees (congressional), 41, 45, 60, 63, 151
Arms control and disarmament, 61, 235-45; agencies concerned with, 159, 222, 227, 229-30, 232, 234; as policy problem, 136, 184, 218, 244; research on, 95, 168, 224, 228, 239-40, 313, 316
Arms Control and Disarmament Agency (ACDA): Establishment, 6, 14, 242-45; need for research in, 95, 228, 239-40, 313, 316; organization of, 238-40; personnel, 339, 363; relations with State, 22, 102, 130-31
Army, 144-45, 151, 164-66, 175; Map Service, 363; Materiel-Command, 151; overseas missions, 267; personnel exchange, 364; research for, 168-69, 315, 317*n;* Signal Corps laboratories, 224*n*
Asher, Robert E., 192*n*
Asia, aid to, 193
Assistant Secretaries: Defense, 147-48, 151, 158-63, 172-73, 175, 177, 196; State, 28, 51, 114-19, 123, 191, 199-201, 204, 207-09, 278
Assistant to the President, 78

DATE DUE

2 26 '81	
2 18 '82	

BRODART, INC.   Cat. No. 23-221